# Australian Monetary Policy
## 1950–1975

# Australian Monetary Policy 1950–1975

*D. C. Rowan*

*Sydney*
GEORGE ALLEN & UNWIN
*London    Boston*

First published in 1980 by
George Allen & Unwin Australia Pty Ltd
8 Napier Street North Sydney NSW 2060
Australia

National Library of Australia
Cataloguing-in-Publication entry:

Rowan, David Culloden, 1918–
  Australian Monetary Policy, 1950–75

  Index
  Bibliography
  ISBN 0 86861 360 6
  ISBN 0 86861 368 1 Paperback

  1. Monetary policy – Australia. I. Title.
332.49'94

Library of Congress Catalog Card No: 79-90343

Set in 10 on 11.5pt Plantin
by Jacobson Typesetters, Auckland, New Zealand
Printed in Hong Kong

# Contents

# *Figures*

# Tables

8

9

*To My Wife*

# *Preface*

This book is a considerably shortened version of a study undertaken from September 1976 to September 1977 when I was fortunate enough to hold a research fellowship generously financed by the Reserve Bank of Australia.

Although my work would not have been possible without the Reserve Bank's support, the views presented are my own and in no way whatever carry the approval or reflect the views of the bank.

During my fellowship I was attached to the Australian National University. Here I incurred a deep debt of gratitude to Professor T. W. Swan, Dr A. R. Hall and other members of the department who not only made my stay extremely pleasant but also gave me the benefit of their advice and criticism. I am also grateful for the help of the department's secretarial and research staff and for the unfailing assistance of the university administration.

A number of other economists have been kind enough to read and criticise this study as it was in late 1977 or, in other ways, to give me help and advice. Not all these can be mentioned by name. I do, however, owe a particular debt to Dr M. Lewis (University of Adelaide), Drs D. W. Stammer and P. D. Jonson (both of the Reserve Bank of Australia), Professor J. O. N. Perkins (University of Melbourne) and Drs A. R. Nobay and K. Schott (University of Southampton). To Dr T. G. Valentine (Australian National University), who held a Reserve Bank fellowship at the same time as I did, I am indebted not only for advice, criticism and very stimulating discussion but also for assistance with computation. None of these persons, is of course, in any way responsible for any errors of fact, analysis or interpretation that the study may contain.

Finally, I am indebted to Dr J. Miller and P. Michael, who helped me with the completion and checking of the data for the tables and charts, and above all to my wife, who so patiently tolerated not only the process of writing but also the more tedious process of revision.

D. C. Rowan
December 1978

# Chapter 1

# Introduction

The aim of this study is to review the conduct of Australian monetary policy over the quarter-century ending in 1975–6.

This is, given the characteristics of monetary policy, a formidable task to attempt within the confines of a single short book. The study therefore makes no claim to offer a comprehensive account or critique of Australian monetary policy over the period under review. Indeed, it is quite deliberately limited to the impact of monetary policy on a small number of macroeconomic variables that have typically been important target variables for the Australian authorities. Thus, by choice, the scope for our study is restricted by treating monetary policy as an element in Australia's overall macroeconomic policy; and in practice it is limited still further by regarding the general macroeconomic policy problem as being to seek to influence the level of economic activity in relation to capacity, the rate of change of prices and the overall balance of payments in ways that the authorities regard as appropriate.[1]

Strictly speaking, the state of the overall balance of payments is not an objective but a constraint that the authorities must take into account in seeking to influence their two (assumed) target variables. Moreover, because cumulative gains in external reserves in most cases bear less rapidly and heavily on domestic policy decisions than do cumulative losses, it is a constraint that operates asymmetrically. Thus, in the usual textbook terms, our approach regards the Australian authorities, in conducting their macroeconomic policy, as seeking to optimise, in terms of their own preference function:[2]

(1) the level of output in relation to capacity; and
(2) the rate of change of prices; subject to
(3) Australia's overall balance-of-payments position. Monetary policy is taken to

be one element in macroeconomic policy, thus narrowly defined.

Just how narrow, and restrictive, this approach is should be obvious. The Australian authorities take many policy decisions that it would be difficult to classify as other than macroeconomic because they attach importance to objectives quite other than (1) and (2). Obvious examples are decisions designed to influence income distribution, the provision of education and health services, the extension of equal pay for men and women in similar employment, and so on. These reflect the high priority that Australia attaches to social equity as an objective of policy — an objective ignored in our (deliberately) narrow definition of target variables.

The justification of our approach is largely that it is convenient; it focuses attention on the *principal* objectives that have influenced the deployment of monetary policy. Moreover, although macroeconomic policy decisions derived from the objective of social equity have *implications* for the conduct of monetary policy, their influence is indirect and will typically be exerted via their implications for target variables (1) and (2) as defined above. Thus, our narrow and somewhat simple approach can be defended on the grounds of relevance and realism, at least in the restricted context of this study.

The central themes of this study are thus: How did the Australian authorities deploy monetary policy in order to optimise the values of the target variables (1) and (2), subject to the constraint of the overall balance-of-payments position? How successful were their attempts to do so? What conclusions (if any) may we derive from our study of the conduct of monetary policy over this quarter-century?

None of these issues is at all simple; and, the state of economic understanding being what it is, few conclusions that we reach are likely to be free from controversy. For example, to evaluate the conduct of Australian monetary policy we first need to describe:

(a) the extent of the overall macroeconomic policy intervention made by the authorities; and

(b) the extent to which monetary policy was used as a means of conducting intervention.

Then we need to compare what *was* done with what it seems it would have been 'optimal' to do.

Given our statement of the objectives of macroeconomic policy, what would have been 'optimal' (in this special sense) must in turn depend upon:

(c) the authorities' ability correctly to diagnose the position of the economy in any period of time;

(d) their ability to forecast crucial exogenous variables over a politically acceptable 'policy horizon';

(e) their understanding (and the reliability of their understanding) of the structure of the economy; and

(f) their understanding (and the reliability of their understanding) of the dynamics of the economic system.

It is these dynamics, together with (e), that will determine the response of the economy, in particular the response of our two target variables and the external restraint, to whatever forms of intervention are undertaken.

Obviously enough, direct information on (c)–(f) is hard to obtain. Moreover, even if it was readily accessible, it would simply enable us to form a judgement as to whether the authorities chose macroeconomic policies that were 'optimal', given (c)–(f) *and* our narrow assumptions regarding their objectives.[3] Since, if the answer was in the negative, this could easily reflect the limitations of the very restricted preferences that we have assigned to the authorities, this judgement might be rather unhelpful. In any case direct information about (c) and (d) is unobtainable,[4] although there are good reasons, as we shall see, for thinking that the authorities do in practice experience considerable difficulties in forecasting such exogenous variables as export proceeds.

Our general methodology, therefore, is to observe the conduct of monetary policy and to inquire whether, in the light of our current knowledge of the structure and dynamic responses of the Australian economy, the policy followed was appropriate. Our answers to this question are bound to be imprecise, i.e. to consist of impressions based upon economic intuition rather than quantitative calculations derived from some econometrically estimated model.[5] As a consequence they seem sure to be controversial and, whether this is so or not, to merit the most careful and sceptical examination that the reader can give them.

Given this approach, there are a number of qualifications that the reader is asked to note.

The first of these is that over a timespan of twenty-five years it would be foolish to expect either the authorities' preferences regarding their ultimate targets or the influences on policy listed as (c)–(f) to remain unaltered. It is, for example, a commonplace that since 1974–5, the relative importance attached to the rate of change of prices as a target of policy has increased not only in Australia but also in highly developed economies. Again, over our timespan, not only did the Australian economy undergo major changes, but in addition there were very marked and closely related changes in Australia's financial structure.[6] It follows that in these circumstances we must expect the use made by the authorities of monetary policy, and their methods of conducting it, also to have changed, since both the role assigned to discretionary monetary action and its techniques must reflect the economic and institutional environment. All that we can ask here is whether the authorities appear to have taken proper account of these changes, i.e. adapted their view of the role of monetary policy and its *modus operandi* in a way that was consistent with the implications of our knowledge of the changing environment in which they had to operate – or rather more precisely, with the findings of economic research regarding these implications.[7] This point is particularly important in view of the susceptibility of contemporary views regarding monetary policy to shifts in intellectual fashion, which in some cases seem to have either rather negligible empirical support or empirical support based upon the experience of countries that are not closely similar to Australia.[8]

The second point to note is that our review of past experience, like any such review, is undertaken with the full and not inconsiderable benefit of hindsight. In short, in some periods it seems clear that the authorities took actions that can now be seen to have been unwise; that is, they made what are now agreed to be errors. This is hardly surprising. We must, however, take care not to assume, either explicitly or implicitly, that any such errors were avoidable at the time when they were made. This is an important, if rather obvious, *caveat*, for we are approaching monetary policy, indeed macroeconomic policy, as a discretionary means of economic stabilisation. Since, as we shall see, the Australian economy during the quarter-century under review, has undergone cyclical fluctuations some of which were severe *despite* the authorities' attempts at stabilisation, we must beware of inferring either that the authorities typically failed in their stabilisation attempts or that, when they did, their failures were avoidable in the then current state of our economic understanding. Still less must we infer, as it is now fashionable to do in some places, that the authorities' interventions, however well intentioned, had the effect of increasing the observed cyclical fluctuations – or more extreme still, were the main cause of them.[9]

Since we are examining monetary policy from the point of view of its contribution to economic stabilisation, our first need must be to give a brief account of Australia's cyclical experience since 1950–1. This is the task of the next chapter.

## Notes: Chapter 1

1   Less formally, this treats macroeconomic policy as being concerned with economic stabilisation.
2   In a democratic system it seems reasonable to expect the authorities' preference function to reflect, although perhaps with some rather unstable lag, the preferences of the majority of the electorate.
3   That is, the authorities were consistent on these assumptions.
4   Economic understanding might be much improved if the authorities were to publish, say some years after the event, the forecasts of major exogenous variables that were available to them. The difficulties of economic forecasting are not widely appreciated; and where this is so, there is always a risk that the authorities will be expected to operate within impractically narrow ranges of error; that is, they will be expected to achieve what is typically impossible. This may well lead to excessive intervention, some of which may prove destabilising.
5   Evidence from the principal available models that are relevant – both developed in the Reserve Bank of Australia – is considered; but in a relatively rapidly changing environment it may be of rather limited value.
6   Some of these are sketched in Chapter 3. A further account is available in the references there cited.
7   On this issue cf. Chapter 5 and its Appendix.
8   Cf. Rowan [144] for a discussion of this issue in the Australian context.
9   The last view assumes that the private sector is stable within narrow limits in the absence of shocks originating in the public sector. It is a matter of controversy between 'Keynesians' and 'monetarists' in the United States; cf. Mayer [99] and the references there cited. Its relevance to Australia is briefly considered in Rowan [144].

# PART ONE

# THE ECONOMIC AND FINANCIAL BACKGROUND

*Chapter 2*

# Economic Fluctuations in Australia, 1950–75

## 2.1 *Introduction*

The emphasis in this study is on monetary policy as a stabilisation device, with stabilisation narrowly defined in terms of only three macroeconomic variables – or more precisely, two variables and a constraint.

The first task of this chapter is to summarise Australia's experience with these variables over the quarter-century under review. In doing this we necessarily pay attention to the Australian cycle and the behaviour of major demand components during upswings and downswings.

This essentially descriptive account does not in any way claim to be more than a rough sketch of Australia's cyclical experience.[1] A full account would require a very sizable monograph. The present purpose is simply to give an outline of the dates and the extent of the main fluctuations in economic activity, in order to form a preliminary judgement of whether there is a strong case for the Australian authorities to continue to pursue policies aimed at anticyclical stabilisation.

The second purpose of this chapter is to reach a preliminary conclusion regarding the scope for monetary action in any overall macroeconomic policy aimed at stabilisation. This raises the obvious difficulty that to provide a sensible, even though approximate, answer to this question requires an understanding of the dynamic response of our macroeconomic target variables to discretionary action by the monetary authorities; that is, it requires an understanding of what is usually called the 'transmission process'.

From this a further difficulty follows in that on quite general grounds, as well as on the evidence reviewed later in Chapter 5, we must expect the transmission mechanism to have changed very significantly during the twenty-five years under review. Hence, if we assume, either explicitly or implicitly, an invariant *and* fairly precisely defined transmission mechanism over the whole period, we shall certainly be in error. The alternative approach, which is to respecify the transmission process throughout this review, is plainly unwieldy. Accordingly, we proceed here by making explicit, but in our view weak and even minimal, assumptions regarding the transmission mechanism over the period.

In outline, our approach is to assess the stabilisation potential of monetary action from the cyclical performance of those elements in private sector expenditure which are, to a significant extent, financed by funds raised, by the units undertaking the expenditure, from outside sources – e.g., by borrowing from banks, non-bank financial intermediaries or the capital market. The two sub-aggregates considered under this head are: (a) gross private expenditure on fixed capital; and (b) consumers' expenditure on durables. Accordingly, we define a subaggregate as

$$\begin{array}{l}\text{Externally financed} \\ \text{Private expenditure}\end{array} \equiv \begin{array}{l}\text{Private expenditure} \\ \text{on fixed capital}\end{array} + \begin{array}{l}\text{Consumers' expenditure} \\ \text{on durables}\end{array}$$

where the description 'externally financed' relates to the dependence of the spending unit on outside funds and does not necessarily imply an overseas transaction.

Two points should be noted about this procedure. The first is that it *assumes*, but does not demonstrate, that these two categories of private expenditure are at the margin dependent on finance by outside funds. Similarly, it assumes that increasing the cost of borrowed funds, or in an imperfect market restricting the ease with which outside funds can be raised, significantly influences Externally Financed Private Expenditures. So far we have offered no evidence to show that these 'cost of borrowing' and 'availability' effects, as they are conventionally known, are either quantitatively important or reliable enough for policy purposes. These issues are reviewed in more detail in Chapter 5 and in econometric terms in Chapter 10. We are at present simply assuming that these traditional effects exist and influence demand, principally via the elements in the subaggregate defined above.

The second point worth noting is that in taking this approach we are certainly not seeking to argue that the transmission process consists in cost and availability effects alone, or even that it is dominated by these two elements. On the contrary, as we shall see, there is evidence to suggest that interest rate changes entail important wealth effects on consumers' expenditure, while the behaviour of some monetary aggregates, or the excess supply of money, may exert a significant influence on business expectations, in particular on expectations regarding the rate of change of prices. In short, our assumed cost and availability approach almost certainly understates the significance of discretionary monetary action and thus understates the scope for its employment as a stabilisation device. Therefore, in utilising our concept of externally financed private expenditures, we are not in any sense taking a position biased *in favour* of there existing a useful role for monetary action aimed at stabilisation; if anything, we are taking the reverse position.

Finally, by adopting our weak assumptions regarding the transmission mechanism, there is a possibility that we may somewhat understate the potential impact of monetary action on the external constraint, particularly upon the capital account.[2]

Theoretically, we should expect the rate of private capital inflow (which dominates the variation of the capital account) to respond to any increase in domestic borrowing costs or any reduction in the local availability of funds; for in these circumstances some borrowers will find it beneficial to borrow overseas (directly or through intermediaries), and some lenders (domestic or overseas) will find it beneficial to switch their lending to the Australian market. These portfolio effects, the magnitude of which is likely to reflect the extent to which the Australian money and capital markets are integrated with those overseas, are simple to comprehend in qualitative terms, even though our present understanding of the quantitative and dynamic response of private capital flows is decidedly limited. It is, however, probably an oversimplication to regard them as arising solely from cost and availability effects. It is *possible*, for example, that monetary policy may, via its influence on monetary aggregates or the excess supply of money, influence expectations regarding the exchange rate and thus the effective *ex ante* interest rates confronting both borrowers and lenders. To the extent that this is so – and at present we have little understanding of how exchange rate expectations are formed – our weak assumptions regarding the transmission mechanism will lead to some understatement of the impact of monetary action on private capital inflows and thus the external constraint.

## 2.2 *Australian Cycles: The Dating Problem*

The first of our macroeconomic target variables is the extent of capacity utilisation. If a cycle is simply defined as a wave-like movement over time, i.e. a wave-like movement with no implication of regular periodicity or amplitude, then by definition cyclical upswings must involve increases in capacity utilisation, and downswings decreases. These fluctuations can be measured by – or more strictly, approximated to by – the values of some index of the ratio of actual output to potential full-capacity output. Unfortunately, although we have official estimates of real gross domestic product (GDP) which though doubtless imperfect are nevertheless the best available, we have no corresponding official estimates of full-capacity GDP. There is therefore no index of capacity utilisation that carries any aura of official approval. Hence we can define, and if we wish calculate, our own cycle in this variable. Not very surprisingly, there is no single correct way of doing this. It is possible to construct a number of capacity estimates, which although similar in broad outline will typically yield different datings (for at least some cycles) of the peaks and troughs in the indexes of capacity utilisation. This is a serious difficulty where the precise dating of turning points in some series is a necessary preliminary to measuring the lead (or lag) of some series over (or behind) another.

Fortunately, however, those who have given systematic attention to the Australian cycle seem, despite their different methods, to agree fairly closely with each other regarding the datings of cyclical peaks and troughs,[3] moreover, in the present context we are not primarily concerned with the precise estimation of leads or lags between series. Hence, we can afford to make the calendar quarter, rather than the month, the basic time unit. Given this rather crude unit, we have, after reviewing the relevant studies, adopted the datings set out in Table 2.1. In some cases the datings are particularly uncertain, e.g. the apparent downswing of 1957-8. This period has accordingly been italicised.

**Table 2.1** *Approximate cyclical dating of the Australian economy*

| Cycle peaks | Cycle troughs |
| --- | --- |
| 1951.II | 1952.IV |
| 1955.II | 1956.II |
| *1957.II* | *1958.III* |
| 1960.III | 1961.III |
| 1965.II | 1966.III |
| 1970.I | 1972.I |
| 1974.I | 1975.II |

*Notes:*
(1)  Years are calendar years.
(2)  Roman numerals refer to quarters.

This table gives our estimates of the most reasonable consensus dating from a number of studies, not all of which are, even conceptually, concerned with capacity utilisation. If therefore follows that the consensus datings in Table 2.1 will not necessarily correspond with any particular index of capacity utilisation. This is a pity; but since capacity indexes do not necessarily correspond and we have no obvious means of saying which index is to be preferred when they do not, this may not matter; for accepting the dating of the Table 2.1, the question that really concerns us is this: Given that Australia has experienced cyclical fluctuations with roughly the pattern shown, how extensively did capacity utilisation fluctuate?

This question cannot be answered unambiguously, since capacity output can be calculated in a number of ways.[4] For example, one simple method is a log-linear interpolation between the peaks of some observed output series. A second is log-linear interpolation between output levels associated with identical percentages of the workforce unemployed. This interpolation gives the assumed constant long-run rate of capacity expansion over the cycle. If this is then applied to the output corresponding to some selected percentage of unemployment defined as full capacity employment, the growth of full capacity output will be defined. Once this is done, comparisons of actual output with the estimated full-capacity output yield estimates of excess capacity, which readily provide a means of calculating the extent of cyclical fluctuations in utilisation.

Both these approaches are oversimplications, and a more refined technique would consist in estimating some appropriate macroeconomic production function and then, from this, estimating full capacity output by making use of the available estimates of labour and capital inputs.

Each method is in some way open to theoretical and practical objections. The output interpolation method, for example, implies that each cyclical peak in the selected output series represents full capacity working. This is almost certainly not the case. Moreover, since the output peak defined (by the method) as full capacity is most unlikely, in peacetime, to exceed the true full-capacity output of the period, the resulting estimates of the extent of fluctuations in capacity utilisation are likely to underestimate the true fluctuations. Against this, the method that interpolates between observations of identical percentages of recorded unemployment implicitly assumes an invariant relation between the recorded percentage of unemployment and the percentage of capacity utilisation. Over a timespan of a quarter of a century it is unlikely that this assumption will hold, either because of technological changes or because of changes in the structure of final demand or because of changes in the structure of the labour market itself. Certainly, in Australia there are good reasons for thinking that the relationship has changed, more particularly in recent years when government policy has sharply modified the relative wages of male, female and juvenile labour. Finally, the production function approach, although in principle considerably more refined, suffers from the difficulty of measuring qualitative changes in factor inputs and the doubt that attaches to the assumption of invariance in the chosen function's parameters over a twenty-five year timespan.

In Figure 2.1 are presented the results (due to Kasper [91]) of applying the linear interpolation process to the Australia and New Zealand (ANZ) Bank's index of industrial production. Precisely because of the limitations of the method no very considerable degree of precision should be attached to this series, which is illustrative only and, for reasons already stated, probably understates the extent to which capacity is underutilised at the cyclical troughs.

22

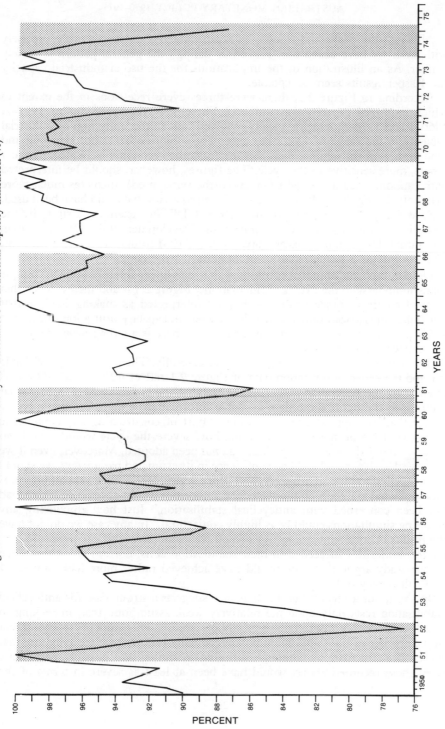

Figure 2.1    The Australian business cycle: fluctuations in industrial capacity utilisation (%)

PERCENT

YEARS

Source: Kasper (91)

Although the peaks and troughs of Kasper's series do not coincide precisely with what we have called our 'concensus dating', the general pattern is closely similar. As an illustration of the implications for the use of industrial capacity the Kasper results seem acceptable.

According to Figure 2.1, there were three severe recessions in the extent to which industrial capacity was utilised.[5] These were the recessions of 1951–2, 1960–1 and 1974–5, which typically involved falls in the utilisation of industrial capacity in the range of 13–22 per cent. These figures are rather alarming and tend to support the familiar view that the Australian economy is, relative to many others, more sensitive to the cycle. The figures, however, should be interpreted with caution, since industrial production (the series used) fluctuates much more markedly during the cycle than other real-output series that could have been used, such as real gross non-farm product or real GDP. For example, a study by the Organisation for Economic Co-operation and Development (OECD), based upon non-farm GDP, estimates excess capacity at the 1961 trough at around 6 per cent, whereas Figure 2.1 suggests a value of some 14 per cent.

Despite this, and mindful of the fact that our linear-interpretation technique tends to understate the extent of fluctuations, Figure 2.1 – and the evidence that is available from other studies – may be interpreted as making it clear that Australia experienced rather sharp fluctuations in capacity utilisation during the study period. From this it may be argued that there is a strong *prima facie* case for anticyclical stabilisation.

This conclusion must be interpreted very carefully. The cycle datings of Table 2.1 and the capacity utilisation data of Figure 2.1 reflect *inter alia* a continuous attempt by the Australian authorities to stabilise the economy by adopting what seemed, in the light of the then available information, a macroeconomic policy stance that was appropriate to this aim. Short of constructing an econometric model we have no means of estimating how severe the cycle would have been *if* these intended anticyclical policies had *not* been adopted. Moreover, even if we possessed such a model and had confidence in its estimated parameters, we should be compelled to give an arbitrary, and hence legitimately controversial, interpretation of what macroeconomic stance the authorities would have taken if they had not been concerned with anticyclical stabilisation.[6] Just how convincing any resulting simulations could be is highly conjectural.[7] In any case we do not have the results of such simulations. As a result we cannot say with any precision how far the authorities succeeded in their stabilisation aims; nor can we at this stage of our study argue that they would have achieved rather more had they acted other than they did.

In short, our assertion that the evidence suggests a strong case for anticyclical stabilisation rests only upon the relatively weak assumption that, in seeking to stabilise, the authorities did not typically destabilise. This amounts to saying that in the absence of the stabilisation policies actually followed we are assuming that the cyclical fluctuations, although differing in timing and possibly periodicity from those recorded above, would have been at least as severe in terms of the related fluctuations in capacity utilisation.

This weak assumption is, of course, provisional. In later chapters we shall discuss the timing and extent of the authorities' actions – more particularly with regard to monetary policy – in an attempt to judge whether the extent, timing and nature of interventions were well or ill chosen.

# 2.3 Demand and the Cycle

In the short run, i.e. within a single upswing or downswing, the extent of capacity utilisation can be regarded as being dominated by demand,[8] since capacity itself is generally assumed to grow rather slowly and smoothly. We shall therefore

**Table 2.2** *Demand behaviour in two upswings*
*(seasonally adjusted quarterly data at 1966-7 prices)*

| Aggregate | 1961.III ($A m.) | 1965.II ($A m.) | Change ($A m.) | % change | Change as % of GDP change | 1972.I ($A m.) | 1974.I ($A m.) | Change ($A m.) | % change | Change as % of GDP change |
|---|---|---|---|---|---|---|---|---|---|---|
| Private consumption | 2,673 | 3,278 | 605 | 22.6 | 50.8 | 4,481 | 5,032 | 551 | 12.2 | 55.5 |
| Gross private fixed investment | 634 | 963 | 329 | 51.9 | 27.6 | 1,195 | 1,360 | 165 | 13.8 | 16.6 |
| Government: | 882 | 1,074 | 192 | 21.8 | 16.1 | 1,480 | 1,599 | 119 | 8.0 | 12.0 |
| of which: Consumption | (459) | (574) | (115) | (25.0) | (9.7) | (837) | (940) | (103) | (13.5) | (10.4) |
| Gross fixed investment | (423) | (500) | (77) | (18.4) | (6.5) | (643) | (659) | (16) | (2.5) | (1.6) |
| Changes in stocks | -122 | 156 | 278 | n.a. | 23.4 | -97 | (441) | 538 | n.a. | 54.1 |
| Exports | 669 | 798 | 129 | 19.4 | 10.9 | 1,394 | 1,339 | -55 | -3.9 | -5.5 |
| Imports | -554 | -931 | -387 | -71.1 | -32.5 | -1,168 | -1,689 | -521 | -44.6 | -62.5 |
| Discrepancy | -42 | 3 | 45 | n.a. | 3.8 | -23 | 175 | 198 | n.a. | 19.9 |
| GDP | 4,150 | 5,340 | 1,190 | 28.7 | 100.0 | 7,261 | 8,257 | 994 | 13.7 | 100.0 |
| Consumers' expenditure on durables* | 167 | 432 | 265 | 158.7 | 22.3 | 517 | 620 | 103 | 19.9 | 10.4 |
| Gross private fixed investment | 634 | 963 | 329 | 51.9 | 27.6 | 1,195 | 1,360 | 165 | 13.8 | 16.6 |
| Externally financed private expenditure | 801 | 1,395 | 594 | 74.1 | 49.9 | 1,712 | 1,980 | 268 | 15.6 | 27.0 |

*Source*: Commonwealth Bureau of Statistics, *Quarterly National Income Estimates*.
* Defined as expenditure on motor vehicles plus household durables.

examine the cyclical behaviour of the major demand components, in particular the behaviour of the variables defined above as externally financed private expenditures. Unfortunately, there are statistical difficulties in doing this, since official quarterly national-income estimates did not become available until 1959. Hence, it is not possible to present data for the upswing ending in 1955.IV or that ending in 1960.III on the basis of official estimates alone. We shall therefore restrict ourselves initially to the upswings ending in 1965.II and 1974.I. The relevant series are set out in Table 2.2.

In the first of the two upswings, which lasted close upon four years, GDP rose by some 29 per cent, i.e. at an annual rate of rather more than 6 per cent. During these years the rate of gross private fixed investment rose by more than 50 per cent and accounted for more than one-quarter of the changes in GDP. During the same period real expenditure on consumer's durables more than doubled, with the increase amounting to about 22.3 per cent of the total change in GDP. Thus, almost exactly one-half of the observed changes in demand was accounted for by these two items and hence by externally financed private expenditure as defined above.

The upswing ending in 1974.I was about half the length of that ending in 1965.II The rise in GDP was some 13.7 per cent – an annual rate only fractionally below 7 per cent.

The contribution of gross private fixed investment to the change in total demand was, however, only about 17 per cent, and that of consumers' expenditure on durables was close to 10 per cent. Thus, externally financed private expenditure, as defined, accounted for some 27 per cent of the change in total demand – not much more than half its contribution to the earlier upswing.

Two additional points are worth noting at this stage. The first is that, in both upswings, changes in stocks accounted for a considerable part of the changes in total expenditure – about 24 per cent in that of 1961–5 and 54 per cent in that of 1972–4. Marginal additions to stocks are in large measure financed by borrowed funds, whether these additions are planned or unplanned. This suggests that, if investment in inventories were included in our definition of externally financed private expenditure, the importance of this variable in accounting for demand changes – and thus, on our earlier arguments, the *prima facie* scope for discretionary monetary action for stabilisation purposes – would be very markedly increased.

There are two reasons why inventory changes have not been included in our definition. The first is that observed changes in inventories are likely to contain an unplanned element. The very simple theory underlying our concept, however, necessarily relates only to planned inventory changes. This is of some importance, since unplanned changes in inventories can be quite large, particularly at or near cyclical turning points, and may well have the opposite sign to the planned changes at some points in the cycle. Thus, the published data, if interpreted as planned changes, seem sure to incorporate an error whose sign and size are, generally speaking, unsure.

Quite apart from this problem there is a theoretical objection to including even the planned element in inventory changes (assuming that it can be identified) in our definition of externally financed private expenditures. This arises because most empirical work in the United States, the United Kingdom and Australia suggests that planned investment in inventories is typically insensitive to monetary conditions, at least where the latter are defined as interest rates. Naturally, since the applied literature is very extensive, it is possible to find studies that *do* find a role for monetary variables. Moreover, even where econometric inquiry finds no significant coefficient on the monetary variables of an aggregate inventory investment equation, undoubtedly the aggregative approach will mask the face that *some* firms do respond to such variables. Thus, although the general findings from inventory models, together with the identification problem already noted, make it sensible to exclude the subaggregate from our concept of externally financed private expenditures, this exclusion must impart a downward bias in its measurement, which may conceivably be significant but is unfortunately unknown.

Table 2.3 finally brings together the evidence from three downswings for which official data are available: 1960–1, 1970–2 and 1974–5. In the first and last of these output fell absolutely; in the second it rose, but more slowly than capacity.

The first point to recall is that, according to our dating, Australian downswings are typically rather short in relation to the upswings. For example, the downswing of 1960–1 lasted only one year, during which GDP fell by just above 3.5 per cent, and perhaps twice this in relation to capacity. About 40 per cent of the observed fall was accounted for by gross private investment in fixed capital, and a further 15.5 per cent by consumers' expenditure on durables. Thus, some 56 per cent of the total decline in demand was accounted for by externally financed private expenditure.

The 1974–5 downswing is not easy to date in terms of real GDP since the official estimates are virtually identical for 1974.IV, 1975.I, 1975.III and 1975.IV. Ironically our earlier consensus dating which puts the trough in 1975.II yields a GDP estimate significantly higher (by some $A 200 million at 1966–7 prices) than any of the four quarters named above and, more ironically still, some $A 200 millions above the cycle peak in 1974.I. We have dealt with this difficulty by retaining our 'concensus' dating and taking 1975.I as the trough. This is admittedly arbitrary and as good a case can probably be made for taking 1975.III or 1975.IV. On our interpretation therefore the 1974–5 downswing lasted a year.

During these four quarters, GDP fell by a little under one per cent, say 4.5–5.0 per cent in relation to capacity. In the same period, gross private investment fell by more than two and a half times the changes in GDP. It is, therefore, not surprising that despite some growth in consumers' expenditure on durables, externally financed private expenditure fell by more than one and a half times the fall in GDP.

In the growth recession of 1970–2, which lasted for two years, real GDP rose

**Table 2.3** Demand behaviour in three downswings (seasonally adjusted quarterly data, at 1966–67 prices)

| Aggregate | 1960.III ($A m.) | 1961.III ($A m.) | Change ($A m.) | % change | Change as % of GDP change | 1970.I ($A m.) | 1972.I ($A m.) | Change ($A m.) | % change | Change as % of GDP change | 1974.I ($A m.) | 1975.I ($A m.) | Change ($A m.) | % change | Change as % of GDP change |
|---|---|---|---|---|---|---|---|---|---|---|---|---|---|---|---|
| Private Consumption | 2,684 | 2,673 | -11 | -0.4 | 7.0 | 4,148 | 4,481 | 333 | 8.0 | 57.4 | 5,088 | 5,213 | 125 | 2.5 | -166.7 |
| Gross private fixed investment | 697 | 634 | -63 | -9.0 | 40.4 | 1,178 | 1,195 | 17 | 1.4 | 2.9 | 1,364 | 1,166 | -198 | -14.5 | 264.0 |
| Government: | | | | | | | | | | | | | | | |
| Consumption | 409 | 459 | 50 | 12.2 | 32.0 | 757 | 837 | 80 | 10.6 | 13.8 | 939 | 980 | 41 | 4.4 | -54.7 |
| Gross fixed investment | 357 | 423 | 66 | 18.5 | -42.3 | 585 | 643 | 58 | 9.9 | 10.0 | 666 | 753 | 87 | 13.1 | -116.0 |
| Changes in stocks | 214 | -122 | -336 | n.a. | 215.4 | 86 | -97 | -183 | n.a. | -31.5 | 412 | -185 | -597 | n.a. | 796.0 |
| Exports | 550 | 669 | 119 | 21.6 | 76.3 | 1,220 | 1,394 | 174 | 14.3 | 30.0 | 1,328 | 1,462 | 134 | 10.1 | -178.7 |
| Imports | -689 | -544 | 145 | 21.0 | -92.9 | -1,171 | -1,168 | 3 | Neg. | 0.5 | -1,689 | -1,443 | 246 | -14.6 | 328.0 |
| Discrepancy | 86 | -42 | -128 | n.a. | 82.0 | -121 | -23 | 98 | n.a. | 16.9 | 86 | 174 | 88 | n.a. | -117.3 |
| GDP | 4,306 | 4,150 | -156 | -3.6 | 100.0 | 6,681 | 7,261 | 580 | 8.7 | 100.0 | 8,193 | 8,118 | -75 | -0.9 | 100.0 |
| Consumer's expenditure on durables* | 191 | 167 | -24 | -12.6 | 15.4 | 530 | 517 | -13 | -2.5 | -2.2 | 620 | 698 | 78 | 12.6 | -104.0 |
| Gross private fixed investment | 697 | 634 | -63 | -9.0 | 40.4 | 1,178 | 1,195 | 17 | 1.4 | 2.9 | 1,364 | 1,166 | -198 | -14.5 | 264.0 |
| Externally financed private expenditure | 888 | 801 | -87 | -9.8 | 55.8 | 1,708 | 1,712 | 4 | Neg. | 0.7 | 1,984 | 1,864 | -120 | -0.6 | -160.0 |

* Defined as expenditure on motor vehicles plus household durables.
Source: Commonwealth Bureau of Statistics, Quarterly National Income Estimates.

by some 8.5 per cent – roughly the sort of rate at which one might expect capacity to expand. Thus, in terms of GDP, as opposed to industrial production, the downswing was extremely mild. In these circumstances it is scarcely surprising that gross private investment in fixed capital rose. The rise, however, was less than 2 per cent of its 1970.I rate and only some 3 per cent of the change in GDP. Consumers' expenditure on durables fell, and the change in externally financed private expenditures was virtually zero. Thus, relative to the rate of growth in capacity, externally financed private expenditures fell by perhaps 8–8.5 per cent – close to 2 per cent of GDP. It thus made a significant contribution to the fall in the level of capacity utilisation.

In all three downswings the fall in the rate of stock accumulation was dramatic.

The cyclical behaviour of economic time series rarely conforms to any regular pattern or permits interpretation in terms of any simple model. Usually, conclusions drawn from contemplating time series need to be cautious. It is therefore suggested that in general there seems to be a good case for arguing that fluctuations in demand were to a significant extent accounted for by fluctuations in externally financed private expenditure.

Clearly, this statement does not always hold, since in 1970–1972 our defined subaggregate moved anticyclically. Equally clearly, if it was possible (and reasonable) to include planned investment in inventories within our definition, the statement would become much less tentative.

In short, the evidence reported supports the view that major elements in private expenditure that are *prima facie* likely to be sensitive at the margin to monetary action play a significant role in the cycle. *Prima facie*, therefore, there is some scope for monetary policies directed at demand stabilisation.

A final word of caution may not be misplaced. It is not being claimed that fluctuations in the components of externally financed private expenditure caused the observed fluctuations in demand. Both gross private investment in fixed capital and consumer's expenditure on durables are endogenous variables within the macrosystem in which the causal elements are either the variables that we assume to be exogenous or shifts in the functions explaining the endogenous variables. Thus, our two elements respond to changes in the exogenous variables, including, of course, those under the direct control of the authorities.

Finally, the preceding discussion has made use of seasonally adjusted data

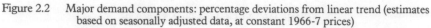
Figure 2.2 Major demand components: percentage deviations from linear trend (estimates based on seasonally adjusted data, at constant 1966-7 prices)

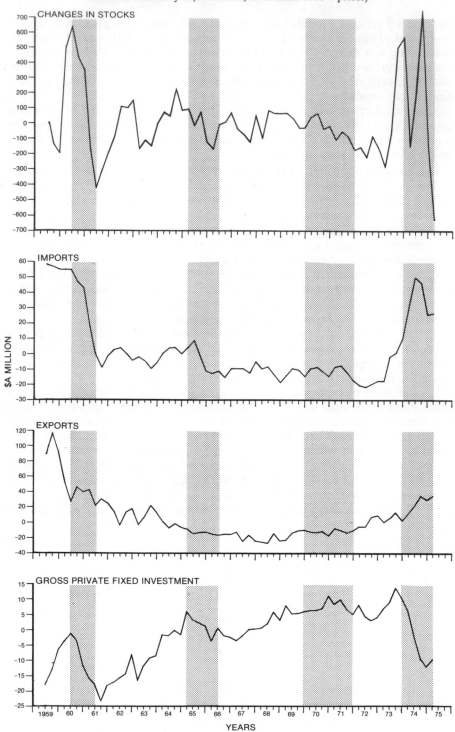

*Source:* Australia Bureau of Statistics, *Supplement to Quarterly Estimates of National Income and Expenditure*

without any attempt to distinguish trend and cyclical components. Figure 2.2 gives estimates of the deviations of some major expenditure components from an imposed linear trend, all data, of course, being at constant (1966–7) prices. Although the trend imposed is clearly crude, the figure provides broad visual support for the discussion in the text.

# 2.4 Housing

In examining demand fluctuations, special interest attaches to this behaviour of investment in dwellings. For this there are a number of reasons.

In the first place, the rate of house construction is a socially, and thus at one remove politically, important variable in most countries. Australia is no exception to this rule. The authorities are therefore sensitive to fluctuations in the rate of investment in housing and commonly take steps, particularly during periods of monetary restraint, to insulate the housing market in some degree. Examples of such concern and consequential intervention are widely found in the United Kingdom and the United States[9] as well as Australia.

In the second place, the construction industry is in many countries one that suffers particularly severely from cyclical fluctuations.[10] Commonly, therefore, the authorities, in the interests of reducing risks in the industry and thus promoting its secular efficiency, will prefer a reduced amplitude of fluctuations in construction. This again directs our attention to the possibility of smoothing the fluctuations in housing investment.

Finally, housing is an extremely long-lived asset. The demand for it is thus closely related to the ability of borrowers to obtain long term finance on reasonable terms from established lenders. This means that at any interest rate the availability of funds from sources of housing finance in the form of mortgages, generally has a marked effect on the rate of starts in housing, and thus on investment in housing and housing completions. Thus, the *organisation* of housing finance becomes an important matter, for it is via this institutional framework that discretionary monetary action influences the flow supply of mortgage finance, and thus starts and investment in dwellings. Clearly, it would be a matter of major concern to the monetary authority if restrictionist policies had their main impact on the housing market. Conversely, the greater is the sensitivity of this market to monetary restraint, the more inhibited is monetary policy likely to be – or alternatively, the more likely are the authorities either to seek ways of insulating the market or to intervene directly in it, thus somewhat reducing the short term efficiency of monetary policy in restraining demand.

The workings of the Australian housing market cannot be examined in any great detail in this study. For our purposes it is sufficient to give a brief review of investment in dwellings during the cyclical phases.

The behaviour of investment in dwellings in real terms is set out in Table 2.4.

31

From this table[11] it is apparent that, with the exception of 1970–2, in which investment in dwellings was unchanged, periods of downswing were generally accompanied by rather rapid rates of fall in housing investment. Similarly, in periods of upswing, investment in housing rose at very appreciable annual rates. This suggests that the housing market in Australia is cyclically sensitive but that the downswing of 1970-2 constituted an exception to this generalisation.

**Table 2.4** *Investment in dwellings: cyclical phases, 1951-75.*

| | Major downswings | | | | Major upswings | | |
|---|---|---|---|---|---|---|---|
| | Investment in dwellings | | | | Investment in dwellings | | |
| Period | Change[a] ($A m.) | % change | Annual rate of change (%) | Period | Change[a] ($A m.) | % change | Annual rate of change (%) |
| 1951.II 1952.IV | - 9[b] | -11·5 | -7·6 | | | | |
| | | | | 1952.IV 1955.II | 14[b] | 20·3 | 8·1 |
| 1960.III 1961.III | -33 | -16·7 | -16·7 | | | | |
| | | | | 1961.III 1965.II | 86 | 52·1 | 13·8 |
| 1970.I 1972.I | 0 | 0·0 | 0·0 | | | | |
| | | | | 1972.I 1974.I | 51 | 14.8 | 7·3 |
| 1974.I 1975.II | -102 | -25·7 | -20·5 | | | | |

[a] At constant 1966–7 prices.
[b] 1951.II prices.
*Sources*:
(1) For 1960.III – 1975.II, Commonwealth Bureau of Statistics, *Estimates of National Income and Expenditure*.
(2) For 1951.II – 1955.II, author's estimates based on Kennedy [92].

In Figure 2.3 are plotted the available data on the flow supply of mortgages and investment in housing. At what is admittedly a rather superficial level, this confirms the expected relationship between the supply of mortgage finance and housing activity.

The series utilised earlier relate to absolute changes in investment in dwellings in real terms. This series is of limited value in assessing the cyclical fluctuations in this variable. Accordingly, Figure 2.4 gives the deviations of this variable from a simple trend – a procedure that, although the trend imposed is necessarily arbitrary, should provide a rather more useful profile of the housing cycle and the extent to which its timing coincides with our concensus cylical dating.

Figure 2.3    Investment in dwellings and the supply of mortgages ($A million at current prices), seasonally adjusted quarterly data, 1959(Q3)—1975(Q4)

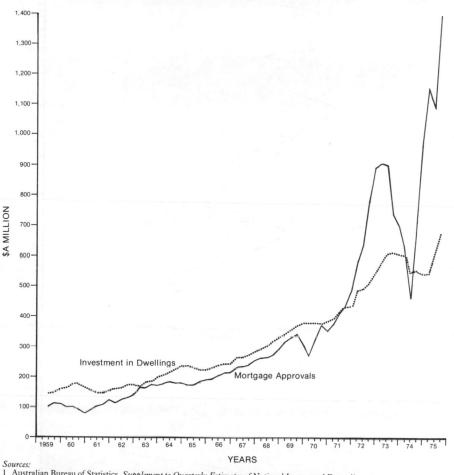

*Sources:*
1  Australian Bureau of Statistics, *Supplement to Quarterly Estimates of National Income and Expenditure (Gross Private Investment in Dwellings).*
2  Reserve Bank of Australia, Activity Section Research Department, *Value of Mortgage Approvals for New and Used Dwellings*

## 2.5  *Preliminary Conclusions*

Thus far we have sought to sketch: (a) Australia's cyclical experience from 1950 to 1975; and (b) the behaviour of the main demand components in the defined cyclical phase.

The first aim was to consider whether the extent of Australia's fluctuations

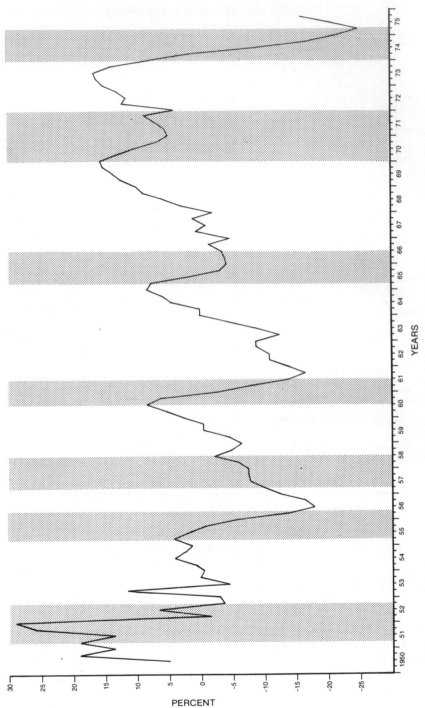

Figure 2.4    Gross private investment in dwellings: percentage deviations from exponential trend (quarterly estimates based on seasonally adjusted data at constant 1966-7 prices, 1950(Q3)-1975(Q4)

PERCENT

YEARS

*Source:* Australian Bureau of Statistics, *Supplement to Quarterly Estimates of National Income and Expenditure.*

suggests a continuing *demand* for anticyclical stabilisation policies. This seems to be established.

The second aim was to consider whether *prima facie* there appears to be a potential role for monetary policy in demand stabilisation. To this purpose we have paid particular attention to the behaviour of demand components typically financed, at least in part, from borrowed funds. This is because such sub-aggregates are in principle susceptible to discretionary monetary action, which makes borrowing more costly (by raising interest rates) or more difficult (by reducing availability). In general these subaggregates, which we have summed to give a new subaggregate defined as externally financed private expenditures, played a significant part in fluctuations during the study period. Thus, even if monetary policy is restricted, in its notional impact, to the cost of capital and availability effects, it undoubtedly has some potential, again in principle, as a stabilisation device. Since the wealth effect can only enhance its potential impact on demand, our method, if anything, understates this scope. So too does our omission to consider the (possible) influence of monetary policy actions on expectations. A rather more elaborate treatment of these matters is given later.

The question implicitly considered thus far is the ability (in principle) of monetary action to influence demand components. Discretionary policy changes are, however, not necessarily aimed at influencing demand. They may in fact be directed at influencing the balance of payments to which we now turn.

## 2.6 *The Balance of Payments*

In this brief account we disaggregate the balance of payments along conventional lines; that is, we consider first the *current account*, then the *capital account* and finally their joint contribution to the change in Australia's external reserves.

Over a single cycle it is a reasonable first approximation to regard Australia's export receipts as exogenous. Hence, the endogenous element in the current account is the import bill. Import prices in foreign currency may similarly be regarded as exogenous. Assuming an exchange rate that is typically pegged, although it experiences occasional jumps determined (proximately) by the authorities, the endogenous import component is the quantity of imports demanded. This depends primarily upon the level of real aggregate demand and, given this, the stage of the inventory cycle. Thus, in as far as discretionary monetary action influences the current balance, it typically does so indirectly, i.e. by influencing real aggregate demand and conceivably (although, as we have seen, far less certainly) the rate of planned investment in inventories.

The behaviour of Australia's current balance is set out in Figure 2.5. Quarterly figures are available only from 1959.III; thus the data do not embrace the cyclical movements in the 1950s, particularly the extremely severe swings that accompanied the Korean War boom and the recession that succeeded it.

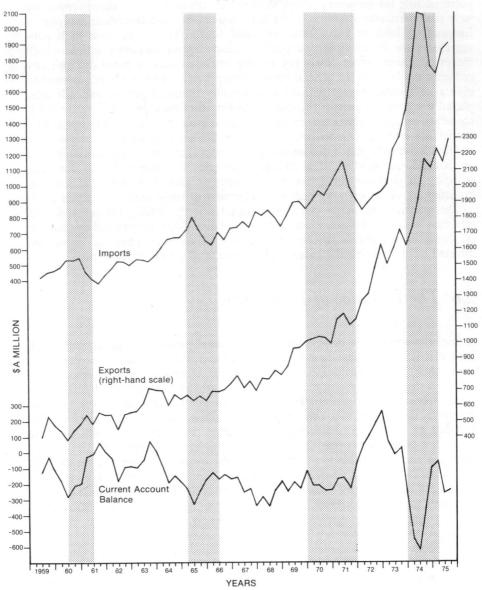

Figure 2.5    Balance of payments: current account ($A million) quarterly data, 1959(Q3)—1975(Q4)

Imports

Exports
(right-hand scale)

Current Account
Balance

$A MILLION

YEARS

*Source:* Reserve Bank of Australia, *Statistical Bulletin*

The sensitivity of the Australian current account to demand fluctuations, in particular to fluctuations in inventory investment, is well known. Prior to 1961 control of the external situation, typically dominated by the current account, was sought partly through the control of aggregate demand and partly by using import restrictions in an attempt to smooth the external impact of the inventory cycle. Thus, the observations prior to 1961 include the impact of the restrictions imposed from time to time, while those after 1961 do not. Because of the demand and inventory effects it is not surprising to find a fairly close correspondence between our cycle peaks and troughs in the current account position (as in 1960 and 1965) and a fairly severe deterioration in the current account in cyclical upswings, even when the role of exports in generating the upswings was important, if not dominant. The swing of 1972–4 was a partial exception to this generalisation, since the very sharp rise in export receipts was not overtaken by imports until virtually the peak of our capacity utilisation cycle, and the trough in the current account deficit did not occur until the September quarter of 1974. Until the mid-1960s these fluctuations were superimposed on a current account position, and *a fortiori* on an external position as a whole, that was commonly believed to be secularly weak.

After the onset of the mineral expansion from about 1964 this position changed sharply both on current account – as mineral exports expanded, sharply reducing Australia's dependence on wool and other agricultural output – and on capital account – with an inflow of private capital that grew fairly steadily until about the middle of 1972. Since that time there have been very considerable fluctuations in the rate of capital inflow, and it is probably quite reasonable to argue that, at least since 1972, the short term problem of managing the external position has become very much one of managing the capital account, i.e. of attempting to match the rate of capital inflow to the requirements of the current balance rather than the reverse, which was typically the case before the mineral expansion.

Before attempting any discussion, however brief, of the capacity of monetary action to influence the rate of capital inflow, it will be useful to have some descriptive data on the capital account. To provide this we shall make use of the following definitions:

Long-term          $\equiv$ Other direct + Portfolio – Australian Investment          (1)
identified private      investment       investment overseas
capital inflow

Short-term          $\equiv$ Non-official + Balancing          (2)
private capital       movements       item
inflow

This excludes the item 'undistributed income', which simply appears as a contra to an identical debit on current account and in any case contributes very little to the variance of the sum of equations 1 and 2 when it is included.

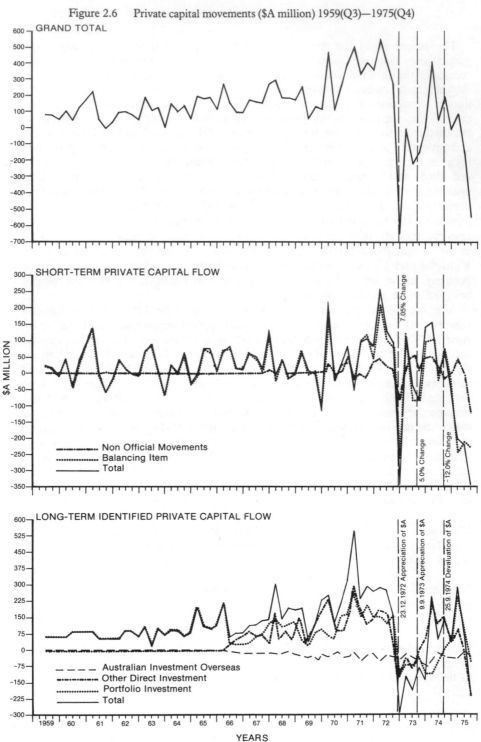

Figure 2.6    Private capital movements ($A million) 1959(Q3)—1975(Q4)

Source: Reserve Bank of Australia, *Statistical Bulletin*

Figure 2.6 presents graphs of the main series in terms of equations 1 and 2. The main points emerging from this figure are:

(1) The long-term identified private capital inflow is dominated by other direct investment and portfolio investment, with Australian investment overseas being generally rather small and stable.

(2) The short-term private capital inflow estimates are dominated by the balancing item, which is, of course, simply a residual here *assumed* to reflect mainly short term capital movements.

(3) The two private inflows seem to move together in the very short term.

(4) There is some suggestion that significant capital movements under both heads occurred in anticipation of the exchange rate adjustments of 1973 and 1974.

Finally, in Figure 2.7 are shown the contribution of private capital movements (as officially defined) and the current balance to explaining the change in overseas reserves.

Given that the behaviour of private capital inflow not only is of increased importance in explaining the balance-of-payments position but must also be expected to become more important as the Australian capital market develops and becomes progressively more closely integrated with the rest of the world, we need to ask how far capital inflow is responsive to discretionary monetary action.

Some part of overseas private investment in Australia is likely to be autonomous with respect to Australian economic conditions, at least over a policy horizon of (say) one or two years, and to be based on calculations regarding world demands, trade policy and world prices. Nevertheless, the precise timing of fund inflows associated with any such investment may still be influenced by Australian monetary conditions, in particular by variation in the effective cost of borrowing abroad rather than in Australia. This is generally a matter of relative interest rates, but the effective interest rate will also be influenced by the anticipation of exchange rate changes and by such administrative devices as the variable deposit requirement (VDR)[12] Quantitatively, these arguments apply with at least equal force to flows of portfolio investment, while short term flows, particularly those originating in leads or lags in payments for imports and receipts from exports, are likely to be sensitive to exchange rate expectations.

Thus, in as far as:

(a) private capital movements are sensitive to relative interest rates;

(b) market rates and effective rates are separable by such devices as the VDR technique;

(c) exchange rate expectations are endogenous; and

(d) exchange rate expectations are directly or indirectly susceptible to influence by monetary policy,

it must, in principle at least, be possible to modify the rate of capital inflow in any desired direction by taking appropriate monetary action. This, of course, could give monetary policy a direct impact on the external constraint via the capital account, which might well prove more significant than its indirect impact

Figure 2.7  Balance of payments: summary ($A million) quarterly data, 1959(Q3)—1975(Q4)

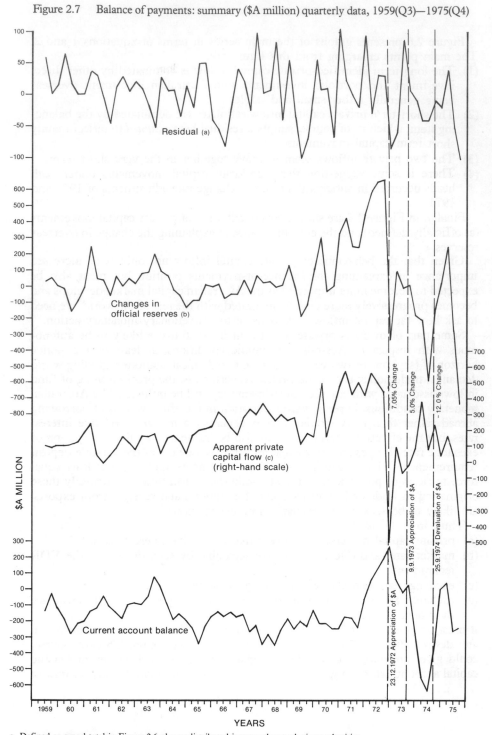

a  Defined as grand total in Figure 2.6 plus undistributed income plus marketing authorities
b  Defined as change in official reserves less current account less apparent private capital flow
c  Increases in reserves shown as positive
*Source:* Reserve Bank of Australia, *Statistical Bulletin*

via the current account.

Qualitatively, both economic theory and rather casual empiricism support this view. However, as is usual in policy matters the essential problem is not qualitative but quantitative. We need to have some quantitative information linking the discretionary devices of monetary policy with the dynamic response of private capital flows. We return to this problem in a later chapter in which an attempt is made to review the present state of economic knowledge in this area.

For the present we draw, however tentatively, the following conclusions.

(1) During the 1950s and early 1960s Australia's external problems arose mainly on current account and in large part reflected the (lagged) response of imports to domestic demand and the inventory cycle.

(2) Since the mid-1960s the capital account has grown in importance, and since the early 1970s fluctuations in the rate of private capital inflow have tended to dominate short-term fluctuations in the external position.

(3) This suggests that, whereas the authorities once sought to adjust the external position by operating on aggregate demand and smoothing the import fluctuations by means of import controls . . .

(4) They may in turn – at least in the medium term of, say, 1975–85 – need to operate more extensively with the aim of influencing private capital flows.[13]

## 2.7 The Rate of Change of Prices

At present (1977) the rate of change of prices is the dominant macroeconomic policy target variable in Australia, as it commonly is elsewhere. Although a more comprehensive account of the theory of the determination of the rate of change of prices in Australia must await a later stage of this study, it is clear that there is a role for both external and domestic factors in explaining inflation.[14]

In Figure 2.8 we have plotted the rate of change of prices experienced in Australia from 1950 to 1975. Clearly, the two main periods of rapid inflation in Australia – 1950–2 and 1972–3 onwards – were closely associated with rapid rates of change in the prices of Australia's exports and imports, i.e. with essentially exogenous overseas impulses. In short, and not very surprisingly since Australia is a relatively small and highly open economy, it seems that a very significant part of Australia's inflation has been imported. This suggests that much of the increase in Australia's prices since the early 1970s has been due to a process of dynamic adjustment to increases in world prices that have not been neutralised by exchange rate changes.

This rather obvious inference should not be interpreted as denying the significance of domestic factors in accounting for the rate of change of prices. Figure 2.9, for example, makes clear the sharp acceleration of the growth in both award wages and earnings in 1973–5. Although the sharp changes in wages recorded in this figure are referred to as 'domestic', it must be stressed that this classification

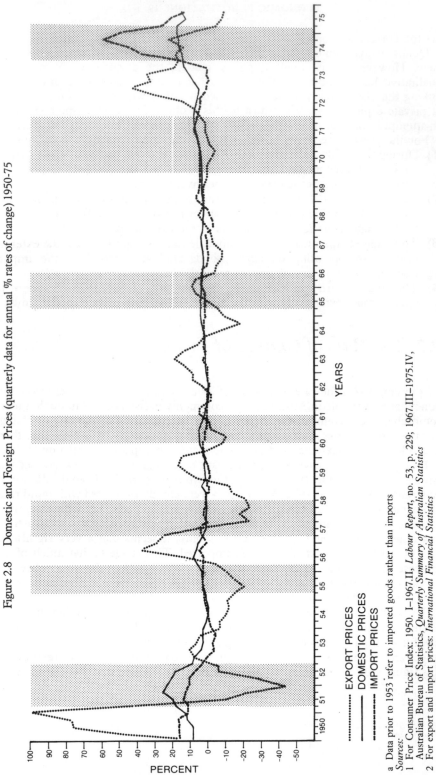

Figure 2.8    Domestic and Foreign Prices (quarterly data for annual % rates of change) 1950-75

EXPORT PRICES
DOMESTIC PRICES
IMPORT PRICES

a  Data prior to 1953 refer to imported goods rather than imports
*Sources:*
1  For Consumer Price Index: 1950. I–1967.II, *Labour Report*, no. 53, p. 229; 1967.III–1975.IV, Australian Bureau of Statistics, *Quarterly Summary of Australian Statistics*
2  For export and import prices: *International Financial Statistics*

is either highly formal or extremely controversial. Controversy arises because the relative importance of external and domestic factors in explaining price increases depends essentially upon whether the decisions of the arbitration bodies – the administrative determinants of wage increases – are themselves strongly influenced *inter alia* by such variables as export and import prices, export receipts and the state of the overall balance of payments. In so far as they are influenced by such variables and respond in a relatively routine way, the arbitration process becomes to that extent endogenised and is typically not to be regarded as an independent domestic factor in the determination of the domestic rate of price increase. The alternative view is that the arbitration process cannot usefully be treated in this way and that the Arbitration Commission, although subject to political, industrial and economic constraints, is nevertheless not compelled by them to respond to economic variables in any routine manner and is hence best regarded as an autonomous domestic influence on price determination. By taking opposed judgements on this point it is possible for investigators, even those using a similar methodology, to reach very different conclusions regarding the relative importance of domestic and external factors in explaining inflation.[15]

This issue, which is partly a matter of semantics, is not one that we need to investigate in the present instance. Our concern is with the capacity of monetary policy to influence the rate of change of the Australian price levels.

The usual theory – essentially an extension of the Phillips curve approach – would immediately concede monetary policy an indirect influence, via aggregate demand, in that evidence exists to suggest that (a) the rate of change of wage earnings, and (b) possibly the mark-up on costs typically applied by firms are both functions of the level of capacity utilisation.

Modern versions of the Phillips analysis, however, attach considerable importance to the rate of change of prices typically expected by wage earners and the rate of change of prices typically expected by firms in determining the outcome for both the rate of change of wage earnings and the rate of change of prices. Hence, in so far as these expected rates of inflation are quantitatively important, it is *possible* that monetary policy actions, by influencing inflationary expectations, have a significant, and possibly more rapid, impact on the rate of inflation than is usually ascribed to the effects occurring via aggregate demand.

At a later stage in this study we attempt to reach a judgement on just how far monetary policy can be expected to moderate inflation by influencing expectations and, of course, a simultaneous judgement on which monetary variables appear to be most important in this context. At this stage, however, it seems fairly clear that, if Australia wishes in an inflationary world to avoid relatively high rates of increase in the domestic price level, its first need appears to be for a means of insulating the domestic wage–price mechanism from inflationary impulses originating overseas.[16]

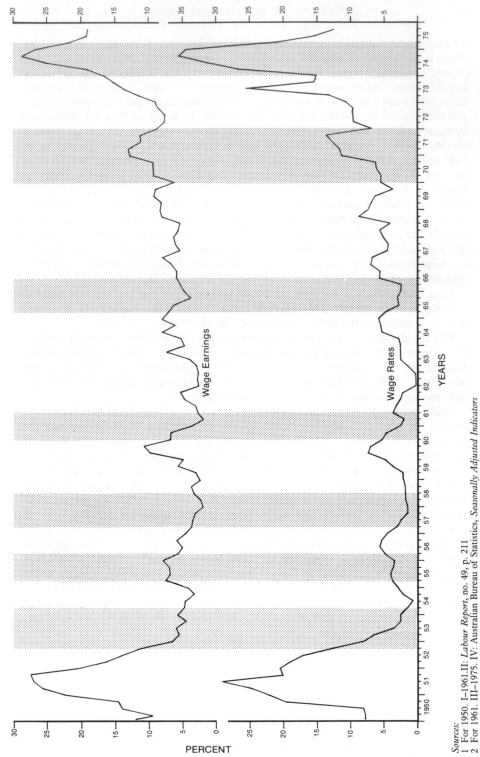

Figure 2.9   Money wage rates and earnings: annual rates of change (%), quarterly data, 1950-75

Sources:
1 For 1950. I–1961.II: Labour Report, no. 49, p. 211
2 For 1961. III–1975. IV: Australian Bureau of Statistics, Seasonally Adjusted Indicators

## 2.7 Conclusions

The aim of this chapter has been descriptive, in that an attempt has been made to give a very brief outline of Australia's cyclical experience – in particular, of the performance of capacity utilisation, the rate of domestic price increase and the state of the overall balance of payments – over the quarter-century from 1950 to 1975.

We have, using what seem to be rather weak theoretical assumptions, put forward the following seven arguments, the first two of which are familiar to the point of being platitudinous:

(1) Past cyclical fluctuations have been sufficiently severe to justify a continuing demand for anticyclical policies aimed at demand stabilisation.

(2) The behaviour of demand subaggregates that are *prima facie* susceptible to influence by monetary means suggests that there may be considerable scope for monetary policy in a macroeconomic policy aimed at demand stabilisation.

(3) The balance of payments is also likely to be responsive to monetary policy both on current account (via domestic demand) and on capital account (via the rate of private capital inflow).

(4) The relative importance and flexibility of the capital account has increased in recent years and is likely to increase further.

(5) Hence managing Australia's short-run external position may for, say, the next ten years or so – be a matter rather more of managing the capital account (and the rate of private capital inflow) than of managing the current account.

(6) Finally, the rate of change of prices in Australia cannot be regarded as being determined exclusively by external influences, in that . . .

(7) Domestic monetary action has some potential influence on Australian inflation, both via its influence on aggregate demand and possibly via its capacity to influence inflationary expectations.

Essentially, the rest of this book is concerned to reach more detailed, and at least very approximately quantitative, judgements on 2–7 and, given these judgements, to try to say what role monetary policy might most usefully be asked to play in the future.

## Notes: Chapter 2

1 There is a fairly considerable litrerature on Australia's cyclical experience since the Second World War. This includes *inter alia*: Barry and Guille [14]; Beck, Bush and Hayes [16]; Bush and Cohen [22]; Haywood [50]; Lewis [96]; Mallyon [98]; Perkins [120]; and Waterman [168] [169].

2 This issue is given extended, if rather inconclusive, discussion in Chapter 11.

3 This is a rather general statement. To see this, compare the datings found by the investigators listed in note 2.

4 There is a useful discussion in OECD [119].

5 Cf. the recent review in Reserve Bank of Australia, *Annual Report* (1977).

6 Experimental simulations of approximately this form are not uncommon. Cf. Pierce [126].

7 Obviously enough, a change in the strategy and tactics of policy may well change economic behaviour in a way excluded by the use of a constant-coefficient econometric model.

8 This assumes a reliable short-run response of output to demand, i.e. a conventional aggregate supply function.

9 Cf. OECD [118].

10 This does not seem to be so much the case in Australia.

11 The data for 1951–2 should be treated with extreme caution.

12 Initially introduced in 1972. Thus far the VDR has been applied only to borrowing overseas not excluded by the partial embargo also introduced in 1972.

13 The temporal qualification reflects the hope that by 1985 the international monetary system may be operating rather more smoothly than at present – a circumstance that should reduce the speculative element in private capital movements.

14 For two views, see Argy and Carmichael [5] and Nevile [105]. Also consult Jonson [71] [73] [76] [77].

15 For example, Argy and Carmichael [5] and Nevile [105].

16 See Kasper [88] [89].

# Chapter 3

# The Financial System

## 3.1 Introduction

The purpose of this chapter is predominantly descriptive. Its twin aims are: (a) to provide an account of the savings–investment nexus; and (b) to provide a brief review of selected financial institutions and markets.

Considerations of space entail that our treatment is skeletal in the extreme and selective, in that we concentrate on those financial institutions which seem, intuitively, to be most susceptible to influences by domestic monetary action. Beyond this only a very short sketch of the responsibilities, powers and technical devices of the Reserve Bank of Australia is provided. Excellent accounts of particular institutions are available in the references cited.

## 3.2 The Savings–Investment Nexus

Quarterly estimates of flows of funds are not available in Australia. Hence, Table 3.1 provides annual estimates of the balances of the main sectors for selected years. Although the conceptual framework of these accounts is not identical with that of the national income estimates, the differences are small. The typical pattern that emerges is, as expected in a developing and highly open economy, that:

(a) non-finance companies and the combined government sectors are usually in considerable deficit, while . . .

**Table 3.1** Sectoral balances in Australia in selected years ($A million).

| Sector | 1964-5 | 1965-6 | 1966-7 | 1967-8 | 1968-9 | 1970-1 | 1971-2 | 1972-3 | 1973-4 |
|---|---|---|---|---|---|---|---|---|---|
| 1 Government | -331 | -521 | -725 | -729 | -503 | -385 | -442 | -831 | -599 |
| 2 Corporate trading enterprises | -621 | -639 | -587 | -371 | -780 | -1,142 | -814 | 304 | -1,487 |
| 3 Subtotal: deficit sectors | -952 | -1,160 | -1,312 | -1,100 | -1,283 | -1,527 | -1,256 | -527 | -2,086 |
| 4 Households | 272 | 249 | 462 | -209 | 177 | 727 | 1,140 | 1,873 | 2,847 |
| 5 Rest of the world | 661 | 772 | 557 | 930 | 756 | 566 | 93 | -997 | 509 |
| 6 Subtotal: main surplus sectors | 933 | 1,021 | 1,019 | 721 | 933 | 1,293 | 1,233 | 876 | 3,356 |
| 7 Other financial institutions | -23 | -8 | 2 | -23 | -1 | -188 | -34 | -294 | -777 |
| 8 Discrepancy (3 + 6 + 7) | -42 | -147 | -291 | -402 | -351 | -422 | -57 | -55 | 493 |

*Source:* Reserve Bank of Australia, *Financial Flow Accounts: Supplement.* (July 1976), tables 1.1-1.10.

**Table 3.2** *Australian corporate trading enterprises:* [a] *financial flows in selected years ($A million)*

| Type of flow | 1964–5 | 1966–7 | 1968–9 | 1970–1 | 1972–3 | 1973–4 |
|---|---|---|---|---|---|---|
| 1 Saving | 1,396 | 1,490 | 2,018 | 2,054 | 2,830 | 3,117 |
| 2 Gross investment | -2,017 | -2,077 | -2,798 | -3,196 | -2,526 | -4,604 |
| 3 Borrowing | -621 | -587 | -780 | -1,142 | 304 | -1,487 |
| 4 Domestic borrowing from: | | | | | | |
| Trading banks | 183 | 108 | 236 | 360 | 800 | 1,008 |
| Financial institutions | 224 | 444 | 705 | 1,036 | 648 | 443 |
| Government | – | – | – | – | – | – |
| Trade credit | 84 | 8 | 36 | 180 | -63 | 324 |
| Other | 127 | -67 | 138 | 115 | 349 | 494 |
| 5 Borrowing from overseas: | | | | | | |
| Advances | | | | | | |
| Other claims | 85 | 105 | 147 | 127 | 21 | 20 |
| 6 Other sources: | | | | | | |
| Equities etc. | 336 | 278 | 527 | 603 | 324 | 308 |
| Debentures, notes etc., | 54 | 122 | 122 | 145 | 63 | 66 |
| 7 Increase in financial assets | -215 | -301 | -726 | -320 | -1,460 | -2,085 |
| 8 Unidentified flows | -257 | -110 | -405 | -1,104 | -986 | -909 |
| **Memorandum** | | | | | | |
| 9 Increase in equities and debentures by rest of the world | 272 | 184 | 529 | 598 | 232 | -151 |

[a] Excludes public trading enterprises.
*Source:* Reserve Bank of Australia, *Financial Flow Accounts: Supplements.*

(b) this deficit is financed partly by the domestic savings of households and unincorporated enterprises, and

(c) partly by the rest of the world through the current account deficit.

Annual data are not particularly helpful in identifying cyclical and other shifts in sector financing. Moreover, the accounts typically display a sizable and, in recent years, variable discrepancy. Nevertheless, it is clear that there is considerable short-term variation around the typical pattern as described above.

Table 3.2 gives a more detailed account of the flow of funds to non-finance companies. Extensive comment on this table is unnecessary. It does, however, make clear the variation in the share of company savings in gross investment and hence the marginal dependence of companies on external funds. Additionally, it emphasises the extent to which corporate investment is financed from overseas.[1]

Table 3.3, which is rather similar, presents data for persons and unincorporated enterprises. The main lesson to be derived from this table is the growth in the importance of lending by building societies and instalment credit.

Given the typical pattern of sectoral balances, our main concern is with the pattern of financial intermediation and the extent of its development. Overall financial development can be roughly proxied by the layering of financial claims and this in its turn is approximately indicated by the ratio of the assets held by the major financial institutions to gross national product (GNP).[2]

We must also expect that, given any rate of financial development in this sense, there will also be changes in the relative significance of financial institutions.

Since both the stages of overall financial development (as proxied above) and the relative importance of different financial intermediaries have very significant implications for the nature of the transmission process relating discretionary monetary action to ultimate economic targets and for the choice of central-banking techniques, Table 3.4 presents data bearing on these issues. Overall, the picture that emerges is one of rapid financial development as proxied by the ratio of the assets of financial institutions to GNP. The process, however, has been uneven. In particular:

(1) The importance of the banking sector has declined, while . . .

(2) Growth has been extremely fast for:

    (a) building societies, in particular for permanent building societies (PBS);

    (b) development finance companies (now reported under the head of money market corporations);

    (d) to a far lesser extent, non-life offices.

We must expect these changes to have implications for the role and *modus operandi* of monetary policy. This is particularly likely in the case of development finance companies, which, as we shall see, are extremely important in linking Australian money and capital markets with those overseas.

**Table 3.3** *Household sector:* ᵃ*flows of funds in selected years ($A million).*

| Type of flow | 1964–5 | 1966–7 | 1969–70 | 1971–2 | 1972–3 | 1973–4 |
|---|---|---|---|---|---|---|
| 1 Gross saving | 2,062 | 2,386 | 2,510 | 3,603 | 4,843 | 6,847 |
| 2 Gross investment | -1,790 | -1,924 | -2,389 | -2,463 | -2,970 | -4,000 |
| 3 Net lending | 272 | 462 | 121 | 1,140 | 1,873 | 2,847 |
| 4 Domestic borrowing: | | | | | | |
| Trading banks | 106 | 255 | 220 | 282 | 1,228 | 950 |
| Other advances | 644 | 661 | 1,191 | 1,331 | 2,235 | 2,334 |
| Other claims | 55 | -52 | 83 | 132 | 181 | 39 |
| 5 Increase in financial assets (-): | | | | | | |
| Bank deposits and notes | 354 | 381 | 402 | 861 | 1,511 | 576 |
| Savings bank deposits | 410 | 510 | 402 | 756 | 1,853 | 951 |
| Shares and debentures | 21 | 208 | 475 | 647 | 1,011 | 911 |
| Government securitiesᵇ | -103 | 22 | -54 | -66 | -74 | 118 |
| Life and superannuation funds | 474 | 567 | 782 | 1,076 | 1,149 | 1,184 |
| Shares in co-operatives | 61 | 68 | 256 | 496 | 674 | 525 |
| Other | 76 | 35 | 173 | 163 | 250 | 467 |
| 6 Unidentified flows | -216 | -465 | -821 | -1,048 | -857 | 1,438 |
| **Memoranda** | | | | | | |
| 7 Increase in equities | -40 | -3 | -19 | 61 | -323 | 158 |
| 8 Increase in mortgages outstanding (PBS)ᶜ | 42 | 47 | 276 | 424 | 760 | 479 |

ᵃ Includes unincorporated enterprises.
ᵇ Includes local and semi-government securities.
ᶜ PBS = permanent building societies.
*Source:* Reserve Bank of Australia, *Flow of Funds Estimates* (July 1976).

**Table 3.4** *Assets and growth rates: selected financial institutions in selected years (new definitions).*

| Type of institution | Assets ($A m.) 1965 | 1970 | 1974 | Proportion held (%) 1965 | 1970 | 1974 | Annual growth rate (%) 1965-70 | 1970-4 | 1964-74 |
|---|---|---|---|---|---|---|---|---|---|
| 1 Trading banks | 5,460 | 8,004 | 15,340 | 23.4 | 21.0 | 22.0 | 8.0 | 17.7 | 11.7 |
| 2 Savings banks | 5,150 | 7,504 | 11,766 | 22.1 | 19.7 | 16.9 | 7.8 | 11.9 | 9.6 |
| 3 Life offices | 3,285 | 5,481 | 8,282 | 14.1 | 14.4 | 11.9 | 10.8 | 10.9 | 10.8 |
| 4 Non-life offices | 938 | 1,799 | 3,062 | 4.0 | 4.7 | 4.4 | 13.9 | 14.2 | 13.8 |
| 5 Finance corporations | 1,555 | 3,633 | 9,023 | 6.7 | 9.5 | 13.0 | 18.5 | 25.5 | 20.6 |
| 6 Building societies | 947 | 1,959 | 4,521 | 4.1 | 5.1 | 6.5 | 15.7 | 23.3 | 19.0 |
| of which: PBS[a] | (276) | (1,082) | (3,571) | (1.2) | (2.8) | (5.1) | (31.4) | (34.8) | (32.9) |
| 7 Short-term money market | 352 | 667 | 488 | 1.5 | 1.8 | 0.7 | 13.6 | -7.5 | 3.0 |
| 8 Money market corporations | 54 | 713 | 2,249 | 0.2 | 1.9 | 3.2 | 67.5 | 33.3 | 46.6 |
| 9 Pension funds | 2,030 | 3,314 | 4,982 | 8.7 | 8.7 | 7.1 | 10.3 | 10.7 | 10.5 |
| 10 Total of 1 to 9 | 19,771 | 33,074 | 59,713 | 84.8 | 86.8 | 85.9 | 10.8 | 15.9 | 13.1 |
| 11 Total: all financial institutions | 23,328 | 38,105 | 69,507 | 100.0 | 100.0 | 100.0 | 10.3 | 16.2 | 12.4 |
| 12 GNP | 19,598 | 29,941 | 50,669 | | | | 8.8 | 14.1 | 11.1 |
| 13 Ratio 11/12 | 1.190 | 1.273 | 1.372 | | | | | | |

[a] PBS = permanent building societies.
*Sources*: Reserve Bank of Australia, *Flow of Funds Estimates* (July 1976); and Australian Bureau of Statistics, *Australian National Accounts, 1974–5*, appendix C, table A, p. 108.

# 3.3 *Australian Trading Banks*[3]

As we have seen, the relative importance of the banking system as a whole, at least as proxied by the shares in total financial assets, has been declining. The implications of this decline, however, need two qualifications.

The first is the obvious point that a fall in the *average* importance of banks, which is inevitable as financial development proceeds, does not entail that, as *marginal* sources of finance, the banks suffer a similar decline. Thus, in the cyclical process the banks are likely to retain importance as a source of finance, although alternative sources of finance to those denied bank advances are likely to emerge on an increasingly competitive basis as financial development proceeds.[4]

The second qualification is that the main trading banks are themselves closely involved, via part ownership, in hire purchase companies, in development finance companies and, as we see later, in savings banks. Thus, the influence of the trading banks as institutions on financial developments within Australia is not well proxied by our simple asset-ratio concept.

The major trading banks dominate the business of the cheque-paying banks in Australia. Their relevant deposit liabilities also dominate the money supply concepts $M_1$ and $M_2$ although, in view of the importance of the savings banks, not the $M_3{}^3$ concept. These points are brought out in Table 3.5.

**Table 3.5** *Trading banks, savings banks and money stock in selected years ($A million).*

| Aggregate | 1960 | 1965 | 1970 | 1975 |
|---|---|---|---|---|
| 1 Current deposits | | | | |
| (all trading banks) | 2,496 | 2,977 | 3,798 | 5,971 |
| 2 $M_1$ | 3,293 | 3,790 | 4,984 | 8,327 |
| 3 Fixed deposits | | | | |
| (all trading banks) | 870 | 1,688 | 2,617 | 6,739 |
| 4 Negotiable Certificates of Deposit | | | | |
| (all trading banks) | | | 145 | 1,144 |
| 5 $M_2$ | 4,163 | 5,478 | 7,747 | 16,211 |
| 6 Savings bank deposits | 3,138 | 4,858 | 7,090 | 12,603 |
| 7 $M_3$ | 7,301 | 10,337 | 14,837 | 28,814 |
| 8 Total deposits | 6,504 | 9,523 | 13,650 | 26,457 |
| 9 Ratio 6/8 (%) | 48·25 | 51·01 | 51·94 | 47·64 |
| 10 Ratio 2/7 (%) | 45·10 | 36·66 | 33·59 | 28·90 |
| 11 Ratio 5/7 (%) | 57·02 | 52·99 | 52·21 | 56·26 |

*Source*: Reserve Bank of Australia, *Statistical Bulletin: Financial Supplement* (October 1975).

If we examine the assets of the major trading banks' balance sheet, we can, ignoring the detailed composition of the groupings, identify a number of sub-aggregates that it is helpful to employ (see Table 3.6). Thus, we can define

$$\begin{matrix} \text{Total} \\ \text{assets} \end{matrix} \equiv \begin{matrix} \text{LGS} \\ \text{assets} \end{matrix} + \begin{matrix} \text{Statutory} \\ \text{reserve} \\ \text{deposits} \end{matrix} + \begin{matrix} \text{Other} \\ \text{securities} \end{matrix} + \begin{matrix} \text{Loans} \\ \text{to} \\ \text{authorised} \\ \text{money-} \\ \text{market} \\ \text{dealers} \end{matrix} + \begin{matrix} \text{Loans,} \\ \text{advances} \\ \text{and} \\ \text{bills} \\ \text{discounted} \end{matrix} + \begin{matrix} \text{Other} \\ \text{assets} \end{matrix}$$

**Table 3.6** *Assets of major trading banks in selected years (yearly averages, $A million).*

| Type of asset | 1955–6 | 1960–1 | 1965–6 | 1970–1 | 1974–5 |
|---|---|---|---|---|---|
| 1 LGS assets | 570·3 | 646·3 | 1,235·9 | 1,540·9 | 3,145·7 |
| of which: | | | | | |
| Australian government securities | (416·1) | (501·5) | (1,075·1) | (1,372·2) | (2,871·0) |
| 2 SRDs | 543·9 | 587·7 | 606·8 | 642·0 | 455·8 |
| 3 Other securities | 17·0 | 47·7 | 81·7 | 168·6 | 395·9 |
| 4 Loans to authorised money-market dealers | n.a. | 47·2 | 70·6 | 93·9 | 143·7 |
| 5 Loans, advances and bills discounted | 1,816·6 | 2,100·1 | 2,708·6 | 4,505·0 | 9,348·4 |
| of which: | | | | | |
| Bills discounted | (n.a.) | (n.a.) | (9·6) | (48·4) | (525·4) |
| Other advances | (1,775·0) | (2,032·5) | (2,393·8) | (3,717·0) | 7,470·5) |
| Total | (1,775·0) | (2,032·5) | (2,403·4) | (3,765·4) | (7,995·9) |
| 6 Other assets | — | — | 54·0 | 51·4 | 42·6 |

*Source*: Reserve Bank of Australia, *Statistical Bulletin: Financial Supplement* (October 1975).

As we shall see, in Australia the quantitative control of the trading banks rests on the existence of a conventional ratio of liquid assets and government securities (LGS) to deposit liabilities that the banks have agreed, with the Reserve Bank, to regard as a minimum. If a bank cannot meet this conventional minimum by other means, it must do so by borrowing from the Reserve Bank at a rate that is in principle penal. Thus, the dynamics of adjustment apart, in so far as the Reserve Bank can control the stock of LGS assets in the hands of the banks, it can control the maximum quantity of deposits that the banks can supply.

Until relatively recently the ability to conduct open market operations was severely limited by the size of the bond market. Hence, the special account device was developed, so that the central bank (then the Commonwealth Bank) could freeze bank reserves by calling them into special account deposits, which were not available to the banks for ordinary reserve purposes. Originally, this device had characteristics that were very different from the typical 'variable reserve ratio' device.[5] By the late 1950s, however, it was being operated as such a ratio; and hence, when by the legislation of 1959 the special account device was replaced by the existing statutory reserve deposit (SRD) system, the change was formal rather than real. Under the present system each trading bank is required to hold a defined and common ratio of the bank's Australian deposits in its SRD with the Reserve Bank. This ratio can be varied by the Reserve Bank at one day's notice (up to 25 per cent of deposits), and in certain conditions and with much longer notice the SRD ratio can be raised above 25 per cent.

It follows that, assuming that the conventional LGS minimum is observed, the SRD device gives the Reserve Bank virtually complete control over the banks' LGS holdings and thus over the maximum deposit supply. Dynamics apart, the slippages in control can only reflect a situation in which the banks typically hold a fairly substantial excess LGS assets and at the same time collectively possess no well-defined and reliable demand function for excess LGS assets.

From this short description it follows that LGS assets (in the main) and SRDs are not simple choice assets to the banks in the sense typically assumed in portfolio theory. The choice assets in this sense are:
(a) other securities;
(b) loans to the short-term money market; and
(c) loans, advances and bills discounted.

Among these the most important item is advances, and it is unfortunately precisely this item over which the banks have the least degree of short term control. This comes about because, under the overdraft system of lending, the banks control the limits to the sums that customers are *authorised* to borrow, not the sums that they *actually do* borrow, which, of course, constitute advances.[6] Thus, a bank attempting to reduce advances by reducing total limits may face a considerable lag in doing so. Moreover, a bank attempting this at a time when the non-finance company sector is increasing its demand for finance may well find that a reduction in outstanding limits is nevertheless accompanied by an increase in advances. In short, simply because of the technical problems involved, the control of advances (as opposed to limits) is likely to exhibit a non-negligible lag, and possibly some unreliability in the form of the lag. This must imply a relatively slow adjustment by the banks (as a group) to changes in LGS holdings, since observed changes in advances will generally differ from those planned by the banks.[7]

The relatively imprecise control that the trading banks can exert over advances is not the only factor making for a relatively slow response by them to changes in LGS holdings. The banks as a group also experience severe seasonal fluctuations, primarily resulting from the impact of government finance but still, to a lesser extent, reflecting the pattern of Australia's trade in agricultural exports. These seasonal patterns appear to be changing, and there have been attempts to moderate the taxation element in them. However, it seems highly probable that the individual trading bank, confronted by a change in its LGS holding, has a difficult problem of diagnosis in determining how far the change is transitory (seasonal or random) and how far it is permanent enough to serve as a basis for seeking to adjust advances. This difficulty will surely have the effect of delaying the trading banks' response to some forms of change in their LGS holdings.

In short, partly because of the nature of the overdraft system of lending and partly because of the diagnosis problem, we must expect the trading banks to respond rather slowly to changes in LGS and probably, although this is less sure, to have a rather unreliable demand function for excess LGS.[8]

# 3.4 The Savings Banks[9]

There are three types of savings banks in Australia:
(a) the Commonwealth Savings Bank;
(b) the savings bank subsidiaries of the private trade banks; and
(c) the state savings banks (including the Trustee Savings Bank of Tasmania).

In total, savings bank deposits are of the same order of magnitude as trading bank deposits. The shares of groups (a)–(c) has changed rapidly since the establishment of the private savings banks in and after 1956. Roughly speaking, state savings banks hold about one-quarter (or a little less) of all deposits, while the Commonwealth Savings Bank and the private savings banks share the remainder roughly equally. Table 3.7 gives figures for total Australian savings-bank deposits, and this makes clear how the dominance of the Commonwealth Savings Bank has been eroded since 1955 by the competition of the private savings banks.

**Table 3.7** *Australian savings banks: shares in deposits in selected years* (%).

| Type of savings bank | 1954–5 | 1959–60 | 1964–5 | 1969–70 | 1973–4 |
|---|---|---|---|---|---|
| 1 Commonwealth Savings Bank | 65 | 52 | 45 | 41 | 38 |
| 2 Trustee and state savings banks | 35 | 30 | 26 | 25 | 24 |
| 3 Private savings banks | n.a. | 18 | 30 | 34 | 37 |
| **Memorandum** | | | | | |
| 4 Deposits[a] ($A m.) | 2,147 | 3,155 | 4,887 | 7,105 | 11,196 |

[a] Average for year, excluding external territories.
*Source*: Commonwealth Statistician, *Australian Banking Statistics*.

Savings bank accounts are used, at least in part, as a substitute for current accounts at the trading banks, although the rate of deposit turnover of savings banks is very considerably less, as one would expect, than that of trading banks. Accounts are not confined to small balances, and the banks offer a wide variety of deposit forms designed to compete effectively with fixed deposits at the trading banks, deposits with building societies and deposits with instalment credit firms. Like the trading banks the savings banks experience a seasonal movement in net increments to deposits, although one that is far less marked than that of the trading banks.

The interest sensitivity of the demand for savings bank deposits has been the subject of a fair amount of research. Various experiments have been conducted, by Lewis and Wallace [97], Valentine [165] and Lewis [96]. The results of these are not easy to summarise. Nevertheless, it seems clear that the demand for savings bank deposits is responsive to rates on fixed deposits, building society deposits and the short term obligations of other non-bank financial intermediaries. Since many of these theoretically competing rates move together, disentangling their individual influences is a difficult matter.

It is, however, interesting to note that the demand for savings bank deposits seems, from some results reported by Lewis and Wallace, to respond not only to changes in the administered rates on competing encashable assets but also to the rates ruling on marketable government securities.

Given these results, it is clear that the composition of the private sector's planned liquid-asset holdings is responsive to shifts in relative rates and that, at least at the margin, changes in relative rates may shift fund flows from (say) instalment credit to (say) the mortgage market.

The asset portfolios of the savings banks are subject to certain minimum requirements. The savings banks are required to maintain funds equal to 100 per cent of deposits in a defined set of assets. Additionally, they are required to hold a minimum proportion of deposits (initially 70 per cent) in liquid assets plus Commonwealth government and public authority securities. Of this figure, 10 per cent of deposits must be held in liquid assets, which since 1962 have been defined to include loans to the short term money market. Both these requirements have been varied from time to time (see Table 3.8).

The savings banks are not subject to the SRD device. In consequence, control of their lending to the private sector can only be affected by:[10]
(a) variations in the rates payable on savings bank deposits in relation to closely substitutable assets;
(b) changes in the LGS and liquid asset ratios that they are required to maintain; and
(c) lending directives from the Reserve Bank.

As lenders, the savings banks are predominantly engaged in: (a) financing the government sector; and (b) providing housing loans. Recently the proportion of housing loans has been rising, while the *composition* of finance to the government sector has also changed, the savings banks typically switching from Common-

**Table 3.8** *Australian savings banks:*
*principal assets in selected years ($A million).*

| Type of asset | 1960-1 | 1965-6 | 1970-1 | 1974-5 |
|---|---|---|---|---|
| 1 Cash | 285·8 | 429·9 | 633·8 | 940·2 |
| of which: | | | | |
| Deposits at Reserve Bank | (277·1) | (419·2) | (615·5) | (907·6) |
| 2 Deposits with trading banks | 89·1 | 129·0 | 106·2 | 391·0 |
| 3 Australian government securities | 1,574·1 | 2,092·7 | 2,287·7 | 2,869·3 |
| 4 Other securities | 622·8 | 1,198·8 | 1,960·6 | 3,296·7 |
| 5 Loans to authorised | | | | |
| money-market dealers | 15·3 | 34·2 | 79·3 | 80·2 |
| 6 Loans and advances | 679·2 | 1,535·0 | 2,603·1 | 5,320·1 |
| of which: | | | | |
| Housing | (612·5) | (1,358·5) | (2,364·3) | (4,717·4) |
| Other | (66·7) | (176·5) | (238·9) | (602·7) |
| 7 Cheques, bills and balances due from | | | | |
| other banks | 0·5 | 0·5 | 183·4 | 294·1 |

*Source*: Reserve Bank of Australia, *Statistical Bulletin* (October 1975).

wealth to state and other public-authority obligations. Finally, there is a relatively small category of other loans – which now includes, personal loans – which also has tended to grow.

Savings banks are collectively just about as important a source of housing finance as the building societies. Moreover, since their lending policies are subject to directives from the Reserve Bank while they typically hold significant excess LGS, they can, and on occasions have been employed to, stabilise, at least in part, the supply of housing finance in periods in which changes in relative rates have inhibited building society lending.[11]

Because of the severe constraints on their operations, the incidence of Reserve Bank directives, and the social factors attaching to housing finance, it must be a matter of some doubt as to how far the portfolio behaviour of savings banks is susceptible to analysis along the usual lines, in which the portfolio manager is assumed to maximise some simple function of expected returns. Nevertheless, an important study by Sharpe [149] [150] of this form has obtained useful results, as has a study by Johnston and Spasojevic [69]. Indeed, both studies suggest that savings banks (as a group) respond to the differential between the mortgage rate and the rates on Commonwealth securities.

To summarise: the savings banks are extremely important intermediaries whose liabilities are either money (on our $M_3$ definition) or quasi-money, if some narrower aggregate is chosen as the empirical definition of the money stock.

Despite the (probably) important convenience elements in the yield on their deposits, they seem to be relatively close substitutes for building society deposits and deposits with other non-bank financial intermediaries. Therefore, the savings banks are to this extent subject to influence via relative rate movements.

On the supply side the savings banks are important and captive lenders to the public sector and of major importance as a source of housing finance.

# 3.5 Building Societies[12]

As we have already seen, the rate of growth of building societies in Australia has been dramatic. This is particularly true of permanent building societies, whose share of housing advances outstanding has risen by a factor of more than 4 since the mid-1950s.

The main sources of funds to building societies are shares and deposits. These two items account for about 92 per cent of their total resources. The remainder consists largely in borrowing from other intermediaries, particularly banks and insurance companies, and borrowing from the government sector.

From the point of view of monetary policy there are three major issues relating to building societies. The first concerns the sensitivity of net flows of funds into the societies to changes in the stance of monetary policy. The second relates to the allocation of funds by the societies, i.e. the sensitivity of their portfolio decisions to rate differentials and the stance of monetary policy. The third, which is closely related to the first, is the financial stability of the societies. This is essentially a liquidity problem, not an insolvency problem; but it is nevertheless an important matter, since the preservation of the stability of the financial system is the primary and over-riding responsibility of the Reserve Bank. Hence, if net inflows of funds are strongly susceptible to (policy-induced) movements in relative rates:

(a) the rate of mortgage approvals will substantially exceed deposit and share inflows plus repayments;

(b) as approvals are drawn down, the societies will have a substantial net cash drain, so that . . .

(c) there is a risk of a run on deposits developing, unless . . .

(d) the societies possess ample liquid assets that can be realised, or unless . . .

(e) they have ready access, on some standby basis, to alternative sources of funds.

Thus, the dynamics of building society operations, which make it difficult for them (as a group) to raise rates rapidly in response to movements in competing rates and their need to grant approvals on the basis of *expected* fund inflows, leads to a potential liquidity risk. As we shall see, the risk became real in 1973–4 when the direction of Reserve Bank policy was shifted sharply to restraint.

There is no published model of the building society sector that provides equations explaining building societies' rate-setting and borrowing equations. Both Sharpe [148] and Johnston and Spasojevic [68] have, however, investigated the asset behaviour of permanent building societies, while it seems a fair inference

**Table 3.9** *Permanent building societies: sources of funds, 1973–5 (monthly data, not seasonally adjusted, $A million).*

| Year / Month | Share capital | | | Unsecured borrowings[a] | | | Secured borrowings | | Change in total |
|---|---|---|---|---|---|---|---|---|---|
| | Received | Withdrawn | Net change | Received | Withdrawn | Net change | From government | From banks[b] | |
| **1973** Jul. | 242.6 | 167.5 | 75.1 | 61.6 | 47.4 | 14.2 | 65.3 | 63.9 | 14.5 |
| Aug. | 235.6 | 162.6 | 73.0 | 76.0 | 47.2 | 28.8 | 65.5 | 53.9 | 1.0 |
| Sep. | 204.5 | 158.2 | 46.3 | 65.3 | 53.3 | 12.0 | 66.2 | 57.0 | - 5.7 |
| Oct. | 271.1 | 206.7 | 64.4 | 66.3 | 62.4 | 3.9 | 66.2 | 48.0 | - 6.2 |
| Nov. | 237.2 | 202.7 | 34.5 | 60.9 | 60.3 | 0.6 | 66.0 | 40.5 | -10.4 |
| Dec. | 237.7 | 202.3 | 35.4 | 98.8 | 69.0 | 29.8 | 66.3 | 33.0 | - 9.2 |
| **1974** Jan. | 213.9 | 162.5 | 51.4 | 69.7 | 47.7 | 22.0 | 66.5 | 22.8 | -13.1 |
| Feb. | 206.6 | 173.2 | 33.4 | 69.5 | 51.2 | 18.3 | 66.4 | 24.0 | - 2.2 |
| Mar. | 222.5 | 194.7 | 27.8 | 71.6 | 55.0 | 16.6 | 66.1 | 26.7 | 1.6 |
| Apr. | 224.3 | 215.0 | 9.3 | 71.2 | 62.1 | 9.1 | 65.8 | 28.7 | - 0.4 |
| May | 263.0 | 257.1 | 5.9 | 72.9 | 83.3 | -10.4 | 65.7 | 37.9 | 13.2 |
| Jun. | 252.5 | 271.0 | -18.5 | 78.8 | 86.2 | - 7.4 | 68.9 | 36.9 | 9.1 |
| Jul. | 331.6 | 259.5 | 72.1 | 95.4 | 81.7 | 13.7 | 64.9 | 29.5 | -10.8 |
| Aug. | 253.8 | 223.5 | 30.3 | 83.7 | 70.5 | 13.2 | 64.7 | 25.4 | - 3.7 |
| Sep. | 239.5 | 226.0 | 13.5 | 92.4 | 69.2 | 23.2 | 64.5 | 23.1 | - 1.9 |
| Oct. | 232.4 | 388.3 | -155.9 | 85.2 | 99.6 | -14.4 | 64.4 | 32.8 | 14.2 |
| Nov. | 237.2 | 182.3 | 55.0 | 70.5 | 59.9 | 10.6 | 64.4 | 35.2 | 14.9 |
| Dec. | 257.5 | 194.1 | 63.4 | 85.5 | 72.7 | 12.8 | 64.1 | 43.6 | - 5.6 |
| **1975** Jan. | 250.4 | 167.7 | 82.7 | 77.0 | 52.4 | 24.6 | 64.1 | 33.0 | - 9.0 |
| Feb. | 241.5 | 179.3 | 62.2 | 87.8 | 62.2 | 25.6 | 63.8 | 31.8 | - 9.1 |
| Mar. | 255.0 | 195.3 | 59.7 | 92.1 | 75.9 | 16.2 | 63.7 | 21.1 | -14.0 |
| Apr. | 305.9 | 258.1 | 47.8 | 108.0 | 94.8 | 13.2 | 63.5 | 21.3 | 0.9 |
| May | 326.3 | 224.0 | 102.3 | 100.4 | 91.1 | 9.3 | 63.6 | 19.0 | 3.2 |
| Jun. | 315.6 | 248.8 | 66.8 | 113.0 | 91.0 | 22.0 | 62.1 | 23.0 | 2.3 |

[a] Includes deposits but excludes unsecured borrowings from banks.
[b] Advances under Commonwealth States Housing Agreement.
*Source:* Australian Bureau of Statistics, *Permanent Building Societies.*

from the available time series and the work of Lewis [96] and Lewis and Wallace [97] that building society liabilities must compete fairly closely with savings bank deposits and the fixed deposits of the trading banks. Econometrically, however, this is a difficult area, and it is not possible to put forward any model of the household sector's asset choices that offers generally acceptable estimates of the response to changes in relative interest rates.

From examining the ratio of loan approvals from the permanent building societies to total approvals for housing from the major lenders, it appears that approvals by permanent building societies are rather more volatile than total approvals. In view of the fact that the societies are specialised lenders (unlike the trading banks and life offices) and are subjected to sharper movements in net fund inflows than savings banks, this is not surprising. Additionally, the steady rise in the societies' share in total approvals reflects their remarkable rate of growth, much of which must have been at the expense of the savings banks.

To supplement this information and illustrate the short run problems involved, Table 3.9 provides data from July 1973 to June 1975 on the sources of building society funds. This table shows that the societies (as a group) experience fairly severe fluctuations in net increments in share capital and unsecured borrowings. There is evidence of a seasonal movement, inflow tending to fall in quarters I and II, and of a cyclical response. It is also clear that secured borrowings tend to move inversely to net inflows on share and deposit account, thus to a limited extent smoothing the total inflow. Despite this, net fluctuations in all three flows can be very severe.

Table 3.10 shows the societies' lending operations for the same period. From this table it is clear that, while the societies can, and do, adjust loan approvals in response to unexpected shortfalls in net fund inflows, loans advanced are harder to control because of their dynamic relation to past approvals. The resultant cash-flow problem is obviously severe; and in the period covered – more precisely, in 1974.III and IV – it was particularly acute in Queensland and, to a lesser extent, South Australia.

From the point of view of monetary policy it would be helpful to have reliable estimates of a dynamic equation, or pair of equations, explaining net inflows of funds. However, as already pointed out, no published model along these lines exists at present.

The absence of estimates of this type is not surprising. The yield on building society liabilities contains a non-pecuniary element in that to hold them, rather than (say) the obligations of trading banks, may increase the probability of obtaining a mortgage in the future and at the same time offer the probability of a rather lower mortgage rate. If these considerations are valid, the formulation of a function explaining deposit inflows will raise some awkward problems about defining the appropriate own rate on deposits and the appropriate rates on competing assets.

**Table 3.10** *Permanent building societies: lending operations, 1973–5 (monthly data, not seasonally adjusted, $A million).*

| Year/ month | | Loans approved[a] | Loans advanced | Change in principal outstanding | Loans approved but not advanced (end of period) | Cancellations of loans |
|---|---|---|---|---|---|---|
| 1973 | Jul. | 65·5 | 72·7 | 38·8 | 178·2 | 4·1 |
| | Aug. | 89·7 | 73·4 | 36·1 | 190·9 | 3·7 |
| | Sep. | 84·7 | 69·5 | 38·0 | 202·0 | 4·2 |
| | Oct. | 89·6 | 81·8 | 44·8 | 206·5 | 2·8 |
| | Nov. | 68·4 | 76·9 | 43·3 | 194·2 | 3·9 |
| | Dec. | 43·7 | 66·4 | 34·6 | 168·9 | 2·7 |
| 1974 | Jan. | 47·9 | 46·0 | 23·5 | 165·8 | 5·1 |
| | Feb. | 60·7 | 55·3 | 29·7 | 167·5 | 3·9 |
| | Mar. | 69·3 | 61·5 | 31·5 | 171·4 | 3·9 |
| | Apr. | 63·7 | 59·0 | 30·0 | 172·8 | 3·4 |
| | May | 66·1 | 73·8 | 38·0 | 161·0 | 4·1 |
| | Jun. | 32·8 | 51·9 | 19·9 | 138·1 | 3·8 |
| | Jul. | 45·9 | 49·2 | 20·2 | 132·4 | 2·4 |
| | Aug. | 39·5 | 46·4 | 20·2 | 122·6 | 2·9 |
| | Sep. | 45·1 | 39·9 | 17·2 | 125·0 | 2·9 |
| | Oct. | 38·6 | 46·4 | 21·8 | 114·0 | 3·3 |
| | Nov. | 34·6 | 42·7 | 17·8 | 102·8 | 3·1 |
| | Dec. | 29·6 | 42·8 | 12·7 | 86·4 | 3·3 |
| 1975 | Jan. | 33·4 | 27·1 | 1·9 | 89·8 | 3·3 |
| | Feb. | 60·4 | 33·4 | -0·6 | 114·7 | 2·4 |
| | Mar. | 70·8 | 45·4 | 10·3 | 135·7 | 4·4 |
| | Apr. | 94·8 | 58·9 | 20·7 | 167·2 | 4·5 |
| | May | 117·9 | 79·8 | 36·6 | 199·0 | 6·4 |
| | Jun. | 126·5 | 87·3 | 42·0 | 223·3 | 4·9 |

[a] Includes capitalised insurance premia and other charges.
*Source*: Australian Bureau of Statistics, *Permanent Building Societies*.

# 3.6 *Instalment Credit Companies*[13]

Like building society lending, instalment credit has expanded very dramatically in Australia. This is apparent in Table 3.11. Our concern with this sector arises, as usual, because of its *potential* response to monetary policy. Since controls over instalment lending (hire purchase) do not exist in Australia in the form in which they exist in the United Kingdom and once existed in the United States, the potential influence of monetary policy on instalment lending must arise, on the supply side, from the sensitivity of fund inflows to interest differentials and the

**Table 3.11** *Finance companies: financial flows in selected years ($A million).*

| Type of flow | 1964–5 | 1966–7 | 1968–9 | 1970–1 | 1972–3 | 1973–4 |
|---|---|---|---|---|---|---|
| 1 Gross savings | 10 | 21 | 43 | 59 | 140 | 51 |
| 2 Gross investments | -16 | -41 | -51 | -91 | -189 | -221 |
| 3 Net borrowing (-) | - 6 | -20 | - 8 | -32 | -49 | -170 |
| 4 Increase in financial assets: | | | | | | |
| Mortgages | – | 3 | 2 | 1 | 174 | 340 |
| Loans to companies | 38 | 19 | 141 | 138 | 365 | 73 |
| Other advances | 118 | 210 | 388 | 396 | 1,286 | 805 |
| Other financial assets | - 5 | 41 | 23 | 0 | 22 | 236 |
| 5 Total | 151 | 273 | 554 | 535 | 1,847 | 1,454 |
| 6 Increase in liabilities: | | | | | | |
| Advances from trading banks | 19 | - 4 | 26 | 5 | -34 | 52 |
| Other advances | 8 | 45 | 38 | 58 | 596 | 102 |
| Sales of equities | 21 | 39 | 71 | 43 | 78 | 235 |
| Debentures, notes and deposits | 106 | 223 | 417 | 457 | 1,219 | 1,127 |
| Trade credit | 2 | -10 | 10 | 4 | 37 | 108 |
| 7 Total | 157 | 293 | 562 | 567 | 1,896 | 1,624 |

*Source:* Reserve Bank of Australia, *Flows of Funds: Statistical Bulletin* (July 1976).

63

possibility of shifts in the instalment credit firms' asset holdings. We shall examine each in turn.

Unfortunately, Australian statistics do not make it possible to provide a series for short term fund flows to instalment credit companies. The *potential* sensitivity of fund flows can therefore only be inferred from the behaviour of the companies' borrowing rates. On the assumption that these rates will be adjusted by the companies to meet potential competition only if there is a significant possibility of changes in net inflows, inferences can be drawn from rates data.

Typically, finance companies' rates move closely with potentially competitive rates. Hence, it seems that they *perceive* the demand for their liabilities to be interest elastic. In the absence of more detailed data this is the most that can be said. Estimates of interest elasticities do not exist, at least in published material.

Data are available in some detail for finance company lending. These are summarised on an annual basis in Table 3.11, again for selected years. Unfortunately, revision of the definitions makes precise comparisons impossible. It is clear, however, that the relative importance to the finance companies of finance for retail sales has been declining fairly steadily. By contrast, other consumer and commercial loans, of which nearly a half constitutes finance for housing, has expanded very fast.

The instalment credit companies provide something over 90 per cent of the credit for retail sales. This credit flow dominates the market in new motor vehicles plus an estimate of the value of used vehicle sales. Other household durables are less dependent on this form of finance; but it seems that new lending was about one-third or rather less (in the second half of the 1960s) of the value of total purchases of household durables, including motor vehicles. According to G. McL. Scott (in Hirst and Wallace [65]), this proportion has been declining and may now be as low as one-quarter. There seems, however, little sign of a serious decline in the importance of instalment finance in the motor vehicle market.

From these figures it is clear that instalment credit, dominated by the lending of finance companies, must exert an important influence on expenditures on consumer durables. Since lending for retail sales is now only about one-fifth of the finance houses' lending, and indeed not appreciably larger than their rate of provision of finance for housing, their importance as sources of private sector finance is beyond doubt.

If our inference that their operations are susceptible to influence by monetary action is correct, the scope for such action will be enlarged while there will be obvious implications for its technical characteristics. We can form some additional impression on this point by examining the time series for amounts financed for 1973–5, which contains, of course, the period in which building societies experienced the sharp fall in their inflow of funds (see Table 3.12).

Clearly, there was a fairly sharp decline in the rate of finance company lending from September–October 1973. Most of this was accounted for by the decline in finance for housing; and a considerable part of the remainder was accounted

**Table 3.12** *Finance companies: amounts financed (monthly data, not seasonally adjusted, $A million).*

| Year/month | | Credit for retail sale | Personal loans | Wholesale and farming | Other consumers and commercial loans | | All Contracts |
|---|---|---|---|---|---|---|---|
| | | | | | Housing | Total | |
| 1973 | Jul. | 97·6 | 27·4 | 155·0 | 148·7 | 392·5 | 672·5 |
| | Aug. | 102·0 | 29·0 | 171·4 | 154·8 | 367·5 | 669·9 |
| | Sep. | 91·3 | 25·8 | 170·7 | 141·0 | 330·7 | 618·5 |
| | Oct. | 107·4 | 30·7 | 181·1 | 153·0 | 367·8 | 687·0 |
| | Nov. | 107·4 | 29·8 | 173·5 | 133·7 | 329·7 | 640·4 |
| | Dec. | 91·2 | 25·1 | 144·8 | 126·3 | 382·6 | 643·8 |
| 1974 | Jan. | 90·3 | 25·3 | 125·7 | 82·8 | 220·7 | 462·0 |
| | Feb. | 82·7 | 28·9 | 149·4 | 118·3 | 252·1 | 513·2 |
| | Mar. | 91·5 | 32·0 | 172·4 | 120·6 | 294·6 | 590·5 |
| | Apr. | 92·1 | 32·1 | 162·7 | 115·7 | 303·3 | 590·1 |
| | May | 108·7 | 33·9 | 215·7 | 116·0 | 296·7 | 655·0 |
| | Jun. | 83·9 | 21·5 | 175·3 | 79·1 | 233·2 | 513·9 |
| | Jul. | 97·1 | 26·8 | 205·2 | 82·1 | 218·9 | 548·0 |
| | Aug. | 97·8 | 30·0 | 199·3 | 64·7 | 210·5 | 537·6 |
| | Sep. | 99·2 | 29·5 | 197·9 | 61·1 | 186·4 | 513·1 |
| | Oct. | 114·0 | 29·3 | 198·3 | 52·6 | 160·7 | 502·2 |
| | Nov. | 99·7 | 24·8 | 174·8 | 37·5 | 129·6 | 428·9 |
| | Dec. | 86·2 | 24·6 | 167·6 | 42·5 | 151·1 | 427·6 |
| 1975 | Jan. | 83·0 | 19·7 | 118·7 | 25·7 | 102·4 | 323·8 |
| | Feb. | 87·3 | 25·7 | 186·4 | 30·7 | 116·2 | 415·6 |
| | Mar. | 86·6 | 26·2 | 200·2 | 32·7 | 144·9 | 458·0 |
| | Apr. | 105·5 | 30·2 | 221·2 | 35·9 | 143·1 | 500·0 |
| | May | 104·2 | 34·2 | 236·3 | 52·9 | 159·4 | 534·2 |
| | Jun. | 94·0 | 34·4 | 220·5 | 55·4 | 181·3 | 530·3 |

*Source:* Australian Bureau of Statistics; reproduced in Reserve Bank of Australia, *Statistical Bulletin* (October 1975).

65

for by the fall in other commercial loans for other purposes, an element of which is also related to housing.

Unfortunately, existing data do not enable us to tell how far this reflected a fall in the *demand* for such finance or a reduction in lending brought about by a fall in the rate of growth in finance companies' resources. almost certainly, both elements were present, but the absence of quarterly fund-flow data prevents the drawing of any firm conclusion.

## 3.7 Development Finance Companies

The growth of development finance companies has been well surveyed by Hirst (in Hirst and Wallace [65]). As we have seen, most of the growth in this sector took place after 1960 – indeed, typically after 1965 – and was closely related to the mineral expansion. As defined for flows-of-funds purposes, this sector contains the merchant banks, the growth of which has been particularly rapid.

In general the development finance companies' central significance from the point of view of monetary policy is that they constitute an important link between the Australian and overseas financial markets. Australian balance-of-payments data do not permit a fine disaggregation of capital movements by type of transaction. A disaggregation is, however, possible on the basis of exchange control approvals, which, since these in total relate fairly well to private capital inflows, may not be too misleading.

It is, of course, a distinguishing feature of private capital movements that they are subject to considerable fluctuations. Nevertheless, the data confirm that the relative importance of overseas borrowing in total capital inflow has been tending to rise, while at the same time there has been an increase in the relative importance of overseas funds to the non-finance corporate sector (see Table 3.13). This is in no sense a measure of the activities of development finance companies, which perform a wide variety of services not reflected in their combined flow-of-funds accounts, such as linking Australian transactors with the Eurocurrency markets.

In short, although this sector is of growing importance as an intermediary on its own account, its major significance for our purposes is as a reflection of the steady integration of Australian financial markets with markets overseas, and thus of the increasing sensitivity of private capital movements to rate differentials and exchange rate expectations.

## 3.8 The Reserve Bank of Australia

Earlier sections of this chapter have provided very brief descriptions of the principal financial institutions currently operating in Australia. The function of pres-

**Table 3.13** *Overseas finance and the corporate sector*[a] *in selected years ($A million)*

| Source of finance | 1964–5 | 1965–6 | 1966–7 | 1967–8 | 1968–9 | 1969–70 | 1970–1 | 1971–2 | 1972–3 | 1973–4 |
|---|---|---|---|---|---|---|---|---|---|---|
| 1 Corporate trading enterprises borrowing | 621 | 639 | 587 | 371 | 780 | 544 | 1,142 | 814 | −304 | 1,487 |
| 2 Institutional borrowing overseas: | | | | | | | | | | |
| Advances by rest of world | 23 | 163 | 117 | 111 | 92 | 82 | 452 | 547 | 22 | −25 |
| Other claims: | | | | | | | | | | |
| Rest of world: | 85 | 91 | 105 | 112 | 147 | 172 | 127 | 138 | 21 | 20 |
| 3 Asset formation overseas | −67 | −13 | 103 | 5 | 23 | 166 | 105 | 139 | 6 | 196 |
| 4 Balance of 2 minus 3 | 175 | 267 | 119 | 218 | 216 | 88 | 474 | 546 | 37 | −201 |
| 5 Sales of equities etc. | 390 | 448 | 450 | 338 | 649 | 776 | 748 | 653 | 387 | 374 |
| 6 Purchase of shares and debentures by rest of world | 276 | 249 | 184 | 512 | 529 | 460 | 598 | 631 | 232 | −151 |
| 7 Sum of 4 and 6 | 451 | 516 | 303 | 730 | 745 | 548 | 1,072 | 1,177 | 269 | −352 |
| 8 Unidentified flows from rest of world | 14 | 240 | 163 | 157 | 113 | 59 | −36 | 465 | 91 | 255 |

[a] Excludes public trading enterprises.
*Source:* Reserve Bank of Australia, *Financial Flows* (July 1976).

iding over this financial system, i.e. of ensuring its financial stability while at the same time promoting its further development, is performed by the Reserve Bank, which under the legislation of 1959 took over the central-banking functions originally performed by the Commonwealth Bank.

As we have seen, the Reserve Bank is able to influence the deposit supply of the banks by operating so as to change the LGS holdings of the trading banks and the reserves of the savings banks. In the former case it relies upon the leverage provided by the LGS convention, and in the latter case on the reserve requirements imposed upon the savings banks, to generate an appropriate response.[14] In controlling the relevant base concept the Reserve Bank is able to employ not only the SRD device but also, particularly in recent years, open market operations.

Policy-engineered changes in bank liquidity influence not only the (appropriately defined) money stock but also the extent of bank lending to the private sector. Under the Banking Act the Reserve Bank has the power to determine the lending policy of both trading and savings banks. Typically, the Reserve Bank has used these powers, both quantitatively and qualitatively, in consultation and co-operation with the banks themselves; and in practice, advances directives since the mid-1950s have been aimed exclusively at quantitative control.

As Arndt and Stammer [8] have pointed out, the form of words in which the use of advances directives are reported differs considerably *inter alia* in the identification of the target variables of the policy as 'bank credit', 'new lending', 'overdraft cancellations and reduction' and 'advances'. On occasions the wording also suggests both greater urgency and greater quantitative precision in Reserve Bank requests. However, in view of the Reserve Bank's close and virtually continuous contacts with the banks it would be surprising if the wording did anything more than give some very rough reflection of interpretations and quantitative targets already explained, discussed and agreed by consultation.[15]

In addition to its ability to influence *market* interest rates by open market operations, the Reserve Bank has the power to determine the rates of interest paid or charged by banks. This power has again been used in an informal way, i.e. by agreement with the banks themselves; and it typically takes the form of determining maximum rates (e.g. on advances), a range of rates according to deposit size and maturity (fixed deposits) and a range of rates varying with the form and size of accounts (savings bank deposits).

The Reserve Bank has no published discount rate, and nothing is known regarding the penal rates that it may charge from time to time on trading bank borrowing; nor does it publish the rate that it charges from time to time on temporary borrowing by authorised dealers in the official short-term money market.

Finally, the Reserve Bank holds Australia's overseas reserves and has technical control of the exchange rate. Australia does not have an active foreign-exchange market; and although forward cover for approved transactions can be obtained through the banks, the banks then cover their net forward position with the Reserve Bank.

The powers of the Reserve Bank were thus fairly extensive at its establishment.

The passing of the Financial Corporations Act (which received the royal assent in August 1974) has in principle greatly extended them; since if part iv of the legislation is proclaimed, regulations may be made empowering the Reserve Bank to make determinations regarding asset ratios, lending policy and interest rates paid and charged by all registered corporations, i.e. effectively by all financial intermediaries[16] of significant size operating in Australia. Up to 1977 this section of the legislation has not been proclaimed. Hence the main importance of the Act has been to the collection and publication of statistical information relating to the operation of financial institutions.

## 3.9  Financial Markets

The rate of development of Australia's financial markets has been considerable since the mid-1950s and particularly rapid since the mid-1960s. If we classify markets by reference to the assets traded in them, Australia now possesses:
(a)  both official (SMM) and unofficial short-term money markets;
(b)  a market in government bonds;[17] and
(c)  a market in longer-term private-sector obligations, i.e. equities and debentures.

These markets have been well surveyed by Hirst and Wallace [65], Rose [139] and Dewald [37]. In the present context our concern with the markets lies, not in their efficiency in the mobilisation and allocation of funds, but in the extent to which (a) they form a single integrated financial mechanism that (b) smoothly transmits interest rate changes engineered by the authorities at the short end of the bond maturity pattern to both long term rates and private sector rates. This, of course, is simply to stress the function of financial markets in the transmission of monetary policy.

It is important at the outset to make it clear that there is no acceptable single statement that can be held to cover the quarter-century under review. The very brief notes that follow refer to the situation during the mid-1970s. It can be assumed that the extent to which the several markets constituted a well-integrated financial mechanism was appreciably less in the 1960s and less still during the 1950s.[18]

The official short term money market (SMM) was created in 1959 when the (then) Commonwealth Bank granted recognition to four dealers[19] operating in the existing short-term money market. Recognition entailed a number of privileges, the most important of which was access to lender of last resort loans from the central bank. In return for these privileges the Reserve Bank was effectively able to control the evolution of the official money market.

The authorised dealers operate along familiar lines, borrowing at short term, and often at call, from a variety of sources, including the banks. With these borrowed funds they hold rather longer-run, but still short-term, assets. The bulk of these consists of short-term government obligations, but since 1965 there has been a rapid expansion in the holding of commercial bills. The dealers have complete freedom to set their own borrowing and lending terms, and as a result the market is strongly competitive.

It seems clear that the existence of SMM in its present form has at least the following consequences for the transmission process:

(1) Since dealers are compelled to take a view about interest rates on government debt, then at least at the short end of the maturity curve it should be possible for the Reserve Bank to influence dealers' expectations and thus rates.

(2) Since dealers also operate extensively in the (bank) bill market, the transmission of rate changes originating in short-term government debt to private sector borrowers will be smooth and rapid.

(3) Finally, the market in government securities, at least for short maturities, now offers considerably increased scope for open market operations.[20]

Much less appears to be known about the unofficial short-term money market.[21] It is, however, believed to be rather larger than the SMM, with which it is extremely closely integrated. The close integration effectively ensures that rate changes are transmitted through the whole spectrum of private-sector short-term borrowing and lending. Since the dealers in the unofficial market are extremely important in arranging intercompany loans, intercompany rates will also be adjusted. Thus, in their present form the official and unofficial short-term money markets seem certain to ensure the smooth transmission of rate changes originating in the official market through the whole range of private-sector short-term rates.

It is possible, but less certain, that the existence of the SMM may also exert an influence on the speed with which the trading banks adjust to changes in their LGS holdings.[22] This is because trading bank loans to the SMM are *not*, by definition, elements in LGS. Hence, for an individual trading bank the recall of funds from the SMM is a simple way of adding to the LGS holding. Given this extra element of flexibility, each individual Trading bank – and hence the Trading Banks as a group – should respond less hesitantly and more homogeneously to changes in aggregate LGS holdings. This argument is strengthened by the reflection that for the trading banks as a group the SMM provides an indirect means of undertaking temporary borrowing from the Reserve Bank, to the extent that the banks, by withdrawing funds from the SMM, can compel authorised dealers to use their borrowing privileges.

Our conclusion that the short term market is sufficiently highly integrated for a smooth transmission of policy changes does not necessarily carry over to the long term market. For example, there is a very considerable captive demand for government securities generated by financial institutions with constrained portfolio choices. The existence of this demand element is certain to reduce switching from public to private sector obligations. Equally, it seems likely to reduce the extent to which substitution between government debt of different maturities is undertaken. Thus, the response at the long end of the rate structure may be slow and uncertain, due to what is in effect a significant element of market segment-ation.[23]

In short, it is arguable (a) that constrained portfolio choice in the bond market slows the response of the rate curve to changes at the short end, due to either open market operations or Reserve Bank operations on market expectations, and (b) that similar influences may retard the response of rates on private sector obligations, such as equities and debentures. Since it is the longer term rates that are generally regarded as the more relevant for private sector expenditure,[24] these contentions, if correct, could have an important bearing on the transmission mechanism and its dynamics.[25]

The dynamics of rate changes cannot be analysed independently of the theory of the rate structure employed in the tests. Empirically, it is not easy to distinguish competing theories of the rate structure, and in particular it is hard to specify the 'market segmentation' hypothesis in an empirically testable form. As a result there is very little published research on these issues in Australia and certainly no established consensus to which we can appeal.

Our judgement, again largely intuitive, is that the transmission of interest movements through the rate curve is slowed by the imperfections sketched in this review, but that these imperfections are probably diminishing. Certainly, research in the Reserve Bank suggests that the supply price of capital (approximately the gross earnings yield in equities) is a relatively reliable function of the medium-term (ten-year) Commonwealth Bond rate. Hence, provided that the medium-term bond rate responds to open market operations or expectation changes, it seems that the market is sufficiently integrated for the effective transmission of an interest rate policy.

At present, it appears that this is the case and that the Australian money and capital markets can consequently, as a first approximation, be regarded as a single entity. In contrast, in the mid-1960s, and certainly before, it appears that imperfections were significant and that the transmission process was therefore substantially different from that of the 1970s.[26]

# Notes: Chapter 3

1 And thus the extent to which the equity market is dependent on portfolio investment from overseas.
2 Cf. the introduction to Hirst and Wallace [65].
3 For a fuller account, consult Arndt and Stammer [8].
4 This development of non-bank financial intermediaries had already proceeded sufficiently far by the second half of the 1950s to modify the problems facing the central bank very considerably. On this point, see Chapter 5.
5 For an excellent review of the special accounts procedure, cf. Hirst [62].
6 On this issue, see Arndt [7] and Arndt and Stammer [8].
7 The processes involved have been modelled by Valentine [164]. The study by Norton, Cohen and Sweeny [113] involves the same problems, but unlike Valentine's it does not seek to estimate an explicit model of both demand and supply effects. The lags in trading bank adjustment have been investigated by Terrell and Valentine [160].
8 This views the variable influencing trading-bank expansion as the excess supply of excess LGS.

9 This section draws heavily on the admirable account of the savings banks by Lewis and Wallace in Hirst and Wallace [65].
10 The asset-holding requirements are typically of major significance not as short-run quantitative controls but as a means of providing an element (controversial) of captive demand for government debt. This point has been well discussed by Lewis and Wallace in Hirst and Wallace [65]. Wallace [65].
11 Commonly in periods of restrictive monetary policy.
12 This section relies heavily on Hill in Hirst and Wallace [65].
13 See Scott in Hirst and Wallace [65].
14 As we have argued, the leverage with respect to the savings banks is not in the usual case very effective in the short run.
15 Both Valentine [164] and Norton, Cohen and Sweeny [113] have found very appreciable lags in the impact of these directives. The lags are in the neighbourhood of four quarters.
16 Including retailers who have a large credit business.
17 The money markets and bond markets overlap in the sense that the extensive trading in short term bonds undertaken by participants in the former is part of the latter.
18 On this issue, cf. Chapter 5 below, particularly the Appendix to it.
19 Since raised to nine.
20 For a fuller account of open market operations, consult Hill [60] and Oram [116].
21 Cf. Allan [3]. I am indebted to Dr Allan for many helpful discussions of money market operations.
22 The attitudes of the trading banks to the SMM is discussed in Arndt and Stammer [8].
23 Market segmentation is best viewed as the limiting case of the 'preferred habitat' theory of the rate curve. Its existence would imply that, to shift the rate curve, the authorities would need to conduct operations in a wide range of maturities, including long term issues.
24 Where they generate both wealth and cost-of-capital effects.
25 How important depends, of course, on the response of private expenditure to rate changes, which, at least in the case of investment in fixed capital, remains a matter of some controversy. On this point, cf. Higgins, Johnston and Coghlan [59].
26 For the authorities' view, cf. Appendix to Chapter 5.

*Chapter 4*

# Monetary Policy:
# An Overview, 1951–75

## 4.1 Introduction

This chapter has two objectives. The first is to place the stance of monetary policy in its cyclical setting, i.e. in relation to the cyclical pattern identified in Chapter 2. The second is to identify the role played by monetary policy in the overall macroeconomic policy mix adopted by the Australian authorities.

These are ambitious aims for a single chapter. The reader is therefore warned that the overview is provided only by examining events from a rather considerable height. This simplifies matters by permitting a correspondingly considerable amount of detail to be neglected. There must remain, however, the problem of whether some of the detail omitted was not in practice more important than the material presented – or to put the same point rather more succinctly, whether the rather descriptive methodology adopted is appropriate. On this issue the reader must form his own conclusions.

## 4.2 Monetary Thrust and Monetary Policy

The impact of monetary variables on the economic system has at least the usual two dimensions, which are, of course, quantities and prices. It is usual to identify the former with one (or more) money-stock concepts and the latter with one (or more) nominal interest rates. When the money stock concepts move closely together over time, it obviously makes relatively little difference which is chosen. The same holds for interest rates. Unfortunately, whatever their relation in the relatively long run (say a decade or more), over the cycle, which is what concerns us in the present context, both individual money-stock concepts and individual interest rates can display dissimilar short-term movements. It follows that, in so far as a single price or quantity concept is adopted as an indicator of the thrust of monetary variables, its choice must be arbitrary, while its performance, at least in some periods, will probably be misleading.

A further difficulty arises in defining price or quantity indicators of monetary *policy* (as opposed to what we shall call 'monetary thrust'). This occurs because most variables that we can consider are endogenous within the system. In theory, therefore, they depend on *all* the exogenous variables of the system, not merely the policy instruments directly controlled by the monetary and other authorities. There is a very considerable literature on this issue; and attempts have been made, at least with the quantity measures, to eliminate the endogenous component and thus generate an approximation to the policy component. Hendershott's [53] 'neutralised' money stock is an example of this method. Considerations of space do not permit a review either of the endogeneity problem or of the related literature on the choice of indicator. However, one brief example will be given to illustrate the problems involved.

Consider a cyclical upswing in which the rate of growth of some quantity indicator (say $M_3$, defined on p. 000) is rising but, at the same time, some price indicator (say the ten-year Commonwealth Bond rate) is also rising. According to the former, monetary thrust is becoming *more* expansionary; according to the latter, *less* expansionary. The indicators are in contradiction with one another, and without additional quantitative knowledge there is no way of resolving the conflict. However, as is well known, such conflicts may easily arise. We may therefore conclude that the usual indicators of monetary thrust are qualitatively reliable only when they qualitatively correspond.

Alternatively, suppose that the indicators *do* correspond qualitatively; that is, the interest rate falls as $M_3$ rises. What of their quantitative implications? To use the same example, suppose that the rate of growth in $M_3$ increases proportionately significantly more than (say) the medium-term bond rate falls. Which is the superior quantitative indicator of monetary thrust in this case? The answer to this question must, of course, depend on the mechanism relating the variables concerned to the level of some endogenous variable – typically gross domestic product (GDP) – selected as the measure of impact, i.e. upon the transmission mechanism that (theoretically) specifies and (empirically) estimates the relationship between price and quantity variables and the selected dependent variable (GDP). It follows that in emphasising either $M_3$ or $r_{GM}$ (see p. 000) as an indicator, some prior (and typically implicit) assumptions are being made about the transmission mechanism and its dynamics. This is an important point, since the transmission mechanism itself changes over time, and we shall argue that it has in Australia undergone very significant changes over the period covered by the study. Thus, the price and quantity indicators cannot be expected to have invariant quantitative implications over time, even if we are prepared to accept (say for the 1950s) a particularly theory of the Australian transmission process.

What of monetary *policy* as opposed to monetary *thrust*? Consider now our first example in which rates rise as $M_3$ rises. Assume that over the period of observation the Reserve Bank is found to undertake no changes in: (a) the interest rate maxima that it is empowered to determine; or (b) the statutory reserve deposit (SRD) ratio. Assume further that the 'banking base', defined as the monetary base less the non-bank public's holdings of notes and coins, is also observed not to change over the period. If these hypothetical conditions hold, we shall have a set of observations such that:

(a) the $M_3$ indicator suggests that monetary policy is expansionary;
(b) the $r_{GM}$ indicator suggests that monetary policy is contractionary;
while . . .
(c) Reserve Bank behaviour suggests that policy should be regarded as unchanged.

Regardless of whether $M_3$ or $r_{GM}$ is chosen as the indicator, either suggests that the Reserve Bank has done something. Nevertheless, the commonsense interpretation of the (hypothetical) Reserve Bank behaviour is that the monetary authority has done nothing. The possibilities for semantic debate are obvious and have been well explored in the literature.

This simple sketch of the problems involved leads to two conclusions:

(1) Variables selected as indicators of *monetary thrust* need to be treated with considerable caution and typically cannot be given a precise quantitative interpretation over any long period of time.
(2) Since even approximately acceptable indicators of *monetary thrust* may well be poor indicators of *monetary policy*, separate indicator(s) seem essential for the latter purpose.

Given the obvious limitations of the indicator approach, we shall define the following indicators of monetary thrust:

**Quantity indicators:**

$M_1$ ≡ currency + demand deposits

$M_3$ ≡ $M_1$ + fixed deposits (including Negotiable Certificate of Deposit NCDs) at trading banks
+ savings bank deposits

$A_{TB}$ ≡ trading bank advances

$A_B$ ≡ $A_{TB}$ + advances of savings banks

**Price indicators:**

$r_{GM}$ ≡ 10-year Commonwealth bond rate

$r_t$ ≡ rate on Treasury bills – Treasury notes

Each of these concepts may be defined in both *nominal* and *real* terms, and in some situations the distinction is important. We shall therefore make use of both nominal and real forms, defining

$\dot{x}_i - \dot{p}$ ≡ real percentage rate of growth in $x_i$ (a quantity indicator)

where

$\dot{x}_i$ ≡ observed percentage rate of growth in $x_i$

$\dot{p}$ ≡ observed percentage rate of growth in the price level

Correspondingly, we define

$r_i - \dot{p}$ ≡ observed real rate of interest on asset $i$.

We now proceed to examine the problem of indicators of *monetary policy* in rather more detail.

## 4.3  Monetary Policy

There are, broadly speaking, two approaches to identifying the stance of monetary policy; these we shall call the '*ex ante*' and the '*ex post*'.

The *ex ante* approach consists in identifying the monetary policy stance over time by examining the *statements* made by the monetary authority – in this case the Reserve Bank of Australia – and classifying these in some systematic way.[1]

This approach has been employed *inter alia* by Poole [129] and the Organisation for Economic Co-operation and Development (OECD) [118] in examining US policy and by Lewis [96] and Lewis and Wallace [97] for Australia. It has been used in this study to give the policy datings set out in Figure 4.1. In examining this figure it must be remembered that the classification is unavoidably arbitrary. This is so because another investigator, even one employing the same classification system, may quite reasonably interpret the Reserve Bank's statements (typically those in its *Annual Report*) rather differently. Fortunately, such differences are less likely to arise over the *direction* of change in policy stance than over the *degree* of change. The unavoidable subjective element in the process may therefore not be a source of any major error in giving some qualitative, as opposed to quasi-quantitative, interpretation of the Reserve Bank's stance, which is all that our index claims to provide.

We call this procedure '*ex ante*' since it is based upon a reading of the Reserve Bank's statements about its policy stance. The alternative approach, here called '*ex post*', simply applies the indicator method of our earlier discussion to Reserve Bank policy. What we seek, therefore, is an indicator (or indicators) that may over the cycle be expected to reflect the Reserve Bank's policy stance.

Assuming that such indicators can usefully be defined, they can provide two pieces of information. In the first place, they provide a direct check on the *ex ante* classification, for a quantitative indicator should in theory correspond both qualitatively and quantitatively with the identified shifts in monetary policy. In the second place, if the two do not correspond, then provided, on re-examination, that the *ex ante* interpretation retains conviction, the conclusion can only be either: (a) that the Reserve Bank behaved inconsistently in the sense that it *chose not* to take actions that would typically be associated with the identified policy stance; or (b) that the Reserve Bank did not in practice have the degree of control over the variable chosen as indicator that was (implicitly or explicitly) assumed in its selection.

The stance of monetary policy in Australia will be reflected in the setting of a number of instruments that the Reserve Bank has under its immediate control. These are:

(a) requests to the trading banks regarding the rate of new lending and the growth of advances;

(b) changes in the SRD ratio (or special account calls);

(c) open market operations (changes in the Reserve Bank's security portfolio); and

(d) changes in the interest rates determined directly by the authorities, in particular the rate on Treasury notes, the maximum rates payable on certain types of trading bank and savings bank deposits and the maximum interest rates chargeable on advances.

Of these, open market operations and the SRD ratio influence the monetary base, and requests seem to exert some slow influence on advances. Neglecting requests, which are difficult to quantify, we are left with a quantity indicator (or indicators) related to the base and a price indicator (or indicators) related to interest rates.

Most students of Australian monetary policy regard the Reserve Bank since 1961-2 as typically seeking to set 'the' nominal interest rate.[2] This is usually taken to mean $r_{GM}$ as previously defined. If the Reserve Bank sets $r_{GM}$ at all precisely, it will become, on some analyses, both an indicator of monetary thrust and an indicator of monetary policy. This is slightly unusual and awkward. Nevertheless, we define the following indicators of monetary policy:

**Quantity indicators:**

Net banking base (NBB)

Net liquidity base (NLB)

**Price indicators:**

Rate on Treasury notes ($r_{TN}$)

Rate on ten-year Commonwealth bonds ($r_{GM}$)

We further define

Net banking base (NBB) $\equiv$ Monetary base (MB) $-$ Notes with non-bank public

Net liquidity base (NLB) $\equiv$ Net banking base $+$ Government securities held by trading banks $+$ Government securities held by savings banks

where, from the liabilities side of the Reserve Bank balance sheet, we define

$$\text{Monetary base (MB)} \equiv \text{Notes with banks} + \text{Notes with non-bank public} + \text{'Free' deposits of trading banks at Reserve Bank} + \text{Deposits of savings banks at Reserve Bank}$$

where Free deposits $\equiv$ Total deposits of trading banks $-$ Statutory reserve deposits (SRDs)

The underlying reason for selecting these indicators is simply that all four (NBB, NLB, $r_{TN}$ and $r_{GM}$) are relatively closely under Reserve Bank/Treasury control. Each should therefore reflect changes in the Reserve Bank's policy stance. It must be emphasised, however, that with some their performance prior to (say) 1961 tends to compare unfavourably with their performance after this date. This is because the Reserve Bank's transmission theory prior to 1961 was primarily a 'credit' rather than a 'monetary theory'. The Reserve Bank (or Commonwealth Bank) did not, as we shall see, then operate extensively on interest rates; rather, it primarily sought to control trading bank advances, via requests and operations with the special account (or SRD) device on trading bank liquidity. Nevertheless, in order to give an overview of the whole period some interest-rate indicators must be included.

In using the net banking base and net liquidity base as indicators of policy we need to employ a proper degree of caution, in that both aggregates include variables that reflect decisions over which the authorities can exert no direct control and that they are therefore compelled to forecast. For example,

$$\Delta NBB \equiv \Delta MB - \Delta \text{non-bank public's holding of notes}$$

Using the Reserve Bank's balance sheet we have

$$\Delta MB \equiv \Delta \text{overseas assets} + \Delta \text{security portfolio} + \Delta \text{other net assets} - \Delta \text{government deposits} - \Delta SRDs$$

Hence, if it seeks to set the value of Δnet banking base, the Reserve Bank will need to forecast Δoverseas assets, Δgovernment deposits, Δother net assets, the non-policy element in ΔSRDs and Δnon-bank public's holdings of notes. Only if these items are (in aggregate) forecast with a high degree of accuracy will the change in the net banking base *planned* by the Reserve Bank correspond closely to the observed change and the net banking base be a reliable policy indicator. Since Δoverseas reserves ≡ Current account balance + Capital account balance neither of which are easy to forecast, close and continuous correspondence between the Reserve Bank's planned Δnet banking base and the observed Δnet banking base cannot be assumed. In short, like all endogenous variables both the net banking base and, even more so, the net liquidity base are far from perfect indicators of policy.

With this warning we now proceed to examine monetary policy in the cycle.

## 4.4 The Cyclical Stance of Monetary Policy

The *ex ante* policy stance of the Reserve Bank (or Commonwealth Bank), as we have identified it, is set out in Figure 4.1. Since we shall argue that the three decades correspond very roughly to three different perceptions of the transmission process, the figure is divided along these lines rather than by cycles, with some degree of overlapping to aid in interpretation.

In examining these data, two main points of interest appear:
(1) At what stage of the upswing did the Reserve Bank institute monetary restraint?
(2) How soon after the cyclical peak was the restrictive stance modified?
The principal underlying assumption of (1) and (2) is, of course, that monetary policy was used, in the main, in an attempt to stabilise demand.

In trying to examine these two issues we need to remember: (a) that our scheme for classifying *ex ante* policy stance is decidedly rudimentary; and (b) that

Figure 4.1    Stance of monetary policy, 1950-75

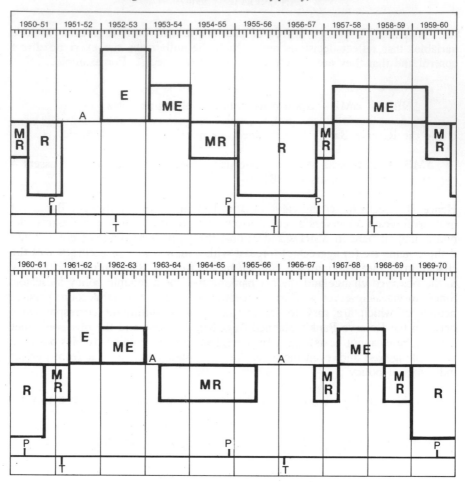

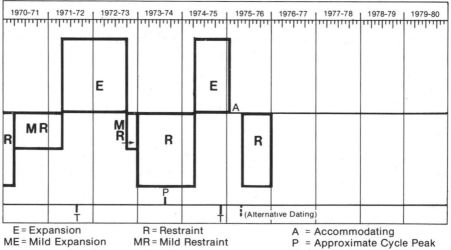

E = Expansion            R = Restraint            A = Accommodating
ME = Mild Expansion      MR = Mild Restraint      P = Approximate Cycle Peak
                                                  T = Approximate Cycle Trough

*Source:* Authors assessments; cycle datings from Chapter 2

demand stabilisation was not always the dominating objective of the monetary authorities.[3]

In the 1950s the Reserve Bank (or Commonwealth Bank) seems to have shifted to restraint – usually from mild restraint – between one and four quarters before the cycle peak. The upswing of 1956–7 constitutes an exception to this timing, since restraint seems to have been maintained virtually from 1955.III to 1957.I or II. The lags in the impact of monetary restraint are for this period largely a matter of guesswork. It seems unlikely, however, that monetary restriction would have an appreciable impact on demand in much less than four quarters. If this is so, restriction was imposed rather too late in the 1950s.

Making some allowance for the uncertainties attaching to our *ex ante* timing, this pattern seems to have repeated itself in the 1960s and early 1970s. In 1960 restraint was intensified virtually *at* the cycle peak. This happened again in 1973.III. The upswing of 1961–5 constitutes a most interesting exception, for in this case the degree of restriction was typically mild (on our assessment) and imposed some six quarters prior to the peak. Since restriction never became severe, this suggests that the 1961-5 upswing represents a rather successful period of demand management.

If we now consider how soon *after* the peaks the (restrictive) policy stance was eased, it is clear that the authorities did not in general modify policy until the downswings (typically short in Australia) were well under way. Indeed, in some instances the emergence of an expansionary stance, even a mild one, came only at the cycle trough or close to it, if at all. This, for example, was the case in 1952, 1961 and 1971.

In short, the evidence (as presented here at least) suggests either that the so-called 'inside lag' of monetary policy is rather long (in relation to the probable lag in the transmission process(es)) or that the simple demand-stabilisation framework that is implicit in our argument is inadequate.[4]

Why should the apparent inside lag be long (in the sense defined above)? The most likely explanation seems to be the difficulties that the authorities have in: (a) diagnosing the current position of the Australian economy; and (b) forecasting important exogenous variables, such as export prices, import prices and at least some elements in private capital inflows; for if (a) and (b) are typically the case, it must be some considerable period before the authorities can feel confident that a cyclical peak or trough has been reached or passed. Our graphical presentation obscures this problem, since the peaks and troughs have already *been* identified with the full benefits conferred by hindsight, which in this area at least are very considerable indeed.

A second reason may arise from the authorities' perception of the transmission process. In so far as this was perceived by them in terms of the availability of funds from major intermediaries, in particular from the trading banks, the authorities may well have identified the impact of policy with the behaviour of the rate of growth of trading bank advances. As we shall see, this variable on the whole tends to lag other possible indicators of monetary thrust. For this reason a restrictive or expansionary stance may have tended to be maintained rather too long.

A third reason, which almost certainly was operative until the early 1960s, was the tendency to see monetary policy, at least in part, as a means of smoothing the cycle in the current balance. This was important since during the 1950s the current balance was seen as secularly weak, while the import bill tended to lag the cycle. Therefore, the monetary authorities may well have maintained a restrictive stance in order that monetary restraint gave support to the attempt to smooth the import cycle by means of import restrictions.

Import restrictions were eliminated in 1961, and the secular weakness of the current account was itself gone by the mid-1960s. After the mid-1960s the external problem became more a matter of the capital account, which has no very clear-cut cyclical pattern. Since the (relatively) slow adjustment of policy in downswings seems to have persisted into this period, this suggests that the inside lag problem arises more from (a) and (b) above than from variation in the assignment of policy to ultimate objectives.[5]

This, of course, is highly conjectural, as indeed is some of the evidence here presented. However, if our argument is correct, it must carry the implication that, in view of the difficulties of *both* economic diagnosis *and* economic forecasting, Australia must offer a rather inhospitable setting for attempts at fine tuning.

# 4.5 Monetary Policy in the Cycle: The Technical Context

Now that we have examined the *ex ante* stance of monetary policy from 1950 to 1975 we need to recall that policy is itself a complex concept, in that it involves the deployment of a number of instruments, notably:

(a) lending requests to the trading banks;
(b) special account calls (or changes in the SRD ratio);
(c) open market operations;
(d) variations in certain interest-rate maxima;
(e) variation (by agreement) in the LGS accepted by the trading banks; and
(f) variation in the required assets ratio of the savings banks.

In short, monetary policy consists in the use of a number of devices, and mix between which is not constant for any given policy stance, since it must depend on the monetary authorities' perception of the transmission process and, probably also on the initial conditions ruling in the financial system.

We begin our brief review of the monetary policy mix by examining two indicators of policy; the net banking base (NBB) and the net liquidity base (NLB) of the Banks.[6]

In Figure 4.2 are set out the quarterly rates of growth in the net banking base

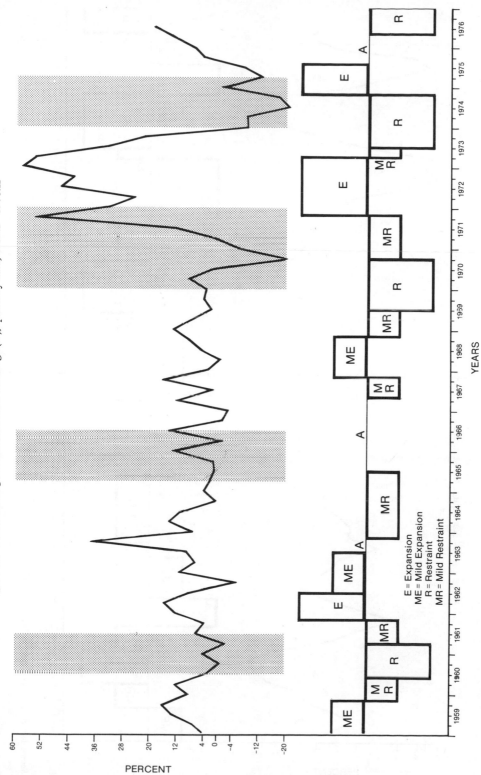

Figure 4.2   Net banking base: annual rates of change (%), quarterly data, 1959.I—1976.II

E = Expansion
ME = Mild Expansion
R = Restraint
MR = Mild Restraint

PERCENT

YEARS

*Source:* Reserve Bank of Australia, *Statistical Bulletin*

Figure 4.3    Net liquidity base: annual rates of change (%), quarterly data, 1959.I—1976.II

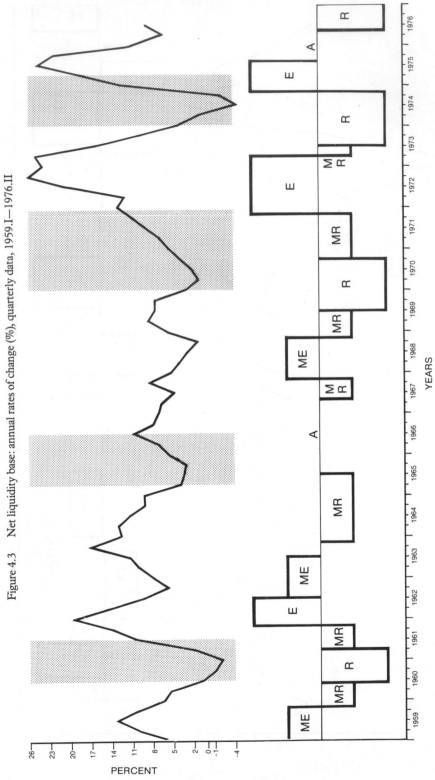

PERCENT

YEARS

*Source:* Reserve Bank of Australia, *Statistical Bulletin*

against (a) the cycle and (b) the *ex ante* stance of the Reserve Bank (or Common-wealth Bank). If the net banking balance is an *ex post* indicator of policy, three things are evident:

(1) Its rate of growth typically turned down well before cycle peaks and generally turned up again during the downswing.

(2) In the downswing of 1970–1 its rate of growth turned upwards rather later than usual.

(3) There is a general correspondence between the behaviour of the percentage rate of growth in the net banking base and our approximate *ex ante* identi-fication of policy stance.

Since the net banking base is closely related to the net liquidity base, it is not surprising that Figure 4.3 shows a very similar pattern to Figure 4.2, although the range of fluctuations in the net banking base is rather greater. Except for the period from mid-1974 to end-1975 the patterns of the rates of growth in the net banking base and the net liquidity base correspond quite closely. The 1974-5 period was, of course, dominated by the sharp rate of expansion in the budget deficit and more importantly, by the special actions that the Reserve Bank was compelled to take to contain an incipient financial panic.[7]

Both figures bring out very clearly the variation in the rates of growth in both the net banking base and the net liquidity base over the cycle. Additionally, they emphasise the severe monetary instability implied by the expansion of 1971–2 and the shift to restraint at the beginning of 1973. Since the rates of growth given are quarterly (at annual rates), it is not difficult to infer that monthly data would show an even greater range of variation. Nevertheless, the quarterly rates not only show a very marked cyclical movement but also make it clear that the *range* of movement in 1971–4 very considerably exceeded what had occurred in the past. *Prima facie* the period appears to have been one of the very marked, and policy-induced, monetary instability. This judgement, of course, implies that the Reserve Bank is able to set the change in the net banking base (over a quarter) within fairly narrow limits, and this in its turn implies that the Bank can neutralise the impact on the net banking base of changes in overseas reserves. Later, we give some evidence that strongly suggests that, thus far at least, the authorities have generally been able to neutralise in this sense.

The net banking base and the net liquidity base are related to the SRD (or special account) instrument and to open market operations. In Figure 4.4 an attempt has been made to summarise the use made by the authorities of their remaining instruments, in particular those called (a) and (d) above.

Before commenting on this figure it is once again necessary to indicate the limitations of the data. Changes in interest rate maxima are relatively well defined and their datings unambiguous. It is otherwise with lending requests. Formal requests to the trading banks appear generally to be reported in the Reserve Bank's *Annual Reports* and/or its *Statistical Bulletin*. There is, however, no way of being sure that *all* such requests *or* formal modifications in them are reported. What is more, the monthly meetings of the governor with the trading banks may

Figure 4.4    Reserve Bank of Australia: Principal Policy Actions

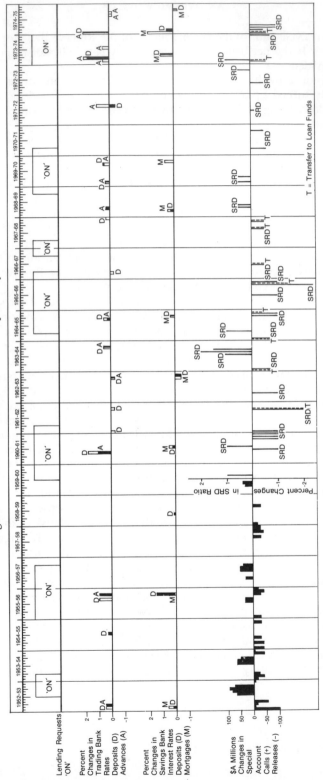

*Sources:* Reserve Bank of Australia, *Annual Reports* and *statistical Bulletin*

on occasions lead to (informal) reinterpretations of earlier formal requests, which may in fact amount to a policy change. Nothing is known about any such changes. There is therefore no obvious means of providing an index of the severity of requests. Accordingly, this issue has been evaded by simply defining periods when requests were *on* and periods when they were *off*; this amounts to defining a fairly typical form of dummy variable and has all the usual crudity of that procedure.

Again, Figure 4.4 shows both the direction and quantitative impact of changes in special accounts and, after 1960, of the SRD ratio. These data are not comprehensive, since changes undertaken for apparently technical reasons have *not* been recorded.[8]

This said, Figure 4.4 presents a fairly convenient summary of the evolution of the Reserve Bank's techniques. For example, the increased reliance after 1962 on changes in interest rate maxima appears fairly clearly. So too does the importance of the SRD (or special account) techniques, designed specifically to enable the Australian authorities to neutralise changes in overseas reserves despite the restricted scope that existed for open market operations until relatively recent years.

Not very surprisingly, the instruments recorded in Figure 4.4 are deployed close conformity with our *ex ante* policy dating, which indeed they helped to determine. Hence, we conclude our brief review of instruments and indicators with a diagram of the Treasury note (or Treasury bill) rate and the medium-term bond yield ($r_{GM}$) (Figure 4.5).

The data are again quarterly, which tends to produce a relatively smooth series. Moreover, Treasury bills were, when in issue, held virtually only by the banks, with the rate on them essentially an administered rate. Treasury notes are available on tap, with the obvious result that the rate is set by the authorities. On the other hand, the medium-term bond rate is technically a market rate, although until the mid-1960s the market was relatively little developed and probably dominated by its perception of the Commonwealth Bank (or Reserve Bank) view.

The behaviour of the short term rate from 1950 through 1960 makes it clear that before 1960–1 the manipulation of short term rates for the purposes of short-term monetary policy was almost non-existent. This is equally true of the medium-term bond rate, for the changes that occurred in this rate before 1961 are best interpreted as changes in which the authorities felt that it wise to allow the market to have its way. Not very surprisingly, therefore, they do not present a time path that is consistent with stabilisation requirements. For example, the sharp increase between 1951 and 1952 occurred, in the main, during the cyclical downswing; the same is true of the (much smaller) increase in 1955–6, while in 1960–1 the rate rose sharply *after* the cyclical peak.

After 1960 the overall picture changed, and the two rates behaved in a way that was broadly consistent with a generally anticyclical policy. This supports the generally accepted position in Australia that the medium-term bond rate ($r_{GM}$)

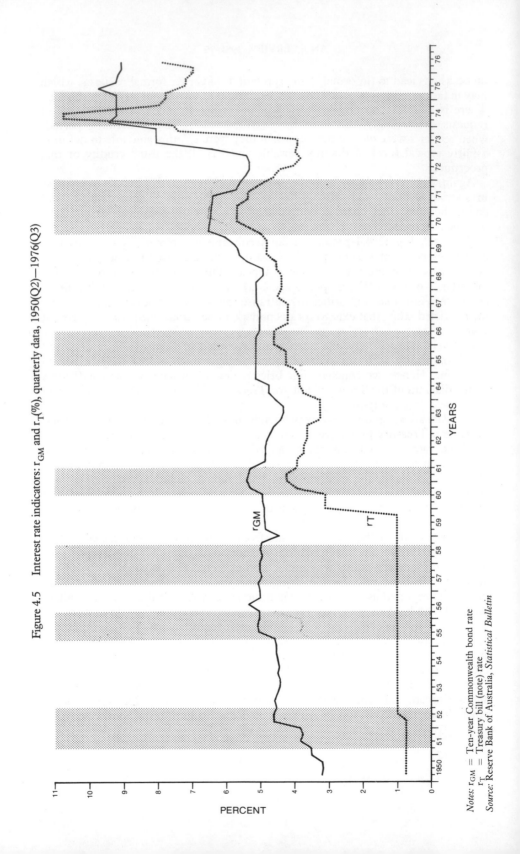

Figure 4.5    Interest rate indicators: $r_{GM}$ and $r_T$(%), quarterly data, 1950(Q2)—1976(Q3)

*Notes*: $r_{GM}$ = Ten-year Commonwealth bond rate
$r_T$ = Treasury bill (note) rate
*Source*: Reserve Bank of Australia, *Statistical Bulletin*

can be treated as a quasi-instrument variable. Thus, in the three upswings of 1961–5, 1966–70 and 1972–4 rates tended to fall in the early stages but to begin to rise, on two occasions quite sharply, well in advance of the cycle peak. Conversely, in cycle recessions rates were either roughly stable (1965–6) or declined.

Since (very roughly) the mid-1960s rates have had an upward trend, doubtless in part explained by the higher rates of inflation both experienced and expected. If some (again very rough) allowance were made for this trend, its result would simply be (a) to increase the extent to which rates were reduced in order to stimulate activity and (b) to reduce the extent to which they were raised in order to contain it. It would also tend to shift the apparent turning points and to make rate increases appear somewhat later in the cyclical process.

The imposition of a trend on rate data has, however, not been undertaken. Additionally, in the absence of a theory that adequately explains, in quantitative terms, the impact of inflationary expectations on nominal interest rates, no attempt has been made to separate the policy element in rate changes from the (assumed) inflationary drift. We are therefore left only with the rather rough interpretation of rate behaviour already given.

In conclusion, the evidence presented seems to show a relatively close qualitative correspondence between both (a) the base indicators and (b) the interest rate indicators and an *ex ante* identification of the monetary policy stance. Beyond this the data suggest a fairly marked shift in technique after (say) 1962, with a much greater relative emphasis being placed upon the manipulation of both the level and structure of rates by the use of direct rate-stting powers and, in relation to bond rates, open market operations. Later, we argue that this shift resulted from a process of reinterpretation of the transmission mechanism that began in the mid-1950s and reached fruition after the experience of 1959–61.

## 4.6 *Monetary Thrust*

Figure 4.6 presents quarterly data for the annual rates of change in $M_1$ and $M_3$ from 1950.II to 1976.III. Two points are immediately apparent: (a) the close correspondence between the time paths of the two series; and (b) the fact that Australia has clearly experienced two periods of extreme instability in monetary growth rates. The first of these – 1950–2 – was associated with the Korean War, the related boom in commodity prices and the lagged response of Australian imports to the sharp, but short-lived, boom in export proceeds. This period has been discussed elsewhere,[9] and that discussion need not be repeated now. The second period is plainly 1971–4. This is considered in some detail in a later chapter, but unlike the earlier period, which was explained primarily by exogenous elements that the (then) Commonwealth Bank could not effectively offset, the later period largely appears to have reflected domestic macroeconomic policy. It is therefore of rather special interest.

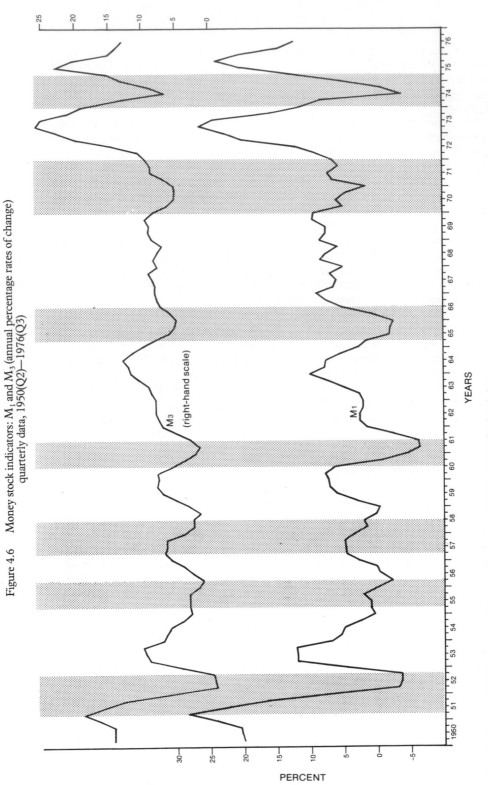

Figure 4.6    Money stock indicators: $M_1$ and $M_3$ (annual percentage rates of change) quarterly data, 1950(Q2)—1976(Q3)

*Note:* for the years 1950-3 data are available only for the second and fourth quarters; for the missing observations the average of the rates in the previous and the following quarters has been taken.

*Source:* Reserve Bank of Australia, *Australian Banking and Monetary Statistics*

In general, the cyclical pattern of both $\dot{M}_1$ and $\dot{M}_3$ show: a rising rate of growth in the early stages of an upswing; a turning point that occurs before (in some cases well before) the cycle peak; a decline that continues into the recession (in some cases virtually through it); followed by a lower turning point that, after 1961 when we argue that the revised perception of the transmission process became effective, occurs well before the troughs. This pattern seems consistent with a reduced emphasis on availability and bank advances and an increased emphasis on interest rates after 1961.

Since most interest attaches to the period after 1961, we shall concentrate our attention to this.

In Figure 4.7 the money stock data are related to the net banking base data for the period 1959.I to 1976.III. Quarterly data have some tendency to smooth lag patterns, as opposed to the monthly data to which we refer later. Nevertheless, there is a clear tendency for the money stock variables to respond to the net banking base variables with a lag. This should cause no surprise, since banks in general cannot be expected to undertake immediate adjustments of choice assets, while in Australia both the very severe seasonal movements and the difficulty that the banks face for purely technical reasons in controlling their advances provide additional explanations for the delay. It is, however, worth noting the implications of this figure:

(1) The money supply function has a fairly long distributed lag.[10]
(2) This lag is due mainly to the lag in the deposit supply function of the trading banks.

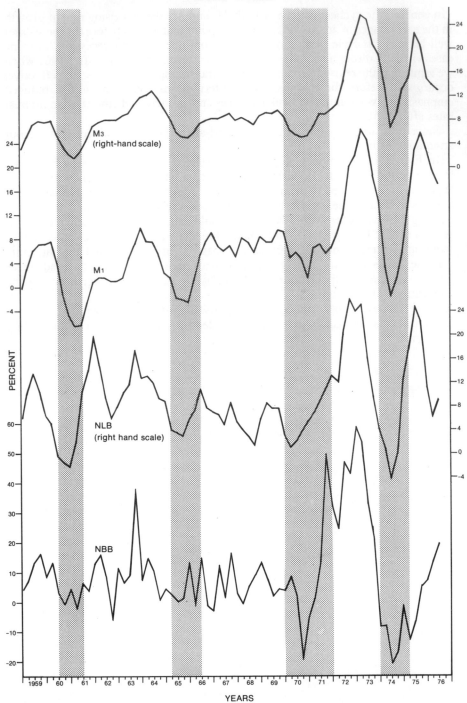

Sources:
1  For $\dot{M}_1$ and $\dot{M}_3$ data: Reserve Bank of Australia, *Australian Banking and Monetary Statistics*
2  For NBB and NLB data: Reserve Bank of Australia, *Statistical Bulletin*

(3) Hence, rapid planned short-term changes in rates of growth either $M_1$ or $M_3$ would require very severe changes in the rate of growth in the net banking base.

Some support for these points is provided by the rate of growth of trading bank advances, which, as Figure 4.8 shows, typically lag the money stock variables and show rather more severe fluctuations.[11]

As indicators of monetary thrust, nominal growth rates are of less interest than their real counterparts. In *ex post* terms these are given in Figure 4.9. These data confirm that after 1961 only the period 1972–4 experienced severe fluctuations in monetary thrust. In this period the rate of growth in real $M_1$ reached nearly 20 per cent in the upswing and then, after a lapse of not much more than a year, declined to -20 per cent. The corresponding fluctuation in $M_3$ was, of course, more modest, but even this relatively broad concept fluctuated between about 17 per cent and -10 per cent. This experience was in very marked contrast to the relatively successful years of macroeconomic performance from 1962 to 1970. Trading bank advances in real terms naturally enough followed a broadly similar path, although in their case the relative stability of the years 1962–70 was even more marked.

We have already examined the behaviour of the medium-term bond rate in nominal terms. In Figure 4.10 this is related to the *ex post* real rate as earlier defined. If this *ex post* real rate is a useful proxy for the relevant *ex ante* rate, and if in turn this has a significant impact on private expenditure, this figure is rather revealing.

In the first place, it sensibly modifies the cyclical timing suggested by the nominal rate. Thus, the real rate declined fairly smoothly throughout the whole of the upswing of 1961–5. During the 1965–6 recession it rose rather than remained constant as did the nominal rate. During the 1966-70 upswing it rose slightly; it peaked before the cyclical peak; and thereafter it declined virtually continuously until the end of 1974, despite the fact that over the same period the nominal rate rose by about 50 per cent of its 1971 level. This, of course, simply reflects the rapid acceleration in the rate of inflation that occurred after the beginning of 1973. Equally clearly, if the rate of inflation and its acceleration were largely independent of monetary action over the period, it would have been entirely impossible for the Reserve Bank to hold the real rate even approximately stable, provided that at the same time it wished to preserve the stability of the financial system. In short, the behaviour of the real rate over this period was not even remotely controllable by the monetary authority, which appears to have conducted a restrictive policy up to the limit of the capacity of the Australian financial system to sustain it.

The principal conclusion that emerges from examining the real rate as an indicator of monetary thrust is that from 1962 to 1970 – a period of relatively successful macroeconomic management – the real rate nevertheless performed less well cyclically than did the nominal rate. It turned up relatively late in the upswing of 1961–5 and to a lesser extent in that of 1966–70, while it was allowed

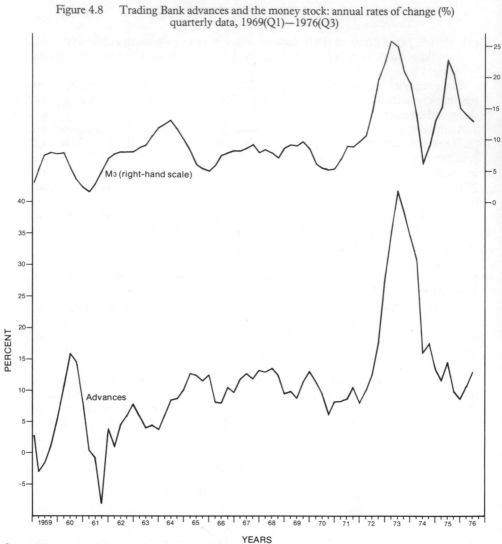

Figure 4.8    Trading Bank advances and the money stock: annual rates of change (%)
quarterly data, 1969(Q1)—1976(Q3)

*Sources:*
1  For M₃ data, Reserve Bank of Australia, *Australian Banking and Monetary Statistics*
2  For advances data, Australian Bureau of Statistics, *Seasonally Adjusted Indicators*

Figure 4.5    Quarterly indicators: real growth rates (%), quarterly data, 1950(3)—1976(2)

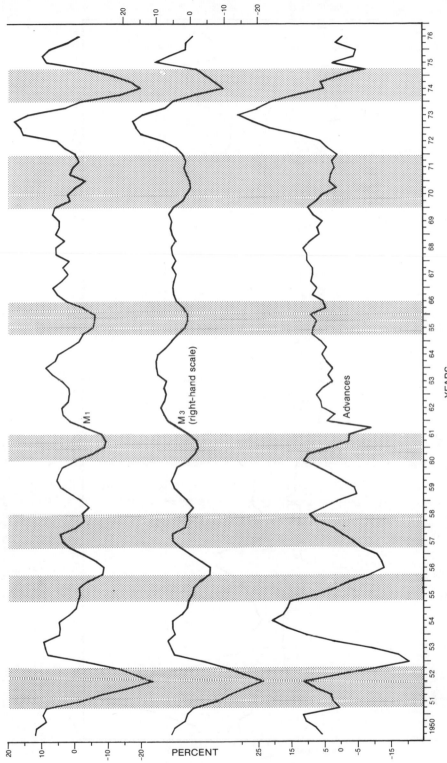

YEARS

*Note:* For the years 1950–3 data are available only for the second and fourth quarters; for the missing observations the average of the rates in the previous and following quarters has been taken.

*Sources:* $\dot{M}_1$, $\dot{M}_3$ and Trading Bank Advances, as in Figure 4.6 and Figure 4.8, *less* the rate of change of the consumer price index, as in Figure 2.8.

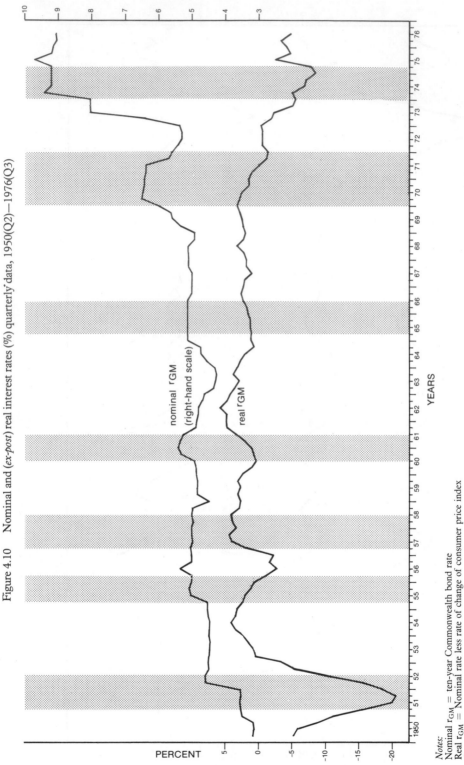

Figure 4.10    Nominal and (ex-post) real interest rates (%) quarterly data, 1950(Q2)–1976(Q3)

YEARS

PERCENT

nominal r<sub>GM</sub>
(right-hand scale)

real r<sub>GM</sub>

Notes:
Nominal r$_{GM}$ = ten-year Commonwealth bond rate
Real r$_{GM}$ = Nominal rate less rate of change of consumer price index
Sources:
1   For Nominal r$_{GM}$, Reserve Bank of Australia, Statistical Bulletin
2   For Consumer Price Index, 1950.I-1967.II, Labour Report, no. 53, p. 229; 1967.III-1975.IV,
    Australian Bureau of Statistics, Quarterly Summary of Australian Statistics

# 4.7 Monetary Policy and Macroeconomic Policy

Monetary policy is simply one of a number of instruments employed by the Australian authorities for macroeconomic purposes. The others are:
(a) fiscal policy;
(b) exchange policy;
(c) quantitative import restrictions (up to 1961); and
(d) methods of influencing private capital movements to and from overseas, including exchange controls, embargoes on certain forms of private capital movements, and the variable deposit requirement (VDR) technique.

Any comprehensive analysis of Australian macroeconomic policy would need to examine each of these and their inter-relations. To do this would take this study far beyond its intended scope. Nevertheless, we shall attempt a short account of the relationship between monetary and fiscal actions over the period of our study, for two main reasons:
(1) Fiscal and monetary policies are often thought of as alternative ways of operating upon the level of domestic demand.
(2) The actual budgetary position (deficit or surplus) is itself an important influence on monetary variables.

Fiscal decisions influence the economy in four main ways:
(1) They have a direct impact on demand via government expenditure on goods and services.
(2) The influence private expenditure via taxation changes, which may modify either the incentive or ability to invest or, by changing personal disposable income, may typically influence private consumption.
(3) They may influence private expenditure by changing expectations, including price expectations.
(4) Since deficits have to be financed, they exert both wealth and liquidity effects on the private sector.

Moreover, these four classifications are far from exhaustive, since it seems almost certain that government expenditure on goods and services is not homogeneous in its impact on demand. It therefore follows that no simple highly-aggregative measure of the fiscal position can of itself be an adequate quantitative indicator of fiscal policy stance.

Assessing the impact of fiscal changes in any one financial year is therefore a complex matter that is likely to require a fairly high degree of disaggregation and a correspondingly considerable research input. Despite the limitations of the available aggregate data we shall try to use it to provide a rather rough and ready assessment of fiscal policy.

The first approximate indicator we provide is the observed deficit. Since it is the observed deficit that has to be financed, this series is a good indicator of the potential liquidity and wealth effect on the private sector.

The actual budget out-turn is, however, not in principle a good indicator of the impact of fiscal policy decisions on aggregate demand, since theory suggests that the relevant concepts here are the exogenous (policy-determined) increases in expenditure and the exogenous shifts in the functions relating tax yields and transfer payments to GNP. Clearly, the actual values of taxation receipts and expenditures contain endogenous elements arising out of changes in economic activity. Hence, the actual values of expenditure and taxation, and *a fortiori* the actual deficit, must in some degree be inaccurate indicators of policy.

Consider, for example, a situation in which with government expenditures and tax functions unchanged – and thus, by definition, fiscal policy unchanged – a sharp recession occurs. Net tax yields will fall severely; and if government expenditure on goods and services is unaltered, the deficit will increase correspondingly. Thus, the observed deficit will suggest a large expansionary change in fiscal policy in a period when, by assumption, fiscal policy has been unaltered. This is, of course, a particular example of the general proposition that we have already met, namely, that endogenous variables are defective indicators of exogenous policy changes, since they are functions of all the exogenous variables in the system.

Given this difficulty, a common procedure has been to construct a series based on the assumption that GDP is either constant or growing along some predetermined path. This eliminates (in the first case) and both reduces and quantifies (in the second) the induced element in expenditures and net tax yields. To the extent that this is done the result is an indicator that is superior, at least conceptually, to the observed values of expenditure and tax receipts and hence their difference. The best known of such indicators is the 'high' or 'full employment' budget.

Unfortunately, the high employment budget is not a concept to which it is easy to give a generally agreed interpretation. Moreover, it is extremely difficult to easure. Also, for non-linear shifts in tax functions, its calculation may lead to very misleading conclusions. Nevertheless, subject to proper caution it seems that *changes* in high employment expenditures, tax yields and hence the deficit are likely to provide a rather better indicator of *changes* in fiscal stance over the cycle than changes in the observed values of the same variables.

Estimates of the full-employment budgetary position for Australia from 1963 through 1974-5 are available.[12] Changes in the estimated 'full employment' deficit and the actual deficit are given in Table 4.1.

It should be noted here that, save for 1965-6 and 1971-2, changes in the actual and full employment surplus are always of the same sign. Both these years were years of recession in which actual tax receipts were less, and unemployment benefits more, than their full employment value. Thus, these years apart, changes in the actual budget out-turn seem in general to be a good indicator of the *sign* of changes in fiscal stance. Quantitatively, the correspondence is less close, and in such cases we should expect changes in the full employment estimates to be a rather better, although imprecise, indicator.

Unfortunately, the full employment concept is highly aggregative and method-

**Table 4.1** *Fiscal indicators, 1955–75.*

| Financial year | Changes in actual deficit | | Changes in full employment deficit | | Nevile's impact effect | |
|---|---|---|---|---|---|---|
| | $A m. | % of NFNP | $A m. | % of NFNP | %of NFNP | Change in % impact |
| 1955–6 | 48 | 0·6 | n.a. | n.a. | 2·2 | 1·3 |
| 1956–7 | − 114 | − 1·3 | n.a. | n.a. | − 0·4 | − 2·6 |
| 1957–8 | 2 | 0·0 | n.a. | n.a. | 1·7 | 2·1 |
| 1958–9 | 228 | 2·2 | n.a. | n.a. | 3·0 | 1·3 |
| 1959–60 | − 54 | − 0·5 | n.a. | n.a. | 2·6 | 0·4 |
| 1960–1 | − 202 | − 1·7 | n.a. | n.a. | 1·2 | − 1·4 |
| 1961–2 | 298 | 2·3 | n.a. | n.a. | 4·4 | 3·2 |
| 1962–3 | 74 | 0·6 | n.a. | n.a. | 3·0 | − 1·4 |
| 1963–4 | 29 | 0·2 | n.a. | n.a. | 3·2 | 0·2 |
| 1964–5 | − 236 | − 1·5 | − 167 | − 1·1 | 3·3 | 0·1 |
| 1965–6 | 72 | 0·4 | − 48 | − 0·3 | 2·8 | − 0·5 |
| 1966–7 | 267 | 1·4 | 271 | 1·5 | 3·1 | 0·3 |
| 1967–8 | 120 | 0·6 | 85 | 0·4 | 2·9 | − 0·2 |
| 1968–9 | − 257 | − 1·2 | − 183 | − 0·8 | 2·3 | − 0·6 |
| 1969–70 | − 194 | − 0·8 | − 132 | − 0·5 | 2·5 | 0·2 |
| 1970–1 | − 181 | − 0·7 | − 239 | − 0·9 | 3·0 | 0·5 |
| 1971–2 | 124 | 0·4 | − 100 | − 0·3 | 2·9 | − 0·1 |
| 1972–3 | 575 | 1·7 | 718 | 2·1 | 4·9 | 2·0 |
| 1973–4 | − 416 | − 1·1 | − 352 | − 0·9 | 4·2 | − 0·7 |
| 1974–5 | 2,274 | 4·9 | 526 | 1·1 | 7·7 | 3·5 |

*Sources:*
(1) For actual deficit from 1954–5 to 1962–3: *Treasury Information Bulletin: Supplement* (August 1964).
(2) For actual and full employment deficit from 1963–4 onwards: Barton, Derody and Sheehan [15].
(3) For Nevile's impact effect, Nevile [103] and private communication.

ologically arbitrary, and to this extent it is suspect. However, we do have estimates, due to Nevile [103], of the impact or first-round effects (i.e. those accruing within the fiscal year in question) of fiscal policy, derived from a model that allows explicitly for the non-homogeneity of expenditure and taxation effects. Nevile's results, stated in terms of percentage changes in non-farm product, are reproduced in Table 4.1 together with the derived first differences, which measure the percentage impact on non-farm product of *changes* in fiscal policy. Except in the years of major policy changes, e.g. 1972-3, 1973–4 and 1974–5, there is no close correspondence between Nevile's estimates and either the high employment or actual changes. This is not entirely unexpected, since quite apart from conceptual differences, unless the aggregate change in policy is fairly substantial, the sign of its impact may be strongly influenced by the *distribution* of expenditure and taxation changes for which Nevile's model allows but the other indicators do not.[13]

In sum, therefore, no entirely satisfactory indicator of fiscal policy changes in Australia is at present available. In what follows we make use, in the main, of the actual budget position on the one hand and Nevile's estimates on the other, although in some cases we refer to the full employment estimates for supporting evidence.

The examination of budget *positions* is not a useful undertaking. What is more helpful is the comparison of annual *changes* in the fiscal indicators. Since Nevile's series, which is almost certainly the most reliable, has been scaled in relation to non-farm product, a similar scaling has been used for the other two series.

The relation between the two policy indicators is, on the whole, unimpressive. Assuming that Nevile's is the more correct, there was a deflationary shift in the period 1955–7, which was reversed in the two following years. The deflationary shift in stance in 1960–1 is well known, as is the sharp reversal of this shift in 1961–2 and *its* reversal in 1962–3. After this date Nevile's estimates suggest rather small changes in fiscal stance until 1972–3, when there was a sharp shift in the direction of expansion. This was reversed in 1973–4 and again in 1974–5.

If we compare the full employment estimates with the actual out-turn, we can see that until 1971-2 they exhibit fair qualitative correspondence and even, in many cases, suggest the same order of magnitude for changes in the policy stance.

After 1971-2 the quantitative correspondence between the two series declines, as the economy moved away from the assumed full-employment figure. In short, until fairly recently the actual budget was probably as good an indicator as an estimated full-employment budget.

As already noted, the two policy indicators are not closely related. Moreover, even where the change in stance was severe, the actual budget tends to perform rather poorly when first differenced to provide an index of the policy shift. This is, for example, typically the case of 1955–8. In later years the performance of the actual budget is somewhat better. In the years of major shifts in stance Nevile's series and the full employment concept tend to agree.

Since only annual estimates are available, it is not easy to fit changes in fiscal stance into the cyclical pattern. Using Nevile's estimates, however, it seems that policy became increasingly restrictive during the downswing of 1955–6 and the subsequent upswing.

The mistiming of the fiscal policy shift in 1960–1 is well known – a mistiming exacerbated by the special measures of November 1960.[14] Finally, in 1971-2 the shift in policy was in a deflationary direction at a time when the economy was in recession. This second piece of mistiming probably contributed to the excessive shift to fiscal and monetary expansion that followed in 1972–3.

Overall, it is difficult to argue that fiscal policy shifts have typically been destabilising rather than the reverse. On the other hand, three of the eight major shifts in stance identified by Nevile seem to have been wrongly timed, while two at best seem doubtful. This suggests that the difficulties of diagnosing, and forecasting, the Australian economy have a similar impact on fiscal policy to that which we have earlier imputed to them in the case of monetary policy. In short, because forecasting and diagnosis are so uncertain, action is delayed so that, when it is taken, rather rapid results are required. This may entail an over-response, as in 1972–3. Alternatively, it may involve what (after the event) can be seen to be a perverse response, as in 1960–1. Thus, Nevile's estimates tend to confirm our earlier judgement concerning the difficulty of fine tuning the Australian economy.[15]

## 4.7 General Conclusions

The overview presented in this chapter is, as we have remarked, unavoidably superficial in part because of the limitations of the available data. Nevertheless, a number of conclusions emerge.

Monetary policy has been used both in an attempt to stabilise aggregate demand and, more commonly perhaps prior to the mid-1960s, in an attempt to moderate the import cycle. This is confirmed both by our *ex ante* dating, the *ex post* policy indicators, and a reading of Reserve Bank reports. If it is defined to *exclude* the VDR technique, then in more recent years it does not seem to have been assigned so commonly to the external objective.[16]

There is some evidence to suggest that the inside lag in policy (as a whole) is rather long. This appears also to be the case with monetary policy, at least in relation to the likely dynamics of the transmission process.[17] This is not surprising in view of the difficulty of both economic diagnosis and economic forecasting, particularly in an economy so open as the Australian. On occasions, however, the result has been what appear to be either excessive policy shifts or even perverse policy shifts, although the latter seem to have related to fiscal rather than monetary policy.

Until 1971–4 the amplitude of fluctuations in indicators of monetary thrust, defined in either nominal or real terms, does not seem to have been very great.

The 1971–4 episode was, however, a clear exception, and in this period it seems that both discretionary monetary action and the monetary indicators were required to respond far too much far too quickly. In short, in this period monetary policy seems to have been used up to, and arguably beyond, the limits of both economic and institutional prudence.

Over the approximately twenty-five years reviewed in this chapter it is clear that the techniques employed in conducting monetary policy markedly changed.[18] In particular there was a relative increase in the emphasis on the manipulation of both administered and market interest rates. The latter development has obviously implied a far greater role for open market operations than was technically feasible in either the 1950s or even the early 1960s.

The brief review of the use made of monetary policy in the authorities' attempts to stabilise the economy suggests a number of issues on which far more detailed information is needed.

The first of these is plainly the transmission mechanism and its dynamic characteristics, for our present treatment of both is based upon assumptions the relevance of which may well be disputed. More precisely, we need to know in quantitative terms the dynamic impact of monetary action on:
(a)  aggregate demand;
(b)  the rate of change of prices; and
(c)  the external constraint; with . . .
(d)  particular reference to the rate of private capital inflow.

Given our views on (a)–(d), we can then ask whether the Australian authorities have generally deployed monetary policy in accordance with its comparative advantage (in relation to fiscal policy, exchange rate policy or administrative devices) in influencing (a)–(c) over the policy horizon. Put another way, we can ask whether monetary policy has been assigned in an appropriate way.

On the basis of our judgement on these matters we can derive a further judgement on the quantitative emphasis placed upon monetary policy, i.e. whether it has typically been expected to do too much or too little.

The reader is asked to note at the very outset that the methodology here employed in attempting to obtain answers to these questions is decidedly eclectic. Naturally, use is made of the evidence from econometric models or individual quantitative studies; but use is also made of simple inspections of time series and other relevant evidence that cannot readily be forced into the econometric framework. Moreover, in weighing the various forms of evidence, much reliance is placed upon economic intuition, which, since it seems certain to be in some degree idiosyncratic, needs to be assessed with caution.

The main purpose of reviewing the past is to improve performance in the future. This is simply a learning process. The final aim of this study is to contribute to this by suggesting, in the light of our review, how monetary policy may be most usefully assigned and conducted over (say) the decade 1980–90.[19] In this area, as we shall see, controversy is unavoidable. However, the attempt will be made to ensure that any controversy that does arise is constructive.

# Notes: Chapter 4

1 Our classification seeks to identify five stances of monetary policy: *expansion* (or *ease*); *mild expansion* (or *mild ease*); *accommodating*; *mild restraint*; and *restraint*. This is less ambitious than the procedure followed by Lewis [96] and Lewis and Wallace [97], but this in no way guarantees greater objectivity.

2 Both the econometric models developed in the Reserve Bank (RB74) and (RB76) follow this approach.

3 On this issue, cf. Jonson, Mahar and Thompson [76].

4 This is a very tentative judgement, since, as pointed out, the cycle peaks and troughs reflect *inter alia* the authorities' attempts at stabilisation by both fiscal and monetary means. To reach a firm conclusion we really need to know what Australia's cycles would have been if the authorities had *not* attempted to stabilise. Theoretically, some indication could be obtained by using an econometric model of the Australian economy to simulate the consequences of 'neutral' i.e. non-stabilising, monetary and fiscal policies. Defining neutral policies is, however, far from easy, while no model generally agreed to be applicable over the period 1950-75 exists. Moreover, the implicit assumption that the model would correctly reflect behaviour in the face of a major change in policy regime is almost certainly erroneous. Thus, the judgement in the text is offered. Doubts concerning the alternative methodology, known as the 'reaction function' approach, are discussed in a later chapter.

5 If monetary policy comes to be used more and more in an attempt to moderate cyclical fluctuations in the rate of change of domestic prices, this will lengthen the apparent lag, since in general the rate of price change lags the typical capacity cycle.

6 Data from which to calculate the net banking base and net liquidity base, as defined, are not available prior to 1959.

7 Cf. Chapter 9.

8 For example, the provision of funds for term and farm development loan funds.

9 Cf. Rowan [140] and Arndt and Stammer [8].

10 A similar result has been obtained by Sharpe [152]. Additionally, preliminary results due to Terrell and Valentine [160], and some as yet incomplete experiments by Valentine and Rowan, suggest a rather slow process of adjustment by the trading banks. Lewis [96], by contrast, has found rather short lags. The issue remains unsettled.

11 The Valentine–Rowan experiments suggest that the observed change in trading bank advances contained an element that was unplanned by the banks and reflected unforeseen changes in the public's utilisation of agreed limits.

12 These are due to Barton, Derody and Sheehan [15]. For some of the difficulties with the full employment concept, consult Carlson [23] and Corrigan [32].

13 Nevile's results relate to federal, state and local government operations in aggregate, the Barton, Derody and Sheehan estimates to the federal budget. This may be important, since in a recent note Nevile [106] has suggested that the Commonwealth position was until recent years typically more stable than the more widely defined 'public sector'.

14 For a further discussion, cf. Nevile [103].

15 Probably political factors, in particular the approach of elections, influence the form and timing of fiscal policy.

16 Since 1975-6 there has been an increasing emphasis on the role of monetary action in restricting the rate of inflation and a parallel tendency to accept the assumption of an appropriate form of the transmission process. These and related points are discussed more fully in Chapter 12.

17 Which we have at present *assumed*, not *demonstrated*.

18 Necessarily so as financial institutions and markets have developed with an associated increase in the importance of non-bank financial intermediaries.

19 We abstract from the immediate future (1977-9) since for various reasons we expect the routine behaviour captured by econometric models to have a limited relevance to it.

*Chapter 5*

# The Australian Transmission Mechanism in Outline

## 5.1 Introduction: The Competitive Model

The transmission mechanism is defined as the dynamic linkage between policy actions taken by the Reserve Bank of Australia (or Commonwealth Bank) and its main ultimate target variables. The latter are simply defined as:
(a) the level of aggregate demand;[1]
(b) the balance of payments, in particular the rate of private capital inflow; and
(c) the rate of change of Australian prices.
This is, of course, oversimplified in that its implicit assumption is that the composition of aggregate demand is not a matter that engages the Reserve Bank's attention, which is clearly not the case.[2]

It is obvious, as we have noted, that the mechanism linking these ultimate targets to Reserve Bank actions is unlikely to have been invariant over our time period. This is so partly because the structure of the Australian economy has changed, partly because the financial system itself has developed very markedly (particularly since the mid-1960s) and partly because there are now some reasons to suppose that, in a period of unusually high rates of inflation, the economic

104

behaviour underlying the transmission process may also have changed in a significant way.

Since this is the case, it makes little or no sense to speak or think in terms of a single theory of the transmission process that is applicable to the twenty-five-year span of our study. This chapter accordingly attempts to give a brief outline of three distinguishable forms of transmission mechanism, which, it seems, were roughly applicable to three stages of financial evolution. Since financial development is a continuous process, the precise dating of these stages must of necessity be arbitrary. However, for reasons given more fully in the Appendix to this chapter, we regard the transmission mechanisms of:

(a) the 1950s as a 'banking' process;

(b) the 1960s as a 'Radcliffe'-type process; and

(c) the 1970s as approximating to a 'competitive' process.

In chapters 6–9 we attempt to review particular periods of Reserve Bank policy. These have been selected to represent each of the three stages defined above.[3] In this chapter we therefore give a very simple and stylised account of the three transmission processes, since these provide the implicit analytical frameworks within which these accounts are given. Most attention is, of course, directed to the "competitive" process, since this approximates most closely to contemporary conditions. Moreover, since financial development is continuing at a relatively rapid rate, the financial system is over time likely to approximate even more closely to this form of model.

Consider now a financial system in which flows of funds from surplus sectors to deficit sectors take place primarily through the medium of financial institutions that are not closely competitive with each other. A simple stereotype of this form of organisation is provided by a hypothetical system in which the institutional structure is dominated by only two classes of financial intermediary: the commercial banks and the life offices. In such a system variation in the supply of finance to deficit units within the private sector is likely to come primarily from variation in the lending of the banking system. We may expect the rates of both private investment and expenditure on consumer durables to be related, at the margin, to the rate of increase in bank advances.

In such a system the banks have, by assumption, no close competitors in the supply of short and medium term finance. Spending units that require bank finance and cannot obtain it typically have no access to alternative sources. Thus, the crucial matter in controlling expenditure in such a system is the control of the banking system. If restrictions are placed upon the composition of bank portfolios by (say) requiring a certain *ratio* of LGS, and upon the total of bank portfolios by controlling the *stock* of LGS, the control of the banking system will, in theory be complete. Moreover, if the rates charged (and paid) by banks are also controlled, the market for bank loans will not clear. There will be disequilibrium rationing or availability effects. Clearly, in such a system, provided that the portfolio choices of the life offices are relatively invariant to the emergence of excess demand for advances, a monetary policy in the usual sense will not be necessary. What may be called a 'banking policy' will, if it is technically efficient in controlling advances, be economically efficient in influencing aggregate demand.

Naturally enough, the Australian financial system in the twenty-five years under review never exhibited the simplicity of this hypothetical illustration.[4] Nevertheless it remains true that in the early 1950s, when the development of non-bank financial intermediaries was comparatively small, the transmission mechanism was perceived as defining the technical problem very much as a matter of controlling the trading banks. Moreover, as non-bank financial intermediaries, in particular instalment finance houses, developed rapidly in the late 1950s, it became an issue whether, should the constitutional position permit it, central banking control should be extended to embrace the emergent forms of finance.[5] The point is that the financial system was perceived to consist in a small number of imperfectly competitive submarkets that were in principle controllable by administrative, as opposed to market, techniques.

As the financial system developed with the growth of non-bank financial intermediaries and the emergence of a money market, the system became susceptible to analysis along essentially Radcliffian lines.[6] We interpret this to mean that market imperfections were still considerable and that in general the submarkets for various forms of finance could not be assumed to clear. Thus, the emphasis remained upon availability. However, it was argued, along essentially Radcliffian lines, that the availability of funds from non-bank financial intermediaries was controllable (at the margin) by official manipulation of the level and structure of interest rates. Thus, a rise in the rates that were payable on deposits with trading banks and savings banks was seen as a means of reducing the ability of non-bank financial intermediaries to supply funds to borrowers – or – in alternative terms, to reduce the observed income velocity of the nominal money stock by reducing the availability of funds.[7]

In both periods there was relatively little emphasis on controlling the nominal money stock. In fact, because of the relation between the growth in advances and the change in the money stock, more emphasis on this variable occurred during the 1950s.[8] In the 1960s attention was devoted to some wider and less clearly defined concept of general liquidity. In the latter period, however, considerable importance was attached, along the familiar Radcliffian lines, to interest rates, whereas, although in the former period the Reserve Bank, through Governor Coombs, was insistent that interest rates must be allowed to vary, this seems to have been due more to the realisation that virtually pegged rates on bonds compelled the Commonwealth Bank[9] to undo, by induced open-market operations, the results of its special account policies.

As already stated, financial development after 1965 was extremely rapid. The imperfections in the financial market were correspondingly rapidly reduced as new forms of asset (such as Negotiable Certificate of Deposit (NCDs)) and additional forms of short term borrowing (notably the recrudescence of the trade bill) emerged. With these developments availability effects became of lesser importance, the element of rationing in the system was reduced, and the system moved towards closer correspondence with a competitive model.

The fully competitive model, like our initial banking model, is, of course, an oversimplification. Its principal characteristic is that it assumes a very wide range of financial intermediaries competing vigorously for funds and, in the process, continually developing new forms of liability designed to attract lenders. Sub-markets for funds are thus closely competitive and typically clear. Disequilibrium rationing or availability effects are (in the limit) absent, and any credit-worthy borrower willing to pay the interest rate demanded can always obtain the funds that he wants. It follows that it is interest rates that are of major importance, not (as in the earlier approach) because they influence availability, but because they allocate the funds between competing borrowers and because changes in them generate wealth effects for holders of long maturity claims. In such a (hypothetical) system fund flows are no longer causal. The transmission variable(s) are interest rates, and the two main transmission processes can be perceived as: (a) cost-of-borrowing effects; and (b) wealth effects.

In practice, of course, no system approximates very closely to this competitive model. Even in the United States and the United Kingdom there is, for example, no effective market in mortgages.[10] As a result availability effects occur in the mortgage 'market' and are usually regarded as an important factor influencing investment in housing. Additionally, when the number of banks is small, as it is in many countries other than the United States, the rates charged for bank advances may be relatively rigid and may on occasion result in the emergence of considerable excess demand. Hence, in the general case we may expect significant availability effects in at least two important markets.

By the early 1970s it seems likely that the Australian system corresponded fairly closely with this modified competitive model. We can therefore regard the Australian transmission mechanism of the 1970s as displaying:

(a) interest rate effects in the form of cost-of-borrowing effects and wealth effects; and

(b) availability effects in at least the markets for bank advances and housing finance.

Given that expectation (b) is correct, it is clear that movements in relative rates, as well as 'the' interest rate in some index number sense, must have a significant influence on both total expenditure and its composition.

Although this assessment of the contemporary Australian transmission process may, if anything, overstate the extent to which it at present corresponds to the competitive model, any such overstatement may, given the nature of financial innovation, be short lived. We shall assume our assessment to be approximately correct.

Thus far we have said nothing of the relationship between the rate of private capital movements and the elements of the transmission process.

Consider, for example, our stereotype of the process in the 1950s. Suppose now that, because of a policy of restraint in bank lending, considerable excess demand occurs. If domestic would-be borrowers had access to external sources of finance, a capital inflow would result. In general, however, a relatively undeveloped domestic financial system lacks close links with financial centres overseas.[11] Thus, during the 1950s we should expect a very weak relation (*ceteris paribus*) between domestic monetary restriction and private capital inflows.

During the (according to us) Radcliffian 1960s financial developments, partilarly those accompanying and following the mineral boom, ensured much closer financial integration with the principal overseas financial centres.[12] The consequence was an emerging relationship between the rate of capital inflow and domestic monetary conditions, defined, of course, to include both availability (excess demand) situations and relative interest costs in Australia and overseas.

By the late 1960s and the contemporary 1970s there could be small doubt that this integration was far advanced. Indeed, one reflection of this integration was the authorities' need to insulate the domestic market in 1972–4 by such devices as an embargo on certain types of external capital transactions and the introduction of the VDR device – a need that recurred at the end of 1976.

In view of the institutional changes and their consequences we must be careful, in analysing the conduct of monetary policy, to recall that the economic, and above-all financial, system in which the observed policy was made has differed very significantly over time. We may well expect this to be reflected in a rather different assignment for monetary policy and in a different emphasis on various monetary policy techniques.

As we have presented matters so far, the competitive-type model has no explicit quantity effects directly derived from changes in the nominal money stock. *Possibly,* although this is uncertain, as we shall see later, this omission is a reasonable approximation to conditions ruling in the early 1970s. With the emergence of extremely high (historically) rates of inflation after 1973 there can be no certainty that, even within the confines of an essentially equilibrium formulation, the expectation-generating process has remained unaltered. Nor can we be sure (from available research results) that the dynamic relationship between the *expected* rates of inflation and actual rates has remained unaltered.[13] These are empirical issues, which we attempt to discuss later. The crucial point, however, is that our exposition of the competitive model leaves out of account some potentially important aspects of the transmission mechanism. Moreover, these are precisely the elements that *may* have been growing more significant in recent years.

## 5.2 Some Cautions

The assertion that the Australian financial system is evolving in the direction of the 'competitive model' should not be misunderstood.

In the first place, this essentially neo-Keynesian approach to the transmission mechanism is not in any sense a denial of the position commonly taken by 'monetarists'. Both 'monetarists' and 'non-monetarists' concur on the role played by rates of return in the transmission process. Controversy arises because non-monetarists typically confine their definition of the relevant rates for empirical purposes to a (relatively) small subset of observable rates on financial assets. By contrast, 'monetarists' regard this specification as too limited. They regard a far wider range of rates of return, including those on real assets, as relevant. Unfortunately, since many of these rates are not observable, a structural specification of the 'monetarist' process is in large measure impracticable. Hence, it is not uncommon for 'monetarist' models to contain no structural specification of the transmission process and to use the money supply (in one of its definitions) as a proxy for the whole range of rates in (say) some reduced-form expression explaining expenditures.[14] Clearly, this kind of procedure, however legitimate, says nothing about the form of the transmission process. It cannot therefore be used as a basis for its analysis. Since our purpose is to relate the transmission mechanism to central bank action, we require an explicit rather than an implicit model. We have therefore adopted a rather conventional neo-Keynesian framework. However, this does not mean that we are thereby denying that additional (monetarist) transmission channels exist and may be significant. We are simply confessing an inability, which (it seems) we share with the monetarists, to include them in a structural framework in a way that not only carries theoretical conviction but also is suitable for empirical work.

Additionally, our argument that the interest rate mechanism is of growing importance in Australia does not imply that the Reserve Bank should use interest rates (in some definition) as its main operating or proximate target. This is a quite separate issue and is discussed in its proper context at a later stage.

Finally, there is, of course, no presumption that the more highly developed is the financial system, the more appropriate, for policy purposes, is the time form of the response of aggregate demand to central bank action likely to be. For stabilisation purposes it is desirable for a high proportion of the total response to take place within the current period (quarter) and for all of it to occur within a short timespan (say four to six quarters). This is simply because long-distributed lags may produce cumulative effects that require sharp policy reversals to offset them. This may lead to an unacceptable measure of instrument variation or even cumulative instrument instability.[15] It is indeed more than likely that the more desirable time form may occur in an undeveloped financial system dominated by rationing. There is certainly no suggestion that the more competitive is the system the faster, or even the more reliable, will be the response.[16] Whether this is so or not is a question of fact.

# 5.3 The Australian Transmission Mechanism in Models

The division of our time period into decades that, as a first approximation, correspond to familiar stereotypes of the transmission process is designed to give only a broad qualitative outline of developments. A rather more precise notion can be obtained by examining econometrically estimated macroeconomic models that contain an identifiable transmission process. In the United States there is a considerable array of such models.[17] Clearly, these models can be employed, typically by conducting policy simulations, to yield information regarding the (average) quantitative and dynamic characteristics of the transmission mechanism, both overall and in whatever degree of detail is specified by the model.

We make use of the results of some simulations of this kind in Chapter 10. For the moment, however, our concern is qualitative rather than quantitative. Accordingly, we now ask: how has the Australian transmission process been modelled?

The range of published macroeconometric models is, as one would expect, considerably smaller in Australia than in the United States. In practice we are restricted to three. Of these, two have been developed in the Reserve Bank and one by the Australian Treasury and Bureau of Statistics. None of these models are official, in the sense that they are accepted by the sponsoring bodies as definitive frameworks for policy formation. Nevertheless, they provide systematic summaries of major, and typically continuing, research efforts by highly skilled researchers. As such they must offer a valuable account of the transmission process.

In the present context most interest attaches to the initial Reserve Bank model constructed by Norton et al. and originally known as RB70. The second model (RB76), constructed in the Reserve Bank by Jonson et al. differs considerably in spirit from RB70 and its later version (RB74). More importantly in the present context, RB76 is a relatively small model in which the financial channels of transmission are treated less explicitly. Thus, although the model is important, it is not a useful indicator of the way in which the transmission mechanism was generally perceived in the late 1960s and early 1970s. In the present context we therefore concentrate upon RB70 and postpone until later any consideration of either RB76 or the Treasury–Bureau of Statistics model (denoted NIF).

The Reserve Bank model (RB70) was constructed initially as long ago as 1970. The construction process, the criteria employed in selecting equations and the theory underlying their specification are reported in a series of Occasional Papers published by the Reserve Bank. For our purposes the most helpful of these is Norton and Henderson [115].[18]

Since its original construction the model has undergone a number of changes, and the most recent report on these is that by Henderson and Norman [57], which incorporates work done by Carmichael and by Norman and Purvis [109]. We consider first the model in its original form, referred to as RB70.

Clearly, if our earlier remarks regarding the rate of financial development in Australia are correct, modelling 'the' financial transmission mechanism is an extraordinarily difficult business, since the implicit assumption of the typical macroeconomic model is of an invariant financial organisation. Thus, in so far as a generally competitive-type model is chosen, it is likely to be a less accurate representation of (say) the Australian system of the late 1950s and early 1960s than of that of later periods. Conversely, if a relatively non-competitive model is specified, it must become progressively less relevant as the development of the Australian money and capital markets proceeds and the system approaches more closely to the competitive type with (in the limit) no important availability effects.[19]

In practice, RB70 was essentially a neo-Keynesian model of a predominantly competitive type. Thus, the principal transmission mechanisms were originally via: (a) the cost of capital, operating through the supply price of capital; and (b) private sector wealth – both of which were influenced by the (policy-determined) changes in interest rates.

Availability or rationing effects were included only in the mortgage market and influenced only investment in dwellings. This was also, it should be noted, a feature of the FRB-MIT model of the US economy originally proposed by the Federal Reserve Board (FRB) and Massachusetts Institute of Technology (MIT).

In sum, therefore, the original model incorporated:

(1) a wealth effect in the equations determining expenditures on:
   (a) consumer durables, defined as motor vehicles plus household durables, and
   (b) investment in dwellings;
(2) cost-of-capital effects in the functions determining:
   (a) investment in dwellings,
   (b) investment in other building and construction, and
   (c) investment in equipment; and
(3) an availability effect in the equation explaining investment in dwellings, which in addition to including the (exogenous) interest rate on mortgages also included mortgage approvals as an explanatory variable.

Since mortgage approvals were an endogenous variable in the model – or more strictly, a variable containing an endogenous component – it is useful to see how they were determined. In fact the model defined

$$\text{Mortgage approvals} \equiv \text{Trading banks} + \text{Savings banks} + \underbrace{\text{Life offices}}_{\text{Mortgage approvals by}} + \text{Building societies}$$

and provided explanatory equations for the trading banks and savings banks terms. In both cases these were simple functions of the deposits of trading banks and savings banks.

These two equations are interesting, since they seem the only point in the model at which the public's holding of deposits (a major component in the money stock) exerts any causal influence, because trading bank deposits are determined, via an identity, by an equation explaining the demand for advances by trading banks. The influence of trading bank advances on expenditure is thus indirect in the sense that, via the identity, it determines trading bank deposits, which in turn determine trading-bank mortgage approvals. At no point does the value of trading-bank advances or new lending appear directly in a function explaining a component of expenditure; nor does any variable representing the excess demand for advances.

Strictly speaking, the function explaining trading bank advances is not a demand function of the private sector but a reduced form incorporating both demand and supply elements. This point has been carefully expounded by Valentine [164]. It therefore incorporates variables representing Reserve Bank requests to the trading banks to restrict either new lending and/or the value of advances outstanding. Thus, in so far as these requests are effective, they influence expenditure not by direct availability effects but by changing the volume of deposits (and thus the money supply), which in turn influences availability in the housing market. Thus, in terms of RB70 the Reserve Bank's requests either can be looked at as an attempt to influence the money supply or as an attempt to influence mortgage availability.

The first interpretation is not easy to reconcile[20] with the basic assumption of the model that the Reserve Bank sets interest rates directly as policy instruments, for this implies that it is willing, via the non-bank public's demand for money function, to allow the public to determine the money stock; and neither interpretation is easy to reconcile with many statements made by the Reserve Bank and its senior officials. It seems that the difficulty arises out of the decision to exclude the possibility of an excess demand for trading bank advances either existing or entering into an expenditure function.[21] Granted the severe difficulties of identifying excess demand situations and modelling the related market process, the method adopted nevertheless seems artificial, particularly for an equation estimated over a period beginning in 1959.IV and including much of a period (1959.III through 1960.IV) in which the Reserve Bank issued requests of both types in increasingly urgent tones. In short, it seems doubtful if the model reflected the transmission process as the Reserve Bank itself saw it in the late 1950s and early 1960s. This does not, of course, necessarily imply that the model was (or is) in error.

Be this conjecture as it may, the monetary instruments of the Reserve Bank are taken to be:
(1) a set of interest rates including:
    (a) rates on fixed and savings bank deposits,
    (b) rates on two-year and ten-year Commonwealth government securities, and
    (c) maximum rates on trading bank advances;

(2) statutory reserve deposits (SRDs); and
(3) requests to the trading banks regarding:
    (a) their rate of new lending, and
    (b) their outstanding advances total.
It is the changes in these instruments that, via the cost-of-capital, wealth and availability effects, influence aggregate demand.

Given these qualitative characteristics of the model, major interest attaches the extent and time form of the responses of aggregate demand and the capital account of the balance of payments to discretionary action.

Apart from the wealth effect on expenditure on consumer durables we must expect the rate of interest effects to be typically rather slow. The economic reason for this is that investment expenditures in general take a long time to plan and, once decided upon, are difficult to modify. Since the three investment functions (for private fixed capital) contained in the model are of the neoclassical type due to Jorgenson [83] [81] and Jorgenson and Stephenson [85] and Bischoff [17], which on econometric estimation habitually give rise to long-distributed lags often with a two or three-quarter delay, we must expect the cost effects of interest rate changes (exerted through changes in the supply price of capital) to occur slowly. Thus, the relatively quick effects are to be expected through: (a) durable consumption (including motor vehicles), via wealth; and (b) investment in dwellings, via mortgage approvals and wealth.

The simplest way to examine this conjecture in quantitative terms is to engage in a simulation. Some simulations with a later version of the model (RB74) are reported in Chapter 10.

The original version of RB70 did not seek to model the capital account of the balance of payments to any extent. Indeed, Norton and Henderson [115] themselves have stressed this deficiency. The single relevant equation explained private capital inflow (other direct investment) as a function *inter alia* of the supply price of capital and thus, indirectly, of the interest rates set by the Reserve Bank.

A model exists to be improved and developed; and RB74 is, as one would expect, an improved version of RB70. It says, however, a good deal for the basic structure of RB70 that the changes reported by Henderson and Norman [57] are typically developments and refinements rather than redesign or major reconstructions. Among the changes of interest in the financial sector are:
(a) the endogenising of mortgage approvals as a function of $M_3$;
(b) the reformation of the supply-price-of-capital equation, including the introduction of inflationary expectations;
(c) the introduction of money stock variables into the equation determining inflationary expectations; and
(d) the introduction of inflationary expectations directly into the equation explaining consumption expenditures.
On the other hand, no important extension of the treatment of the capital account has been reported by Henderson and Norman.

## 5.4 The External Impact

Australia is an extremely open economy. Since this is the case, it is clear that, via the demand for imports and the associated demand for services, discretionary monetary action must exert some influence on the balance of payments on current account. This channel is modelled in RB74, which contains an equation explaining major elements in imports. Therefore, if exports are regarded as exogenous, a restrictive (expansionary) monetary policy that, via the transmission mechanism, changes aggregate demand must, via the import demand function, decrease (increase) imports and thus improve (worsen) the current balance.

This influence, although it is clearly important, does not, of course, exhaust the impact of Australian monetary policy on the balance of payments. As already noted, Australia now possesses a highly developed financial system, which embraces increasingly well-developed money and capital markets. These markets are closely linked through banking, merchant banking and the operation of multinational companies with corresponding markets overseas. In these circumstances we must expect the capital account of the balance of payments to react to discretionary monetary policy, in so far as such policy alters the relative attractions of investing funds in Australia (a) by changing the relation between Australia's interest rates and the rates ruling in major countries overseas, and/or (b) by influencing expectations regarding Australia's future rate of exchange.[22]

These capital account influences were not modelled in RB70. However, work by Norman [110] [108] has developed a number of equations designed to explain major items in the capital account. These equations are, of course, experimental. Nevertheless, they can be incorporated into RB74 and therefore used, with this model, to simulate the external consequences of discretionary monetary policies. Such simulations are, of course, in no sense to be taken as definitive or assumed to carry with them any penumbra of Reserve Bank approval. They are nevertheless of some interest, since they give an indication (however crude) not only of the sensitivity of the capital account to domestic monetary action but also of the time form of its response.

Information of this kind is essential if we are to make any worthwhile assessment of the most useful role for discretionary monetary policy. This becomes clear if we consider an extreme hypothetical situation in which the Australian money and capital markets are assumed to be fully integrated with the corresponding markets in major financial centres overseas. In such a case any discrepancy (neglecting exchange rate expectations) between Australia's interest rates and those overseas would stimulate a capital inflow that would tend to eliminate it. Alternatively, any discrepancy between the demand for, and supply of, money in Australia would, either by changing domestic interest rates or by direct portfolio adjustments, lead to an offsetting capital movement. If such responses were rapid, it is difficult to see any scope for an independent Australian monetary policy, since even over a relatively short period neither the level of domestic interest rates nor the level of the domestic money stock could be effectively set by domestic action with the instruments at present under review.

This simple example suggests two obvious conclusions. The first is that, in assuming a potential role for Australian monetary policy under a system of a pegged exchange rate, we are assuming that Australian markets are imperfectly integrated in the sense outlined above. The second is that the critical issue is not the *existence* of imperfection in this sense (which most observers would accept) but its *degree*, for it is the degree of imperfection that will influence the relative efficiency of monetary policy as a means of influencing either the balance of payments on capital account or aggregate demand. Where imperfections are small and, as a result, capital account responses are rapid – as they were, for example, in the case of Britain during much of the nineteenth century – the comparative advantage of monetary policy tends to lie with the control of the capital account. This issue – an aspect of the so-called 'assignment' problem – is one to which we return at a later stage. Finally, it is important to note that, where the degree of imperfection is relatively small (so that capital inflows respond quickly to relative rate changes), monetary policy is likely to be a relatively inefficient means of controlling aggregate demand.

Thus far the discussion has proceeded on the implicit assumption of a pegged rate of exchange in which the peg is shifted, at discrete intervals, by the authorities as a deliberate act of policy. This is in accordance with the Australian practice over the period of this study. Since November 1976 this position has, however, been modified by a discretionary devaluation of 17.5 per cent, coupled with the introduction of what is in effect a managed float.

## 5.5 The Rate of Change of Prices

Earlier sections of this chapter have sought to sketch, in very broad terms, the transmission process linking Reserve Bank instruments to aggregate demand and the overall balance of payments. Traditionally, these two ultimate targets have received major attention. However, since the rapid acceleration in world inflation from 1972, major emphasis has come to be placed on the ability of macroeconomic policy measures, particularly discretionary monetary action, to influence (typically, of course, to moderate) the rate of change in prices, defined (say) as the rate of change in the implicit gross domestic product (GDP) deflator.

The extent to which discretionary monetary action can reduce the rate of change of prices, the mechanism by which it does so and the time form of the response involved are controversial issues on which a professional consensus has not yet been reached. Moreover, the literature, in particular the applied literature on the inflationary mechanism and its sensitivity to monetary action, is large and rapidly growing. The following discussion is thus in no sense an attempt to review the literature. Its aim is the more limited one of indicating in broad terms what appear to be the crucial elements in the problem, in order that the simulation results reported in Chapter 10 can be viewed in an appropriate perspective.

Early macroeconomic models commonly employed a Phillips curve approach to the determination of the rate of change of prices.

This regarded the rate of change of wage earnings as being a positive function of the pressure in the labour market and the expected rate of price change, usually proxied by some distributed lag on past rates of price change. In very early formulations the influence of the second element was often ignored; that is, its coefficient was set equal to zero. In later formulations it was introduced, and its coefficient was estimated to be positive but less than unity. In more recent experiments the coefficient has frequently been estimated to be close to unity and, in the statistical sense, insignificantly different from it, thus conforming to the Friedman [43] prediction. In outline, therefore, the amended (or augmented) Phillips curve appears to suggest that the percentage rate of change of wage earnings is a positive function of (a) the pressure in the labour market (proxied for empirical purposes in a variety of ways), and (b) the expected rate of change of prices, with the coefficient on the latter in the near neighbourhood of unity.

If the rate of change of prices is then regarded as the weighted sum of the rate of change of export prices, import prices and domestic prices, with the last element explained by a mark-up process on wage costs, we will be left with a simple theory of inflation, since the rate of change in wage costs can be approximated by the rate of change of wage earnings less the rate of change of productivity.

This very elementary outline is put forward simply as a framework within which to review the overall problem. In no sense can it be regarded as a model, or even as the skeletal outline of a model, of the Australian inflationary process, since it abstracts from the role of the arbitration processes (both state and Commonwealth) in determining the rate of change of wage rates, the impact of these on earnings and the difficult problem of the appropriate specification of the employers' perception of the rate of change in productivity.

Despite these limitations the framework is sufficiently complete to make it clear that discretionary monetary action must exert its influence on the rate of change in prices through:

(a) its impact on labour market pressures
(b) its impact on the expected rate of change in prices:
(c) its impact on the perceived rate of change in productivity; or
(d) its impact on the mark-up applied to costs.

Of these channels (a) and (c) are derived from the response of real (non-farm) GDP to discretionary monetary action; however, (b) constitutes what is essentially a separate mechanism not directly related to the cost-of-capital, wealth and availability effects already discussed. Clearly, if (b) were quantitatively sig-nificant, discretionary monetary action could be an effective means of influencing the rate of change of prices, even if (a) and (c) were quantitatively negligible. Very clearly, the significance of this for the efficient use of monetary policy would be of major importance, particularly with respect to the assignment problem.

To see this, consider a purely hypothetical case in which the wealth, cost-of-capital and availability effects were close to zero over some policy horizon of (say) six to eight quarters but the expectation effects, i.e. (b) above, were significant. Although changes in the expected rate of change in prices resulting from discretionary monetary action would ultimately have some influence on aggregate demand in real terms, these would in all probability be slow to materialise; the important impact of monetary action within the policy period would be on the expected rate of inflation and thus, with some distributed lag, on the actual rate of change of prices via the wage earnings relationship.[23] In this extreme, and probably implausible, case it would be natural to assign monetary policy to the control of inflation and leave aggregate demand to be controlled by other means, probably fiscal action. Thus, the expectational impact of discretionary monetary action (in this restricted sense) is a matter of major significance, and we need to consider the empirical findings with regard to it with great care.

There are at least three major elements in the problem:

(1) Does a macroeconomic concept of 'the' expected rate of inflation exist?[24]

(2) If it does, how far is it a function of monetary variables under the immediate or proximate control of the monetary authority?

(3) Which monetary variables, satisfying (2), are significant in this respect?

Of these problems (1) is, virtually by compulsion, answered in the affirmative by model builders; for even where 'the' expected rate is assumed to be heterogeneous between transacting sectors, it must nevertheless be assumed to be unique for any single sector. This may not be valid, particularly when the rate of inflation is at a level that is historically very high. However, if this latter possibility is excluded and 'the' expected rate regarded as a single number, at least as a first approximation, we are then able to concentrate attention on (2) and (3), i.e. upon the issue of precisely how expectations regarding the rate of change of prices are formulated.

The expected rate of change of prices is not a directly observable variable. There are therefore essentially two approaches to the problem of securing empirical information about the structure of the expectation-generating function.

The first of these is to construct a series for the expected rate of change of prices typically from surveys of the expectations of transacting groups. This has been done by a number of investigators, including Jonson and Mahoney [77], Danes [33] and Taylor [158] [159]. An explanation can then be sought for this series in terms of: (a) other macroeconomic variables, including variables under the immediate or proximate control of the monetary authority; and (b) past rates of change in prices.[25]

The second approach is to argue that the expectation-generating process is such as to minimise the forecasting error – or more strictly, to minimise the variance of the expected rate of inflation around the observed rate. In this case we seek an expectation equation that essentially explains the actual rate well. The equation is 'rational', in the restricted sense that it minimises the variance. Typically, such formulations rely upon a distributed lag on past rates of inflation plus some additional variables, including those under the direct or indirect control of the monetary authority. In short, the second approach is a variant of the first, which eliminates the unobservable expected rate by additional assumptions regarding the form and size of the forecasting error.[26]

As an alternative to the *structural* methods outlined above, a *reduced form* approach can be employed. In this case the expected rate of change of prices is written as a function of observable variables, including those controlled by the monetary authority, and these variables are then inserted into the equations explaining the observed rates of change in wage earnings and/or prices. This method yields no direct information on the expected rate of change of prices, and the model may not permit the identification of the underlying (implicit) expectation-generating function.

Both the structural and reduced form approaches have been used in the development of models within the Reserve Bank. In RB70 – the initial model – the approach is structural in the sense of the earlier discussion. In RB74 – a later development of RB70 – the method is the same. By contrast, RB76 follows an essentially reduced-form approach, the expectation of the rate of change of prices being proxied by an expression for the excess real supply (demand) for money and by a term involving the discrepancy between the real wage and its equilibrium value.

Precisely because of their critical importance the influence of monetary variables (however defined) on inflationary expectations, and the influence of the latter (via the wage and/or price-setting equations) on the actual rate of price change, are typically the subjects of a major research effort. Australia is no exception to this generalisation, and in addition to the papers cited there is already available a further research report by Jonson and Taylor [80] relating specifically to this problem.

Dogmatism on this issue, as it affects Australia, would plainly be out of place, particularly since work in progress but not yet available that would sensibly modify our present understanding might appear at any moment. At present, (1978), the available research on the price–wage mechanism seems to indicate two things:
(1) The form of any monetary influence on price expectations is not yet well established.
(2) Considerable doubt remains concerning the dynamics of the response of the actual rate of inflation to inflationary expectations.
The preliminary nature of this judgement must be stressed. We discuss the evidence for it in rather more detail in Chapter 10. The reader is, however, warned that the issue here is what conclusions can be supported by professional economic research, *not* what conclusions are nowadays typically accepted by 'influential opinion'. This can well be a distinction of great importance, since influential opinion is frequently dominated by fashion, and fashions in economic

thinking often have little theoretical or empirical basis.

## 5.6  Conclusions

This chapter has attempted to provide a non-quantitative sketch of the transmission process linking discretionary monetary action to the authorities' ultimate target variables.

Since the transmission process itself has changed, we have made use of three illustrative stereotypes, each of which we have associated, very roughly, with one of the decades of our study period.

Since rather more interest attaches to the neo-Keynesian competitive stereotype we have reviewed this, in the Australian context, through a short qualitative account of the competitive neo-Keynesian model developed in the Reserve Bank by Norton *et al.* This does not imply that this model is correct. In particular, we do not exclude that there may well be important channels, sometimes excluded or given little emphasis in the neo-Keynesian approach, through which monetary action may influence important target variables, in particular the rate of change of prices.

The following chapters supplement our brief overview of Australian monetary policy in that for four selected periods, they seek to analyse the impact of particular Reserve Bank policies. The framework of the latter four chapters derives rather loosely from the account of the transmission mechanism presented in this chapter, with the proviso that the underlying transmission process is implicitly assumed to be a good deal more competitive in the later periods examined than in the earlier. This seems to be in general accord not only with observation but also with the Reserve Bank's own views, as the Appendix to this chapter seeks to show.

# APPENDIX:  The Transmission Process: the Reserve Bank Perception[28]

In the qualitative sketch of the transmission process presented in Chapter 5 we have pointed out that the mechanisms that are implicit in it have changed over time as the Australian economic and financial structure has developed. This evolutionary process is difficult to document or express simply and quantitatively. Nevertheless, it is possible to provide some account of how the Reserve Bank itself has perceived developments by examining a series of important statements made by Dr H. C. Coombs (governor of the Reserve Bank from 1949 to 1968) and Sir John Phillips (governor from 1968 to 1975). These sources and related papers are included in the Bibliography.

Clearly, since the process of evolution is continuous, it is impossible, without being arbitrary, to say when the governors made significant changes in their perception of the transmission mechanism. However, the following conclusions may be drawn from the governors' statements:

(1) Until 1960–1 the transmission mechanism was seen, although with increasing misgivings, to be primarily a matter of controlling the lending of the trading banks. Broadly then, the 1950s constituted a decade of banking policy rather than monetary policy, as we have used these terms.

(2) During the 1960s steadily increasing emphasis was placed on interest rate movements, including movements in *relative* rates. In this period the under-lying theory of the transmission mechanism seems to have been essentially Radcliffian (at least as Rowan [143] has interpreted Radcliffian monetary theory).

(3) Towards the end of the 1960s, and lasting perhaps until the mid-1970s, the Radcliffian approach seems gradually to have developed into a neo-Keynesian-type analysis, in which the role of imperfections in financial markets was much less emphasised and availability elements were thus given reduced prominence.

(4) Finally, from about 1975–6 onwards the neo-Keynesian approach of the early 1970s seems gradually to have acquired some monetarist overtones. However, this is a very much more speculative judgement, since the present governor (H. H. Knight) has not as yet expressed himself in public on the theory of the transmission mechanism, and the only evidence is provided by occasional comments in the *Annual Reports.*[29]

Before we review, very briefly, the governors' positions, it must again be emphasised that our datings are rather arbitrary. Also, our interpretations are derived from literary detective work quite as much as economic analysis. Which of these two is currently the less able to provide clear-cut conclusions it is hard to say. What is sure, however, is that assigning interpretations to published statements has an unavoidable subjective element and is, on this account, always to be treated with some additional measure of scepticism.

# THE BANKING POLICY PERIOD: 1950–61

During this decade the Australian economy faced very severe fluctuations in its external position, with corresponding changes in overseas reserves.[30] Since the securities market was relatively undeveloped and there was small public tolerance of the need to accept changes in market interest rates on Commonwealth obligations, the first requirement was for an instrument that would enable the central bank (then the Commonwealth Bank) to sterilise changes in overseas reserves with respect to their impact on the 'base' of the banking system (the LGS base). The special account technique was developed for this purpose, and it is clear from Coombs's statements that it was a technically efficient means of doing so [28, esp. paras 18–34 and 38]. This is further attested by Australia's experience in 1950–2, reviewed elsewhere by Rowan [140].

Beyond the ability to influence LGS in this way, matters were a good deal less satisfactory, in the sense that the trading banks, both prior to the establishment of a minimum agreed LGS ratio and after, responded very slowly to changes in LGS holdings. This was particularly true with respect to advances. On this point Coombs remarked that 'months elapse before a change in policy towards lending shows itself in actual debit balances' [25, p. 10]. Clearly, the governor was dissatisfied with the slippage in the ability of the authorities to influence bank advances. It seems, however, that he expected the introduction of an effective agreed LGS convention to reduce this.

It is not entirely clear whether Coombs regarded the control of bank advances primarily as a means of controlling the availability of finance or primarily as a means of controlling the nominal money stock.[31] He did, however, at some points emphasise both aspects of banking control. However, it was undoubtedly the case that, whichever aspect of advances expansion was in fact regarded as the more significant, the *modus operandi* of domestic policy was that of a banking policy.

Coombs was fully aware of the limitations of such an approach to the transmission process. Indeed, he not only emphasised the significance, in this context, of the growth of non-bank financial intermediaries but also asserted that 'to the extent that monetary policy relies primarily on action through the banking system, it is operating in a steadily contracting field' [26, p. 36]. He also gave some weight to the argument that, if controls fall primarily on the traditional banking system this itself will stimulate the growth of non-bank financial intermediaries [29, p. 10].

The principal theme in the governor's observations was, however, the need to provide the central bank with a greater scope for open market operations, partly by developing the securities market itself but, more importantly, by obtaining general acceptance of the proposition that market interest rates on Commonwealth debt must be allowed to vary. Thus, he asserted that there could be no 'effective open market operations in the restraint of inflation unless we also adopt more flexible attitudes towards interest rates' [26, p. 26] and argued that 'it was imperative that the public and political parties should regard interest rate variations as a normal and necessary feature of the market' [26, p. 28].

Clearly, with interest rates virtually pegged the central bank could at any time be required to monetise Commonwealth debt, either by the non-bank public or, in the absence of an effective LGS convention, by the banks. It could thus be compelled to undertake induced open-market operations that would negate its special account policy. This was certainly one element in Coombs's concern. It seems also that he regarded variation in interest rates as an essential element in the transmission mechanism. There are, however, no explicit statements to the effect that variations in the level and structure of rates were means of restricting the availability of funds from non-bank financial intermediaries along the lines of Radcliffian monetary theory.[32]

Thus, on our interpretation, by the late 1950s the central bank saw the transmission mechanisms in broad terms as embracing:

(a) quantity (money stock) effects;
(b) price (interest rate) effects; and
(c) availability effects.

There was, however, no explicit argument relating (c) to (b).


# THE RADCLIFFIAN PERIOD: 1961—70


In 1964 Phillips [124] reviewed the development of monetary policy in Australia. Significantly, he began his review by pointing out that 'the last few years have been marked by a greater readiness on the part of the authorities to take the initiative in varying monetary policy, particularly in the field of interest rates' [124, p. 5].'

Next, he stressed the role of intermediaries in the 1959–61 boom and argued that this came about essentially because 'the community's demand for liquid assets was being largely satisfied by the rapid expansion of money substitutes by the non-bank intermediaries' [124, p. 10].

His actual conclusions were virtually pure Radcliffian. He argued that the 'focus of monetary policy must extend beyond the quantity of money to the state of general liquidity' [124, p. 13] and that 'it was no longer feasible to rely only on the traditional approach of endeavouring to maintain financial stability and to influence expenditure by controlling the capacity of the banks to increase the money supply' [124, p. 13]. The position was linked directly with interest rate variation by a further statement. 'It was the recognition of these elements of the problem and the progress which had been achieved in developing the bond market that opened the way for a more flexible approach to interest rates' [124, p.13].

It is also plain that Governor Phillips saw the availability of funds from non-bank financial intermediaries as a function of relative rates. This is implied by his discussion of the theory of asset demand and is explicit in his statement that 'scope to vary interest rates means that steps can be taken to make bank deposits more competitive with other short-term instruments' [124, p. 14]. It should be noted that the Reserve Bank acted in precisely this way in April 1964 [124, p. 17].

In view of these quotations, and similar passages in some of the Reserve Bank reports, it seems reasonable to argue that during the 1960s the Reserve Bank thought on Radcliffian lines. In short, it thought in terms of general liquidity rather than the money stock, thus implicitly emphasising the role of $V_y$ ($\equiv$ income velocity) rather than M in determining $MV_y$, and regarded availability from non-banks as a function of relative interest rates.[33] This, at least on some interpretations, is virtually the essence of Radcliffian monetary theory.

In one sense, however, the Reserve Bank seems to have taken a position quite opposed to Radcliffe. Despite words of caution on the need for accurate economic diagnosis and forecasting, Governor Phillips seems to have believed that monetary action was a potentially effective means of influencing aggregate demand over the short period. The Radcliffe Report argued otherwise [135, para. 511].

## THE NEO-KEYNESIAN PERIOD: 1970—5

In his 1971 Mills Memorial Lecture Governor Phillips set out to review developments in monetary theory and policy. Starting with the statement that 'In Australia the reaction of the monetary authority to the various developments (in monetary economics) has been to progressively shift the emphasis of monetary policy away from direct controls over the banking system and towards measures that operate more widely through the market' [125, p. 11], he went on to outline the theory of portfolio choice, to assert that the supply of money cannot be controlled simply by controlling the monetary base [125, p. 16] and to outline a neo-Keynesian transmission mechanism [125, p. 16]. This distinguished:
(a) interest rate effects;
(b) availability effects;
(c) wealth effects;
(d) expectation effects; and
(e) a money stock effect (a direct impact on expenditure).
Phillips went on further to argue that monetary policy must be managed eclectically and to deny the strong monetarist[34] view by saying: 'I do not think the evidence which has been produced on the length and variability of lags proves that a counter-cyclical policy will not reduce fluctuations in the economy' [125, p. 41].

Thus, Governor Phillips's analytical framework and his empirical judgement on the issue of lags were both neo-Keynesian. Indeed, the former corresponded closely with the structure of the Reserve Bank model (RB70) and the rather similar structure of the original FRB-MIT model of the US system. It is therefore not surprising to find references to the latter model, as well as the former, occurring in his lecture and used to support his view of the lag issue.

This outline of the transmission mechanism was followed by an interesting, but in this context not strictly relevant, review of the implications of his earlier analysis for policy (including the assignment problem) and a brief review of the Reserve Bank's employment of its principal instruments [125, pp. 20–3].[35] It is interesting, in comparison with the period of the late 1950s, that he argued that the Reserve Bank had 'been coming to regard open market operations as the key instrument of monetary policy'. This, together with the reduced emphasis given to changes in the relative rates as a means of influencing availability, seems to confirm that by 1971 the early Radcliffian imperfect-capital-market approach had been largely abandoned in favour of a competitive neo-Keynesian framework.

Phillips's lecture was delivered in April 1971. It is a matter for conjecture whether his relative optimism concerning the efficiency of monetary policy as a stabiliser of demand or capital inflows would have been as great had it been given in 1974; for as we see in Chapters 8 and 9, the period 1971–4 was one in which both monetary and fiscal policy, in an attempt at anticyclical stabilisation, were probably destabilising.

## Conclusions

We must expect the authorities' view of the transmission process to reflect three main types of influence:
(a)  changes in the economic and financial environment;
(b)  developments in monetary theory; and
(c)  the results of economic research.
The influence of (a) is apparent throughout all three periods. However, it seems possible, to put it no higher, that the apparent acceptance of the neo-Keynesian competitive framework in the early 1970s was the result less of research findings than of the requirements of model building.[36] If this was so, (b) probably dominated (c) in influencing the Reserve Bank's view of the transmission process in the early 1970s.

Apart from (a), the most important influence in revising the Reserve Bank's views must have been neither (b) nor (c) but the failure of monetary policy in the mid-1950s[37] and the repetition of the failure in 1959–60.[38] We have yet to have any clear indication of how the unhappy experiences of 1971–5 will influence the Reserve Bank's thinking. It will, however, be rather surprising if the neo-Keynesian approach reflected in models RB70 and RB74 is not significantly modified.

## Notes: Chapter 5

1 Since the current account is primarily a function of exogenous variables and the level of aggregate demand, it is in effect incorporated in the latter.
2 Cf. the Reserve Bank's repeated concern with the supply of housing finance.
3 Major emphasis has for obvious reasons been placed on more recent episodes.
4 In some respects the Japanese system of the 1960s approximated to this simple model. On this point, cf. OECD [117].
5 In other words, whether the administrative approach to monetary management should be extended.
6 Radcliffian monetary theory is here interpreted along the lines of Rowan [143].
7 An essentially similar interpretation has been given by Lewis and Wallace [97].
8 Cf. Coombs [25] and Phillips [124].

9 Reserve Bank and Commonwealth Bank are synonymous terms in this period.
10 On the Australian position, see Hill in Hirst and Wallace [65] and references there cited.
11 Save for multinational enterprises or where the economy is financially dependent on some major overseas centre.
12 Cf. Hirst [64] in Hirst and Wallace [65].
13 Intuitively, this seems most unlikely.
14 For a particularly well-known example, cf. Andersen and Jordan [4].
15 Cf. Gramlich [45].
16 There is some presumption that, the more competitive is the system, the more probable is *ceteris paribus* relative stability in crucial functional relations. Recent experience with money demand functions in the United States, however, throws doubt on this. On this point, cf. Goldfeld [44].
17 For a review, consult Christ [24].
18 Further references are given in later chapters.
19 This throws some doubts on the contemporary and prospective relevance of simulations with these models.
20 It is, however, to be found by implication in Coombs [28] and Phillips [124] [125].
21 This is a complex problem, since under the overdraft system it can be argued that the stock of advances outstanding is demand determined subject only to the constraint imposed by the value of outstanding limits. For a discussion, see Arndt [7] and Valentine [164].
22 For a brief discussion of this issue, see Swan's [156] review of Treasury Economic Paper, No. 1.
23 Or, in a less simplistic approach, the mark-up relation.
24 Roughly, this implies a single mode for any probability distribution for the expected rate.
25 For an example of this approach, see Jonson and Mahoney [77].
26 A third possibility is to obtain an equation explaining the expected rate of change of prices from a prior theory of the transactors' behaviour in a field in which the expected rate of inflation is regarded as a significant variable. For examples of this method, consult Rowan and Edwardes [145], where equations are derived from the application of rate structure theory. This is a variant of the reduced form approach.
27 Some preliminary experiments made personally suggest negligible influence for monetary variables, but those results, since they are preliminary, should be treated with great caution.
28 An excellent and more comprehensive review of these issues is in Lewis and Wallace [97].
29 Cf., for example, *Annual Report, 1976–7,*, pp. 9–41.
30 These fluctuations arose mainly on current account.
31 Cf. Lewis and Wallace [97 p. 6] for emphasis on this point.
32 Cf. Rowan [143] where Radcliffian monetary theory is interpreted as regarding the capital market as imperfect and availability as a function of the level and structure of rates.
33 Cf. Lewis and Wallace [97] for a fuller discussion of this point.
34 ' Strong monetarism' is identified with the Friedman position on lags and the argument for a money stock 'rule'.
35 Cf. also Norton [112].
36 Imperfect markets are difficult to model. This is because they essentially involve non-price elements, disequilibria and discontinuities. As a result model building tends to emphasise market processes.
37 Cf. Rowan [142] and Lewis and Wallace [97].
38 Lewis and Wallace [97, pp. 6–7] where this period is described as a miserable failure.

PART TWO

# MONETARY POLICY IN ACTION: A REVIEW OF TIME SERIES

# Chapter 6

# Monetary Restraint, 1958–60

## 6.1 *Introduction*

The cyclical upswing experienced by Australia in 1958–60 is now two decades in the past. It is nevertheless a period of considerable interest for monetary policy, since it occurred after a period of very rapid development in the Australian money and capital markets. It was the expansion of 1958–60, coupled with the realisation of the extent and momentum of financial development, that encouraged the Reserve Bank of Australia to modify its techniques of monetary management after this date by moving, admittedly with some caution, towards a more explicitly market-based approach.

The evidence offered for this interpretation is relatively straightforward. On the basis of our *ex ante* dating of the Reserve Bank's policy stances, monetary policy was typically easy from June 1957 through September 1959. Admittedly, this ease was sometimes qualified. Nevertheless, it seems clear that the Reserve Bank moved from ease to a mildly restrictive stance in October 1959[1] and maintained this stance, and indeed intensified it, until approximately May-June 1961. This was a period, then, of nearly two years of *ex ante* monetary restriction.

What makes this period particularly instructive is that, although the restrictive stance continued throughout, the techniques employed by the Reserve Bank fell fairly readily into two types, each of which was associated with a particular subperiod of restraint. Broadly, from October 1959 to October 1960 the Reserve

129

Figure 6.1    Policy stance and principal actions, 1958-61

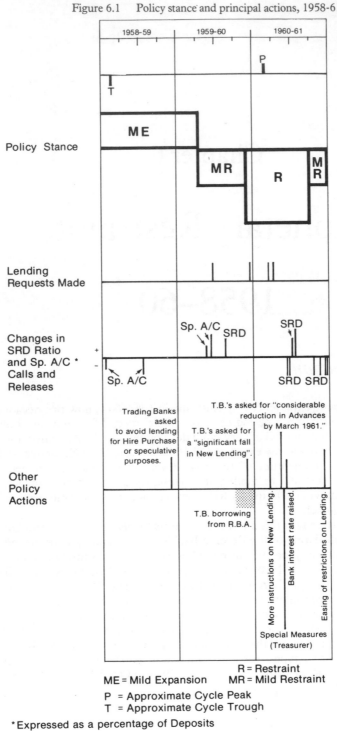

ME = Mild Expansion         R = Restraint
                           MR = Mild Restraint
P = Approximate Cycle Peak
T = Approximate Cycle Trough

*Expressed as a percentage of Deposits

*Source:* Reserve Bank of Australia, Annual Reports, and Statistical Bulletin, various issues

Bank conducted not a monetary policy but a banking policy. That is, it sought to restrict the availability of finance from the banks by the familiar device of operating on bank liquidity – the banks' holdings of liquid assets and government securities (LGS) – and at the same time issuing to the banks quantitative requests aimed initially at influencing new lending and later at reducing advances outstanding.[2] These quantitative requests typically contained qualitative advice aimed at the selective influence of bank lending (see Figure 6.1).

After October 1960, however, in particular after the somewhat draconic intervention by the Commonwealth Treasurer in November, the banking policy was buttressed by changes in (maximum) rates[3] controlled by the Reserve Bank and by a policy that may well have promoted, and certainly acquiesced in, movements in market rates on Commonwealth obligations. In short, after November 1960 monetary control was no longer seen, technically, as combining a banking policy with a virtually unchanged set of rates on time deposits, savings deposits and government debt. In future discretionary monetary action was to be broader in concept and to meet more openly the problems raised by the rapid development of Australia's financial institutions.

Whether this shift came about because the Reserve Bank was by its experience compelled to admit that Australia's developing financial institutions demanded a wider technical attack if monetary restriction was to become effective, or because the Treasurer's rather belated essay in overkill entailed the abandonment of what many believed to be his department's attachment to stable interest rates, is not known and perhaps may never be.[4] What matters is that after 1960 the Reserve Bank was never again so strictly constrained by a requirement (or a wish) to keep rates unchanged.

We now examine the period in somewhat greater detail.

## 6.2 Initial Conditions and Macroeconomic Policy

The stance of monetary policy is, as we have seen, an important element in the overall macroeconomic-policy position. In this section we therefore attempt to give a very brief account of: (a) the thrust of budgetary operations and fiscal policy; and (b) the initial conditions ruling at the time of the Reserve Bank's policy shift in October 1959.

In order to keep the initial conditions manageable descriptively Figure 6.2 presents data relating to:
(a) the position in the labour market;
(b) the behaviour of real output; and
(c) the rate of change in prices and wage earnings.
Before discussing these data it is worth making two points. First, the figure conveys a limited picture in that it provides only a minute proportion of the information that was available to the authorities at the time of the change in

## Figure 6.2  Initial economic conditions

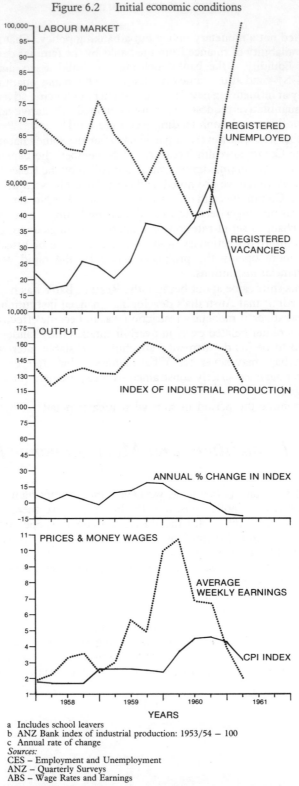

a  Includes school leavers
b  ANZ Bank index of industrial production: 1953/54 – 100
c  Annual rate of change
*Sources:*
CES – Employment and Unemployment
ANZ – Quarterly Surveys
ABS – Wage Rates and Earnings

policy stance. Second, since the data are *ex post*, they overstate, at least by implication, the reliability of the information that was available to the authorities on any given date, since they are purged of any errors, some of which may well have been significant, contained in preliminary estimates or forecasts.

This skeletal account of the initial conditions is later supplemented in two ways: (a) by data relating to changes in non-farm stocks and to the rate of investment in dwellings; and (b) by data relating to the major items in the balance of payments. Of these (a) is included in the belief that changes in non-farm stocks is an important cyclical indicator that is certain to be taken into account in formulating overall macroeconomic-policy stance. The relevance of the rate of investment in dwellings is slightly less sure; it is included in the expectation that, given the political importance of housing and the probable sensitivity of investment in dwellings to monetary action, the stage of the housing cycle may influence the fiscal–monetary mix. The inclusion of (b) needs no explanation in view of the significance of the external constraint for Australian policy.

In terms of our definition of the initial conditions we now examine the situation prevailing just prior to the Reserve Bank's policy shift in October 1959. Since quarterly national-income estimates are not available, for the national product data we substitute the index of production of the Australian and New Zealand (ANZ) Bank.

If we consider the figures for persons unemployed and registered vacancies, the evidence suggests that the labour market was tightening from 1958.II and tightening at an increasing rate after 1959.II. This is broadly borne out by the behaviour of the ANZ Index of Production and its annual rate of change, although the noisiness of the series makes the pattern unclear in detail. Thus, at the end of 1959.III – the date of the policy shift – it appeared that expansion was well under way and probably accelerating.

During 1958 the rate of (annual) price change was virtually constant at 1.7 per cent, but for the first three quarters of 1959 the rate accelerated to 2.6 per cent. Moreover, there is roughly similar evidence of an increase in the (annual) rate of change in average weekly earnings. For example, over 1959.II and III the average rate of change in earnings was just over 4.3 per cent against approximately 2.9 per cent in the corresponding period of 1958. Thus, the expansion appears to have been generating a significantly faster rate of growth in both prices and wage earnings.

Because of the absence of official quarterly estimates it is not possible to give figures for either the increase in the volume of stocks or for the quarterly rate of real investment in dwellings. However, current price estimates are available and, for what they are worth, are set out in Table 6.1. Since the rate of change of prices was relatively slow, at least by contemporary standards, these may give some rough indication of what was happening to key items in private sector expenditure. However, even if this is so, they may not correctly proxy whatever estimates were available to the authorities in 1959.III.

**Table 6.1** *Investment in dwellings and inventories, 1958–61*
*($A million at current prices)*

| Year / quarter | | Gross fixed capital expenditure | Investment in dwellings | Increase in value of non-farm stocks | Current account of balance of payments |
|---|---|---|---|---|---|
| 1958 | III | 657 | 137 | 83 | − 163 |
| | IV | 734 | 131 | − 25 | − 76 |
| 1959 | I | 704 | 129 | 46 | − 68 |
| | II | 873 | 137 | 54 | − 78 |
| | III | 749 | 149 | 74 | −133 |
| | IV | 807 | 145 | − 12 | − 33 |
| 1960 | I | 782 | 150 | 72 | −107 |
| | II | 988 | 162 | 125 | −186 |
| | III | 878 | 177 | 192 | −282 |
| | IV | 926 | 171 | 118 | −218 |
| 1961 | I | 819 | 157 | 146 | −201 |
| | II | 964 | 151 | − 6 | − 36 |

*Source*: Commonwealth Bureau of Census and Statistics, *Supplement to Quarterly Estimates of National Income and Expenditure*, no. 22 (December 1965).

Quarterly balance-of-payments data for this period are not available. Table 6.2 therefore gives the data, in simplified form, for the first and second halves of 1958 and the first half of 1959. These figures suggest that the current account was improving, largely due to the lag in the response of imports to the substantial (21 per cent) growth in export receipts between June 1958 and June 1959. Similarly, including the balancing item, apparent private capital inflow was also rising fast, the June–June rate of growth being 34 per cent.

**Table 6.2** *The external constraint, 1958–9 (half-yearly data, $A million)*

| Year/month | | Exports | Imports | Current account balance | Capital inflow Official | Private | Balancing Item | Change in Reserves |
|---|---|---|---|---|---|---|---|---|
| 1958 | Jun. | 360 | 395 | − 140 | 8 | 17 | 51 | − 64 |
| 1958 | Dec. | 389 | 399 | − 128 | 16 | 28 | 59 | − 25 |
| 1959 | Jun. | 438 | 397 | − 79 | 4 | 28 | 63 | 16 |

*Source*: Australian Bureau of Statistics, *Balance of Payments*.

Overseas reserves fell in 1958 by $A89 million. In the first half of 1959 they rose by $A16 million. Since the level of reserves was relatively high, the external position did not of itself compel any sharp shift to restraint. Import restrictions were relaxed in August 1959, and the overall strategy appeared to be to encourage increasing imports to offset domestic demand pressures and (marginally) to increase competition while using monetary policy to contain domestic expansion.

Estimates of the full-employment budget position do not exist for this period. However, neither Nevile's calculations nor the budget changes suggest any significant shift in fiscal policy in 1959–60 (see Table 6.3).

**Table 6.3** *The fiscal impact, 1957–60*

| Financial year | Change in budget deficit | | Nevile's impact effect | |
|---|---|---|---|---|
| | $A m. | % of NFNP | % of NFNP | Change in % impact |
| 1957–8 | 2 | 0·0 | 1·7 | 2·1 |
| 1958–9 | 228 | 2·2 | 3·0 | 1·3 |
| 1959–60 | − 54 | −0·5 | 2·6 | −0·4 |

*Source:* Table 4.1.

It thus seems reasonable to conclude that the authorities placed their major reliance on monetary policy to contain the expansion in domestic demand while allowing the balance of payments, via the import bill, to reduce any excess demand for importables that developed.

This strategy rested upon the assumption that monetary policy could be made effective in restraining the rate of growth in demand within a relatively short period (say four quarters). As we shall see, in practical terms it proved untenable.

# 6.3 Reserve Bank Policy and Monetary Thrust

The *ex ante* dating of Reserve Bank policy is given in Figure 6.1 together with a dating of the Reserve Bank's main policy actions. This dating, although subjective, seems unambiguous. We now turn to consider the behaviour of the main indicators of monetary thrust as defined in Chapter 4. We shall begin by examining the money stock indicators.

Examination of Figure 6.3 suggests that the percentage rates of growth in $M_1$ and $M_3$ began to decline by about 1960.II. The fact that $M_3$ turned down before $M_1$ – perhaps two to three months before – suggests that changes in monetary thrust, for which $M_3$ is probably the superior indicator, began to be significant some nine months *after* the shift in policy stance. In so far as $M_1$ reflects demand factors, in particular the rate of expansion in nominal GNP, it may indicate a lag of nine to ten months in the response of real factors to monetary action.

Figure 6.3    Money stock indicators: annual rates of change (%)

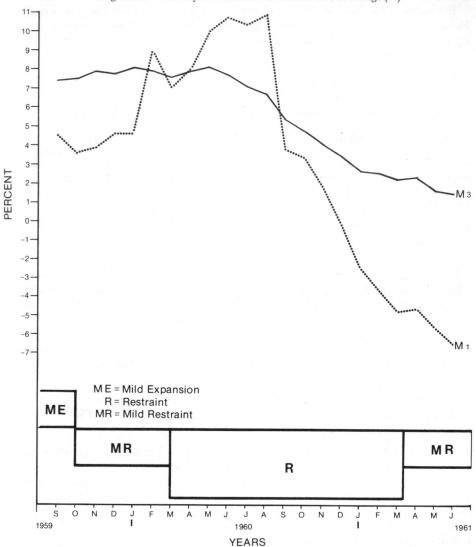

*Source:* Reserve Bank of Australia, *Statistical Bulletin*

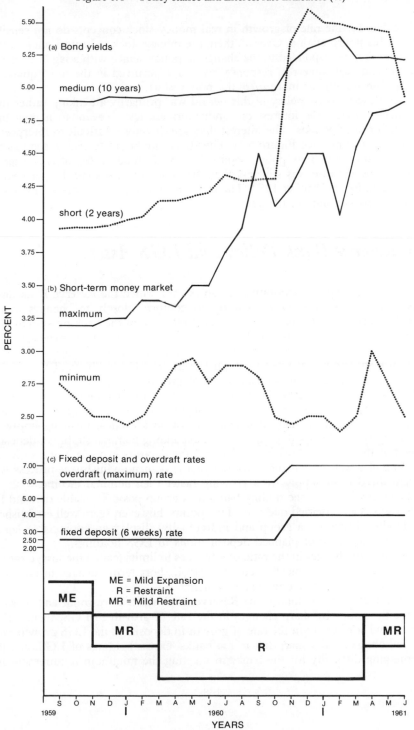

Figure 6.4    Policy stance and interest rate indicators (%)

*Source:* Reserve Bank of Australia, *Statistical Bulletin*

The data for the rate of growth in real money-stock concepts do not sensibly modify this interpretation. Overall, then, the money stock indicators suggest that monetary factors responded to the change in policy stance with a lag of over two quarters and that some real response may have occurred in the third quarter – perhaps ten months or more *after* the policy shift.

Since Reserve Bank policy in this period was primarily a banking rather than a monetary policy, the interest rate indicators are less relevant to it than they become for later periods. The interest data are therefore difficult to interpret in the present context (see Figure 6.4). The short rate began to rise as soon as the Reserve Bank shifted its policy stance; but by October 1960, after a year of restraint, the increase was still less than 40 basis points – some 10 per cent of the value ruling in October 1959. The medium rate was even more sticky, rising by only 7 basis points in the year.

# 6.4  Reserve Bank Policy and LGS Assets

It is natural to expect quantitative variables over which the Reserve Bank has a considerable measure of direct control to conform closely to changes in the Reserve Bank's *ex ante* policy stance. The LGS base of the banking system and, in particular, the LGS base of the trading banks are two such variables. This section is in the main concerned with their behaviour. We should therefore expect the policy shift to be reflected very quickly in the LGS holdings of the trading banks – or more precisely, in their rates of growth.

Against this, the Reserve Bank's policy entailed the maintenance of virtually unchanged rates on Commonwealth securities. Given this condition, a stable demand function for money, if it exists, must on a cyclical upswing imply an expanding nominal stock of money and an expanding nominal supply of deposits. Indeed, if the income elasticity of demand for deposits exceeds unity, only the rationing of advances and the dynamics of the demand adjustment process will prevent the deposit supply from growing faster than nominal income.

The extent to which the trading banks as a group possess a stable demand for LGS assets is an unsettled question. Two points, however, seem well established:
(1)  Trading banks (as a group and individually) display an appreciable lag in their adjustment of planned deposit totals to LGS holdings.
(2)  Because of changes in the ratio of advances to limits (called the 'usage ratio'), which the banks typically cannot control, short term changes in advances contain a significant unplanned element.
It is therefore probable that, if the Reserve Bank shifts to restraint and seeks to enforce the policy by sharp changes in the rate of growth in LGS, then, rather than a rapid adjustment in the rate of growth in deposits to the LGS growth rate, we shall observe: (a) a sharp fall in the banks' excess holdings of LGS; and (b) an emerging difficulty for the banks in meeting the minimum requirement for

the ratio of LGS holdings to deposits.

In fact, given a sufficiently violent change in the rate of expansion in LGS and a sufficiently imperfect capacity on the banks' part to control the rate of expansion in advances, there is no reason why some, or all, trading banks should not be compelled to undertake distress borrowing at penal rates from the Reserve Bank to meet the required LGS convention. Thus, trading bank borrowing may occur simply because of the technical difficulties facing the trading banks rather than because of their defiance of Reserve Bank policy.

We now define:

$$\begin{matrix} \text{LGS} \\ \text{holdings} \\ \text{of} \\ \text{trading banks} \end{matrix} - \begin{matrix} \text{Excess} \\ \text{LGS holdings} \\ \text{of} \\ \text{trading banks} \end{matrix} \equiv \begin{matrix} \text{Required} \\ \text{LGS holdings} \\ \text{of} \\ \text{trading banks} \end{matrix} \equiv \begin{matrix} \text{Deposits} \\ \times \\ \text{Minimum} \\ \text{conventional} \\ \text{ratio} \end{matrix} \quad (1)$$

and

$$\begin{matrix} \text{Net} \\ \text{free LGS} \\ \text{holdings} \end{matrix} \equiv \begin{matrix} \text{Excess} \\ \text{LGS holdings} \end{matrix} - \begin{matrix} \text{Borrowing} \\ \text{from} \\ \text{Reserve Bank} \end{matrix} \quad (2)$$

It follows that the pressure on the banks to restrain their expansion of choice assets and, in particular, advances is theoretically best measured by net free LGS holdings rather than LGS holdings. Unfortunately, this quantity can only be estimated very approximately, since no figures for borrowing from the Reserve Bank are available.[5] The estimates used are taken from Davis and Wallace [34].

Although borrowing is here presented as a disequilibrium phenomenon, it seems likely that some borrowing arose from the unwillingness of banks in relatively illiquid LGS positions to risk the loss of customers, via the refusal of advances, to competitor banks with relatively strong LGS positions. This is the more likely since banks are rather typically concerned with long run profits while the initial LGS positions of the individual trading banks did in fact differ sharply. We return to these points later. For the moment, however, we turn to examine the behaviour of the LGS holdings. This is given in Figure 6.5, which gives data on:

(a) LGS holdings of the major trading banks,
(b) excess LGS holdings;
(c) (estimated) net free LGS holdings; and
(d) the (annual) rate of change in LGS holdings

At the shift of policy to restraint in October 1959 the annual rate of growth in the major trading banks' LGS holdings was close to 30 per cent. On the same basis deposits were growing at around 6 per cent. Excess LGS holdings were

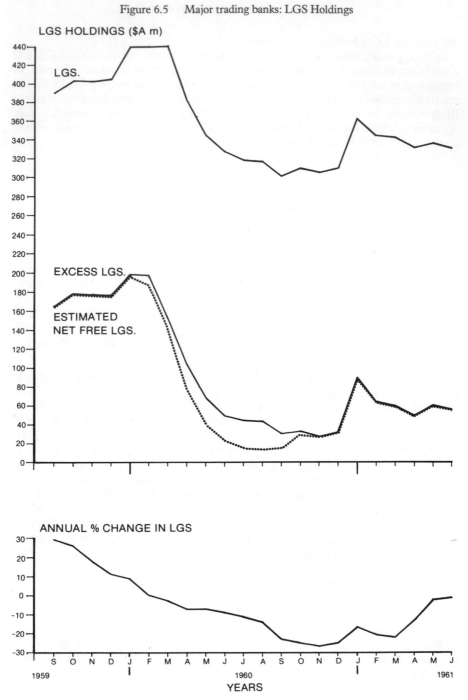

Figure 6.5    Major trading banks: LGS Holdings

LGS HOLDINGS ($A m)

LGS.

EXCESS LGS.

ESTIMATED
NET FREE LGS.

ANNUAL % CHANGE IN LGS

1959    1960    1961

YEARS

*Sources:* Reserve Bank of Australia, *Statistical Bulletin*
Davis and Wallace [35]

therefore rising and at $A164 million were already very substantial, amounting to some 10 per cent of deposits.

With the advent of restraint the rate of growth in LGS assets fell very sharply. It reached approximately zero in February 1960. Thereafter, it continued to decline, falling to an annual rate of -26 per cent in December 1960. The later months saw a reversal of this sharp swing, and by June 1961 the rate of growth was once more positive.

Excess LGS holdings were affected not only by calls to special account and the adjustment of the statutory reserve deposit SRD ratio but also by an agreed increase in the conventional LGS/deposit minimum ratio from 14 to 16 per cent in March 1960. Thus, Reserve Bank actions brought about a very rapid decline in excess LGS holdings, which reached their trough in November 1960.

Borrowing appears to have begun in January 1960 and peaked in July. At the peak, which was partly seasonal, the estimated borrowing amounted to some 10 per cent of LGS holdings. At this date net free LGS holdings for the banks as a group amounted to less than 1 per cent of deposits. For some banks net free LGS holdings were, of course, negative. Thus, in a little over two quarters Reserve Bank operations had: (a) reduced net free LGS holdings from around 10 per cent of deposits to less than 1 per cent; and (b) compelled the banks as a group to borrow some 8 – 10 per cent of their overall LGS holdings. This was accomplished while maintaining both short and long-term rates on Commonwealth obligations relatively stable.

As a quantitative indicator of Reserve Bank policy, therefore, the banks' LGS position performed in line with its *ex ante* policy stance and, in terms of banking liquidity, indicated severe restraint. Thus, the technical capacity of the Reserve Bank to bring about rapid changes in the banks' LGS position is not in doubt, nor is the consistency of the Reserve Bank's operations and its *ex ante* policy stance.

On the other hand, the figures already presented for the nominal money-stock concepts suggest a fairly mild response in the rate of growth in deposits to shifts in the banks' LGS position. This is confirmed in Figure 6.6, which plots the rate of growth in trading bank deposits. This makes it clear that the rate of growth in deposits continued to rise (on an annual basis) until February 1960 and did not fall *below* its rate of growth *prior* to restraint until July – nearly a year after the policy shift. This figure therefore emphasises the rather long lags in the planned adjustment of deposits to LGS holdings and the very considerable element of slippage.

## 6.5 The Financial Transmission Process

As we have seen earlier, prior to late 1960 the Reserve Bank operated on what may be called an availability theory of monetary policy, which in effect reduced

Figure 6.6    The behaviour of deposits

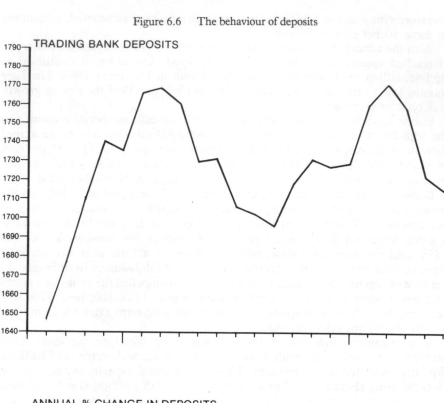

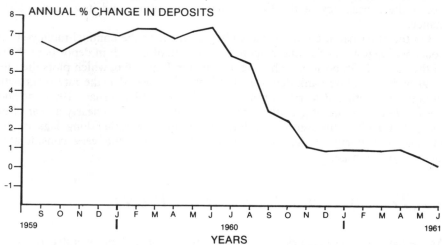

Source: Reserve Bank of Australia, *Statistical Bulletin*

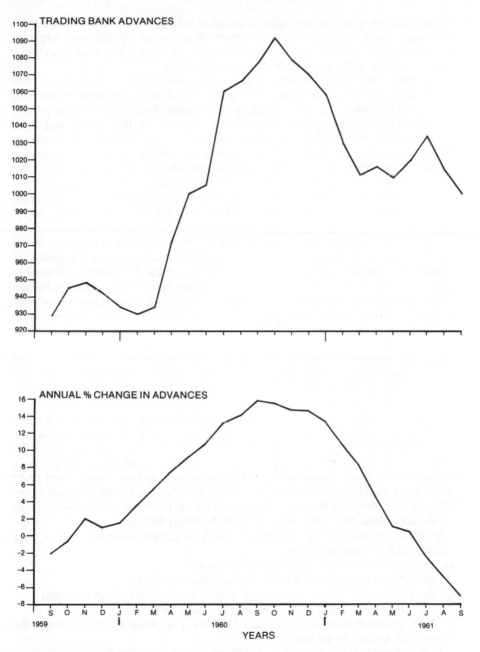

Figure 6.7    The behaviour of advances

*Source:* Reserve Bank of Australia, *Statistical Bulletin*

it to conducting what we have called a 'banking policy'. Thus, the Reserve Bank's proximate target, through which it aimed to influence its ultimate target of private expenditure, was the rate of new lending by banks or – what is a closely related variable – the stock of advances outstanding.

The behaviour of the advances of the major trading banks is set out in Figure 6.7. This shows that, at the time when the Reserve Bank moved to restraint, total advances were below the figure ruling a year earlier. Indeed, the rate of growth over the corresponding period in 1958 was negative in the second and third quarters. After the introduction of restraint in October the rate of growth in advances rapidly accelerated. The acceleration continued until September– October 1960, reaching a peak of an annual rate close to 16 per cent. After the Treasurer's intervention the rate fell and ultimately became negative in July 1961. Over the two-year period from September 1959 to September 1961 advances rose by slightly over 7.6 per cent – an annual rate, over the two years, of close to 3.7 per cent.

It thus appears that, despite the fact that the new lending and advances of the trading banks were the Reserve Bank's main proximate targets, the policy of restraint was ineffective until *after* the intervention of the Treasurer in November 1960. Since, as we have seen, the Reserve Bank brought about a major reduction in the trading banks' net free LGS holdings (as defined above), this seems, and in fact is, an astonishing outcome. Why did the Reserve Bank, operating on essentially orthodox lines, find itself unable to exert any effective influence on bank lending?

In broad outline, the principal reasons for the Reserve Bank's failure are well known. The first is that the aggregate figures for the trading banks – whether of LGS holdings, excess LGS holdings, or net free LGS holdings – are misleading, since individual banks had widely differing LGS and excess LGS ratios in October 1959. For example, the Commonwealth Trading Bank was nearly three times as liquid and the Bank of New South Wales around twice as liquid as the least liquid of the other large banks (the ANZ). Given the competitiveness of the banks and the pressure to increase advances, the less liquid banks had either to run the risk of losing business, perhaps permanently, to their competitors or to satisfy their minimum LGS requirement by distress borrowing at penal rates. Thus, at least three banks expanded so rapidly on the basis of borrowing from the Reserve Bank that their net free LGS holdings became negative.[6]

In short, the inability of the Reserve Bank to impose effective control over trading bank lending arose out of:
(a) the heterogeneity of banks' initial positions;
(b) the intense competition within the banking oligopoly;
(c) the dominance of long-term profit considerations over short-run; and
(d) the banks' own inability to control the usage ratio.
In these circumstances, as Davis and Wallace [34] have shown, quantitative control was certain to be ineffective.

This technical inefficiency of banking policy was undoubtedly a major reason for the Treasurer's belated and overdraconic action in November 1960. By the same token the authorities' earlier belief that sooner or later, and in any case soon enough, banking restriction *must* bite meant that, when the disillusionment came, action was excessive.

It would, of course, be an error to concentrate on the trading banks as the only institutional source of funds to the private sector. Accordingly, we now consider the supply of funds via:
(a) instalment credit;
(b) the mortgage market; and
(c) the capital market.

Unfortunately, quarterly series for flows of funds are not available in Australia. The data that follow are therefore incomplete. Moreover, since trading banks lend to non-bank financial intermediaries[7] and make loans for housing, the data arc not simply additive with the data already given for advances. In short, they contain elements of double counting, which can be roughly estimated but not calculated at all precisely, since the distribution of advances is available only on a half-yearly basis.

Consider first the record of instalment credit for retail sales. The amount financed per quarter was growing at 10 per cent per annum at the onset of restraint. This rate of growth had more than doubled by the first quarter of 1960. Thereafter, a rapid decline followed, with the amounts financed in the first two quarters of 1961 being some 20 per cent *below* the corresponding quarters of 1959. Thus, the rate of growth of the flow of hire purchase finance turned down in June 1960. This was rather more than one quarter before the rate of growth

**Table 6.4** *Instalment credit for retail sales: hire purchase*

| Year/quarter | Amount financed | | Change in balances outstanding[b] |
| | $A m. | % change[a] | $A m. |
| --- | --- | --- | --- |
| 1959 III | 85·5 | 9·8 | 18·9 |
| IV | 102·2 | 15·9 | 36·8 |
| 1960 I | 89·1 | 23·6 | 14·0 |
| II | 90·8 | 16·0 | 14·7 |
| III | 94·3 | 10·3 | 15·9 |
| IV | 95·8 | − 6·3 | 26·2 |
| 1961 I | 64·5 | −27·6 | −21·3 |
| II | 60·9 | −32·9 | −21·0 |

[a] % change over the corresponding quarter of the previous year.
[b] Change over the previous quarter.
Source: Reserve Bank of Australia, *Statistical Bulletin: Financial Supplement* (September 1963).

in advances started to decline. Since the figures for advances to other finance (which includes hire purchase) were still growing between June and December 1960, this does not suggest that the downturn was due to hire purchase companies reacting to a reduced availability of bank advances. It follows that, if the downturn was a supply-dominated phenomenon, it must have been due to the reduced flow of funds from other sources (see Table 6.4).

The behaviour of new money raisings by Australian companies is difficult to interpret, since raisings in 1956–7 and 1957–8 were at levels well below trend. Raisings in 1958–9 were about 56 per cent above those of 1957–8, while raisings in 1959–60 were about 35 per cent above those of 1958-9. The available figures, which are quarterly, are given in Table 6.5 together with the index of equity prices. From these figures it is clear that new money raisings peaked in the third quarter of 1960; that is, they continued to rise, at rising annual rates (as defined), until the Treasurer's intervention in November. By this time stock market prices had already begun to fall from the September peak. After the Treasurer's intervention new money raisings fell sharply, the figure for the June quarter of 1961 being roughly 25 per cent below that of the corresponding quarter of 1959. Two points thus seem clear:

(1) New money raisings were virtually unaffected by the monetary restraint from October 1959–60;

(2) It was the Treasurer's intervention that brought about the downturn.

This interpretation is given a measure of support by the sharp change in the *composition* of new raisings after November 1960. Since this, at least, was mainly a response to the Treasurer's proposals to modify the tax treatment of interest costs rather than a reaction to changes in the relative gross costs of equity and debt finance, it may well be that the basic response of new raisings was of the same kind, i.e. in conformity with (2).

On the other hand, equity prices began to fall in October – before the Treasurer's intervention. This is compatible with the interpretation that equity prices responded to restraint with a lag of about a year. This may have been the case, just as it is possible that the equity boom *during* restraint, which increased prices by more than 20 per cent, might have been more rapid still if the Reserve Bank had followed a less restrictive policy. Without a quantitative model of the economy, or at the very least an equity price equation into which policy-determined variables enter, it is hard to see how this interpretation can be tested. Events seem to indicate however, that the major reason for the equity price decline was the rapid deterioration of the current account balance following upon the progressive relaxation of import restrictions. It must be emphasised, however, that, while some evidence that is consistent with this interpretation can be assembled,[8] it derives in the main from the intuition of the investigator.

**Table 6.5** *New money raisings, 1958–61, and equity prices, 1959–61 (share price index, 1952–3 = 100)*

| Year/ month/quarter | | Share price index (SPI) | Annual %* change in SPI | New money raisings (NMR) ($A m.) | | | Annual change* in NMR ($A m.) | Annual %* change in NMR |
|---|---|---|---|---|---|---|---|---|
| | | | | Equity | Other | Total | | |
| 1958 | IV | | | 16·2 | 46·0 | 62·2 | 31·5 | 90·8 |
| 1959 | I | | | 12·5 | 30·2 | 42·7 | 12·0 | 39·1 |
| | II | | | 22·5 | 33·2 | 55·7 | 18·0 | 47·7 |
| | III | | | 15·8 | 52·3 | 68·1 | 13·8 | 25·4 |
| Sept. | | 206 | 31·2 | | | | | |
| Oct. | | 217 | 40·9 | | | | | |
| Nov. | IV | 216 | 38·4 | 23·6 | 61·5 | 85·1 | 18·9 | 28·5 |
| Dec. | | 219 | 37·7 | | | | | |
| 1960 Jan. | | 234 | 42·9 | | | | | |
| Feb. | I | 234 | 40·2 | 17·6 | 47·1 | 64·7 | 22·0 | 51·5 |
| Mar. | | 227 | 37·6 | | | | | |
| Apr. | | 231 | 35·9 | | | | | |
| May | II | 236 | 33·3 | 26·2 | 51·3 | 77·5 | 21·8 | 39·1 |
| Jun. | | 240 | 32·6 | | | | | |
| Jul. | | 242 | 27·4 | | | | | |
| Aug. | III | 244 | 21·4 | 31·7 | 62·2 | 93·9 | 25·8 | 37·9 |
| Sep. | | 245 | 18·9 | | | | | |
| Oct. | | 231 | 6·5 | | | | | |
| Nov. | IV | 207 | − 4·2 | 38·1 | 51·7 | 89·8 | 4·8 | 5·6 |
| Dec. | | 197 | − 10·0 | | | | | |
| 1961 Jan. | | 202 | − 13·7 | | | | | |
| Feb. | I | 205 | − 12·4 | 26·0 | 30·6 | 56·6 | − 8·1 | − 12·9 |
| Mar. | | 206 | − 9·3 | | | | | |
| Apr. | | 212 | − 8·2 | | | | | |
| May | II | 216 | − 8·4 | 34·9 | 5·2 | 40·1 | − 37·4 | − 48·3 |
| Jun. | | 222 | − 7·5 | | | | | |

*Defined as changes over corresponding period in previous year.

*Sources:*
(1) For new money raisings, Australian Bureau of Statistics.
(2) For equity prices, Reserve Bank of Australia.

**Table 6.6** *Main demand components (quarterly data, seasonally adjusted, $A million at 1966–7 prices)*

| Year/quarter | | Gross private fixed investment | | | | Private consumption | | Change in Stocks |
| --- | --- | --- | --- | --- | --- | --- | --- | --- |
| | | Total | Dwellings | Other building and construction | Other | Total | Durables[a] | |
| 1959 | III | 565 | 172 | 116 | 277 | 2,550 | 350 | 35 |
| | IV | 597 (22·7) | 174 (4·7) | 123 (24·1) | 300 (33·2) | 2,596 (7·2) | 366 (18·3) | −25 |
| 1960 | I | 641 (29·5) | 182 (18·4) | 128 (16·3) | 332 (42·7) | 2,640 (6·8) | 375 (9·8) | −14 |
| | II | 669 (17·5) | 189 (15·4) | 131 (9·4) | 350 (21·7) | 2,678 (5·8) | 383 (8·5) | 187 |
| | III | 697 (16·7) | 198 (19·0) | 137 (18·3) | 362 (13·7) | 2,682 (0·7) | 385 (2·1) | 214 |
| | IV | 690 (−4·0) | 197 (−2·0) | 136 (−2·9) | 357 (−5·5) | 2,681 (0·0) | 373 (−12·5) | 183 |
| 1961 | I | 649 (−23·8) | 182 (−30·5) | 137 (2·9) | 331 (−29·1) | 2,657 (−3·6) | 337 (−38·6) | 159 |
| | II | 636 (−8·0) | 174 (−17·6) | 139 (5·8) | 323 (−9·7) | 2,645 (−1·8) | 320 (−20·2) | −21 |

[a] Household durables plus motor vehicles.
*Note*: Figures in parentheses give the percentage change over the previous quarter, multiplied by 4.
*Source*: Australian Bureau of Statistics, *Supplement to Quarterly Estimates of National Income and Expenditure* (December 1975).

# 6.6 The Behaviour of Demand Components

Retaining our assumption that public sector expenditure is exogenous, Table 6.6 shows the behaviour of the main components of private sector expenditure.

Initially, consider gross private investment in fixed capital. As an aggregate this element continued to expand until the September quarter of 1960, i.e. until just before the Treasurer's November 1960 interventions. Its rate of expansion (quarter on previous quarter) had, however, begun to fall after the March quarter of 1960. It is thus arguable that the investment boom was already tapering off by 1960.II, i.e. more than one quarter before the Treasurer's intervention. It is thus not unreasonable to infer that monetary restraint may have influenced gross private investment in fixed capital, at least marginally, by 1960.II – a lag of about $2^1/_2$ quarters.

This overall view, however, conceals some interesting information concerning the subaggregates. Both other investment and other building and construction experienced severe falls in their rate of growth as early as 1960.II. The effect of this was, however, somewhat masked by the behaviour of the dwellings component; the rate of growth for this held up until 1960.III, after which the rate of change became negative and the rate of decline very severe.

There are a number of possible interpretations of this pattern of behaviour. first is that, partly in response to monetary restraint, gross private investment was already approaching a turning point by the end of the financial year 1959–60. However, this interpretation, although plausible, must meet the difficulty that investment in housing, which is usually one of the first components to react to monetary restraint elsewhere, continued its increasing rate of growth for a further quarter. Unless special factors can be found to explain this apparent discrepancy in timing, this suggests that monetary restriction may have had rather little to do with the dampening of the investment boom. The fact that all three elements in investment had negative growth rates in 1960.IV – the quarter in which the Treasurer intervened – lends a measure of superficial support for this rather sceptical interpretation. On the other hand, expenditures on fixed capital formation typically have a lengthy decision period. It is therefore unlikely that the downturn of 1960.IV resulted mainly from the Treasurer's intervention in November, although doubtless the severity of the downturn that developed was partly due to businessmen's extremely adverse reaction to the Treasurer's actions.

It seems, therefore, that the policy of restraint did have an impact on gross private investment in fixed capital with a lag of roughly two to three quarters but, rather surprisingly, that the lag was at the upper limit in the case of investment in dwellings.[9] This interpretation does not appear to be weakened by the examination of the estimates for private consumption, in which the rate of growth had already started to decline by 1960.I.

Examination of the movements in time series is always a relatively risky undertaking, since it is only too easy to mistake an observed change in some

149

variable for a particular partial derivative. In later sections, therefore, we seek to supplement the present discussion by an examination of the econometric evidence relating to dynamic consumption and investment functions.

## 6.7 Econometric Evidence

The econometric evidence concerning the dynamic form of investment functions derives largely, but not exclusively, from work undertaken by the Reserve Bank in the estimation of RB70. This work typically disaggregates gross private investment into three components:
(a) investment in dwellings;
(b) investment in other new building and construction (defined as 'construction'); and
(c) all other investment (defined as 'equipment investment').
Each of these subaggregates is then explained by a separate equation.

Postponing examination of (a), it should be recalled that the functions explaining (b) and (c) in RB70 are variants of the neo-classical approach. In such functions there is no role for any such concept as the availability of funds. Financial variables exert their influence through the cost ( ≡ implicit rental price of capital services) of capital, which in its turn is a function of the supply price (per cent per annum) of capital services. This supply price of capital is in its turn related, via an identity, to the market value of capital stocks, and it is this variable that is *inter alia* a function of the Commonwealth government two-year bond rate. In short, any change in the bond rate exerts its influence by changing the relative price of output to capital services. The response of investment then depends upon its elasticity with respect to this ratio and upon the time form describing the reaction of the business sector to the changed conditions.

Generally speaking, empirical estimates of investment functions of this type involve a very slow response to changes in the cost of capital. Commonly, there is a delay of one or two quarters before any reaction occurs, and this is followed by a distributed lag involving perhaps a further ten to twelve quarters. The rationale of this finding is, of course, the long planning period involved in private investment decisions and the short period inflexibility of such decisions once made. The form of the distributed lag emerging from estimates thus often implies an average lag of around ten quarters.

Broadly speaking, these findings are applicable to the functions explaining investment in construction and equipment investment in the RB70 model, although the construction function has no delay and the equipment function a delay of only one quarter. Thus, the functions suggest that, in so far as the Reserve Bank's policy of restraint raised the ten-year bond rate, it can only have had a small and slow effect on these two components of private investment. Moreover, as we have already seen, the rise in the relevant bond rate between

October 1959 and the Treasurer's intervention in November 1960 was very small. Thus, the Reserve Bank's economic studies suggest that the downturn in equipment investment after 1960.III must have been due in the main to causes other than the central bank's restrictive policy. This analysis is perhaps rendered the more plausible by the fact that Investment in Construction did not turn down at all but merely ceased to grow after 1960.III.

Investment in dwellings is slightly more complicated, since, although the basic theory of the demand for housing in RB70 is neoclassical, the rate of investment is also postulated to be a function of the availability of mortgage finance as well as its cost. For this availability element the lags are typically shorter. Thus, the availability variable does not suffer from any delay, while the mean lag is of the order of only two quarters. Against this, the mortgage rate of interest has a delay of three quarters and a mean lag of some $6^1/_2$ quarters. This confirms the conventional wisdom that the response of investment in dwellings to monetary restriction is initially a response to diminished availability.

As we have seen, investment in dwellings reached its peak rate of growth (19 per cent) in 1960.III, fell slightly in 1960.IV and thereafter fell relatively rapidly until 1961.IV. Reconciliation of this pattern with the econometric model is not difficult. The policy of advances restriction began to have appreciable effects (according to the time series) by 1960.III. Some of the restriction clearly had an impact on mortgage availability. After the Treasurer's intervention in November the Reserve Bank raised the maximum rates on fixed deposits with the trading banks. This had an impact on the demand for savings bank deposits[10] and restricted those institutions' ability to grant mortgage approvals. Thus, by the March quarter of 1961 the reduced availability of mortgage finance, together with the impact of the Treasurer's statement on confidence, had generated a downturn in a series that had in any case already reached a level considerably in excess of the normal long-run rate. On this interpretation, Reserve Bank action had its main impact on investment in dwellings in 1960.IV and 1961.I. Until then its contribution was minor.

## 6.7 Conclusions

The period reviewed here ended, in a sense, in a double failure for monetary policy. This was because, although monetary policy had probably begun to influence real aggregate demand by 1960.II, its impact was small and difficult to perceive, even if we are correct in arguing that it was there at all. The unexpectedly long lags in the impact of monetary policy and the failure to appreciate that the expansion had already peaked in 1960.III, led as we have seen, to the fiscal overkill of November 1960. Thus, the inability of monetary action to meet the authorities' expectations led to errors in overall macroeconomic policy that made the downswing of 1960–61 more severe than necessary.

The principal cause of this failure was, it now appears, a misconception of the transmission mechanism, which by emphasising availability effects attempted to combine restraint with a relatively stable set of nominal interest rates. This did not, as we have seen, reduce the technical ability of the Reserve Bank to control trading bank liquidity (LGS). On the other hand, it did weaken the (potential) impact of wealth and cost-of-capital effects. This not only reduced the impact of policy as a whole but probably also contributed to maintaining the *demand* for advances, with obvious consequences for the rate of deposit growth, which in all probability in turn somewhat reduced the availability effects in the housing market below what they would otherwise have been.

From this experience the Reserve Bank gradually revised its perception[11] of the transmission process along neo-Radcliffian lines. This process of revision led, as we know, to a more flexible rate policy, to increased emphasis on open market operations and to a reduction in the relative importance attached to advances rationing.

# Notes: Chapter 6

1 This is asserted in the Reserve Bank's *Annual Report, 1960–1*, p. 20.
2 The dating of requests is not always a simple matter, since there is no single comprehensive source. However, requests seem to have been made on the following dates: February 1959; May–June 1960; August 1960; and October 1960, while in November 1960 the October position was reaffirmed. The October request asked for a considerable reduction in the banks' advances before the end of March 1961 (Reserve Bank, *Annual Report, 1960–1*, p. 20).
3 Maximum overdraft rates were raised from 6 to 7 per cent on 17 November and the permissible average from $5^1/_2$ to 6 per cent. Interest rates on fixed deposits were raised to a maximum of $4/_2$ per cent. Savings bank rates followed in January 1961.
4 The then Governor (Dr H. C. Coombs) must surely have been pressing for a relaxation of the interest rate peg. On this point, cf. Coombs [25] [26] [27]. When it came, however, the change generated a considerable amount of overexcited comment.
5 The end–June positions of the banks as a group are given in Reserve Bank *Annual Reports* in the form of charts. From these it seems that the banks were borrowing at end–June in 1956, 1957, 1958 and 1960.
6 Cf. Davis and Wallace [34].
7 In this period requests usually asked the banks *not* to lend to hire purchase or instalment credit.
8 *Ad hoc* assumptions about the expectation generating process are often plausible, often tempting, but essentially dangerous.
9 The housing market was, in the later stages of the boom, strongly influenced by speculation.
10 The rate on savings bank deposits was raised in January 1961.
11 Cf. note 4. It may well be that the Reserve Bank did not so much revise its own perception as revise that of the Treasury.

*Chapter 7*

# Monetary Restraint 1966–70

## 7.1 *Introduction*

The second period chosen for an examination of the Reserve Bank's capacity to conduct a successful policy of monetary restriction is 1967–71. The cyclical trough of the economy came in 1966.III or IV.[1] The trough, however, was relatively shallow and involved, in terms of industrial production, not much more than 6 per cent of excess capacity compared with about 15 per cent in the troughs of 1961.III and 1975.II and about 22 per cent in the trough of 1952.III. Thus, in the earlier part of this period the Reserve Bank's policy aim was to promote a recovery from the 1966.III trough, while ensuring that the recovery did not accelerate sufficiently to produce a situation of serious excess demand. In short, the aim was one of relatively fine tuning.

From this it followed that in 1967–8 monetary policy was directed towards maintaining the position of approximate domestic balance. In more specific terms, monetary policy was conceived as providing essentially complementary flexibility to the stimulus originating in the budget. Thus, policy in that year was in the main accommodating or mildly expansionary.

Towards the end of 1968 and throughout much of 1968–9 the monetary stance became more cautious as economic revival proceeded. Initially, this caution took

Figure 7.1    Policy stance and principal actions, 1967-71

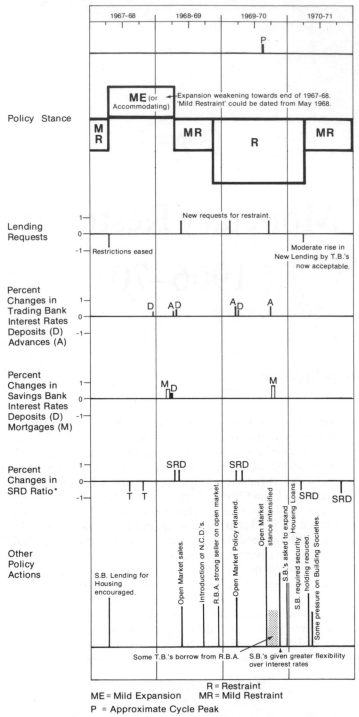

ME = Mild Expansion
P = Approximate Cycle Peak
R = Restraint
MR = Mild Restraint

*Changes marked 'T' are technical and relate to transfers to Term and Farm Loan
Development Funds.

*Source:* Reserve Bank of Australia, *Annual Reports* and *Statistical Bulletins*, various issues

the form of mild restraint, but in the last quarter of 1968–9[2] the mildness was abandoned and the Reserve Bank's policy became one of restraint. This new stance was maintained until the end of the first quarter of 1970–1 and was intensified in the second half of 1969–70.

The cyclical peak came in 1970.I – roughly a year after policy became fully restrictive. Nevertheless, restraint was maintained until the end of the first quarter of 1970–1, almost certainly out of a desire to contain the rate of increase in prices, which had accelerated fairly sharply. The subsequent downswing, which lasted about a year, was less severe (again in terms of industrial production) than that of either 1960–1 or 1974–5 and generated excess capacity of the order of 10–11 per cent.

In broad terms, therefore, there is a parallel between 1958–60 and 1968–70, although in terms of GDP the authorities came a good deal closer to successful fine tuning in the second period than in the first.

The degree of success attending the authorities' efforts at fine tuning is not, however, our primary concern in the present context. This is with the technical characteristics and economic impact of the Reserve Bank's actions. In particular we are interested in the extent to which, rather less than a decade after its experiences in 1958–60, the Reserve Bank had successfully adapted its techniques to the new financial environment.

Figure 7.1 shows our dating of Reserve Bank policy stances and its principal actions over the relevant period. We now examine events in rather more detail.

## 7.2 Initial Conditions and Fiscal Policy

Our interpretation dates the two Reserve Bank policy shifts as (a) in May (or October) 1968, a shift to mild restraint; and (b) in May 1969, a shift to restraint.

Figure 7.2 presents the initial conditions up to and including 1969.II, employing for this purpose the limited definition explained earlier. Unemployment began to fall after the first half of 1968. At roughly the same date, registered vacancies began to rise. Both movements continued and were still continuing at the time of the Reserve Bank's shift to restraint; over the same period the rates of change in wage earnings and the consumer price index were relatively stable, with perhaps some very slight tendency to acceleration in the former. Finally, GDP (at constant 1966–7 prices) began to rise rather faster than the usual estimate of the rate of growth in capacity by mid-1968.

Since the rate of growth in non-farm stocks (again at constant prices) did not suggest any sharp upturn in the inventory cycle, the shift in stance to mild restraint seems unexceptionable. Clearly, an upswing was under way, which by 1968.II showed no signs of unacceptable acceleration.

The external situation was also not such as to compel any rapid adjustment in policy. Admittedly, the current account deficit for the first half of 1968 was some

## Figure 7.2    Initial economic conditions

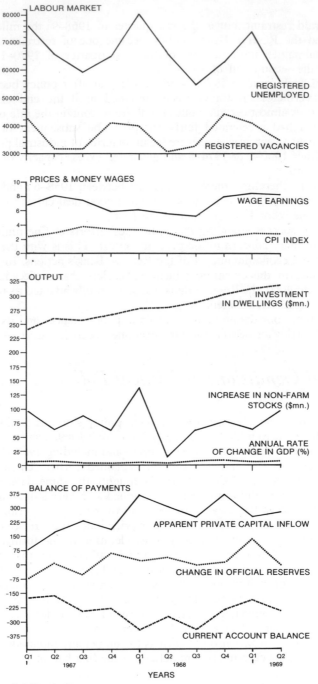

a  Including school leavers
b  Including the Balancing Item, Undistributed Income, Marketing Authorities and Non-Official
   Monetary Sector transactions

*Sources:*
Panel 1 – CES – Employment and Unemployment
       – ABS – Quarterly Summary of Australian Statistics
       – ABS – Supplement to Quarterly Estimates of National Income and Expenditure
       – RBA – Statistical Bulletins

**Table 7.1** *Fiscal impact and stance, 1966–71*

| Financial year | Changes in actual deficit | | Changes in full employment deficit | | Nevile's impact effect | |
|---|---|---|---|---|---|---|
| | $A m. | % of NFNP | $A m. | % of NFNP | % of NFNP | Change in % impact |
| 1966–7 | 267 | 1·4 | 271 | 1·5 | 3·1 | 0·3 |
| 1967–8 | 120 | 0·6 | 85 | 0·4 | 2·9 | −0·2 |
| 1968–9 | −257 | −1·2 | −183 | −0·8 | 2·3 | −0·6 |
| 1969–70 | −194 | −0·8 | −132 | −0·5 | 2·5 | 0·2 |
| 1970–1 | −181 | −0·7 | −239 | −0·9 | 3·0 | 0·5 |

*Source:* Table 4.1.

157

$A290 million above that for the corresponding period of 1967, but this was more than offset by a rise in the rate of apparent private-capital inflow of some $A420 million. The change in reserves was therefore negligible but distinctly an improvement over the fall experienced in the corresponding period of 1967.

The three indicators of fiscal policy that are available are given in Table 7.1. In general the indicators agree that changes in fiscal stance were expansionary in 1966–7. According to Nevile, the change in first-round effects (over 1965–6) amounted to some 0.3 per cent of non-farm national product. This is broadly supported by the full-employment budget calculations, which put the increase in the deficit at some $A270 million – rather over 1 per cent of GNP. By contrast the 1967-8 budget provided no increase in the fiscal element in aggregate demand; indeed Nevile's calculations suggest a fall of 0.2 per cent. The full employment budget, however, suggests a slight ($A85 million) stimulus. In the face of these conflicting estimates perhaps the best guess is that 1967–8 constituted no change in fiscal policy over 1966–7.

Clearly, when the Reserve Bank made its initial policy shift, the budget for 1968–9 had not been brought down. It seems, however, likely that the Reserve Bank had some information on the probable direction of any shift in policy stance. In the event the change in fiscal policy was restrictive according to both Nevile and the full-employment budget calculations. The extent of the shift, however, was not dramatic, although it was certainly not negligible. The fiscal policy shifts were consistent with the stage of the Australian cycle, readily comprehensible in terms of the initial conditions and complementary with Reserve Bank policy shifts.

## 7.3 Monetary Policy and Indicators

In this section we again present *ex post* indicators of monetary thrust. These take the same form as before: (a) two variants of the nominal money stock ($M_1$ and $M_3$); and (b) two interest rates on Commonwealth obligations: the short (two-year) and medium (ten-year) bond rates. In addition to (b) we also provide data for the average rate paid by the official short-term money market and the rate on finance company debentures. Unfortunately, official data on other private sector rates are not available.[3]

Consider first Figure 7.3, which gives the data for $M_1$ and $M_3$ (seasonally adjusted) and also the annual growth rate of the two series. The Reserve Bank moved to a policy of restraint in May 1969. In 1969.I $M_1$ was rising at roughly 6.5–7 per cent per annum. After the introduction of restraint the annual rate of increase of $M_1$ accelerated to reach over 9 per cent in December 1969 and again in March 1970. Thereafter, the rate of growth in $M_1$ declined fairly steadily until April–May 1971. Thus, if the rate of growth is taken as the appropriate indicator, it seems that: (a) it responded to restraint with a lag of around four quarters; and

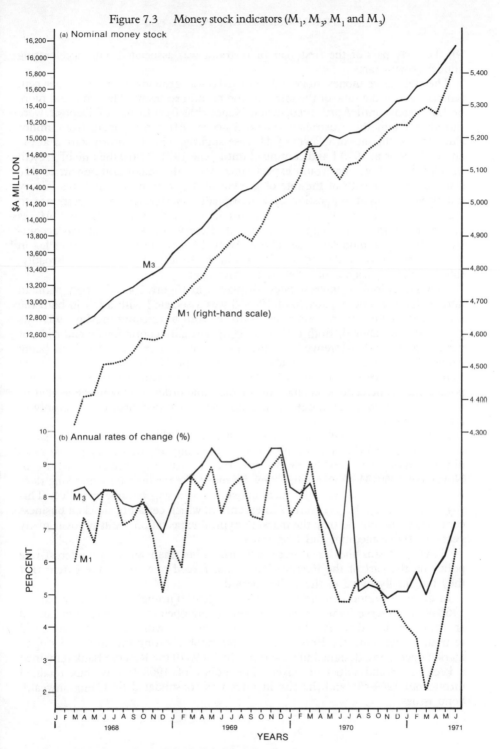

Figure 7.3 Money stock indicators ($M_1$, $M_3$, $M_1$ and $M_3$)

(a) Nominal money stock

$A MILLION

M3

M1 (right-hand scale)

(b) Annual rates of change (%)

M3

M1

PERCENT

J F M A M J J A S O N D J F M A M J J A S O N D J F M A M J J A S O N D J F M A M J J
1968              1969              1970              1971

YEARS

*Source:* Reserve Bank of Australia, *Statistical Bulletin (seasonally adjusted data)*

(b) the early part of the first year of restraint was associated with accelerating annual growth rates.

The alternative money stock indicator ($M_3$) was growing at around 8 per cent (annual rate) at the time of the introduction of mild restraint. This rate held more or less steady until April 1969, when Negotiable Certificates of Deposit were introduced into the Australian financial scene. After this, apart from minor fluctuations, the rate of growth of $M_3$ rose slightly. The downturn started at the end of 1969 or in 1970.I and continued until June 1971. Thus, the rate of growth in $M_3$ followed, as one would expect since $M_1$ is the major component of $M_3$, fairly closely the path of the rate of growth of $M_1$, with only – and this is very doubtful – a slight suggestion of a marginally shorter lag in its response to restriction. There is therefore no important conflict between $M_1$ and $M_3$ as indicators. Both in fact suggest that *ex ante* Reserve Bank restraint was accompanied by *ex post* monetary ease; alternatively, both suggest a four-quarter lag in the response of $M_1$ or $M_3^4$ to the changes in the Reserve Bank's stance. Broadly, this was the experience of 1959–61 all over again.

Now let us look at interest rates, displayed in Figure 7.4. The first point to note is that the mild expansion of 1967–8 was associated with a fall in both the short- and medium-term bond rates. With the shift to restraint in May 1969 this picture rapidly altered. Both rates moved up virtually continuously and did not peak until 1970.II. Moreover, the increases in rates were very far from being negligible. The rate on short bonds rose by close on 170 basis points – a change somewhat in excess of 35 per cent. The rise in the medium rate was 174 basis points, and its percentage change was of the same order of magnitude as that of the shorts. Moreover, although the medium-short gap declined, it did so only to a trivial extent.

It follows that the behaviour of interest rates in 1968–70 was in very sharp contrast to their behaviour in the 1958–60 upswing. In the earlier period rates did not move appreciably until *after* the Treasurer's special measures of November 1960. Moreover, when they did move, the medium term and long rates were relatively sticky, and the medium–short yield gap became negative. This suggests that even the Treasurer's intervention, which certainly shocked business confidence, did not destroy the market's typical expectation, built up over many years, of stable medium and long rates.

Finally, it *was* the Treasurer's actions, rather than an active interest-rate policy on the part of the Reserve Bank, that forced rates up to the extent that they did finally move in the earlier period.

In the later period matters were very different. Throughout the early part of 1968–9 the Reserve Bank was already conducting open market operations aimed at absorbing liquidity. At the end of the year, i.e. with the shift from mild restraint to restraint, the Reserve Bank undertook a strong initiative in its open market operations, designed to raise rates. In 1969–70 the Reserve Bank remained a keen seller and reluctant buyer. The policy of 1968–9 was thus retained throughout 1969–70, and the rise in rates was consolidated by Commonwealth bond issues.

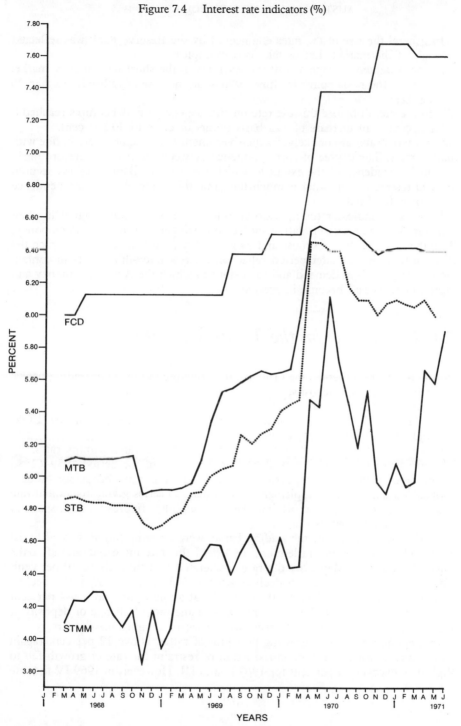

Figure 7.4    Interest rate indicators (%)

FCD

MTB

STB

STMM

YEARS

PERCENT

a  Average rate
b  Rebatable
*Source:* Reserve Bank of Australia, *Statistical Bulletin*

In general the rise in the rates engineered by the Reserve Bank was reflected throughout the market. Let us take two examples:

(1) The weighted average of call money rates in the short-term money market rose by 160 basis points by June 1970 – an increase of rather more than 35 per cent.

(2) In the month before this the rate on finance company debentures reached 8 per cent – an increase of 175 basis points or close to 30 per cent.

Administered rates are unlikely, by their very nature, to rise precisely in line with market rates. The degree of correspondence between the two is therefore fairly convincing evidence of the extent to which the Reserve Bank's actions secured a broad response – or, what is much the same thing, the close interdependence of markets for funds.

Used as an indicator (or indicators), interest rates provide a signal in close conformity with the *ex ante* dating and *ex ante* stringency of Reserve Bank policy. Both the speed of their response and its generality reflect the extent to which the Reserve Bank in this later period relied on interest rate adjustments to contain the rate of growth in demand and the extent to which the Australian money and capital markets had become integrated.

## 7.4 The Impact on the Trading Banks

In Figure 7.5 are presented the principal data relating to the major trading banks:

(a) a series for total deposits;

(b) a series for advances;

(c) a series for both holdings of liquid assets and government securities (LGS) and excess LGS holdings;[5] and

(d) data for both new lending by the banks and the advances/limits ratio.

The two latter series are not available for the whole of the period 1959–61; so (d) provides additional information regarding trading bank behaviour. Where applicable each series is supplemented by a derived series giving its annual rate of growth. In each case the original data, i.e. monthly figures without seasonal adjustment, have been used.

In 1968 the deposits of the trading banks were growing (on an annual basis) at around 7 per cent or a little more. In 1969.I this rate increased, and after the shift to restraint in May 1969 the rate accelerated to a little above 10 per cent. The rate of growth began to decline after 1970.I; and thereafter the decline persisted through December 1970, stabilising at a rate of around 3.5–4 per cent in the first half of 1971. Thus, on the basis of the rate of change of deposits, it seems that restraint became effective with a lag of roughly three quarters.

In 1968 advances were growing at a rate of rather above 12 per cent (again on an annual basis). After the introduction of restraint the rate of growth fell to slightly in excess of 9 per cent for 1969.II and III. However, in 1969.IV the rate

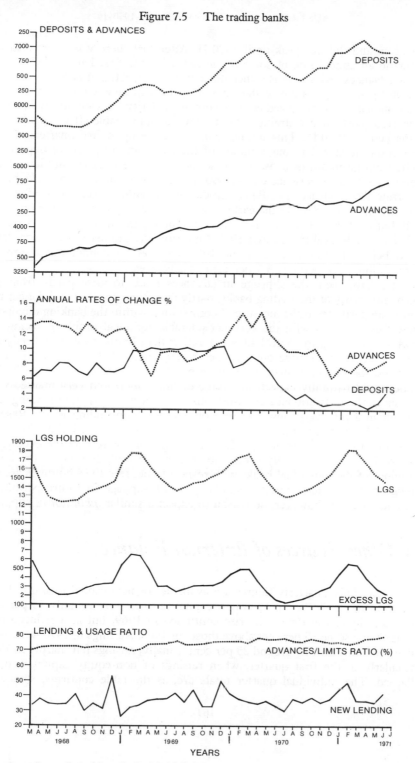

Figure 7.5    The trading banks

*Source:* Reserve Bank of Australia, *Statistical Bulletin*

rose again and did not peak until 1970.II. After that there was a fairly steady decline to an annual rate of some 8 per cent over the first half of 1971.

The advances series is thus rather difficult to interpret, and no real assistance is given by an examination of the rates of growth in new lending, which even on an annual basis displayed very severe irregularity. A cautious judgement, however, suggests that restraint began to have an appreciable effect on advances by the end of 1970.II. This implies a lag of close upon five quarters – very considerably longer than our estimate of the lag in the response of deposits.

The slippage in advances is, of course, not entirely surprising in view of the essentially similar experience of 1958-60. It seems that the trading banks began to borrow from the Reserve Bank coincidentally with, or very soon after, the introduction of restraint. In the early stages of restraint borrowing was probably small, but by 1969.III it was growing very rapidly, and it certainly persisted at a relatively high level throughout 1970. Our estimates are necessarily hazardous, but we believe that borrowing in mid-1970 may well have amounted to around $A160 million, i.e. perhaps 3.5 per cent of advances.

As we have seen, the slippage in advances tends to arise partly from the non-homogeneity of the trading banks, partly from their concern with longer run profits and partly from the measure of competition within the banking oligopoly. These factors, allied with the very considerable technical problems facing the banks in attempting to control advances rather than limits, explain not only the extent of advances slippage but also the greater length of the advances response lag. Thus, the rate of growth in limits responded to restraint fairly rapidly; but as one would naturally expect, the usage of limits increased very markedly.

In short, the institutional framework and the overdraft system of lending tend to result in a relatively slow response of advances outstanding to the Reserve Bank's LGS policy and the consequential behaviour of excess LGS holdings and the unobservable variable net free LGS holdings. In this respect the experience of 1969–70 was qualitatively similar to that of 1958–60; and where the initial conditions of the individual banks with respect to net free LGS holdings are not homogenous, we must expect a similar *form* of slippage in future periods of restraint. There is, however, no reason to expect a similar *quantitative* slippage.

## 7.5 *Other Sources of External Finance*

Once again, only quarterly figures are available for new capital raisings. These are set out in Table 7.2. In 1968 new capital raisings were roughly 75 per cent above the figure for 1967. The rise continued in 1969, but at a reduced rate, raisings being some 35 per cent above those for 1968. Raisings in 1970 were again above 1969, this time by around 25 per cent. Finally, raisings fell sharply in 1971, particularly in the first quarter, when raisings of non-equity capital virtually collapsed. The individual quarter totals are, as the table confirms, somewhat

**Table 7.2** *New capital raisings and share prices, 1968–71 (Sydney share price index, 1966–7 = 100)*

| Year/quarter | | New capital raisings ($A m.) | | | Sydney share price Index |
|---|---|---|---|---|---|
| | | Equity | Other | Total | Index |
| 1968 | I | 33·8 | 93·3 | 127·1 (53·9) | 141 (41·0) |
| | II | 54·3 | 92·0 | 146·3 (132·6) | 168 (61·5) |
| | III | 60·2 | 166·8 | 227·0 (112·1) | 182 (51·2) |
| | IV | 93·1 | 130·4 | 223·5 (40·1) | 169 (25·2) |
| 1969 | I | 83·0 | 101·7 | 184·7 (45·3) | 189 (34·0) |
| | II | 171·6 | 80·9 | 252·5 (72·6) | 184 (9·5) |
| | III | 74·8 | 143·4 | 218·2 (−3·9) | 172 (−5·5) |
| | IV | 110·9 | 177·6 | 288·5 (29·1) | 182 (7·7) |
| 1970 | I | 149·4 | 114·0 | 263·4 (42·6) | 190 (0·6) |
| | II | 187·2 | 63·1 | 250·3 (−1·0) | 167 (−9·2) |
| | III | 115·4 | 236·5 | 351·9 (61·3) | 175 (1·7) |
| | IV | 156·8 | 156·7 | 313·5 (8·7) | 164 (−9·9) |
| 1971 | I | 78·4 | 14·4 | 92·8 (−64·8) | 152 (−21·0) |
| | II | 80·2 | 123·4 | 203·6 (−18·5) | 152 (−9·0) |
| | III | 94·0 | 254·1 | 348·1 (−3·1) | 111 (−17·7) |

*Note:* Figures in parentheses give annual percentage changes over corresponding period in the previous year.
*Sources:* Reserve Bank of Australia, *Statistical Bulletin: Financial Supplement.*

165

erratic. It is therefore a hazardous proceeding to attempt to infer the lag in their response to Reserve Bank restraint. Our tentative interpretation is that the main response came after 1970.III, i.e. about two quarters *after* the turning point in the rate of growth in advances. This suggests a lag of six quarters. If, however, the actual rate of raisings rather than its rate of change is utilised as an indicator, the lag pattern suggested will be identical. Thus, the estimated lag of six quarters may be tentatively accepted.

Some support for this estimate is provided by the series for share prices. Technically, the stock market peaked in 1970.I, but the sustained fall in the index did not begin until after 1970.III – virtually in parallel with the series for new capital raisings. On the other hand, the rate of growth of share prices, which had been of the order of 45 per cent during 1968, became negligible after the introduction of restraint at the end of 1969.I. It seems arguable, therefore, that the Reserve Bank's policies at least checked share speculation sufficiently to prevent the emergence of extrapolative expectations. The fact that the market *declined* after 1970.III rather than *collapsed* tends to support this interpretation. Since a stable share market cannot be expected to inhibit new capital raisings, this is consistent with the observation that the downturn in raisings coincided with the fall in the market.

The time series for new instalment credit is given in Table 7.3. The series is defined as

$$\text{Instalment credit} \quad \equiv \quad \begin{array}{c} \text{Instalment credit} \\ \text{for} \\ \text{retail sales} \end{array} \quad + \quad \begin{array}{c} \text{Other consumers} \\ \text{and} \\ \text{commercial loans} \end{array}$$

This series again exhibited a fair amount of noise. Nevertheless, it is clear that it peaked in 1970.IV. If the examination is based upon rates of change, however, the peak of the series was in 1969.I – in effect the same quarter in which the Reserve Bank switched to restraint. It is thus possible to interpret this series as suggesting: (a) that the shift to restraint had some, almost immediate, impact in reducing the rate of growth in new instalment credit granted; but (b) that the level of new credit granted per period remained high until 1970.IV. Both interpretations are highly conjectural. Moreover, the available data do not enable us to determine whether the time path of new instalment lending was primarily a supply or a demand phenomenon.

Finally, we turn to the market in mortgages. Table 7.4 presents data for:
(a) mortgage approvals;
(b) the mortgage rates as proxied by the rate on private mortgages registered in New South Wales and by the rate charged by permanent building societies; and
(c) the permanent building societies' deposit rates.
Looking initially at approvals, it is clear that these were rising strongly until 1969.IV. There was then a fairly considerable fall until 1970.II. After that,

**Table 7.3** *Instalment credit: finance companies, 1968–71*
*(amounts financed, $A million)*

| Year/month/quarter | | Monthly | | Quarterly | |
|---|---|---|---|---|---|
| 1968 | Jan. | | 133·6 | (18·6) | | |
| | Feb. | I | 128·8 | (14·8) | 138·2 | (18·5) |
| | Mar. | | 152·1 | (21·7) | | |
| | Apr. | | 143·4 | (27·2) | | |
| | May | II | 179·4 | (31·8) | 157·3 | (20·7) |
| | Jun. | | 149·0 | (4·9) | | |
| | Jul. | | 180·5 | (35·1) | | |
| | Aug. | III | 155·5 | (4·9) | 165·5 | (15·4) |
| | Sep. | | 160·6 | (7·7) | | |
| | Oct. | | 189·5 | (33·5) | | |
| | Nov. | IV | 198·6 | (21·7) | 192·9 | (25·9) |
| | Dec. | | 190·5 | (23·4) | | |
| 1969 | Jan. | | 160·5 | (27·6) | | |
| | Feb. | I | 181·5 | (40·9) | 180·6 | (30·7) |
| | Mar. | | 199·9 | (31·4) | | |
| | Apr. | | 177·3 | (23·6) | | |
| | May | II | 195·8 | (9·2) | 186·5 | (18·6) |
| | Jun. | | 186·5 | (25·2) | | |
| | Jul. | | 213·5 | (18·3) | | |
| | Aug. | III | 191·6 | (23·2) | 205·8 | (24·4) |
| | Sep. | | 212·2 | (32·1) | | |
| | Oct. | | 223·9 | (18·2) | | |
| | Nov. | IV | 201·9 | (1·7) | 223·5 | (15·9) |
| | Dec. | | 244·7 | (28·5) | | |
| 1970 | Jan. | | 196·4 | (22·4) | | |
| | Feb. | I | 224·8 | (23·9) | 212·4 | (17·6) |
| | Mar. | | 215·9 | (8·0) | | |
| | Apr. | | 239·8 | (35·3) | | |
| | May | II | 221·8 | (13·3) | 229·8 | (23·2) |
| | Jun. | | 227·8 | (22·2) | | |
| | Jul. | | 244·8 | (14·7) | | |
| | Aug. | III | 219·9 | (14·8) | 232·8 | (13·1) |
| | Sep. | | 233·6 | (10·1) | | |
| | Oct. | | 259·7 | (16·0) | | |
| | Nov. | IV | 241·3 | (19·5) | 268·9 | (20·3) |
| | Dec. | | 305·7 | (24·9) | | |
| 1971 | Jan. | | 237·4 | (20·9) | | |
| | Feb. | I | 231·9 | (3·2) | 244·2 | (15·0) |
| | Mar. | | 263·3 | (22·0) | | |
| | Apr. | | 258·2 | (7·7) | | |
| | May | II | 245·4 | (10·6) | 261·3 | (13·7) |
| | Jun. | | 280·4 | (23·1) | | |

*Note:* Figures in parentheses give annual percentage changes over corresponding period in
previous year.
*Source:* Reserve Bank of Australia, *Statistical Bulletin.*

**Table 7.4** *The mortgage market, 1968–71*

| Year/quarter | Mortgage Approvals ($A m.) | Mortgage rate (%) NSW | Mortgage rate (%) PBS | PBS deposit rate (%) |
|---|---|---|---|---|
| 1968  I | 257 | 9·2 | 7·1 | 5·8 |
| II | 264 | 9·2 | 7·1 | 5·8 |
| III | 263 | 9·1 | 7·2 | 5·9 |
| IV | 273 | 9·3 | 7·2 | 5·9 |
| 1969  I | 296 | 9·3 | 7·2 | 5·9 |
| II | 320 | 9·3 | 7·3 | 5·9 |
| III | 332 | 9·3 | 7·4 | 5·9 |
| IV | 347 | 9·6 | 7·5 | 6·0 |
| 1970  I | 314 | 9·8 | 7·5 | 6·0 |
| II | 271 | 9·8 | 7·4 | 6·0 |
| III | 324 | 10·4 | 7·4 | 6·0 |
| IV | 373 | 10·5 | 8·1 | 6·6 |
| 1971  I | 356 | 10·8 | 8·1 | 6·6 |
| II | 375 | 10·8 | 8·1 | 6·6 |

*Notes*:
NSW = New South Wales (private mortgages).
PBS = permanent building societies.
*Sources*: Reserve Bank of Australia, *Statistical Bulletin*; and Australian Bureau of Statistics, *Monthly Review of Business Statistics*.

growth was resumed through 1971.[6] It thus appears that, if the Reserve Bank's shift to restraint had an impact on approvals, the lag involved was probably two to three quarters. Moreover, the impact was relatively short lived, lasting for three quarters at the most.

In examining this pattern it is notable that the permanent building societies' borrowing rate rose by only 10 basis points between 1968.III and 1970.III, the rise actually taking place in 1969.IV.[7] However, in 1970.IV the deposit rate was raised by 60 basis points to 6.6 per cent and remained at this level until 1972.II. It is thus likely that the slowdown in approvals was occasioned by the reduced rate of inflow to deposits and by a reduction in the certainty regarding them, both reflecting the relative stickiness of building society rates as against those on competing assets. It also seems possible that an element in the slowdown was some readjustment of building society portfolios. There is some evidence that this may have occurred in 1969–70. Unfortunately, it is not clear precisely why the adjustment occurred when it did. On the face of it it seems unlikely that building societies reacted simply to a change in the relative rates of return on mortgages and government securities. Nevertheless, it remains true that building societies' share in total mortgage approvals fell sharply from 1969.IV and did not recover its (approximate) trend value until three to four quarters later.

It thus appears that monetary restraint may have generated a fairly sharp, although deliberately short lived, reduction in mortgage approvals which, in the main, reflected the behaviour of the building societies.

## 7.6 The Behaviour of Demand

The information regarding the main demand components is set out in Figure 7.6.

Consider first gross private investment in fixed capital. In aggregate, this series peaked in 1971.III. This was more than a year after the peak in investment in dwellings (1970.I) and perhaps two quarters after the peak in construction (1971.I). The remaining element in gross private fixed investment, namely, equipment, peaked in either 1971.I or III. Thus, if the timing of the peak is imputed to monetary action, there was a lag of some four quarters for investment in dwellings and perhaps eight quarters for the remaining two elements. Speaking very broadly, these datings make intuitive sense and in the latter two components are roughly consistent with the implications of econometrically estimated investment functions.

Not very surprisingly, private consumption expenditure rose throughout the period. The rate of growth, however, fell to virtually zero in the second half of 1970 and did not recover its earlier momentum until the second half of 1971. This behaviour seems consistent with our earlier series for instalment credit, and it also agrees fairly well with the fall in stock market prices after 1970.I. In short, the pattern of consumption behaviour was consistent with some wealth effect together with a response to the increased cost of instalment credit. This conclusion is strengthened if consumption is disaggregated and expenditure on consumer durables is considered.

From the time series it is virtually impossible to do more than guess at the impact of restraint from 1969.I to the cycle peak of 1970.I, partly because tuning was relatively fine. Clearly, the rate of growth of private investment was slowed by 1970.I, as was the rate of growth in consumption. However, it is conceivable that this was at least in part attributable to the shift in fiscal stance. Presumably, the issue could be resolved in terms of an econometric model by a simulation. Unfortunately, this cannot be undertaken.[8] An intuitive guess would put the impact of monetary restraint in 1969–70 at around 0.5 per cent of GDP.

## 7.7 The Technique of Monetary Restraint

The period 1967–70 came virtually at the end of the decade in which, on our interpretation, the Reserve Bank perceived the transmission process in Radcliffian terms. It is therefore of some interest to consider how the techniques employed in this later period differed from those of 1958–60 – virtually the end

Figure 7.6    Main demand components ($A million) (1966-7 prices)

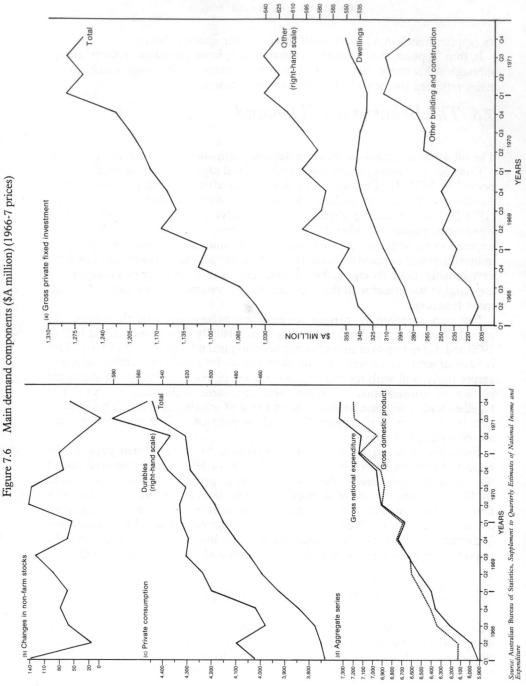

Source: Australian Bureau of Statistics, Supplement to Quarterly Estimates of National Income and Expenditure

of what we have called the 'banking policy' period.

The most interesting aspect of this issue is the Reserve Bank's manipulation of interest rates, in which it very clearly took the initiative in the period under review, in marked contrast to 1958–60.

Consider, for example, the shift to mild restraint, which we have dated in May–June 1968. During the second half of 1967–8 bank liquidity tightened fairly appreciably. The Reserve Bank did not offset this process; nor did it reinforce it by SRD calls. Instead, it began its policy shift by raising trading bank rates (in June) and savings bank rates (in July). A further upward movement in rates came in October, when the maximum rate on trading bank advances was raised by 0.25 per cent. The issue rate on Treasury notes was also raised slightly, and in November the trading banks were told that some tapering down in their rate of new lending would be appropriate and warned that the SRD ratio would be operated so as to restrain bank liquidity.

These rate changes were small. Nevertheless, they show the Reserve Bank initiating mild restraint by changes in relative rates – aimed at raising the ability of the banks to attract funds away from non-bank intermediaries – and in the process operating on market expectations regarding rates.

In March–April 1969 the Reserve Bank approved two institutional changes, which were likely to exert a similar influence: (a) the introduction of NCDs (with a maximum rate of 4.75 per cent); and (b) approval for the savings banks to introduce progressive savings accounts yielding a rate of return of 1 per cent above their usual deposit rates. Finally, in May 1969 the Reserve Bank sharply shifted its stance in the bond market to become a more active seller. Simultaneously, the issue rate on Treasury notes was raised by 0.25 per cent.

Remarkably little information is available from official sources on private-short-term borrowing rates, e.g. those ruling in the unofficial money market and the intercompany market. Some privately constructed series, however, suggest that these Reserve-Bank-initiated interest movements were followed by increases in market rates; and this is confirmed by the response of official short-term money-market rates, which rose after March 1969, and finance company two-year debentures, which rose by about 0.5 per cent from August 1969.

We have dated the shift to restraint in May–June 1969. According to the Reserve Bank's *Annual Report*, this period opened by the Bank taking an even firmer reluctant buyer – willing seller position in relation to the bond market. In August 1969 the rate maxima for *both* trading banks and savings banks were increased, and at the same time both groups were asked to moderate their lending. The SRD ratio was raised by 1 per cent over August and October 1969, and in March–April 1970 the Reserve Bank again raised the rate maxima for both trading banks and savings banks and intensified its willing seller attitude to the bond market. Additionally, in April the trading banks were requested to reduce their rate of new lending and maintain a high rate of cancellations of limits.

As we know, the cycle peak came in 1970.I. It follows that the Reserve Bank was still intensifying its restrictive policy at the peak; but in view of the extreme difficulty of identifying cycle peaks (or troughs) this is readily comprehensible. Moreover, although restraint was on our dating maintained until roughly September 1970, the Reserve Bank had already moved in July to ensure that trading banks and life offices maintained their rates of lending for housing purposes and to arrange for savings banks to *increase* their rate of lending. In short, our policy-phase dating tends to conceal a significant measure of flexibility in the Reserve Bank's approach.

From the point of view of technique, 1968–70 thus offers a clear-cut contrast with 1958–60. Compared with the earlier period it is clear that the Reserve Bank:

(a) placed far greater emphasis on interest rates and used *both* its direct control of certain administered rates *and* its open-market policy to lead the market to a markedly higher rate structure;

(b) put much less emphasis on requests to the trading banks, although the apparatus was still employed; and

(c) showed a capacity to act flexibly with regard to the housing market.

In the absence of data on quarterly fund flows and short term rates in the private sector it is not possible to make even a rough guess at the quantitative impact of these techniques on the flows of funds through non-bank financial intermediaries. The technical success of the Reserve Bank's policies can therefore only be inferred from the (relative) success of macroeconomic policy as a whole; and in this context it seems that, although the tuning of the economy was not *ex post* as fine as one might wish, given the difficulties of economic diagnosis and the associated difficulties of forecasting major variables in Australia, macroeconomic policy in general and monetary policy in particular must in this period be counted as relatively very successful.

# Notes: *Chapter 7*

1  The former on the basis of industrial production, the latter on the basis of non-farm GDP.

2  We date this from May 1969, when the Reserve Bank shifted its stance in relation to the bond market and there was an upward adjustment of the Treasury note rate.

3  Some information is obtainable from a chart published in the *Australian Economic Review*, No. 3 (1970), p. 41.

4  There is nothing surprising in this in view of the dynamics of the money supply process.

5  Strictly, we need estimates of Net Free LGS $\equiv$ Excess LGS $-$ Borrowing from Reserve Bank. Since we have little confidence in our estimate, of this variable, we offer no such series.

6  Significantly, this followed sharply on Reserve Bank action in July 1970 aimed at increasing the flow of mortgage lending.

7  The approvals of permanent building societies fell more than proportionately to those of savings banks. There was a virtual halt in lending in West Australia.

8  For purely technical reasons, policy simulations with either of the models developed in the Reserve Bank could not be conducted.

# Chapter 8

# Monetary Expansion 1971–3

## 8.1 *Introduction*

This chapter gives an account of a period in which the Reserve Bank followed an expansionary monetary policy aimed at stimulating demand. It therefore offers some evidence concerning the ability of discretionary monetary action in Australia to expand, as opposed to restrict, economic activity.

There are at least two reasons why evidence on this point is of interest. In the first place, macroeconomic models typically suggest approximately symmetric responses to discretionary changes in monetary instruments over a short (say four to eight quarters) policy-planning horizon. Thus, in the Reserve Bank model RB74 an $\chi$ per cent *rise* in interest rates generates a dynamic path that is fairly close, with the sign reversed, to the path generated by an $\chi$ per cent *fall* in rates. The reason for this is that, although some variables, notably capacity utilisation, enter the model in a non-linear form, they respond rather slowly to policy changes. Hence, over a relatively short horizon the dynamic path is very little influenced by them. In short, models that reflect not only the real world, but also the assumptions imposed by model builders for theoretical or econometric reasons, imply that discretionary monetary action is roughly as efficient in generating an expansion as in enforcing a restriction.

# Figure 8.1  Policy stance and principal actions, 1970-4

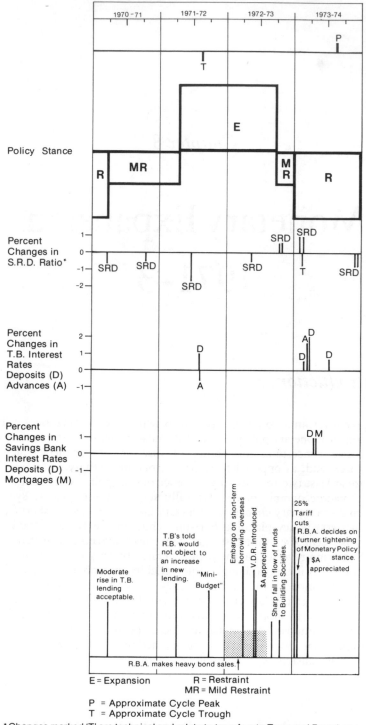

E = Expansion
R = Restraint
MR = Mild Restraint
P = Approximate Cycle Peak
T = Approximate Cycle Trough

*Changes marked 'T' are technical and relate to transfers to Term and Farm Loan Development Funds.

*Source:* Reserve Bank of Australia, *Annual Reports and Statistical Bulletins*

This view is not shared by all economists. Indeed, the position is commonly taken that monetary action is less efficient in promoting an expansion. It seems probable that this view derives from an interpretation of the transmission process that implicitly emphasises availability effects rather than cost-of-capital effects, wealth effects and expectational effects. Nevertheless, it is of potential importance, since it may influence the authorities' perception of the comparative efficiency of monetary and fiscal devices and thus impose a bias on the macroeconomic policy mix. Any such bias is, of course, likely to be magnified by the entirely understandable preference of Treasurers for using fiscal policy rather more intensively when the overall macroeconomic policy stance is strongly expansionary and rather less intensively when the reverse is the case.

According to our *ex ante* dating of Reserve Bank policy, this was shifted from restraint to ease in October 1971. Figure 8.1 provides, as usual, our *ex ante* policy datings and a summary of the principal actions taken by the Reserve Bank over the period.

We turn now to consider the initial conditions, i.e. the economic situation and the authorities' perception of it at the beginning of the financial year 1971–2.

# 8.2 The Initial Conditions and the Macroeconomic Policy Stance

The initial conditions are set out in Table 8.1 in terms of those variables which – it seems highly likely – would either enter the authorities' disutility function as targets or be approximate indicators of the behaviour of the target variables. No extensive comment on these is necessary. Both the labour market and the growth rate of output suggest that a move towards recession was well under way by June 1971. Moreover, the accumulation of non-farm stocks during the calendar year 1970 and financial year 1970–71 did not suggest that demand in 1971–2 would be sustained by an upswing in the stock cycle. The case for some stimulus to demand was thus relatively clear-cut in terms of employment, output and the phase of the inventory cycle.

In contrast to this, the rate of change of the consumer price index showed clear signs of accelerating in 1970–1. Additionally, in the second half of that year the rate of change in wages and salaries had more than doubled over the second half of 1969–70, with a corresponding acceleration in the rate of change in labour costs that was not by June 1971 fully reflected in prices. The authorities were thus presented with the familiar problem of determining the rate at which they would trade off real expansion against inflation on the then current assumption of a relatively stable augmented Phillips curve.

Despite the signs of strain in the international monetary system the state of the overall balance of payments was extremely favourable. This is made clear in

**Table 8.1** *Initial conditions, 1969–71*

| Year/month/quarter | | (a) Labour market | | (b) Prices and money wages (annual % rates of change) | | Annual rate of change in GDP (%) | (c) Output[a] | | | (d) Balance of payments ($A m.) | | |
|---|---|---|---|---|---|---|---|---|---|---|---|---|
| | | Registered unemployed (no.) | Registered vacancies (no.) | CPI index | Wage earnings | | Increase in non-farm stocks ($A m.) | Investment in dwellings ($A m.) | | Current account balance | Apparent private capital inflow (b) | Change in official reserves |
| 1969 Jan. | | 63,578 | 46,321 | | | | | | | | | |
| Feb. | I | 59,491 | 40,745 | 2·9 | 8·4 | 8·0 | 64 | 313 | | −187 | 264 | 133 |
| Mar. | | 53,422 | 38,635 | | | | | | | | | |
| Apr. | | 54,625 | 35,602 | | | | | | | | | |
| May | II | 54,145 | 35,379 | 2·9 | 8·2 | 8·9 | 92 | 321 | | −252 | 285 | −2 |
| Jun. | | 52,834 | 34,996 | | | | | | | | | |
| Jul. | | 47,801 | 38,312 | | | | | | | | | |
| Aug. | III | 43,303 | 42,399 | 3·1 | 9·3 | 6·7 | 127 | 331 | | −191 | 108 | −184 |
| Sep. | | 39,454 | 46,736 | | | | | | | | | |
| Oct. | | 38,972 | 54,012 | | | | | | | | | |
| Nov. | IV | 40,261 | 56,482 | 2·8 | 9·0 | 5·7 | 62 | 339 | | −231 | 193 | −110 |
| Dec. | | 45,105 | 61,437 | | | | | | | | | |

| | | | | | | | | | | | | |
|---|---|---|---|---|---|---|---|---|---|---|---|---|
| 1970 | Jan. | I | 55,147 | 64,749 | 3·2 | 6·1 | 4·3 | 54 | 345 | −125 | 175 | 106 |
| | Feb. | | 49,341 | 58,258 | | | | | | | | |
| | Mar. | | 44,238 | 54,507 | | | | | | | | |
| | Apr. | II | 44,929 | 49,495 | 3·7 | 9·1 | 5·9 | 142 | 342 | −213 | 507 | 306 |
| | May | | 48,477 | 44,446 | | | | | | | | |
| | Jun. | | 49,852 | 39,865 | | | | | | | | |
| | Jul. | III | 48,783 | 40,140 | 3·8 | 9·2 | 4·6 | 136 | 340 | −214 | 161 | −34 |
| | Aug. | | 45,658 | 42,538 | | | | | | | | |
| | Sep. | | 45,960 | 47,236 | | | | | | | | |
| | Oct. | IV | 42,898 | 51,814 | 4·9 | 9·2 | 3·4 | 71 | 332 | −245 | 319 | 7 |
| | Nov. | | 42,930 | 58,468 | | | | | | | | |
| | Dec. | | 47,647 | 59,554 | | | | | | | | |
| 1971 | Jan. | I | 60,829 | 64,287 | 4·9 | 12·2 | 6·7 | 80 | 332 | −241 | 478 | 343 |
| | Feb. | | 60,834 | 49,979 | | | | | | | | |
| | Mar. | | 59,273 | 40,537 | | | | | | | | |
| | Apr. | II | 60,370 | 36,442 | 5·4 | 12·4 | 3·0 | 41 | 339 | −173 | 576 | 426 |
| | May | | 62,368 | 34,426 | | | | | | | | |
| | Jun. | | 64,020 | 31,771 | | | | | | | | |

*a* Seasonally adjusted, 1966–7 prices.
*b* Including the balancing item, undistributed income, marketing authorities and non-official monetary-sector transactions.

Sources:
(a) Australian Bureau of Statistics, *Seasonally Adjusted Indicators, 1976.*
(b) Australian Bureau of Statistics, *Quarterly Summary of Australian Statistics.*
(c) Australian Bureau of Statistics, *Supplement to Quarterly Estimates of National Income and Expenditure* (December 1975).
(d) Reserve Bank of Australia, *Statistical Bulletin.*

Table 8.1, which shows that in the second half of the financial year 1970–1 the increase in official reserves was close to $A800 million.

Additionally, the *level* of reserves gave no cause for anxiety, since by June 1971 they amounted to about six months' imports. The current acount deficit was approximately on trend, and the rate of private capital inflow was more than ample. Thus, although any moves to expansion would necessarily have increased the import bill both directly, after some lag, and via stock accumulation, rather later, the figures suggest that the external position could not have significantly constrained policy.

This judgement, however, must be considered subject to the realisation that it contains an element of hindsight. In June–August 1971, when the major policy decisions were taken, the international monetary system based on Bretton Woods was virtually disintegrating. In these circumstances the external out-turn, which in more normal times would beyond doubt have been highly reassuring, must have carried a very considerable load of uncertainty. This was the more likely since private capital flows are readily reversible and were, in the international monetary climate of mid-1971, particularly difficult to forecast.

As we have pointed out, no unambiguous fiscal policy indicator of general acceptability exists. However, an examination of Nevile's estimates reveals that the impact of fiscal decisions in 1971–2 was, if anything, marginally less than in 1970–1. Thus, the *change* in the impact of fiscal decisions from 1970–1 to 1971–2 was, according to Nevile, marginally deflationary – or, given the unavoidable imprecision of the estimates, roughly neutral. A qualitatively similar conclusion emerges from the change in the full-employment budget position estimated by Barton, Derody and Sheehan [15]. This puts the change in the full employment surplus at $A100 million in current prices, or about 0.3 per cent of current GNP. This is rather more than three times Nevile's estimate and suggests that the change in fiscal impact was in fact perceptibly deflationary rather than neutral.

Initially, there is no doubt that the fiscal stance was aimed at containing demand rather than expanding it. The general line adopted by the Treasurer was that the dominant policy problem was to restrain the rate of growth in prices. Additionally, he appears to have expected a fairly sharp increase in private consumption and a continuation of the expansion in construction investment. How far this approach represented a shift in the preference function of the authorities rather than a reaction to the uncertainties of the international situation it is impossible to say; nor is it possible to estimate how far it arose out of errors in economic forecasting. What is clear is that the budget brought down on 17 August planned for a reduction in the deficit of around $A65 million (on a conventional basis) and asserted that monetary policy would remain restrictive, and from the Treasurer's remarks it also seems clear that official forecasters were expecting an increase in aggregate demand from domestic sources. Since these forecasts must have been made around the end of the financial year 1970–1, i.e. approximately four calendar quarters *after* the cyclical peak in output, the 1971–2 budget provides a clear example of the difficulty of macroeconomc diagnosis and

Table 8.2 *Fiscal impact and stance, 1969–74*

| Financial year | Changes in actual deficit | | Changes in full employment deficit | | Nevile's impact effect | |
|---|---|---|---|---|---|---|
| | $A m. | % of NFNP | $A m. | % of NFNP | % of NFNP | Change in % impact |
| 1969–70 | −194 | −0·8 | −132 | −0·5 | 2·5 | 0·2 |
| 1970–1 | −181 | −0·7 | −239 | −0·9 | 3·0 | 0·5 |
| 1971–2 | 124 | 0·4 | −100 | −0·3 | 2·9 | −0·1 |
| 1972–3 | 575 | 1·7 | 718 | 2·1 | 4·9 | 2·0 |
| 1973–4 | −416 | −1·1 | −352 | −0·9 | 4·2 | −0·7 |

*Source:* Table 4.1.

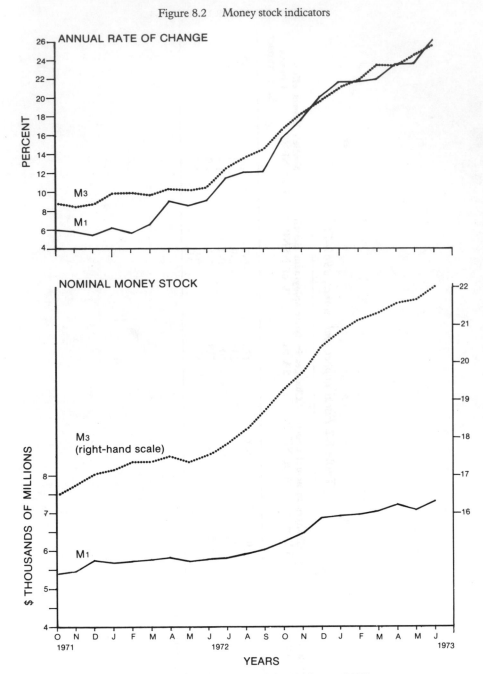

Figure 8.2    Money stock indicators

*Source:* Australian Bureau of Statistics, *Seasonally Adjusted Indicators (1976)*

forecasting in Australia.

In the event fiscal policy was marginally eased during 1971-2 more or less coincidentally with the Reserve Bank's shift in stance in October 1971.[1] However, in 1972-3 fiscal policy changed very sharply in favour of expansion. Thus according to Nevile the change in the impact of fiscal policy on non-farm product amounted to a full 2 per cent. This was almost identical with the shift between the years 1956-7 and 1957-8 and nearly two-thirds of the largest expansionary shift estimated by Nevile, namely, that for 1960-1 to 1961-2.

Using the full employment estimates, the change in the deficit amounted to $A718 million – roughly 2 per cent of non-farm product. This was a marginally larger change than Nevile's estimates suggest. Nevertheless, the correspondence is close. The change in the actual budget deficit was $A575 million; and the deficit itself, which is the relevant concept from the point of view of liquidity, amounted to $A701 million. These figures are summarised in Table 8.2.

It follows that the fiscal background to the Reserve Bank's expansionary stance was initially one of marginal restraint, easing gradually and becoming in 1972-3 one of very considerable direct stimulus to demand, involving a *potential* liquidity impact in 1972-3 of around 30 per cent of the liquid assets and government securities (LGS) holdings of the trading banks.

# 8.3 Monetary Thrust: Ex Post Indicators

As usual, *ex post* indicators of monetary thrust are now presented in the form of two nominal money stock concepts ($M_1$ and $M_3$) and a subset of interest rates (see Figure 8.2). During 1970-1, as in 1969-70, both $M_1$ and $M_3$ grew relatively slowly, the former at almost exactly 6.6 per cent (annual rate) and the latter at 7 per cent. With the shift to ease in October 1971 the response of both aggregates was relatively slow. $M_1$ indeed initially grew rather more slowly; but by April 1972 the rate of expansion of $M_1$ had reached 9 per cent, and after the sharp shift in the fiscal stance in the September quarter of 1972 the rate expanded rapidly. By June 1973 the annual rate of expansion in $M_1$ had reached 26.3 per cent. $M_3$, as Figure 8.2 shows, followed a very similar pattern, and by June 1973 this aggregate was also rising at close to 26 per cent.

The interest rate indicators tell a very similar story, at least until calendar 1973.I. The rates on two-year and ten-year bonds declined steadily from June 1971. For the period June–October 1971 this decline was presumably to be explained in terms of declining activity rather than the impact of monetary expansion. After the change in the stance of monetary policy both rates fell further, reaching their trough values in 1973.I. Overall, these two rates fell by roughly 1 per cent – 100 basis points. In the case of two-year bonds this was a fall of some 19 per cent, in the case of ten-year bonds of some 13-14 per cent. These changes were considerably less, both absolutely and proportionately, than

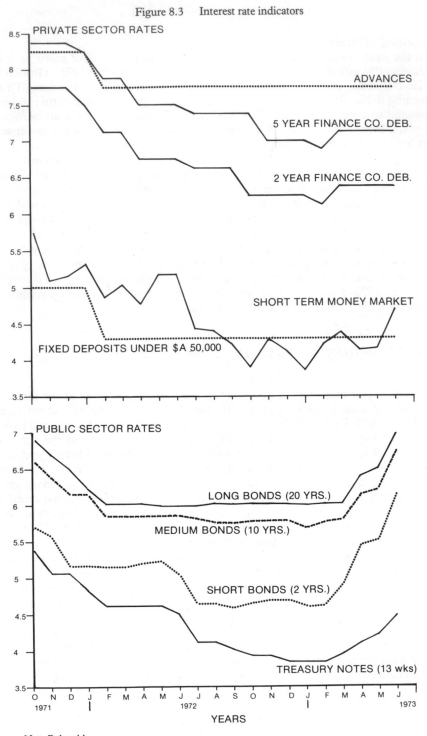

Figure 8.3    Interest rate indicators

PRIVATE SECTOR RATES

ADVANCES

5 YEAR FINANCE CO. DEB.

2 YEAR FINANCE CO. DEB.

SHORT TERM MONEY MARKET

FIXED DEPOSITS UNDER $A 50,000

PUBLIC SECTOR RATES

LONG BONDS (20 YRS.)

MEDIUM BONDS (10 YRS.)

SHORT BONDS (2 YRS.)

TREASURY NOTES (13 wks)

O   N   D   J   F   M   A   M   J   J   A   S   O   N   D   J   F   M   A   M   J
1971                              1972                                    1973

YEARS

a  Non-Rebatable
b  Average rate
Source: Reserve Bank of Australia, Statistical Bulletin

the corresponding change in the Treasury note rate, which amounted to 152 basis points – or in proportional terms, rather more than 39 per cent.[2]

As one might expect, the long rate (twenty-year bonds) behaved very similarly to the medium (ten-year) rate, although somewhat surprisingly its trough value occurred as early as May–June 1972, i.e. before the marked shift in fiscal policy. Its actual fall from October amounted to 99 basis points – a proportional decline of 14 per cent.

In February 1973 the Reserve Bank modified its policy stance to what we have called 'mild restraint', in particular by changing its attitude to bond purchases. This was reflected fairly quickly in yields on government securities.

Private-sector interest rates, typically administered rates, followed official rates down. Apart from the market-determined short-term money-market rate they did not, however, rise after February 1973. In contrast, other market-determined private rates, e.g. those on intercompany loans and bank bills, did (see Figure 8.3).

The two sets of *ex post* indicators are therefore in fair agreement about the direction, and even the extent, of monetary thrust until the end of the calendar year 1972. After this date the money stock indicators suggest continuing and even increasing ease, while the interest rate indicators suggest an emerging tightness. Of the two, because of the lags in the responses of the money stock measures, the interest rate indicators seem to give a superior indication of timing in 1973.I and II. Against this, however, they almost certainly give an erroneous qualitative indication of monetary thrust in the period June–October 1971.

## 8.4 The Major Trading Banks

The annual rate of growth in trading bank deposits in June 1971 was slightly over 4 per cent; in October the rate had risen to just under 8 per cent. After the shift to expansion there was no very marked change in deposit growth until calendar 1972.I.[3] After mid-1972, when the shift to an overall macroeconomic stance of expansion occurred and fiscal policy, as we have seen, became markedly expansionary, the rate of growth accelerated very markedly. By December 1972 it had reached 25.5 per cent, and in June 1973 – some four months after the Reserve Bank had moved to mild restraint – the growth rate was nearly 34 per cent. These developments are set out in Figure 8.4.

As we have seen, the existence of a stable demand function for excess LGS assets or net free LGS assets on the part of the major trading banks remains a matter of doubt. It is, however, clear that the rate of growth in LGS assets rose very considerably after the October 1971 shift in monetary stance and accelerated very sharply after the mid-1972 overall policy shift. By October 1972 LGS assets were growing at rather more than 58 per cent per annum. With the shift to mild restraint in 1973.I the growth rate declined. By June 1973 it was down to 24 per

Figure 8.4    The trading banks

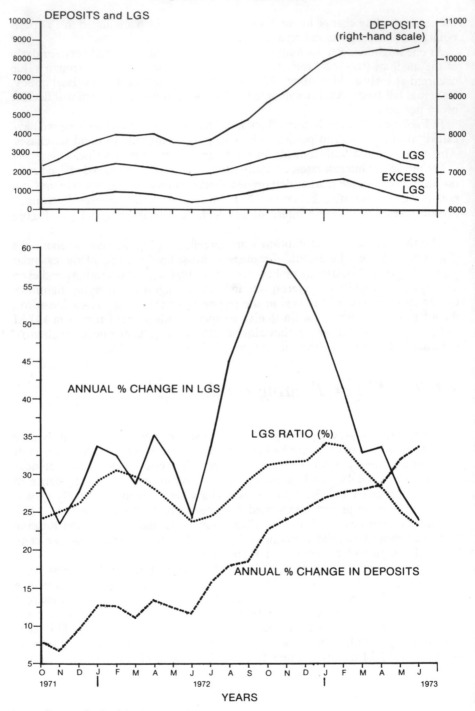

*Source:* Reserve Bank of Australia, Statistical Bulletin

Figure 8.5    Trading bank new lending and limits

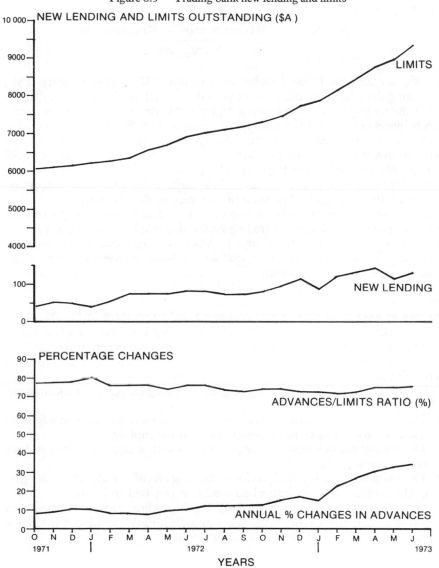

*Source:* Reserve Bank of Australia, Statistical Bulletin

cent – a rate that was not significantly different from that ruling at the onset of expansion in October 1971. If we define the amplitude of the growth rate over a certain period as

$$\frac{\text{Amplitude}}{\text{growth rate}} \equiv \frac{\text{Maximum rate} - \text{Minimum rate}}{\text{Average rate}}$$

the result for the period from October 1971 to June 1973 is close to unity. This, considering the relative shortness of the period involved, is a large figure. Plainly, even if the trading banks did possess a highly stable demand function for excess LGS holdings or net free LGS holdings, they would have faced a very formidable problem in adjusting earning assets speedily enough to preserve their desired portfolio allocation. As it is, the sharp expansion in the growth rate of LGS holdings, the relatively slow response of deposits and the persistence of rising rates of deposit growth after February 1973 all support the earlier judgement that there is a strongly lagged adjustment on the part of the trading banks.

In considering the behaviour of advances – the trading banks' principal earning asset – we need to recall that the trading banks' decision variables are in practice new lending and cancellations (of limits). Data on cancellations are not available for the period before July 1972. New lending did, however, respond quite rapidly to the Reserve Bank's expansionary stance, and by mid-1972 it was running at a rate roughly twice that of October 1971. The rate of growth in advances, by contrast, did not accelerate very markedly until 1972.III, while the ratio of advances to limits (the usage ratio) declined from 80 per cent in October 1971 to 73 per cent in January–February 1973. Not very surprisingly, when policy shifted to mild restraint in February 1973, the usage ratio began to rise, and the rate of growth in advances roughly doubled over the January 1973 figure to reach nearly 35 per cent in June 1973 (see Figure 8.5).

This examination of the main trading-bank aggregates serves to confirm our earlier findings:

(1) The Reserve Bank seems to experience little technical difficulty in adjusting the LGS growth rates to its policy stance quite rapidly.[4]

(2) The trading banks adjust to changes in LGS with a lag, which may or may not be fairly stable.[5]

(3) The existence of a lag partly reflects the absence of the ability on the part of the trading banks to control advances, as opposed to limits.

The overall consequence is a fairly long lag in trading bank adjustment – a circumstance that must reduce the short run flexibility, in all but a narrow technical sense, of some forms of monetary policy.

## 8.5 Other Financial Institutions

The data on instalment credit by finance companies is not easy to interpret because of changes in definition among the subaggregates. The main data that are available, i.e. data for amounts financed, is given in Table 8.3. The break in

**Table 8.3** *Instalment credit: finance companies, 1971–3*
*(amounts financed, $A million)*

| Year/month | | Retail finance | Total[a] |
|---|---|---|---|
| 1971 | Oct. | 94.7 | 209.6 |
| | Nov. | 100.9 | 222.8 |
| | Dec. | 104.2 | 251.4 |
| 1972 | Jan. | 80.0 | 178.0 |
| | Feb. | 83.8 | 198.2 |
| | Mar. | 94.0 | 241.2 |
| | Apr. | 82.1 | 206.8 |
| | May | 101.0 | 242.3 |
| | Jun. | 90.9 | 303.2 |
| | Jul. | 91.7 | 251.3 |
| | Aug. | 94.6 | 259.6 |
| | Sep. | 91.6 | 271.6 |
| | Oct. | 103.5 | 276.4 |
| | Nov. | 106.4 | 322.9 |
| | Dec. | 101.8 | 332.4 |
| 1973 | Jan. | 96.3 | 277.8 |
| | Feb. | 89.0 | 305.7 |
| | Mar. | 102.8 | 381.7 |
| | Apr. | 91.4 | 327.6 |
| | May | 120.9 | 410.5 |
| | Jun. | 103.9 | 467.1 |

[a] Instalment credit for retail sales plus other consumers and commercial loans.
*Note*: — indicates break in series.
*Source*: Reserve Bank of Australia, *Statistical Bulletin: Finance Companies.*

the series occurs at the end of June 1972. Because of series breaks as well as the rather noisy nature of the monthly data, annual growth rates are not presented.

The rate of lending for retail finance – the single continuous series – showed no identifiable response to the stance of monetary policy, save perhaps a somewhat paradoxical tendency to expand after the shift to mild restraint in February 1973. On the other hand, other consumer and commercial loans clearly did grow fairly markedly from October 1971 through June 1972. Comparing July 1972 with June 1973 on the basis of the new definitions adopted by the Commonwealth statistician, it is plain that this expansion continued at, if anything, a slightly higher rate and was not reduced by the shift to mild restraint in February 1973.

## Table 8.4 Finance for housing, 1971–3

| Year/month/quarter | | Savings banks and major Life offices | | PBS[a] | Total | Finance companies | Mortgage rate NSW[b] | Mortgage rate PBS[a] | Deposit rate of PBS[a] |
| | | Savings banks $Am | Total $Am | $Am | $Am | $Am | % | % | % |
|---|---|---|---|---|---|---|---|---|---|
| 1971 Oct. | IV | 49·1 | 75·9 | 53·7 | 129·6 | n.a. | 11·2 | 8·1 | 6·6 |
| Nov. | | 50·1 | 75·2 | 57·1 | 132·3 | n.a. | | | |
| Dec. | | 55·5 | 81·5 | 52·5 | 134·0 | n.a. | | | |
| 1972 Jan. | I | 49·2 | 78·2 | 43·9 | 122·1 | n.a. | 11·3 | 8·1 | 6·6 |
| Feb. | | 54·1 | 93·6 | 55·7 | 149·3 | n.a. | | | |
| Mar. | | 63·9 | 112·5 | 58·2 | 170·7 | n.a. | | | |
| Apr. | II | 55·5 | 95·3 | 53·0 | 148·3 | n.a. | 10·8 | 7·9 | 6·5 |
| May | | 70·1 | 118·4 | 69·1 | 187·5 | n.a. | | | |
| Jun. | | 58·5 | 98·9 | 70·2 | 169·1 | n.a. | | | |
| Jul. | III | 61·5 | 104·1 | 79·5 | 183·6 | 63·3 | 10·6 | 7·9 | 6·5 |
| Aug. | | 67·6 | 119·6 | 92·9 | 212·5 | 69·7 | | | |
| Sep. | | 66·8 | 111·8 | 106·1 | 217·9 | 71·5 | | | |
| Oct. | IV | 69·8 | 122·4 | 108·6 | 231·0 | 70·4 | 10·5 | 8·0 | 6·5 |
| Nov. | | 90·4 | 111·5 | 117·3 | 228·8 | 76·5 | | | |
| Dec. | | 72·9 | 118·0 | 93·9 | 211·9 | 83·0 | | | |
| 1973 Jan. | I | 88·2 | 160·0 | 95·6 | 255·6 | 67·3 | 10·6 | 8·0 | 6·5 |
| Feb. | | 97·3 | 163·3 | 112·2 | 275·5 | 82·4 | | | |
| Mar. | | 110·6 | 184·5 | 128·8 | 313·3 | 106·6 | | | |
| Apr. | II | 98·9 | 161·2 | 78·4 | 239·6 | 94·3 | 10·6 | 7·8 | 6·2 |
| May | | 127·1 | 228·3 | 77·8 | 306·1 | 128·5 | | | |
| Jun. | | 125·4 | 209·8 | 53·2 | 263·0 | 137·6 | | | |

[a] PBS = permanent building societies.
[b] NSW rate = rate on private first mortgages registered in New South Wales.

Sources:
(1) For loans approved: Reserve Bank of Australia, Statistical Bulletin: Finance for Housing and Finance Companies.
(2) For interest rates: Reserve Bank of Australia, Statistical Bulletin; and Australian Bureau of Statistics, Monthly Review of Business Statistics.

**Table 8.5** *New capital raisings and share prices, 1971–3 (Sydney share price index,[a] 1966–7 = 100)*

| Year/month/quarter | Share price index[a] Monthly | Quarterly | New capital raisings ($A m.) Equity | Other | Total | Listed companies[b] ($A m.) |
|---|---|---|---|---|---|---|
| 1971 Oct. | 132·5 | | | | | |
| Nov. IV | 127·3 | 134 | 80·4 | 209·5 | 289·9 | 227·2 |
| Dec. | 141·4 | | | | | |
| 1972 Jan. | 151·3 | | | | | |
| Feb. I | 156·9 | 160 | 60·0 | 144·8 | 204·8 | 240·2 |
| Mar. | 170·3 | | | | | |
| Apr. | 174·2 | | | | | |
| May II | 175·7 | 179 | 86·2 | 143·2 | 234·4 | 226·6 |
| Jun. | 187·2 | | | | | |
| Jul. | 178·6 | | | | | |
| Aug. III | 180·6 | 178 | 50·0 | 141·3 | 191·3 | 148·0 |
| Sep. | 174·8 | | | | | |
| Oct. | 176·3 | | | | | |
| Nov. IV | 182·9 | 182 | 82·2 | 164·9 | 247·1 | 180·4 |
| Dec. | 186·2 | | | | | |
| 1973 Jan. | 190·4 | | | | | |
| Feb. I | 179·0 | 182 | 51·6 | 153·6 | 205·2 | 234·3 |
| Mar. | 175·8 | | | | | |
| Apr. | 167·6 | | | | | |
| May II | 165·2 | 168 | 75·7 | 193·8 | 269·5 | 260·1 |
| Jun. | 172·1 | | | | | |
| Jul. | 171·7 | | | | | |
| Aug. III | 166·7 | 162 | 77·0 | 345·5 | 422·5 | 352·0 |
| Sep. | 147·7 | | | | | |
| Oct. | 145·6 | | | | | |
| Nov. IV | 144·5 | 141 | 105·7 | 478·9 | 584·6 | 437·8 |
| Dec. | 132·7 | | | | | |

[a] All ordinaries.
[b] Seasonally adjusted data.
*Source:* Reserve Bank of Australia, *Statistical Bulletin.*

The pattern in housing finance, excluding finance company lending, is broadly similar, with lending beginning to expand fairly sharply in 1972.II and continuing its expansion until 1973.II (see Table 8.4). In general there was no marked shift in the structure of housing finance. From October 1971 lending by permanent building societies had risen by 132 per cent by March 1973; the corresponding figure for savings banks was 125 per cent and for savings banks and major life offices 143 per cent. The overall lending expansion in the same period, again excluding finance companies, was 139 per cent. In short, the expansion in housing finance was more or less equally distributed between the major lending institutions.

This suggests that it reflected general monetary conditions rather than a marked shift in the private sector's asset preferences in favour of savings banks or permanent building societies. In these circumstances it seems reasonable to attribute it, at least in large measure, to the monetary expansion.

New capital raisings made no appreciable response to the expansionary monetary policy. Indeed, the main increase in the rate of new raisings accrued after February 1973, when policy had shifted from expansion to mild restraint. This, as we see when examining the main demand components, is not entirely surprising, since apart from housing gross private fixed investment fell in real terms by about 10 per cent. What is perhaps rather more surprising is that the growth in the rate of new raisings took place when equity prices were falling. However, the expansion occurred primarily in debt issues (see Table 8.5).

The overall judgement must be that if – and it is a large 'if' – new raisings responded to monetary expansion at all, they did so only with a lag approaching eight quarters. On the other hand, equity prices began to recover one quarter after the policy change and peaked in 1973.I, when policy was reversed. By this time they had risen by nearly 36 per cent, which must have ensured a substantial wealth effect.

# 8.6 Aggregate Demand, the Labour Market and the Rate of Price Change

As we know, the cyclical peak came in 1973.II. At this date GDP at constant 1966–7 prices was roughly 10 per cent above its value in 1971.II – the quarter in which monetary expansion began. Private consumption expanded rather faster than this (12.8 per cent), and expenditure on durables expanded faster still (16.5 per cent). By contrast, gross private investment in fixed capital rose by only 1 per cent. The fact that it did not fall was entirely due to the expansion of investment in dwellings, which rose by 21.5 per cent. Both the remaining elements in gross private investment in fixed capital fell, other building and

**Table 8.6** *Main demand components, 1971–3 (seasonally adjusted data, $A million at 1966–7 prices)*

| Year/quarter | Private consumption | | Gross private fixed investment | | | | Change in non-farm stocks | GDP |
|---|---|---|---|---|---|---|---|---|
| | Total | Durables[a] | Total | Dwellings | building and construction | Other | | |
| 1971 I | 4,299 | 544 | 1,288 | 332 | 314 | 642 | 80 | 7,138 |
| II | 4,317 | 534 | 1,269 | 339 | 306 | 625 | 41 | 7,117 |
| III | 4,434 | 581 | 1,304 | 350 | 312 | 642 | −3 | 7,340 |
| IV | 4,442 | 553 | 1,269 | 357 | 286 | 626 | 58 | 7,339 |
| 1972 I | 4,464 | 539 | 1,198 | 349 | 275 | 575 | 0 | 7,295 |
| II | 4,535 | 549 | 1,246 | 381 | 256 | 608 | −32 | 7,397 |
| III | 4,617 | 555 | 1,224 | 380 | 255 | 589 | −26 | 7,459 |
| IV | 4,717 | 578 | 1,214 | 383 | 249 | 582 | −43 | 7,627 |
| 1973 I | 4,791 | 608 | 1,242 | 403 | 238 | 602 | −27 | 7,812 |
| II | 4,870 | 622 | 1,284 | 412 | 251 | 621 | 34 | 7,844 |

[a] Household durables plus motor vehicles.
*Source:* Australian Bureau of Statistics, *Quarterly Estimates of National Income and Expenditure.*

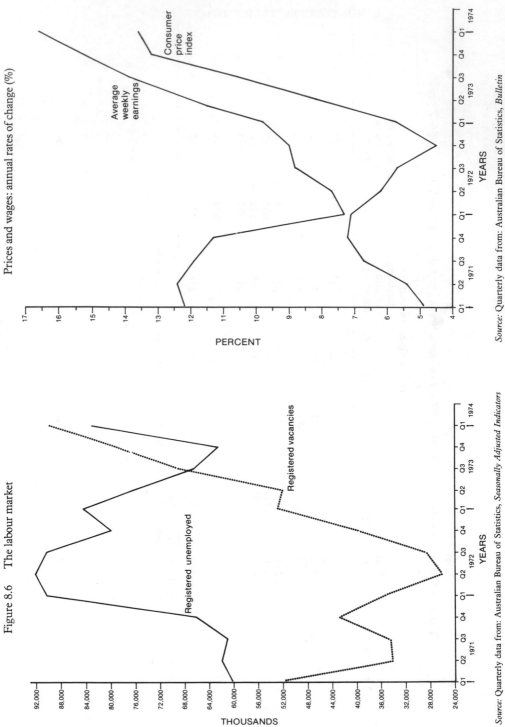

Figure 8.6   The labour market

THOUSANDS

Registered unemployed

Registered vacancies

Q1 Q2 Q3 Q4 | Q1 Q2 Q3 Q4 | Q1 Q2 Q3 Q4 | Q1
1971          1972          1973          1974
YEARS

*Source:* Quarterly data from: Australian Bureau of Statistics, *Seasonally Adjusted Indicators*

Prices and wages: annual rates of change (%)

Average
weekly
earnings

Consumer
price
index

PERCENT

Q1 Q2 Q3 Q4 | Q1 Q2 Q3 Q4 | Q1 Q2 Q3 Q4 | Q1
1971          1972          1973          1974
YEARS

*Source:* Quarterly data from: Australian Bureau of Statistics, *Bulletin*

construction quite sharply (18 per cent). The change in the rate of change of non-farm inventories is notoriously difficult to interpret in this way; but if we compare the average of 1971.II and III with the average of 1973.I and II, the change appears small (see Table 8.6).

The contribution of monetary expansion to this process can, apart from a simulation, only be assessed extremely roughly. If, however, we credit monetary expansion with the whole of the increase in investment in dwellings and the bulk of the increase in expenditure on durables, this amounts to some $A160 million at 1966–7 prices, or about 2 per cent of GDP over two years. To these there should probably be added some unobservable reduction in the fall in the other two components of gross private fixed investment. Since share prices followed the curve of monetary expansion very closely, wealth effects must have been considerable. This assessment may therefore not be too wide of the mark. It then follows that the bulk of the stimulus came from the export boom and the expansion of government expenditure. Monetary expansion simply accompanied and intensified a boom originating in the public sector and overseas, and in doing so it may have added (say) some $1^1/_2$ per cent to total demand, the greater part of which developed after 1972.I, i.e. with a discrete lag of approximately two quarters from the initial policy change.[6]

Cyclically, the labour market is a lagging indicator. Hence, unemployment continued to rise until 1972.III. After that it fell sharply, registered vacancies rose sharply, and there was a rapid expansion in civilian employment. Indeed, in terms of the labour market, the reversal of conditions was exceptionally rapid (see Figure 8.6).

The rate of change in wage earnings showed a slight acceleration in 1972–3. This, however, was more than offset by the growth in productivity that typically accompanies cyclical upswings. Hence, labour costs rose no faster in 1972–3 than in 1970–1 and rose more slowly than in the second half of 1971–2. The rate of change of prices, however, did accelerate in the last two quarters of 1972–3, partly because of the sharp rise in the price of exportables and partly because the effects of the appreciation of the Australian dollar in December 1972 seem to have been absorbed by the end of 1973.I. It seems unlikely that domestic demand factors played any major role in this acceleration (see Figure 8.7).

## 8.7 The Balance of Payments

Our main concern with the balance of payments is the behaviour of the capital account, in particular of private capital movements (see Table 8.7). This is because, as argued earlier, the ability of the Reserve Bank to conduct an independent monetary policy depends crucially on how closely the Australian money and capital markets are integrated with corresponding markets overseas. Theoretically, if integration is close to complete and portfolio behaviour both at

**Table 8.7** *Balance of payments, 1971–4 ($A million)*

| Year/quarter | | Current account | | | Capital account | | Change in official reserves |
|---|---|---|---|---|---|---|---|
| | | Exports | Imports | Balance | Official | Private[a] | |
| 1971 | I | 993 | 909 | −241 | 26 | 478 | 343 |
| | II | 1,152 | 981 | −173 | −23 | 576 | 426 |
| | III | 1,185 | 1,047 | −169 | 8 | 426 | 256 |
| | IV | 1,112 | 987 | −233 | −10 | 505 | 251 |
| 1972 | I | 1,154 | 913 | −65 | 1 | 424 | 453 |
| | II | 1,275 | 845 | 56 | −59 | 558 | 585 |
| | III | 1,316 | 893 | 116 | 43 | 501 | 649 |
| | IV | 1,486 | 940 | 191 | 14 | 440 | 662 |
| 1973 | I | 1,629 | 960 | 264 | −58 | −505 | −327 |
| | II | 1,504 | 1,016 | 68 | −63 | 87 | 95 |
| | III | 1,602 | 1,234 | −22 | 79 | −74 | −9 |
| | IV | 1,729 | 1,302 | 27 | −11 | −22 | 12 |
| 1974 | I | 1,624 | 1,472 | −259 | −10 | 85 | −181 |

[a] Including the balancing item, undistributed income, marketing authorities and non-official monetary-sector transactions.
*Source:* Reserve Bank of Australia, *Statistical Bulletin.*

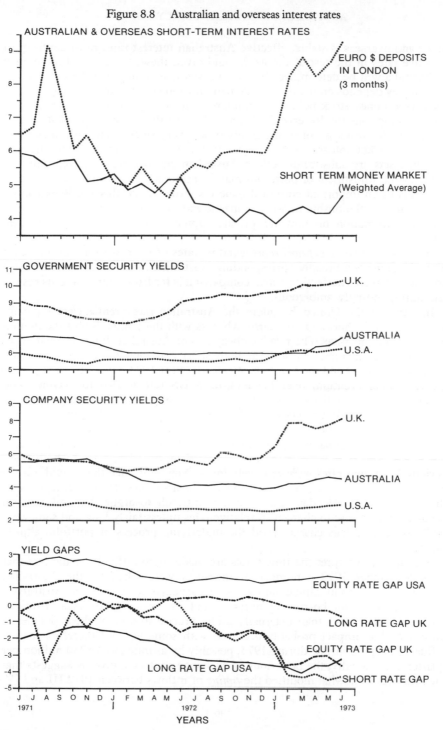

Figure 8.8    Australian and overseas interest rates

AUSTRALIAN & OVERSEAS SHORT-TERM INTEREST RATES

EURO $ DEPOSITS
IN LONDON
(3 months)

SHORT TERM MONEY MARKET
(Weighted Average)

GOVERNMENT SECURITY YIELDS

U.K.

AUSTRALIA
U.S.A.

COMPANY SECURITY YIELDS

U.K.

AUSTRALIA

U.S.A.

YIELD GAPS

EQUITY RATE GAP USA

LONG RATE GAP UK

EQUITY RATE GAP UK

LONG RATE GAP USA

SHORT RATE GAP

J J A S O N D J F M A M J J A S O N D J F M A M J
1971            1972            1973

YEARS

*Sources:*
Reserve Bank of Australia, *Statistical Bulletin*; Financial Supplement, October 1975 (Government
Security Yields)
Bank of England, Quarterly Bulletin (F.T. – Actuaries, Industrial Ordinary Shares)
Survey of Current Business (Moody's – Industrial Common Stocks)
Melbourne Stock Exchange: Dividend Yield: 50 Leading Companies

home and overseas is stable, effective Australian interest rates must conform to effective rates in the rest of the world, and given these, the demand for money in Australia will be determined. In such a system, assuming that the demand for base money depends on the public's demand for money, the Reserve Bank cannot conduct a money stock policy, or an interest rate policy. Indeed, in the limit of these assumptions the Reserve Bank can only vary the composition of its assets.

Clearly, Australia is not in the position of a very small financially-integrated country. Market integration is not complete;[7] and in so far as domestic and foreign assets are substitutes both to Australian and overseas portfolio holders, the dynamic adjustment of portfolios may be rather a slow business. It nevertheless remains an important empirical issue just how far the Reserve Bank can go in varying the relationship between domestic and foreign rates. We therefore need reliable information on how far private capital flows are responsive to rate differences.[8]

In Figure 8.8 some *a priori* representative rates of interest ruling overseas are plotted against the broadly corresponding Australian rates. Since overseas rates are not themselves perfectly related, comparison is far from simple, and its results are correspondingly ambiguous.

In terms of the United Kingdom the Australian rate premia were typically negative at both short and long term, whereas with the United States the premia were typically positive. The relative cheapness of Australian funds in relation to the UK funds increased steadily at both short and long term throughout the calendar year 1972 and the first half of calendar year 1973. Over the same period the Australian premium over the long-term US rate tended to decline. The behaviour of the relative equity rates is rather less clear-cut. Broadly speaking, however, the overall tendency was for Australian funds to become relatively cheaper throughout 1972 and early 1973.

By contrast, the apparent private capital inflow was very considerable throughout 1971 and 1972. A sharp reversal occurred in 1973.I and II. In both these periods Australian rates were relatively low – a circumstance that would, on the usual arguments, promote outflows and diminish inflows. However, in view of the experience of calendar year 1972 it is difficult to argue that this reversal occurred in response to changes in relative rates unless fairly long and somewhat oddly structured lags characterised the underlying process of portfolio adjustment.

Attempts to interpret the time series are made more difficult by the fact that from September 1972 a number of measures were taken by the Australian authorities to contain capital inflows – in particular to discourage Australian-resident firms from borrowing overseas and to encourage overseas firms to borrow locally rather than externally.[9] The precise impact of these policies is uncertain. The impact probably occurred with some lag and therefore mainly influenced capital inflow during 1973, possibly by as much as $A230 million per quarter. Additionally, the behaviour of exchange control approvals suggests that the measures somewhat modified the *timing* of inflows between 1972.III and IV.

In 1972.IV there was undoubtedly an inflow due to the expectation of a change in the exchange rate. The Reserve Bank's overbought forward position rose sharply. So did the balance-of-payments residual. In December the Australian dollar was appreciated, formally by just under 5 per cent but effectively by just over 7 per cent. Predictably, the result was a sharp outflow as speculators took their profits. Speculation *against* the US dollar became important in January 1973. Reserve Bank net new forward purchases rose sharply again towards the end of January. The US dollar was devalued in February, and the Australian dollar did not follow. Thus, from December the Australian dollar rose from 1.191 US dollars to 1.417 US dollars – an appreciation of 19 per cent relative to the US dollar.

In view of this rather complex set of short run and speculative influences the time series are extraordinarily hard to interpret. Because of this it is difficult to do more than guess at the response of private capital inflows to the fall in Australian rates. Indeed, even guessing is difficult, since the change in private capital movements was in general not closely related to the direction of Australian rate changes. Hence, the only sensible judgement is probably that the interest policy of the Reserve Bank must have had small influence over the period under review, compared with the shifts in exchange rate expectations, exchange control policy and exogenous factors. However, this judgement is necessarily very tentative, and we review this problem again in a later chapter.

## 8.8 *Monetary Policy and Expansion*

The quantitative interpretation of time series is, as we have repeatedly stressed, a most hazardous undertaking. It does seem, however, that the monetary expansion did make an appreciable impact on GDP over the two years from 1971.II – an impact of some 1.5 – 1.75 per cent. This suggests that monetary expansion was roughly of the same quantitative importance as fiscal policy – or perhaps of marginally smaller quantitative importance than fiscal policy – in providing a domestic stimulus over the two-year period. Certainly, there is no suggestion that the Reserve Bank was 'pushing on a string'.

Clearly, with hindsight the timing of both fiscal and monetary policy shifts was ill judged. We do not know, but it seems more than probable that the authorities' apparent errors of timing and stance arose in large measure out of forecasting failures on the one hand and an incorrect interpretation of labour market data on the other. Certainly, the period and, more particularly, its aftermath tended to emphasise the difficulties of fine tuning and the risks unavoidably related to attempts to fine tune within narrow limits.

The expansion of 1971–3 was followed, as we shall see, by a period of severe restraint. This entailed a very sharp reversal of policy and a consequently dramatic change in the rate of expansion in the banking base and the LGS base.

Indeed, this reversal was so severe that it led to a short period of financial instability in which the Reserve Bank had to take extraordinary steps to relieve certain institutions and certain markets and thus to forestall the emergence of a financial crisis.

We may thus argue that 1971–5 demonstrated that the so-called 'flexibility' of monetary policy is largely an illusion. It is, of course, true that monetary policy is technically flexible, in the sense that the rate of growth in LGS holdings can be quite rapidly reduced or increased. The same argument holds with respect to nominal interest rates. The economic impacts of relatively draconic changes of this type do not, however, occur all that quickly; and – what is more important – sharp reversals of monetary policy, by running the risk of promoting a financial crisis that may easily be cumulative, put at risk the stability of the very financial structure through which the Reserve Bank must influence the economy and which it is any central bank's primary duty to preserve.

In short, 1971–4 confirmed that the technical flexibility of monetary policy does not imply the ready reversibility of its economic impacts. This is, of course, a familiar story. It also suggests that any attempt to enforce economic flexibility may soon run into the constraint imposed by the need to preserve the institutional structure; but this too is not an unfamiliar finding from US experience.

## Notes: Chapter 8

1   The process of easing the fiscal stance began in December. The mini-budget of April 1972 continued the easing by *inter alia* reducing the income tax levy from 5 per cent to $2^1/_2$ per cent.
2   There were downward adjustments to the Treasury note rate in January, November and December 1972. Trading bank interest rates were reduced in February 1972.
3   The Reserve Bank attempted to reduce the lag in the trading banks' response to the policy shift by removing all restraints on lending and deliberately operating so as to raise already fairly high LGS ratios. The object of the latter exercise was stated to be the reduction of uncertainty.
4   Australia's buoyant external position made this task technically simple over the period under discussion.
5   Direct evidence on this issue is scanty. Cf. Terrell and Valentine [160].
6   That is, it may have added to demand at a rate slightly in excess of 0.75 per cent per annum. This estimate, which is probably on the high side, is by no means negligible.
7   The Reserve Bank, in its *Annual Report, 1970–1* and *1971–2*, has emphasised the growing integration of domestic and overseas financial markets and also the very considerable development of the domestic financial structure. A similar view occurs in Snape [154].
8   We discuss this issue more fully in later chapters.
9   In December 1972 the Australian dollar was appreciated. At the same time the coverage of the existing embargo (introduced in September 1972) on certain forms of borrowing was extended and the VDR introduced. The embargo was broadened again in February 1973. In July 1973 there was a general (25 per cent) cut in tariff rates and September 1973 a further (5 per cent) appreciation in the Australian dollar.

*Chapter 9*

# Monetary Restraint in 1973–4

## 9.1 *Introduction*

Our *ex ante* dating of Reserve Bank policy for the cycle from the trough of 1972.I to the trough of (say) 1975.III is set out in Figure 9.1. According to this dating the Reserve Bank shifted from expansion to mild restraint (as defined on p. 000) in 1973.II[1]. This was only one quarter before the cyclical peak, as measured by the index of industrial production. Moreover, the change in stance occurred after unemployment had been falling sharply for more than six months and unfilled vacancies rising even more sharply for rather longer.

In 1973.III mild restraint gave way to restraint. This was precisely the quarter in which the cycle peak in industrial production occurred.

The subsequent cycle trough is not easy to identify. It can be placed in either 1975.III or IV. The last date corresponds very closely with the Reserve Bank's shift from a policy of expansion, introduced in 1974.IV during the cyclical downswing, to a policy of restraint – a policy maintained until 1976.IV, when in early November it was intensified despite the rather weak recovery in economic activity and the developing political pressures for action that would expand domestic demand and, in particular, for a devaluation of the Australian dollar.

Examined against the background of the approximate cyclical dating, the timing of these policy shifts is unusual. For example, the shift to restraint came

199

Figure 9.1    Policy stance and principal actions, 1971-6

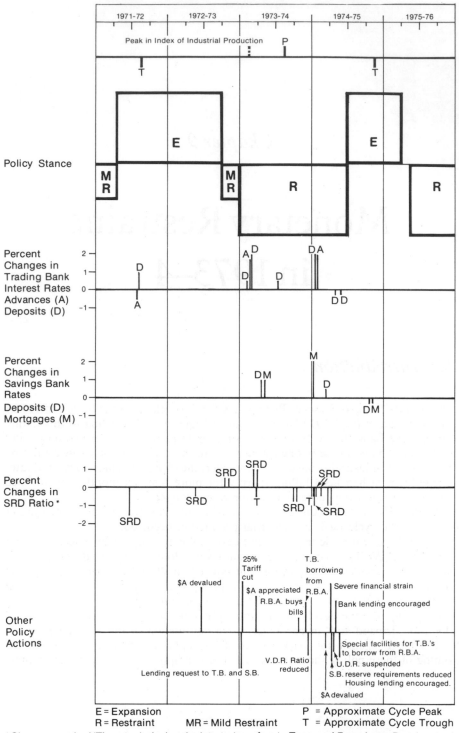

E = Expansion                                           P = Approximate Cycle Peak
R = Restraint          MR = Mild Restraint             T = Approximate Cycle Trough

*Changes marked 'T' are technical and relate to transfers to Term and Farm Loan Development
  Funds.

*Source:* Reserve Bank of Australia, *Annual Reports and Statistical Bulletin*

some two quarters before our estimate of the overall cycle peak and coincided with the cyclical peak in industrial production – a circumstance that suggests either a failure in forecasting or a shift in policy objectives. Again, the shift from restraint to expansion did not occur until roughly a year after the cycle peak. By then unemployment had already risen very sharply, and registered vacancies had fallen to very low levels compared with 1973–4, when the labour market was admittedly overheated. In the same way the intensification of restraint in November 1976 appears at first sight surprising, since it came at a time when the government was increasingly under criticism for the (unexpectedly) weak recovery.

This apparently inappropriate timing is, however, less inappropriate than it appears. The recovery from the relatively shallow trough of 1972.1 was, as seen in Chapter 8, not only unusually rapid but also accompanied by unprecedented rates of monetary expansion. The upswing was the shortest of any of Australia's post war cycles and was considerably aided by a continuing rise in export prices and receipts, which produced a large current-account surplus in 1972–3 and the first half of 1973–4. The monetary effects of this surplus were buttressed, in the first half of 1972–3, by a high rate of private capital inflow. It seems probable that the speed of this short upswing was not well forecast by the authorities and that, in consequence of this and of the difficulty in offsetting the monetary impact of the buoyant external position,[2] the move to restraint was made at a date that now, with full benefit of hindsight, appears to have been too late.

The persistence with restraint well into the downswing is explicable in terms of a shift in the relative weighting of the employment and price stability objectives of the authorities in favour of the latter. It is this shift, together with an increasing concern to use monetary policy as a means of controlling the capital account of the balance of payments and thus avoiding an unwelcome, inflationary and largely ineffective devaluation of the Australian dollar, that explains the reintroduction of restraint at approximately a cyclical trough and its intensification in November 1976.

In short, the Reserve Bank's *ex ante* policy shifts appear to be quantitatively inappropriate only if it is assumed that economic forecasting in a highly open economy is a relatively simple matter and that discretionary monetary policy is typically to be interpreted as being aimed primarily at the maintenance of low rates of unemployment. Economic experience makes it clear that there is no warrant for the first assumption, while economic theory implies no warrant for the second in a regime of a pegged exchange rate.

Acceptance of the qualitative shifts in policy does not, however, necessarily imply that either the quantitative extent of the policy shifts or the precise timing of the shifts was also broadly correct. This is an issue to which we must and do return later.

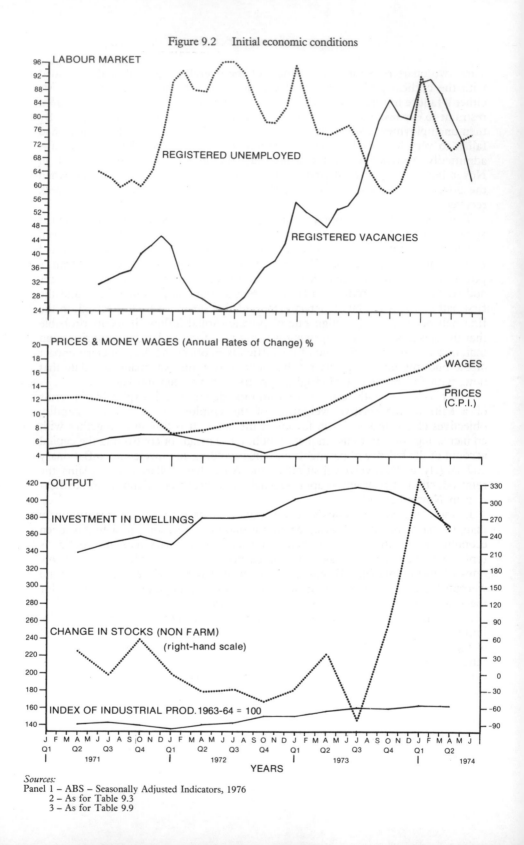

Figure 9.2    Initial economic conditions

LABOUR MARKET

REGISTERED UNEMPLOYED

REGISTERED VACANCIES

PRICES & MONEY WAGES (Annual Rates of Change) %

WAGES

PRICES
(C.P.I.)

OUTPUT

INVESTMENT IN DWELLINGS

CHANGE IN STOCKS (NON FARM)
(right-hand scale)

INDEX OF INDUSTRIAL PROD. 1963-64 = 100

J F M A M J J A S O N D J F M A M J J A S O N D J F M A M J J A S O N D J F M A M J
Q1    Q2    Q3    Q4    Q1    Q2    Q3    Q4    Q1    Q2    Q3    Q4    Q1    Q2
      1971              1972              1973              1974
                              YEARS

*Sources:*
Panel 1 – ABS – Seasonally Adjusted Indicators, 1976
        2 – As for Table 9.3
        3 – As for Table 9.9

## 9.2 The Initial Conditions and Overall Policy

During 1972–3 the Australian economy expanded very rapidly from the relatively shallow cyclical trough of 1972.I. This is made clear in the summary of the initial conditions given in Figure 9.2. This figure shows a rapid fall in unemployment and rise in registered vacancies, which, since the labour market lagged output, points to rapid rates of growth in real GNP in the recent past. Moreover non-farm stocks fell during 1972–3 – a circumstance that suggested that an upturn in planned stock accumulation could not be far away.

The rate of change of prices accelerated somewhat in the second half of 1972–3, mainly due to a very sharp rise in the rate of growth in food prices. Although wage earnings rose rather faster in 1972–3 than in 1971–2, the change was far from dramatic. Moreover, as is commonly the case with sharp expansions in output, apparent productivity per man employed rose at a rate very much faster than the average of recent years. Consequently, labour costs rose by rather less. Nevertheless, since there was every likelihood of the rate of change in wage earnings adjusting to the recent acceleration in the rate of price changes, while there could be no reasonable expectation of a similar rate of increase in productivity, the prospect was for a rising rate of inflation.

The very rapid expansion of 1972–3 was not accompanied by any deterioration in the external position. Australia moved into current account surplus in the last quarter of 1971–2. Export prices rose extremely fast in 1972–3, and the current account surplus grew to a record level in 1973.I. Since private capital inflow in 1972.III and IV remained at close to the average level for 1971–2, the overall surplus in the first half of 1972–3 was extremely large. In the second half of the year, partly as a result of official action – including an appreciation in December of the Australian dollar by a formal percentage of 4.85 and an actual percentage of just over 7 – a capital outflow developed. After the devaluation of the US dollar in February 1973, which Australia did not follow – but which increased the appreciation of the Australian dollar against the US dollar to nearly 19 per cent – the outflow continued. Nevertheless, for 1972–3 as a whole there was still a net capital inflow of roughly $A500 million.[3] Since the current balance, although deteriorating, remained favourable, over 1972–3 Australia gained some $A1,100 million of reserves. Thus, at the beginning of 1973–4 Australia possessed extremely high reserves, much of the short term unwinding of speculative positions taken in anticipation of parity changes had been completed, the authorities could contemplate, without any serious anxiety, a considerable rise in the import bill and even a sizable loss in reserves during 1973–4 (see Table 9.1).

The change in fiscal policy between 1972–3 and 1971–2 had been extremely expansionary. According to the full-employment budget calculation the change in fiscal stance added some $A720 million to demand – something rather below 2 per cent of GNP. This is in fairly close agreement with Nevile's estimate, which gives the change in the first-round fiscal impact as 2 per cent of non-farm

**Table 9.1** *Balance of payments, 1972–5 ($A million)*

| Year/quarter | | Current account | | | Capital account | | Change in official reserves |
|---|---|---|---|---|---|---|---|
| | | Exports | Imports | Balance | Official | Private[a] | |
| 1972 | I | 1,154 | 913 | −65 | 1 | 424 | 453 |
| | II | 1,275 | 845 | 56 | −59 | 558 | 585 |
| | III | 1,316 | 893 | 116 | 43 | 501 | 649 |
| | IV | 1,486 | 940 | 191 | 14 | 440 | 662 |
| 1973 | I | 1,629 | 960 | 264 | −58 | −505 | −327 |
| | II | 1,504 | 1,016 | 68 | −63 | 87 | 95 |
| | III | 1,602 | 1,234 | −22 | 79 | −74 | −9 |
| | IV | 1,729 | 1,302 | 27 | −11 | −22 | 12 |
| 1974 | I | 1,624 | 1,472 | −259 | −10 | 85 | −181 |
| | II | 1,734 | 1,745 | −557 | −62 | 391 | −206 |
| | III | 1,917 | 2,100 | −627 | −34 | 80 | −587 |
| | IV | 2,165 | 2,087 | −359 | −2 | 227 | −141 |
| 1975 | I | 2,111 | 1,758 | 1 | −22 | 44 | 26 |

[a] Including the balancing item, undistributed income, marketing authorities, and non-official monetary-sector transactions.
*Source:* Reserve Bank of Australia, *Statistical Bulletin.*

**Table 9.2** *Fiscal impact and stance, 1971–5*

| Financial year | Changes in actual deficit | | Changes in full employment deficit | | Nevile's impact effect | |
|---|---|---|---|---|---|---|
| | $A m. | % of NFNP | $A m. | % of NFNP | % of NFNP | Change in % impact |
| 1971–2 | 124 | 0·4 | −100 | −0·3 | 2·9 | −0·1 |
| 1972–3 | 575 | 1·7 | 718 | 2·1 | 4·9 | 2·0 |
| 1973–4 | −416 | −1·1 | −352 | −·9 | 4·2 | −0·7 |
| 1974–5 | 2,274 | 4·9 | 526 | 1·1 | 7·7 | 3·5 |

*Source:* Table 4.1.

205

product. The actual budget, as it must in an expansion, suggested a rather smaller figure for the change, amounting to some $570 million. However, all three indicators are in close agreement, and there can be no doubt that the expansionary shift in fiscal policy in 1972–3 made a major contribution to the upswing (see Table 9.2).

In short, at the end of 1972–3, the economy was close to full capacity, inflation was accelerating both at home and overseas, and the external position was strong.

Given these initial conditions, it seems clear that the authorities' major aim in 1973–4 was to contain the rate of inflation as far as possible. Fortunately, there was no *qualitative* contradiction between the policies implied by this objective and the policies implied by the phase of the Australian cycle. The novelty lay perhaps in the emphasis placed upon the role of imports, not only in meeting domestic demand, but also in providing a direct element of domestic price restraint by competition and in the further discretionary appreciation of the Australian dollar in September 1973 with the aim of insulating the domestic economy from overseas inflation, at least to a limited extent.

Indeed, monetary policy was in 1973–4 an element in an unusually comprehensive package of policies, which included:
(a)  a general (25 per cent) cut in tariff rates;[4]
(b)  a further discretionary appreciation;[5]
(c)  a strengthening of earlier measures to contain net private capital inflow;[6] and
(d)  a marked deflationary shift in fiscal stance.
To this package the Reserve Bank added a strongly restrictive monetary policy.

Clearly, with a policy package of this kind there must always be a risk of overkill. In part this is because of the difficulty of forecasting exogenous variables, e.g. exports, import prices and the exogenous element in private capital flow; but in part it must arise also because new *types* of policy cannot be modelled in the usual way. Their quantitative impact is therefore extremely difficult to forecast.

Of this package, apart perhaps from the tariff cut and the appreciation, all the measures were concerned to influence aggregate demand or, in the case of (c), to enhance the authorities' ability to influence it. Thus, the missing element in a comprehensive anti-inflationary operation was the absence of any complementary wage or incomes stance.[7]

In the event this missing element probably contributed very greatly to the severity of the downturn that occurred after 1973.III and to the continuation of relatively low levels of capacity utilisation and relatively high levels of unemployment; for as shown in Table 9.3, the rate of change in wage earnings was extremely rapid in both nominal *and* real terms. From this table it can be seen that, between the second halves of 1973 and 1974 real wages rose by about 10–11 per cent – roughly three times the typical annual rates of growth. Even if the view is taken that the rate of profit is a largely conventional phenomenon rather than the narrowly defined outcome of an economic process, it is difficult to believe that so rapid a shift could be digested by businessmen without a sharp reduction

**Table 9.3**

*Annual rate of change of money wages and real wages, 1972–5 (%)*

| Year/quarter | | Money wages | Real wages |
|---|---|---|---|
| 1972 | II | 7·7 | 1·5 |
| | III | 8·8 | 3·1 |
| | IV | 9·0 | 4·5 |
| 1973 | I | 9·8 | 4·1 |
| | II | 11·5 | 3·3 |
| | III | 13·9 | 3·3 |
| | IV | 15·3 | 2·1 |
| 1974 | I | 16·6 | 3·0 |
| | II | 19·2 | 4·8 |
| | III | 25·4 | 9·3 |
| | IV | 27·9 | 11·6 |
| 1975 | I | 27·3 | 9·7 |
| | II | 21·7 | 4·8 |

*Source*: Australian Bureau of Statistics, *Bulletin: Average Weekly earnings and Consumer Price Index.*

in planned output and planned investment.

The explanation of this real wage explosion lies outside the scope of this study. In particular we are not concerned with the question of whether the shift was, in an importance sense, domestic or external in origin, i.e. autonomous with respect to external conditions or induced by them. A superficial judgement suggests that perhaps two-thirds of the real wage change may reasonably be regarded as having been autonomous. If this is even roughly correct, domestic wage policy must have contributed largely to the very unsatisfactory outcome of 1974 through 1976.[8]

# 9.3 *Monetary Indicators*

According to our *ex ante* dating, the Reserve Bank shifted its policy stance from ease to mild restraint in 1973.I and from mild restraint to restraint at roughly the end of 1973.III. These datings, together with the main policy actions in each phase of Reserve Bank policy, are set out in Figure 9.3. As usual, two sets of *ex post* indicators of monetary thrust are provided: (a) a group of nominal money-stock concepts; and (b) a subset of interest rates.

From June 1972 to June 1973 all the nominal money-stock concepts reported here had very fast rates of growth: $M_1$ grew by more than 26 per cent; $M_2$ by

Figure 9.3    Policy stance and principal actions, 1971-6

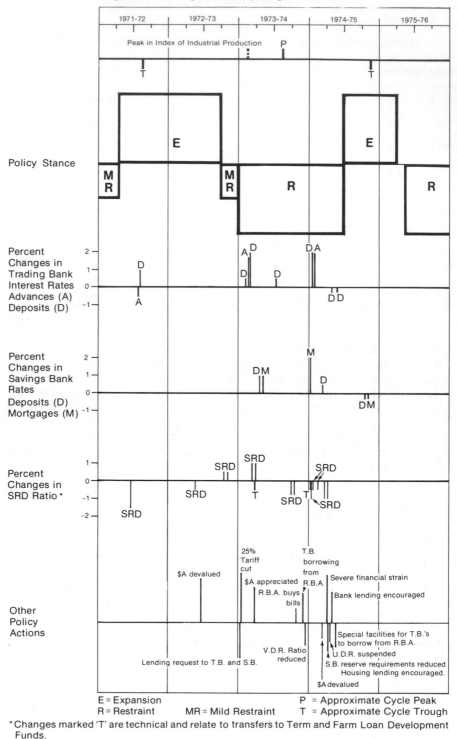

E = Expansion                                      P = Approximate Cycle Peak
R = Restraint          MR = Mild Restraint          T = Approximate Cycle Trough

*Changes marked 'T' are technical and relate to transfers to Term and Farm Loan Development
Funds.

*Source:* Reserve Bank of Australia, *Annual Reports and Statistical Bulletin*

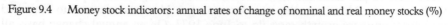

Figure 9.4     Money stock indicators: annual rates of change of nominal and real money stocks (%)

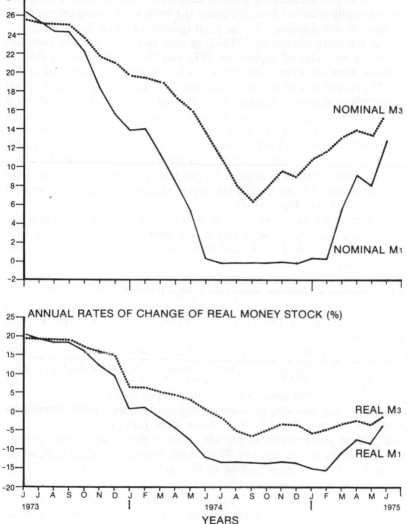

*Source:* Australian Bureau of Statistics, *Seasonally Adjusted Indicators*

more than 29 per cent; and $M_3$, which includes savings bank deposits, by close to 26 per cent. Moreover, the introduction of mild restraint seems to have had no impact on these growth rates up to June 1973. On an annual change basis all three series experienced accelerating growth rates over 1972–3; while if monthly changes (in seasonally adjusted data) are made the basis of the comparison, there is no clear sign of any slowdown in the final quarter of 1972–3.

However, in the early months of 1973–4, growth rates stabilised or even fell slightly. After the measures of September 1973 and the Reserve Bank's shift to restraint, growth rates fell even more rapidly. The fall in the growth rate of $M_1$ from nearly 25 per cent annual rate in September 1973 to only 1 per cent by June 1974 was particularly dramatic. The fall in the rates of growth of $M_2$ and $M_3$ were less severe, although the growth rate of $M_3$ was roughly halved between August 1973 and June 1974 and that of $M_2$ reduced by about one-third. Since prices were rising faster in 1973–4 than in 1972–3, the impact on the implied rates of growth in *real* balances was even more severe. For example, in the last quarter of 1972–3 $M_1$ was in real terms growing at around 16 per cent per annum; by June 1974 it was *falling* at around 12 per cent. This rate of decline accelerated to around 16 per cent in 1975.I (see Figure 9.4).

In short, as Figure 9.4 shows, in nominal terms – and even more in real terms – the money stock indicators display a very severe swing in monetary thrust, with the rates of growth in nominal stocks reflecting the authorities' policy shift with a relatively short lag.

The interest rate indicators, in nominal terms, tell an essentially similar, and in some cases even more dramatic, story (see Figure 9.5).[9] Broadly speaking, rates fell during the first three quarters of 1972–3 and began to rise shortly after the introduction of mild restraint. During 1973–4 the rise, in nominal terms, became very rapid indeed.

In the period from June 1973 to June 1974 the changes were:
(a) Treasury notes rose by 566 basis points (nearly 110 per cent);
(b) short bonds rose by 474 basis points (some 78 per cent); and
(c) long bonds rose by 250 basis points (some 36 per cent).
These changes, not surprisingly, produced a negatively sloped yield curve, with shorts enjoying a premium over longs of more than 1.25 per cent.

The same pattern was repeated in private sector interest rates, where the rise in rates was commonly of the order of 70 per cent. Indeed the NCD rate, which was freed from its Reserve Bank ceiling in September 1973, rose from slightly above 6 per cent to over 17 per cent.[10]

Short rates typically peaked at the end of 1973–4 or in the first quarter of 1974–5 and then declined sharply. Medium term and long rates did not in general follow them down. Hence, by the end of 1974–5 the rate curve had resumed a more typical form, with long rates once more above short rates by a margin of the order of 1·5 per cent – 150 basis points.

The Reserve Bank switched its policy from restraint to ease in September–October 1974, and at approximately the same time it took a number of steps to

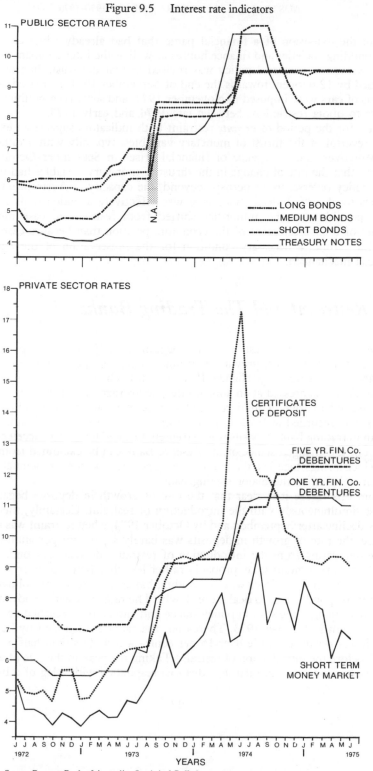

Figure 9.5    Interest rate indicators

PUBLIC SECTOR RATES

N.A.

LONG BONDS
MEDIUM BONDS
SHORT BONDS
TREASURY NOTES

PRIVATE SECTOR RATES

CERTIFICATES
OF DEPOSIT

FIVE YR. FIN. Co.
DEBENTURES

ONE YR. FIN. Co.
DEBENTURES

SHORT TERM
MONEY MARKET

J J A S O N D J F M A M J J A S O N D J F M A M J J A S O N D J F M A M J
1972            1973              1974              1975
YEARS

*Source:* Reserve Bank of Australia, *Statistical Bulletin*

prevent the extension of a financial panic that had already adversely affected some building societies and finance houses as well as the inter company market.[11] At the same time external policy was revised in that the Australian dollar was devalued by 12 per cent towards the end of September 1974, increased tariffs on imports of cars were imposed in November 1974, and some commodities became subject to quota restrictions between late 1974 and early 1975.

Thus, for the period of *ex ante* restraint both indicators suggest an extremely sharp reversal of the thrust of monetary variables, typically with a rather short lag. Moreover, the emergence of financial crises in September–October 1974 suggests that the rate of change in the thrust of monetary variables had probably taken policy reversal to, or perhaps beyond, the capacity of Australia's financial markets to absorb. Indeed, since ease was effectively abandoned in 1975.I, it seems possible that the authorities shifted from restraint to ease much less because of their assessment of the economic position than because ease was, at least for a time, a necessary condition for the preservation of the Australian financial mechanism.

# 9.4 Restraint and The Trading Banks

At the reintroduction of restraint at the beginning of 1973–4 the deposits of the major trading banks were growing at around 34 per cent per annum, on the basis of year-on-year percentage change. If the monthly change in seasonally adjusted deposit data is expressed at an annual rate, the average rate of growth in 1973.II – the second quarter of mild restraint – was over 36 per cent. This was the highest rate recorded in 1972–3. Thus, restraint was introduced when the rate of growth in trading bank deposits was extremely fast and tending to accelerate. The impact of the changed stance of the Reserve Bank can be examined from Figure 9.6, which brings together the main series (and their percentage annual rates of growth) relating to the major trading banks.

From this figure it is clear that the rate of growth in deposits began to fall almost simultaneously with the introduction of restraint. Certainly, there was a steady decline after September; and by October 1974, when restraint was replaced by ease, the rate of growth in deposits was barely 1 per cent per annum. Thus, taking our dating from the introduction of restraint, deposits responded with a lag of up to two months, i.e. probably rather less than half a quarter.

Predictably enough, in view of the trading banks' imprecise control over them, advances responded a good deal more slowly. The rate of growth in advances rose fairly sharply *after* the shift in policy stance and annual basis reached no less than 42·3 per cent in October 1973. Thereafter, the rate declined, and by September 1974 it was down to a little over 16 per cent – a little less than half of the rate ruling before the introduction of restraint.Taking the peak in the rate of advances expansion as our response dating, advances responded with a lag of a little over

Figure 9.6    The trading banks

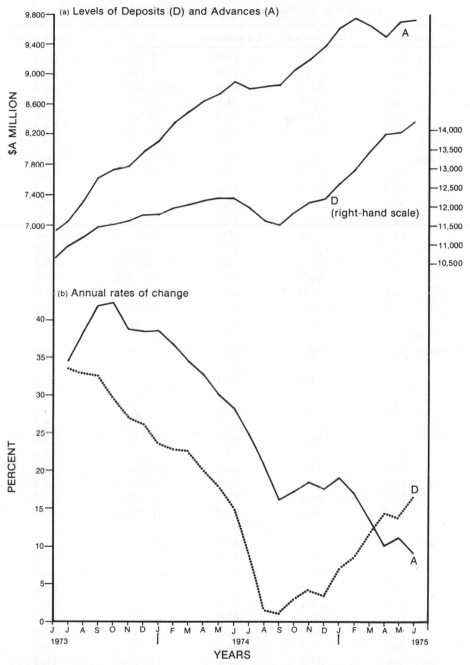

(a) Levels of Deposits (D) and Advances (A)

$A MILLION

9,800
9,400
9,000
8,600
8,200
7,800
7,400
7,000

A

D
(right-hand scale)

14,000
13,500
13,000
12,500
12,000
11,500
11,000
10,500

(b) Annual rates of change

PERCENT

40
35
30
25
20
15
10
5
0

D

A

J J A S O N D J F M A M J J A S O N D J F M A M J
1973                    1974                    1975

YEARS

*Source:* Seasonally adjusted monthly data from: Reserve Bank of Australia, *Statistical Bulletin: Financial Supplement (October 1975)*

**Table 9.4.** *Trading bank lending, 1972–5 ($A million).*

| Year/month | | New lending | Cancellations | Limits | Net new lending |
|---|---|---|---|---|---|
| 1972 | Jul. | 74·2 | 45·9 | 7,023·9 | 28·3 |
| | Aug. | 67·5 | 41·4 | 7,128·7 | 26·1 |
| | Sep. | 67·5 | 51·5 | 7,208·9 | 16·0 |
| | Oct. | 76·1 | 44·9 | 7,333·8 | 31·2 |
| | Nov. | 90·9 | 51·3 | 7,492·2 | 39·6 |
| | Dec. | 105·1 | 47·6 | 7,780·0 | 57·5 |
| | | | | | |
| 1973 | Jan. | 83·2 | 54·1 | 7,896·8 | 29·1 |
| | Feb. | 109·2 | 52·5 | 8,180·6 | 56·7 |
| | Mar. | 122·3 | 48·6 | 8,475·3 | 73·7 |
| | Apr. | 130·0 | 52·0 | 8,787·1 | 78·0 |
| | May | 109·6 | 40·1 | 9,065·1 | 69·5 |
| | Jun. | 123·3 | 68·6 | 9,338·3 | 54·7 |
| | Jul. | 127·2 | 73·0 | 9,427·3 | 54·2 |
| | Aug. | 109·1 | 63·3 | 9,610·5 | 45·8 |
| | Sep. | 99·2 | 63·6 | 9,788·5 | 35·6 |
| | Oct. | 91·0 | 59·5 | 9,914·5 | 31·5 |
| | Nov. | 89·8 | 76·2 | 9,982·9 | 13·6 |
| | Dec. | 86·0 | 60·0 | 10,086·7 | 26·0 |
| | | | | | |
| 1974 | Jan. | 72·3 | 62·7 | 10,125·0 | 9·6 |
| | Feb. | 74·9 | 60·9 | 10,195·1 | 14.0 |
| | Mar. | 91·0 | 75·1 | 10,258·7 | 15·9 |
| | Apr. | 98·0 | 46·8 | 10,463·5 | 51·2 |
| | May | 75·6 | 60·1 | 10,525·6 | 15·5 |
| | Jun. | 62·9 | 62·5 | 10,527·2 | 0·4 |
| | Jul. | 45·5 | 67·5 | 10,439·4 | −22·0 |
| | Aug. | 34·8 | 53·7 | 10,345·0 | −18·9 |
| | Sep. | 34·3 | 48·3 | 10,289·1 | −14·0 |
| | Oct. | 34·7 | 38·0 | 10,276·0 | −3·3 |
| | Nov. | 66·1 | 54·3 | 10,335·1 | 11·8 |
| | Dec. | 88·6 | 47·7 | 10,498·4 | 40·9 |
| | | | | | |
| 1975 | Jan. | 80·9 | 49·8 | 10,623·1 | 31·1 |
| | Feb. | 100·2 | 53·5 | 10,856·4 | 46·7 |
| | Mar. | 119·6 | 71·6 | 11,048·6 | 48·0 |
| | Apr. | 117·5 | 50·3 | 11,517·3 | 67·2 |
| | May | 121·1 | 58·9 | 11,628·4 | 62·2 |
| | Jun. | 106·1 | 53·5 | 11,838·0 | 52·6 |
| | Jul. | 93·8 | 61·2 | 11,968·4 | 32·6 |
| | Aug. | 83·2 | 68·2 | 12,043·6 | 15·0 |
| | Sep. | 85·2 | 66·0 | 12,120·5 | 19·2 |
| | Oct. | 98·3 | 54·0 | 12,287·5 | 44·3 |
| | Nov. | 90·2 | 66·2 | 12,417·7 | 24·0 |
| | Dec. | 93·0 | 52·1 | 12,581·4 | 40·9 |

*Source:* Reserve Bank of Australia, *Statistical Bulletin.*

a quarter. However, if the response lag is dated from the first month *after* the introduction of restraint in which the rate of growth in advances fell *below* that ruling at the time of the policy change, the lag will be ten to eleven months or approaching four quarters. On the whole, the latter interpretation seems slightly more sensible where a process which is likely to be characterised by a distributed lag form is being described in terms of a single discrete response lag. We thus put the lag at around four quarters.

We can analyse the behaviour of advances rather more precisely by examining the data for new lending and cancellations of limits by the major trading banks. These are given in Table 9.4. New lending, on a seasonally adjusted basis, peaked in April 1973. On a quarterly basis the peak came in 1973.II. Net new lending (new lending minus cancellations) peaked in 1973.II, i.e. *before* policy moved from mild restraint to restraint. It can thus be argued that the banks' lending policy, as reflected in the variables over which they can exert control, responded to mild restraint. During restraint net new lending declined; and by the September quarter of 1974, just prior to the adoption of ease, it was negative. A rapid recovery followed the change in policy stance in 1974.III.

It follows that the continued expansion of advances once again reflected a sharp increase in the usage ratio. At the introduction of restraint this ratio was 75 per cent. At the shift to ease it was some 88 per cent. Moreover, it did not peak (at 90 per cent) until January 1975 – roughly one quarter after the policy reversal. Arithmetically, the increase in the usage ratio accounted for a shade over 60 per cent of the increase in advances up to October 1974.

The behaviour of trading bank deposits and advances reflects in part the banks' adjustment to their position regarding LGS. Accordingly, Figure 9.7 sets out the behaviour of LGS assets and excess LGS assets. In interpreting this figure it must be recalled that in theory the appropriate series is not excess LGS assets but net free LGS assets, where

$$\text{Net free LGS assets} \equiv \text{Excess LGS assets} - \text{Borrowing from Reserve Bank}$$

Unfortunately, although borrowing seems to have occurred from April 1974, attempts to estimate it have proved unsatisfactory. Therefore, no series for net free LGS assets is presented, and we are compelled to rely upon the theoretically less relevant concept of excess LGS assets.[12]

Consider now the rate of growth in LGS assets. At the shift to restraint this was of the order of 25 per cent per annum. With the shift in policy stance the rate of growth declined very rapidly. By October 1973 it was negative, and it remained negative through December 1974. In January 1975 – rather more than a quarter after the shift from restraint to ease – it became positive. Thereafter, it rose rapidly, averaging indeed rather more than 60 per cent for 1975.II.

These movements imply, of course, consequential changes in holdings of excess LGS and net free LGS. The minimum LGS convention remained unal-

Figure 9.7    The LGS position

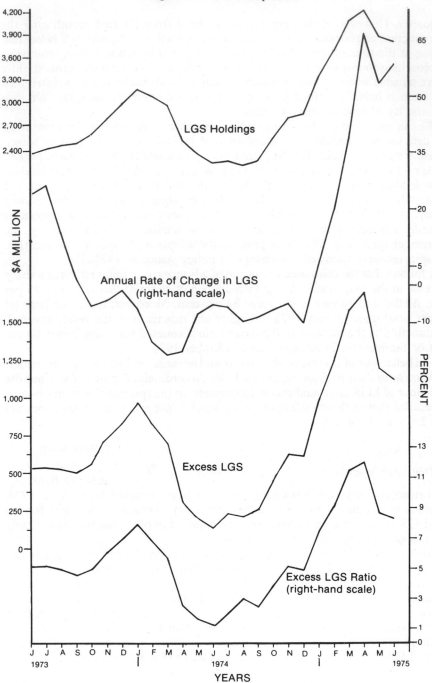

*Note:* Minimum LGS ratio required = 18%
*Source:* Monthly data from: Reserve Bank of Australia, *Statistical Bulletin: Financial Supplement (October 1975)*

tered throughout this period. Not seasonally adjusted, the excess LGS ratio peaked in January 1972, and by June 1973 it was not markedly different from that of June 1972. Thereafter, in comparison with the same month in the previous year, it declined. It appears that borrowing began in April 1974. By May the net free LGS ratio was probably virtually zero, and on our very crude estimates it seems to have been negative for the next three months.

On a monthly basis it may well be that the Reserve Bank's technical ability to control the LGS assets of the trading banks is incomplete, since shifts in government balances and borrowing by the banks or by money market dealers may be difficult to forecast[13] and thus to offset. Nevertheless, the movements in LGS, as revealed above, are obviously consistent with those to be expected from our *ex ante* policy classifications. This statement is, of course, qualitative. Quantitatively, if LGS assets are regarded as an indicator of Reserve Bank policy, it will be clear that the policy shifts were very severe, and arguably excessive.

As we have seen, a policy of restraint typically compels some borrowing by members of the major trading banks. It is unlikely that our estimates of borrowing are accurate; but even if they were, they would understate the turn of events, since in and after May 1974 the Reserve Bank began to purchase bank-accepted bills from the market. As far as we can trace, this step was unprecedented, and it gives some indication of the pressure exerted on the banks and short term markets by the severity of the policy reversal. The position in mid-1974 is illustrated by the movements in private-sector short-term rates reported in Table 9.5.[14]

Not very surprisingly, companies compelled to roll over short term debt at extremely high interest rates experienced severe cash-flow problems. Two major companies failed in 1974.III, and by October 1974 there was an emerging risk of financial panic as investors – it seems typically small investors – sought to switch from finance house and building society obligations into bank deposits. As a result the Reserve Bank was compelled in October to provide the trading banks with a special drawing facility amounting to $A112.5 million that was available for 180 days. Somewhat earlier, the banks were asked to look sympathetically on requests for assistance. By these means, and SRD releases, the incipient crisis was contained. Nevertheless, it seems clear that the speed of the policy reversal had reached and perhaps exceeded the limits of prudence. Indeed, it seems possible that, if the authorities had not acted effectively in October 1974, some permanent damage might have been done to Australia's financial system.

This point is stressed because the series for the trading banks suggests a relatively smooth, although lagged, adjustment, accompanied, if our estimates are correct, by only a short period of distress borrowing at the Reserve Bank's unknown penal rate(s).

The response of the trading banks cannot effectively be considered simply in terms of asset ratios, as we have done here, for one element in the response was the banks' willingness to offer remarkably high rates on NCDs. For the banks as a whole this aggressive bidding creates no additional funds, save in so far as the authorities are prepared to finance switches out of marketable public debt into

**Table 9.5** *Selected short-term market rates, 1972–5* (%)

| Year/month | NCDs 3–6 months | Bank bills[a] 90 days | Commercial bills 90 days | Inter-company market 90 days | Finance companies[b] 90 days | Official short-term money market 60 days |
|---|---|---|---|---|---|---|
| 1972 Jan. | 5·25–5·50 | 6·68–7·10 | 6·25–6·50 | 6·00 | 5·25–5·50 | 5·25 |
| Feb. | 5·25–5·50 | 6·60 | 5·75 | 5·75 | 5·00 | 4·80 |
| Mar. | n.a. | n.a. | n.a. | 5·75 | 5·25 | 4·90 |
| Apr. | n.a. | n.a. | n.a. | n.a. | 5·25 | n.a. |
| May | n.a. | 7·35 | 6·50 | 6·25 | 5·25 | 5·25 |
| Jun. | 6·00 | 7·60 | 6·25 | 6·00 | 5·25 | 5·13 |
| Jul. | 4·80 | 6·60 | 5·50 | 5·50 | 5·13 | 4·50 |
| Aug. | 4·25 | 6·10 | 5·25–5·50 | 5·50 | 5·25 | 4·70 |
| Sep. | 4·25–4·50 | 6·00 | 4·75–5·00 | 5·25 | 5·25 | 4·25–4·40 |
| Oct. | 4·05–4·10 | 5·90 | 4·75 | 4·75 | 5·00 | 4·25 |
| Nov. | 4·00–4·10 | 5·90 | 4·75 | 5·00–5·25 | 4·75 | 4·23 |
| Dec. | 5·75–6·00 | 5·50 | 4·75 | 4·75–5·00 | 4·75 | 4·20 |
| 1973 Jan. | 3·90–4·70 | 6·00 | 4·75 | 4·75–5·00 | 4·75–5·0 | 4·10 |
| Feb. | 4·10–4·80 | 6·60 | 5·50 | 5·50 | 4·75 | 4·20 |
| Mar. | 4·75–5·25 | 7·10 | 5·75 | 6·00 | 5·50 | 4·25 |
| Apr. | 5·50–5·60 | 7·55 | 6·55 | 6·15 | 6·00 | 4·60 |
| May | 6·25–6·50 | 8·10 | 6·75 | 6·50 | 7·00 | 4·65 |
| Jun. | 6·50 | 8·35 | 7·20 | 7·10 | 7·00 | 5·10 |
| Jul. | 6·50 | 8·25 | 7·10 | 7·25 | 7·00 | 5·25 |
| Aug. | 6·50 | 8·30 | 7·10 | 7·25 | 7·00 | 5·50 |
| Sep. | 8·00 | 11·10 | 10·75 | 9·25 | 9·23 | 6·75 |
| Oct. | 8·75–9·00 | 10·85 | 10·00 | 9·50 | 9·78 | 7·50 |
| Nov. | 9·27 | 9·00 | 10·00 | 9·50 | 9·00 | 7·50 |
| Dec. | 9·23 | 9·25 | 9·25 | 9·25 | 9·25 | 7·00 |
| 1974 Jan. | 9·33 | 9·40 | 9·50 | 9·25 | 9·25 | 7·00 |
| Jan. | 9·35 | 9·50 | 10·00 | 9·50 | 9·50 | 7·10 |
| Mar. | 9·65 | 9·75 | 10·40 | 9·75 | 9·50 | 7·60 |
| Apr. | 13·00 | 16·00 | 17·00 | 12·00 | 14·00 | 8·25 |
| May | 18·20 | 21·00 | 22.00 | 19·00 | 18·00 | 8·25 |
| Jun. | 13·00 | 18·50 | 19·50 | 20·75 | 19·00 | 8·25 |
| Jul. | 12·50 | 15·50 | 15·50 | 15·50 | 13·50 | 10·25 |
| Aug. | 11·88 | 14·25 | 15·00 | 15·50 | 15·00 | 10·25 |
| Sep. | 11·94 | 12·75 | 15·75 | 16·25 | 14·50 | 10·15 |
| Oct. | 10·39 | 10·60 | 14·00 | 16·25 | 15·00 | 9·00 |
| Nov. | 10·11 | 10·30 | 14·60 | 15·95 | 14·00 | 8·50 |
| Dec. | 9·41 | 9·50 | 11·75 | 13·00 | 11·50 | 7·50 |
| 1975 Jan. | 9·32 | 9·00 | 10·50 | 11·00 | 11·23 | 7·75 |
| Feb. | 8·96 | 9·00 | 10·25 | 10·75 | 9·75 | 7·75 |
| Mar. | 9·10 | 8·90 | 9·25 | 10·25 | 9·75 | 7·75 |
| Apr. | 9·64 | 10·25 | 11·00 | 10·25 | 10·50 | 7·00 |
| May | 9·16 | 8·85 | 9·75 | 10·00 | 9·75 | 7·00 |
| Jun. | 9·12 | 8·85 | 9·60 | 10·50 | 10·25 | 7·00 |
| Jul. | 8·68 | 8·25 | 9·00 | 9·25 | 9·00 | 7·00 |
| Aug. | 8·73 | 8·10 | 8·75 | 9·00 | 8·75 | 7·00 |
| Sep. | 8·23 | 8·10 | 8·75 | 9·00 | 8·75 | 6·75 |
| Oct. | 7·94 | 7·85 | 8·75 | 9·00 | 8·75 | 6·75 |
| Nov. | 8·13 | 8·10 | 8·75 | 9·00 | 8·75 | 7·00 |
| Dec. | 7·84 | 7·65 | 9·00 | 9·00 | 8·75 | 7·25 |

[a] Cost to borrower.
[b] Trading Bank controlled.
*Source*: R. H. Allan (private communication).

NCDs. The high NCD rates are nevertheless an index of the pressure felt by individual banks – and of their willingness to compete very strongly when they feel the need to do so.

As already noted, the banks borrowed from the Reserve Bank in 1974.II and might have borrowed rather more, and for rather longer, if the Reserve Bank had not bought bills and provided its Special Drawing Facility. With so severe a shift in policy some borrowing seems almost certain, since the banks' ability to adjust their portfolios, in particular their advances, at all quickly is limited. Hence, unplanned (by the banks) increases in advances occur as the result of unforecast-able (by the banks) increases in the usage ratio, and this seems the most plausible explanation of the banks' borrowing. In fact over the relevant period the rise in the percentage utilisation of limits added around $A600 million to advances. If the banks had forecast only about half of this, it would have accounted for most of their distress borrowing, at least on the basis of our very approximate estimates.[15]

If this argument is correct, the emergence of borrowing in 1974 cannot be taken as evidence either: (a) that the trading banks as a group do not possess a relatively stable demand function for excess LGS assets together with a relatively well-defined dynamic-adjustment process; or (b) that borrowing implies some reluctance, as opposed to technical inability, to comply with official policy. It may simply reflect the fact that in the short term actual deposits and advances changes differ from the banks' planned quantities, so that, where LGS policy changes rapidly as an element in restraint, distress borrowing seems an unavoidable concomitant of the adjustment process.

Whether trading bank behaviour can be explained by a simple portfolio-type model with a relatively simple adjustment process is debatable. The experience of 1973–4 does not preclude it. On the other hand, if this experience were to be repeated too often, the banks might well feel compelled to raise their typical excess LGS ratio fairly considerably, simply to ensure that, without recourse to distress borrowing, they could, consistently with their own capacity for adjustment, adapt to changes in LGS holdings.[16]

# 9.5 *Other Private Finance*

The quarterly estimates of new capital raisings, together with the index of share prices, are given in Table 9.6. Looking at the matter quite formally, new raisings peaked in 1973.IV after rising strongly from 1972.III. The downturn, however, did not become severe until 1974.III. Thus, for the first half of 1974–5 new capital raisings, in nominal terms, were about 63 per cent of the corresponding figure for the first half of 1973–4 – a decline of well above one-third. For the second half of 1974–5 they were less than 57 per cent. The decline was shared about equally between equities and debt.

**Table 9.6** *New capital raisings and share prices, 1972–5 (share price index, 1966–7 = 100)*

| Year/quarter | New capital raisings ($A m.) | | | Listed companies ($A m.) | | Share price index |
| | Equity | Other | Total | Non-seasonally adjusted | Seasonally adjusted | |
| --- | --- | --- | --- | --- | --- | --- |
| 1972 IV | 82·2 | 164·9 | 247·1 | 222·9 | 180·4 | 104·4 |
| 1973 I | 51·6 | 153·6 | 205·2 | 177·1 | 234·3 | 104·3 |
| II | 75·7 | 193·8 | 269·5 | 234·2 | 260·1 | 96·6 |
| III | 77·0 | 345·5 | 422·5 | 383·8 | 352·0 | 93·0 |
| IV | 105·7 | 478·9 | 584·6 | 511·1 | 437·8 | 80·9 |
| 1974 I | 43·0 | 202·4 | 245·4 | 228·2 | 304·7 | 88·1 |
| II | 80·7 | 334·1 | 414·8 | 391·4 | 429·0 | 80·4 |
| III | 56·0 | 236·1 | 292·1 | 270·0 | 252·6 | 56·8 |
| IV | 58·0 | 281·9 | 339·9 | 314·3 | 246·3 | 52·6 |
| 1975 I | 16·5 | 260·0 | 276·5 | 255·9 | 343·3 | 60·0 |
| II | 86·8 | 208·3 | 295·1 | 279·6 | 304·5 | 63·0 |
| III | 53·3 | 245·3 | 298·6 | 286·9 | 282·5 | 64·5 |
| IV | 74·5 | 306·5 | 381·0 | 360·5 | 287·2 | 73·1 |

*Source:* Reserve Bank of Australia, *Statistical Bulletin.*

**Table 9.7** *Finance companies, 1972–5 (amounts financed, $A million)*

| Year/month | | Retail sales | Housing | Other consumers and commercial loans | Total |
|---|---|---|---|---|---|
| 1972 | Jul. | 91·7 | 67·2 | 159·6 | 381·9 |
| | Aug. | 94·6 | 72·2 | 165·0 | 413·8 |
| | Sep. | 91·6 | 76·3 | 179·1 | 411·6 |
| | Oct. | 103·5 | 71·8 | 172·9 | 427·4 |
| | Nov. | 106·4 | 79·7 | 216·5 | 487·5 |
| | Dec. | 101·8 | 86·5 | 230·6 | 487·8 |
| 1973 | Jan. | 96·3 | 67·3 | 181·0 | 386·4 |
| | Feb. | 89·0 | 82·4 | 216·7 | 442·5 |
| | Mar. | 102·8 | 106·6 | 278·9 | 546·1 |
| | Apr. | 91·4 | 94·3 | 262·2 | 471·5 |
| | May | 120·9 | 128·5 | 289·6 | 602·7 |
| | Jun. | 103·9 | 137·6 | 363·2 | 625·7 |
| | Jul. | 97·6 | 148·7 | 385·2 | 665·3 |
| | Aug. | 102·0 | 154·8 | 361·0 | 663·6 |
| | Sep. | 91·3 | 141·0 | 324·7 | 612·8 |
| | Oct. | 107·4 | 153·0 | 362·2 | 680·7 |
| | Nov. | 107·4 | 133·8 | 323·4 | 633·4 |
| | Dec. | 91·2 | 126·3 | 377·3 | 638·3 |
| 1974 | Jan. | 90·3 | 82·8 | 220·7 | 462·0 |
| | Feb. | 82·7 | 118·3 | 252·1 | 513·2 |
| | Mar. | 91·5 | 120·6 | 294·6 | 590·5 |
| | Apr. | 92·1 | 115·7 | 303·3 | 590·1 |
| | May | 108·7 | 116·0 | 296·7 | 655·0 |
| | Jun. | 83·9 | 79·1 | 233·2 | 513·9 |
| | Jul. | 97·1 | 82·5 | 219·2 | 547·8 |
| | Aug. | 97·7 | 65·2 | 210·8 | 537·3 |
| | Sep. | 99·1 | 62·0 | 186·8 | 512·6 |
| | Oct. | 113·9 | 53·0 | 160·8 | 501·7 |
| | Nov. | 99·8 | 38·2 | 129·7 | 428·5 |
| | Dec. | 86·2 | 42·7 | 151·0 | 428·8 |
| 1975 | Jan. | 83·0 | 25·7 | 102·4 | 323·8 |
| | Feb. | 87·0 | 30·7 | 116·2 | 415·6 |
| | Mar. | 86·6 | 32·7 | 144·9 | 458·0 |
| | Apr. | 105·5 | 35·9 | 143·1 | 500·0 |
| | May | 104·2 | 52·9 | 159·4 | 534·2 |
| | Jun. | 94·0 | 55·4 | 181·3 | 530·3 |

*Note*: — indicates break in series.
*Source*: Reserve Bank of Australia, *Statistical Bulletin: Finance Companies*.

Equity prices began to fall as early as the second half of 1972–3, roughly coincidentally with the rise in short rates. The fall, however, was far from smooth, and the trough occurred late in the first quarter of 1974–5, i.e. rather *before* the trough in new capital raisings. If, as can be done, the comparison is based upon seasonally adjusted rather than raw data for new capital raisings, the troughs in share prices and new capital raisings will occur virtually together. What is interesting, and perhaps rather surprising, is that new capital raisings continued to rise strongly from 1973.I to IV despite the fact that share prices were typically falling fairly fast.

Because of definitional changes the data relating to finance companies are extremely difficult to interpret. This can be checked by an examination of Table 9.7. A consistent series of total amounts financed is available from July 1972 to June 1973, while the numerical consequences of the definitional change in July 1973 appear to be rather small. It therefore seems reasonable to place the peak in the series in October 1973, i.e. in 1973.III – one quarter after the shift from mild restraint to restraint. From this point the series underwent a fairly continuous decline until 1975.I. By the time the Reserve Bank shifted to ease the overall amounts financed per period were about 25 per cent below their peak figures, while by their trough in January 1975 the decline was close to 53 per cent.

Examination of the main heads of amounts financed is also made rather hazardous by definitional changes. Broadly speaking, the peaks of the three series given all appear to have occurred at or close to October 1973. Apart from instalment credit for retail sales, however, the percentage falls in the separate elements was far greater than the percentage decline in overall amounts financed, and typically in excess of 70 per cent. This, of course, reflects a shift in finance company lending into the finance of wholesaling.

Broadly, therefore, both new capital raisings and finance company lending reached their peaks about two quarters after the shift to restraint, and their troughs in 1975.I came six quarters later and about one quarter after the Reserve Bank's shift to ease. The proportionate decline in finance company lending was, however, greater, and this suggests that the period contained a revision of lenders' risk assessments.

As we have seen, the finance companies' lending for housing declined by some 75 per cent between August 1973 and November 1974. A roughly similar pattern was shown by the housing finance made available by the major long-term lenders (see Table 9.8). The total finance provided by banks, major life offices and building societies reached a peak of some $A330 million (monthly rate) in August 1973. This coincided with the peak in the savings bank–life offices element but was about two quarters after the peak in lending by building societies.

From August 1973 housing finance generally declined, reaching a trough exactly a year later. By this date the fall amounted to some 63 per cent of the peak figure, while for building societies lending alone the decline from the peak (in March 1973) to their trough (in December 1974) was over 78 per cent.

**Table 9.8** *Finance for housing: main sources, 1973–5 ($A million)*

| Year/month | | Banks, life offices and building societies | | | Finance companies (2) | Total (1+2) |
|---|---|---|---|---|---|---|
| | | Banks and life offices | Building societies | Total (1) | | |
| 1973 | Jan. | 160·0 | 95·6 | 255·6 | 67·3 | 322·9 |
| | Feb. | 163·3 | 112·2 | 275·5 | 82·4 | 357·9 |
| | Mar. | 184·5 | 128·8 | 313·3 | 106·6 | 419·9 |
| | Apr. | 161·2 | 78·4 | 239·6 | 94·3 | 333·9 |
| | May | 228·3 | 77·8 | 306·1 | 128·5 | 434·6 |
| | Jun. | 209·8 | 53·2 | 263·0 | 137·6 | 400·6 |
| | | | | | — | |
| | Jul. | 203·6 | 53·4 | 267·0 | 148·7 | 415·7 |
| | Aug. | 239·3 | 88·0 | 327·3 | 154·8 | 482·1 |
| | Sep. | 185·9 | 82·3 | 268·2 | 141·0 | 409·2 |
| | Oct. | 194·3 | 84·0 | 278·3 | 153·0 | 431·3 |
| | Nov. | 149·8 | 66·5 | 216·3 | 133·8 | 350·1 |
| | Dec. | 114·5 | 42·6 | 157·1 | 126·3 | 283·4 |
| 1974 | Jan. | 160·4 | 46·6 | 207·0 | 82·8 | 289·8 |
| | Feb. | 151·3 | 65·9 | 217·2 | 118·3 | 335·5 |
| | Mar. | 155·6 | 66·5 | 222·1 | 120·6 | 342·7 |
| | Apr. | 134·8 | 58·7 | 193·5 | 115·7 | 309·2 |
| | May | 146·0 | 64·1 | 210·1 | 116·0 | 326·1 |
| | Jun. | 102·3 | 30·6 | 132·9 | 79·1 | 212·0 |
| | Jul. | 101·7 | 44·2 | 145·9 | 82·5 | 228·4 |
| | Aug. | 89·9 | 38·2 | 128·1 | 65·2 | 193·3 |
| | Sep. | 88·6 | 42·0 | 130·6 | 62·0 | 192·6 |
| | Oct. | 135·3 | 36·8 | 172·1 | 53·0 | 225·1 |
| | Nov. | 161·6 | 33·5 | 195·1 | 38·2 | 233·3 |
| | Dec. | 199·7 | 28·5 | 228·2 | 42·7 | 270·9 |
| 1975 | Jan. | 239·8 | 32·1 | 271·9 | 25·7 | 297·6 |
| | Feb. | 248·2 | 57·6 | 305·8 | 30·7 | 336·5 |
| | Mar. | 242·1 | 67·6 | 309·7 | 32·7 | 342·4 |
| | Apr. | 254·1 | 91·1 | 345·2 | 35·9 | 381·1 |
| | May | 234·0 | 113·3 | 347·3 | 52·9 | 400·2 |
| | Jun. | 209·0 | 122·5 | 331·5 | 55·4 | 386·9 |

*Note:* — indicates break in series.
*Source:* Reserve Bank of Australia, *Statistical Bulletin: Finance for Housing and Finance Companies.*

Thus, the evidence suggests a fairly rapid and dramatic response by housing finance to monetary restraint, with a lag of a quarter or less and a response that in percentage terms exceeded the responses of both capital raising and finance company lending. In this connection it is worth noting that this fall took place with the evident approval of the Reserve Bank, which did not take any clear steps to limit the decline until the period September–November 1974. In these months the regulations governing savings-bank asset holdings were amended to reduce from 60 per cent to 50 per cent the proportion of deposits to be held in liquid assets and public securities and from 10 per cent to 7.5 per cent the proportion to be held in Treasury notes or as deposits with the Reserve Bank. These changes were made in September. In November 1974 the Reserve Bank asked the savings banks to increase their lending for housing, and in December 1974 the savings banks were granted a special government loan of $A150 million additional housing finance. Thus, there was no attempt to mitigate the effect of restraint on housing finance until it had fallen by close upon two-thirds of its peak value.

## 9.6 The Behaviour of Demand Components

The behaviour of the major demand components, excluding exports, is set out in Table 9.9. In real terms, gross private investment in fixed capital rose by 6 per cent during 1972–3. The expansion continued after the move to restraint, but the peak came relatively quickly in 1973.IV. Thus, during mild restraint and the first two quarters of restraint gross private investment in fixed capital rose by rather more than 14 per cent.

After the peak in 1973.IV the rate of investment declined, initially very slowly but subsequently, in 1974–5, rather rapidly. The trough was reached in 1975.I. By this date the fall from the peak amounted to 15 per cent of the peak figure.

If the subaggregates are considered, it is clear that investment in dwellings, which had risen rather faster than the other components in 1972–3, reached its peak first. This occurred in 1973.III – only one quarter after the shift to restraint and virtually coincidentally with the peak in the series for housing finance. Thereafter, investment in housing declined continuously through 1973–4 and 1974–5. Measured from the peak, the decline was of the order of 28 per cent. This was, of course, substantially less than the percentage fall in housing finance. Nevertheless, it was nearly three times as rapid as the decline in the other components of gross private fixed investment.

By contrast with housing, other construction peaked later (by one quarter) and declined proportionately far less – in fact by only some 7 per cent from its peak (in 1973.IV or 1974.I) to its trough (in 1974.II). By 1975.II other construction was showing a slight recovery. So too was investment in equipment, which rose by some 22 per cent to its peak in 1973.IV and then declined by about 13 per cent to its trough in 1975.I.

**Table 9.9** *Major demand components, 1972–5 (seasonally adjusted data, $A million at 1966–7 prices)*

| Year/quarter | | Gross private fixed investment | | | | Change in stocks | | | Private consumption | | Gross non-farm product | Imports |
|---|---|---|---|---|---|---|---|---|---|---|---|---|
| | | Total | Dwellings | Other building and construction | Other | Total | Farm | Non-farm | Total | Durables[1] | | |
| 1972 | III | 1,224 | 380 | 255 | 589 | −139 | −113 | −26 | 4,617 | 555 | 6,856 | 1,101 |
| | IV | 1,214 | 383 | 249 | 582 | −138 | −95 | −43 | 4,717 | 578 | 7,043 | 1,172 |
| 1973 | I | 1,242 | 403 | 238 | 602 | −25 | 2 | −27 | 4,791 | 608 | 7,131 | 1,282 |
| | II | 1,284 | 412 | 251 | 621 | 123 | 90 | 34 | 4,870 | 622 | 7,240 | 1,362 |
| | III | 1,305 | 416 | 245 | 644 | 3 | 86 | −83 | 4,913 | 656 | 7,390 | 1,435 |
| | IV | 1,387 | 412 | 261 | 713 | 255 | 173 | 82 | 5,005 | 679 | 7,463 | 1,549 |
| 1974 | I | 1,360 | 395 | 261 | 705 | 441 | 101 | 339 | 5,032 | 663 | 7,644 | 1,689 |
| | II | 1,300 | 374 | 243 | 683 | 308 | 57 | 250 | 5,067 | 693 | 7,421 | 1,788 |
| | III | 1,259 | 338 | 248 | 673 | 393 | 92 | 301 | 5,030 | 693 | 7,233 | 1,882 |
| | IV | 1,192 | 316 | 247 | 629 | 385 | 99 | 287 | 5,027 | 688 | 7,334 | 1,709 |
| 1975 | I | 1,175 | 303 | 248 | 623 | −90 | 76 | −166 | 5,102 | 698 | 7,317 | 1,443 |
| | II | 1,212 | 299 | 252 | 662 | −127 | −23 | −104 | 5,197 | 728 | 7,476 | 1,448 |

[1] Household durables plus motor vehicles.
*Source:* Australian Bureau of Statistics, *Supplement to Quarterly estimates of National Income and Expenditure* (1975, 1976).

Thus, of the fall in gross private investment in fixed capital – $A212 million at 1966–7 prices – slightly over one-half was due to housing and slightly over 40 per cent to investment in equipment. Other construction, by contrast, was relatively stable.

It is, of course, a remarkably risky procedure to attempt any assessment of the impact of monetary measures on either private investment or expenditure on consumers' durables on the basis of an examination of time series. On the other hand, it is difficult to believe that the sharp reversal in the stance of monetary policy in 1973.II was not an important factor in first checking the rate of housing investment and next, via a rapid decline in housing finance, in reducing it. In this context it may well be significant that the rate of fall in housing investment accelerated fairly markedly in 1974.I through IV – a period that included the mini-crisis in the flow of deposits to the building societies. A tentative conclusion would be that housing investment was particularly hard hit by restraint – a conclusion given indirect support by the special measures taken in November–December 1974 to encourage the flow of housing finance.

It is less simple to draw inferences regarding investment in equipment. Undoubtedly, the switch to restraint had some impact, but it must be recalled that there was a remarkably large shift in real wages between December 1973 and December 1974. This must have reduced profit expectations and, as a result, the willingness to undertake investment. Moreover, it seems unlikely that the influence of an autonomous change in the real wage of the magnitude experienced would be adequately captured in the typical investment function employed in Australia, since in the main these functions are derivatives of Jorgenson's essentially neoclassical formulation. If this is so, not only will such functions tend to overpredict investment from roughly the end of 1973, but they will also be rather little help in any attempt to isolate the contribution of monetary restriction to the observed fall in investment in equipment. Thus, we may have to rely upon interpretation of the time series rather than a model to estimate the impact of monetary restriction. Assuming that this is so, it seems reasonable to argue that the bulk of the fall in investment in equipment should be attributed to what may be called 'real wage shock'. But this tentative judgement is essentially intuitive and may well be shown to be entirely misguided by later research.

Generally, do not regard planned investment in stocks as being susceptible to monetary influences. Moreover, there are good reasons for thinking that the increase in the rate of accumulation in non-farm stocks after 1974.I contained a significant unplanned element as well as a very substantial import component. We thus do not assign any important role to the monetary restriction in the explanation of the behaviour of investment in non-farm stocks.

# 9.7 *Provisional Conclusions*

The period examined in this chapter contained an unusually sharp, severe and sustained shift in the stance of monetary policy from mild restraint to restraint. As such it probably represented something like a maximum in the speed and severity with which monetary policy can be reversed in the direction of restraint. This view is given greater strength by the fact that there were undoubtedly signs of financial crisis in mid- and late-1974. The signs included: the introduction of special borrowing facilities for trading banks (in October 1974); Reserve Bank purchases of bank bills (from June 1974); trading bank borrowing from the Reserve Bank (in April–May 1974); and an outflow of funds from building societies and finance companies (during July–December 1974). This experience was not entirely dissimilar to that of the United States in periods in which there was a sharp move in the direction of monetary restriction, although in the case of the United States the difficulties facing the authorities were exacerbated by the fact that in the United States a mortgage is in general not only a cash flow hedge but also an interest rate hedge – a circumstance that puts the stability of housing finance institutions at more severe risk.

The structure and wisdom of the anti-inflationary package deployed by the authorities in June–September 1973 is, of course, a matter of controversy. In part, indeed probably in large part, it represented a response to the expansion of 1972–3, the rapidity of which was certainly not well forecast and the extent of which was probably not fully appreciated when the macroeconomic policy decisions of June–September 1973 were taken. In retrospect, i.e. given the extensive advantage of hindsight, it now seems clear that monetary policy was excessively easy in the ease and even in the mild restraint of 1972–3 and that as a consequence of this it became excessively restrictive in the restraint of 1973–4 and early 1974–5.

Economic forecasting is always a hazardous undertaking. As argued earlier, it is particularly so where, as in Australia, the economy is highly open on both current and capital account. Where forecasting is so hazardous, there is always a double risk. The first is that macroeconomic policy adjustments will be delayed for purely technical reasons deriving from lack of confidence in the available economic diagnosis and forecasts. The second is that action, when taken, will aim at a rapid result and thus consist in doing rather too much, rather too late and possibly for rather too long. In broad terms this seems to have occurred in Australia over the period 1972–5.[17]

Where the aim is restriction, it is important that the contribution of monetary policy to any overall package is carefully considered. Restrictive budgetary policies are not politically very appealing. There is therefore a continuing risk that too much may be asked of discretionary monetary action. As a result monetary restriction may be pushed to the extent that the financial system, through which monetary policy operates and for the stability of which the Reserve Bank carries the final responsibility, may be endangered. In the first half of 1974–5 Australia seems to have reached such a position.

Pushing monetary policy to, or even beyond, its limits in the pursuit of belated fine or coarse tuning carries awkward consequences for financial institutions and tends to weaken, or even temporarily destroy, routine responses to financial stimuli. Where this occurs, transactors' behaviour becomes less predictable, and as a consequence the monetary control mechanism itself becomes less reliable. In short, the reliability, for control purposes, of the responses of transactors almost certainly depends crucially on the range and speed of policy-induced changes in financial variables to which they are compelled to adjust. It seems unlikely that, for example, a money demand function will remain stable if there are severe and rapid changes in the rate of monetary expansion and the level and structure of interest rates.

If these arguments are correct, it is one obvious judgement on 1971–5 that monetary policy was expected to do too much and tried too hard to do it. In the process it may well have impaired its capacity to make a more modest, but more reliable, contribution to macroeconomic management in the future, if it is in fact to be deployed as a means of controlling aggregate demand.

The second judgement is that, despite the severity of the shift in policy stance, monetary action seems to have had its main impact on only two major demand-components: investment in dwellings, and expenditure on consumer durables. This intuitive judgement, of course, assumes that the decline in investment in equipment was primarily the result of the autonomous revision of real wages. Thus, quick effects from monetary policy, amounting to perhaps 1.5 per cent of GNP,[18] were obtained at a fairly severe cost in terms of the housing market. This leaves it open to us to argue that a similar total reduction in aggregate demand might more usefully have been obtained by a greater use of fiscal policy and with a consequentially less severe reversal in monetary policy and a wider industrial impact.

In a later chapter we use simulations from model RB74 and some related results from model RB76 to check our interpretations of the time series. In examining these it should, however, be noted that, if we are correct in arguing that the investment functions in the former model (other than for dwellings) do not effectively incorporate the impact of the autonomous real-wage change, they may by the same token incorporate an inadequate specification of the new (1973–4 onwards) dynamic response to interest rate changes.[19] In short, the simulation results may be a less reliable guide to the experience of 1973–4 than to that of earlier years, and very possibly an even less reliable guide to the economy's behaviour in the late 1970s.

# Notes: Chapter 9

1 On our assessment there was a short period in which policy was accommodating.
2 This does not necessarily mean that the Reserve Bank cannot technically control the base; it simply means the Bank may regard the costs of completely neutralising inflows as excessive.
3 During much of this period both the embargo and the VDR were in operation.
4 In July 1973.
5 In September 1973. The appreciation was 5 per cent, and the occasion was taken to abandon the link with the US dollar in favour of trade-weighted basket of currencies.

6 The VDR ratio was not lowered to 25 per cent (from 33) until the last weeks of June 1974. It was reduced to 5 per cent in August and suspended in November when the embargo, formerly on transactions two years or less to maturity, was reduced in coverage to transactions of half a year or less. This followed the devaluation of 12 per cent in September 1974.

7 The appreciations were, of course, directed at reducing the rate of growth in prices.

8 The argument is not necessarily reversible in the sense that it will require the restoration of the former (pre-1973) share of wages to restore business willingness to invest; nor is it necessarily the case that, if the pre-1973 share *is* restored, business will regain either its confidence or its elan.

9 Some additional data on private sector short-term rates are given in Table 9.5.

10 See Table 9.5.

11 These are briefly discussed in the next section. For a more comprehensive account of the period, see Allan [3].

12 The estimates were obtained by combining the results of some regression equations with intuition. Typically, the regression results were unconvincing. For this reason the estimates are not given.

13 So too may changes in external assets. However, it seems that the Reserve Bank can usually control the monetary base fairly accurately over a quarter. For the LGS base this seems less certain.

14 Private communication suggests that in mid-1974 some quotations recorded were nominal in that no transactors were able to purchase the obligations offered.

15 Presumably, if the authorities engineer a sufficiently rapid change in LGS holdings, any bank, however skilled in portfolio management and rapid in its response, can be driven to borrow and hence compelled (at least in theory) to pay a penal rate. In a branch banking system, portfolio adjustments must involve lags of an administrative as well as an economic character. If this point is neglected and the banks are fairly frequently compelled by over-rapid (in this sense) shifts to restraint to undertake distress borrowing, this may weaken the LGS convention.

16 That is, neutralise the convention, at least in part.

17 It is arguable that the relieving actions taken by the Reserve Bank in May 1974 *et seq.* might have, with advantage, been taken earlier.

18 This intuitive estimate is, if anything, rather high, since some unavoidably crude experiments with RB74 and RB76 suggest that, if interest rates had *not* risen in this period of restraint, real output would have been about 1.5 per cent higher after *eight* quarters.

19 The recent performance of investment functions is not reassuring. Cf. Higgins, Johnston and Coghlan [59].

PART THREE

# THE CHARACTERISTICS OF MONETARY POLICY: A REVIEW OF FINDINGS

# Chapter 10

# The Evidence from Models

## 10.1 *Introduction*

It will not have escaped the reader that the analysis of the preceding chapters has two obvious and serious limitations.

The first of these arises because its methodology, typically the review of selected time series, relies heavily on judgement. Judgement may easily be idiosyncratic in the sense that other investigators reviewing the same evidence might well reach different conclusions with at least as plausible a set of reasons for doing so. This is because the quantitative aspects of the model upon which the judgements of the earlier chapters are based are implicit rather than explicit, while the dynamics are crude in the sense that complex distributed lags are treated as discrete and estimated by the inspection of time series rather than by more systematic statistical techniques.

This limitation is extremely important, since policy issues are essentially concerned with the quantitative responses, and their distribution over time, of the main macroeconomic target variables to the authorities' settings of their instruments.

The second limitation arises because the reviews contained in Chapters 6–9 are in the main concerned with the response of aggregate demand to discretionary monetary action. Relatively little attention has been given to the response of the other macroeconomic targets, which we have defined as the rate of change of prices and the state of the overall balance of payments. This is a serious omission, since the relative efficiency of monetary action in influencing these three variables must, at least in theory, be a major element in determining the way in which monetary policy should be used as a part of overall macroeconomic policy, i.e. its place in the optimal mix of policies.

233

Because of these deficiencies it is essential to supplement the earlier chapters by a review of the results of more systematic quantitative economic research into the workings of the Australian economy. Failure to do this would be an invitation to sceptical readers to regard our earlier judgements as based on little more than casual empiricism. More than this, if we neglect alternative evidence, we shall be simultaneously neglecting a potentially useful check on our own intuitions and thus presenting them more strongly (or perhaps more tentatively) than the available evidence warrants.

For these reasons the central aim of this and the following chapter is to review the results suggested either by:
(a)  existing macroeconometric models of the Australian economy;
(b)  econometric studies of single structural equations; or
(c)  similar studies of individual sectors of the economy.
At this stage the reader is asked to note very carefully that this review is of necessity extremely brief. It does not purport to give a full account, let alone a full critique, of the macroeconometric models; nor does it do more than sketch some of the results of other applied work. Moreover, since the models are in the process of continuous development, some of the results reviewed here, which typically derive from models available in 1976–7, may be misleading, for later versions of the same basic model may easily give significantly different results.

# 10.2 Models and Simulations

Three large macroecometric models that are suitable, at least in principle, for a more systematic examination of the impact of monetary policy have been constructed in Australia. Two of these, designated RB74 and RB76, were, as noted in Chapter 5, developed in the Research Department of the Reserve Bank of Australia. The third, the so called NIF model, has been jointly developed by the Treasury and the Australian Bureau of Statistics. Although all three models have been constructed under official auspices, this, as already said, must *not* be taken to mean that any of the models carries with it an aura of official approval; nor should it be inferred that despite this formal disclaimer one of these models is in practice accepted by the authorities as the main basis for policy decisions. The models are best looked at as systematic and sustained research efforts, which, it is believed, will provide some useful information about the *typical* responses of the Australian economy and, to this extent, a valuable check on the consistency and relevance of policy proposals generally generated by other means.

The impact of selected policies on the economy is usually investigated by means of model simulations that change some exogenous (policy-determined) variable from its actual historical value in a defined way at a particular date. The model then generates the values of the endogenous variables in future periods. The resultant dynamic path for any endogenous variable is then compared with the path taken by the same variable when the policy change is *not* imposed, i.e. with the so-called 'control' path. This is defined as the path that the model generates when all the exogenous variables take their actual historical values. By definition the resulting deviations from the control path give the response over time of the endogenous variables to the policy change.

There is, of course, no reason why simulations should be restricted to changing a single policy-controlled variable.[1] Indeed, many simulations that involve more complex policies are undertaken; nor are simulations restricted to changes in policy variables.[2] Any exogenous variable may be changed in an analogous way and its dynamic consequences computed from the model.

A simulation therefore is conceptually a simple and appealing way of undertaking policy and other experiments with the model that cannot in reality be undertaken with the economic system itself.

What are the limitations of simulation experiments?

The first is, of course, the model employed. If the model performs poorly in the sense that, when the exogenous variables take their historical values, the values of the endogenous variables emerging from the model do not correspond closely with their observed values – that is, the model 'tracks' poorly – we may reasonably be sceptical about the simulated results of policy changes. In short, if the model tracks inefficiently, we shall not be so interested in policy-induced deviations from the track, since we shall have decidedly limited confidence in the model's construction.

The second limitation is that by their very nature models reflect average performance as determined from the sample period used in their estimation. *Within* this sample period, a model that tracks acceptably may give, via simulation, a useful estimate of the response to any defined policy changes, provided that the changes are sufficiently small and sufficiently familiar in form not to modify the routine economic behaviour that the model reflects. It is, however, far less certain that the model will be useful when applied to periods *outside* its data sample, since the behaviour of the transacting sectors specified in the model may have changed. For example, it would be rather rash to assume that the importance of the expected rate of inflation in Australia from (say) 1974 to 1977 was what it was from (say) 1961 to 1970 or that Australian transactors formed their inflationary expectations in precisely the same way in both periods. Yet, this is the sort of thing that models in general must assume.

The fact that models generate simulations on the basis of exact values of estimated coefficients is from the policy aspect a further limitation. Strictly, the values of the endogenous variables generated by the model are expected values that are subject to a range of error. Unfortunately, the range of error is not known, in the sense that for any preassigned degree of probability we cannot define the upper and lower limits of any value generated for an endogenous variable. In short, there is no clear-cut way of estimating the error range. All that we can do is to remember that one must exist and to be correspondingly cautious in assessing the apparently precise estimates of the response of the system to changes in the exogenous variables.[3]

Clearly, a model will, as a matter of arithmetic, generate values for the endogenous variables for any period for which values of the exogenous variables are available. Thus, at the moment of writing, it would probably be possible to extend the simulation of any policy change up to and including 1977.IV. It would thus be conceivable to inquire into the consequences of an assumed policy change undertaken in 1966.III, for example, over a period of some eleven years or forty-four quarters. We thus need to consider over what timespan we are primarily interested in the dynamic path of the system.

Although for some purposes we might be interested in the macrosystem's reponse over some medium term of (say) five to seven years, it seems highly probable that in determining macroeconomic policy the authorities would have a far shorter horizon in mind. We shall define our policy horizon as having a maximum length of eight quarters (two years) and argue that within this period particular weight is probably given to the four-quarter (one-year) response. We are thus looking to the macroeconometric models to give us quantitative information of the average dynamic response of the Australian economy to particular changes in monetary policy, over a policy horizon that is relatively short in simulation length. [4]

We now turn to examine the inferences that may be drawn from the models.

# 10.3 Simulations with RB74

The RB74 model is a neo-Keynesian structure initially developed in the Reserve Bank by Norton and others as RB70. Like most models it has spawned a considerable literature and since its initial completion has been modified and extended. The main developments are those by Norton and Henderson [115], Henderson [56], Henderson and Norman [57] and Norman [108]. The results quoted below are those obtained by Norman using a development of the published version of RB74, which differs from it mainly in two ways:

(1) The non-bank public's demands for demand and time deposits are estimated directly.

(2) The modelling of the capital account of the balance of payments is disaggregated in order to provide explanatory functions for:
   (a) other direct investment ($\equiv$ FIOD);
   (b) institutional loans ($\equiv$ FIIL); and
   (c) portfolio investment ($\equiv$ FIP).

Since Henderson and Norman's [57] earlier extensions of the model emphasised the role of inflationary expectations in influencing consumer spending, award wages, the supply price of capital and financial asset choices, the model is reasonably general in that the transmission process contains not only the familiar cost-of-capital and wealth effects but also availability effects (in the housing sector) and expectational effects.

For present purposes we are not primarily concerned with the relative import-ance of these four channels of monetary influence. Simulations of the full model, such as we are here reporting, are not well designed to give information on this point. Typically, however, the wealth effect is quick relative to both the cost of capital and availability. After a time – often substantial, since the functions explaining private investment in fixed capital are typically neo-classical – the cost-of-capital effect becomes of major importance in influencing investment.[5]

In the simulations reported below the change in monetary policy is defined as increasing a subset of domestic interest rates by one percentage point (100 basis points) and maintaining them above their historical values by this amount through the simulation. For convenience we shall use the medium-term Commonwealth-bond rate (RGM) as a proxy for this subset of rates. Hence, we shall discuss the simulation in terms of a 1 per cent (100 basis points) increase in RGM. Since the change is assumed to occur in 1967.I, the proportionate

**Table 10.1** *Intermediate financial variables:*
*simulation response for RB74 (Norman)*

| Quarter | Supply price of capital (RHO) % | 90-day Common-wealth bill rate (R.Bill) % | Private sector wealth ($W_p$) $A mm | Broad money stock ($M_3$) $A mm | Mortgage approvals (MA) $A mm |
|---|---|---|---|---|---|
| 1 | 1·252 | 1·683 | −1,833·3 | −53·1 | −0·92 |
| 2 | 1·252 | 1·683 | −2,079·9 | −105·4 | −1·83 |
| 3 | 1·252 | 1·683 | −2,279·7 | −155·2 | −3·00 |
| 4 | 1·252 | 1·683 | −2,444·9 | −201·6 | −3·73 |
| 5 | 1·252 | 1·683 | −2,567·1 | −240·8 | −4·24 |
| 6 | 1·252 | 1·683 | −2,598·6 | −279·9 | −5·37 |
| 7 | 1·252 | 1·683 | −2,744·3 | −319·0 | −6·69 |
| 8 | 1·252 | 1·683 | −3,189·5 | −365·5 | −7·70 |
| 27 | 1·252 | 1·683 | −4,823·4 | −1,027·9 | −24·62 |
| Maximum | 1·252 | 1·683 | −6,734·2 | −1,027·9 | −27·93 |
| (Quarter) | (n.a.) | (n.a.) | (24) | (27) | (24) |

| Elasticity with respect to RGM [a] | | | | | |
|---|---|---|---|---|---|
| 4 quarters | | | −0·24 | −0·09 | −0·17 |
| 8 quarters | 0·49 | 1·74 | −0·31 | −0·35 | −0·35 |
| Maximum | | | −0·66 | −0·44 | −1·26 |

[a] All elasticities are defined with respect to initial values.
*Notes*: Proportionate change in RGM = 0·199.
*Source*: Norman [108].

increase in RGM is of the order of 20 per cent. It is with respect to this change that the reported elasticities are calculated.

Since the transmission process contained in the model is of the familiar neo-Keysian form, we provide only a single table showing the response, in both elasticity and absolute terms, of the main intermediate financial variables (Table 10.1). Extensive comment on this table is unnecessary. Two points, however, are worth noting. The first is that, apart from the supply price of capital, the three main intermediate variables attain their maximum response only after some six or seven years. An implication for this is that, if monetary policy (as defined) is to be used for short-period stabilisation purposes, then, since its impact on financial variables is fairly slow to develop, policy may have to be modified fairly quickly, if the implicit medium-term variations in intermediate variables are unacceptable. In short, a severe change in monetary policy, defined in form as in the simulation, may in the medium term imply changes in (say) private sector wealth ($W_p$) or the flow of mortgage approvals (MA), which would bring an unacceptable risk of financial instability either overall or in particular financial markets.

The second point is that, although private sector wealth, the nominal money stock and the flow of mortgage approvals all react fairly slowly, the last variable is the slowest of the three. Indeed, by the eighth quarter it has changed by only about 25 per cent of its maximum response, whereas private sector wealth has responded by nearly 50 per cent of its maximum and the broad money stock ($M_3$) by some 35 per cent. This relatively slow response of mortgage approvals is a little surprising, but the magnitude of its final response provides a good explanation of the Reserve Bank's obvious readiness to ease the impact of restraint in this market as soon as possible.

The response of the main demand components is set out in Table 10.2. Once again, apart from investment in non-farm stocks, most demand components reach their peak response after some six and a half to seven years. According to the model, however, this is not true of private investment either in other building and construction or in equipment, both of which reach their maxima after around three and a half to four years. In short, these two series exhibit oscillatory behaviour, as does investment in non-farm stocks.

According to the transmission process of RB74, both consumption and gross private investment in fixed capital respond directly to monetary action. Taking the sum of these two subaggregates, the four-quarter change amounts to close on $A38 million at constant 1966–7 prices; this is about 0·8 per cent of its initial value. Over two years the change is almost precisely doubled (1·6 per cent) and amounts to about half of the maximum change (3·1 per cent) that occurs after approximately seven years. Thus, the main elements in private sector expenditure respond fairly slowly, even though about half of the maximum effect is already reached by the eighth quarter. The distribution of these changes over the elements of expenditure is what might be expected. Proportionately, the most sensitive element is investment in dwellings, followed by investment in other

**Table 10.2** *Major demand and components: Simulation results for RB74 (Norman)*
*(at constant 1966–7 prices)*

| | Consumption ($Am.) | | | | Investment ($A m.) | | | | | Imports |
|---|---|---|---|---|---|---|---|---|---|---|
| Quarter | CND | CHD | CMV | C | ID | IC | IE | I | INFS | ($A m.) |
| 1 | −2·7 | −1·8 | −0·04 | −4·54 | −2·78 | −4·6 | 1·4 | −5·9 | 1·5 | −0·8 |
| 2 | −7·6 | −4·1 | −0·66 | −12·36 | −6·08 | −3·5 | 0·2 | −9·4 | 1·0 | −1·9 |
| 3 | −11·6 | −4·9 | −1·74 | −18·24 | −7·0 | −3·2 | −1·0 | −11·2 | −1·2 | −3·5 |
| 4 | 15·7 | −5·5 | −2·68 | −23·88 | −8·0 | −3·7 | −2·4 | −14·3 | −3·1 | −4·5 |
| 5 | −18·0 | −6·0 | −3·49 | −27·49 | −9·3 | −2·7 | −4·6 | −16·6 | −5·0 | −6·4 |
| 6 | −23·2 | −6·4 | −4·28 | −33·88 | −10·4 | −4·0 | −6·3 | −20·6 | −5·6 | −8·1 |
| 7 | −27·5 | −6·6 | −4·88 | −38·98 | −11·4 | −4·9 | −8·0 | −24·3 | −6·6 | −9·7 |
| 8 | −33·8 | −7·1 | −5·34 | −46·24 | −12·6 | 7·2 | −9·7 | −29·5 | −6·5 | −10·2 |
| 27 | −85·2 | −9·4 | −8·62 | −103·22 | −29·8 | −2·4 | −8·5 | −40·7 | −4·1 | −23·3 |
| Maximum | −93·4 | −12·5 | −8·71 | −103·22 | −31·5 | −14·0 | −18·2 | −40·7 | −10·1 | −23·3 |
| (Quarter) | (24) | (24) | (26) | (27) | (25) | (16) | (14) | (27) | (15) | (27) |
| Elasticity with respect to RGM[a] | | | | | | | | | | |
| 4 quarters | −0·02 | −0·09 | −0·008 | −0·033 | −0·16 | −0·10 | −0·02 | −0·07 | n.a. | −0·03 |
| 8 quarters | −0·05 | −0·12 | −0·153 | −0·064 | −0·26 | −0·19 | −0·09 | −0·15 | n.a. | −0·07 |
| 27 quarters | −0·14 | −0·16 | −0·248 | −0·142 | −0·60 | −0·06 | −0·07 | −0·20 | n.a. | −0·15 |
| Maximum | −0·15 | −0·21 | −0·250 | −0·142 | −0·64 | −0·37 | −0·16 | −0·20 | n.a. | −0·15 |

[a] All elasticities are defined with respect to initial values.
*Notes:* CND = consumption of non-durables
      CHD = consumption of household durables
      CMV = consumption of motor vehicles
      C = CND + CHD + CMV
      ID = investment in dwellings
      IC = investment in other building and construction
      IE = investment in equipment
      I = ID + IC + IE
      INFS = investment in non-farm stocks
*Source:* Norman [108].

building and construction, although both elements in consumers' expenditure on durables display a marked response. Indeed, our proxy (defined in Chapter 3) for the potential scope for monetary policy, which is

| Externally financed private expenditure | ≡ | Gross private investment in fixed capital | + | Consumers' expenditure on durables |
|---|---|---|---|---|

declines by nearly 32 per cent of its initial value by the eighth quarter of the simulation.

Overall, the behaviour of the major demand components offers some support for the view of the transmission process implicitly assumed in Chapters 7–9 and for our *a priori* identification in Chapter 2 of elements that are sensitive at the margin to cost-of-capital and availability effects.

Our main interest, however, is the impact of the monetary restriction on our two macroeconomic target variables and on the external constraint of the balance of payments. Norman's [108] results for the former are given in Table 10.3. The

**Table 10.3** *Ultimate target variables: simulation results for RB74 (Norman)*

| Quarter | Real GNP Constant 1966–7 $A million | Unemployment ('000) | % unemployment | GDP Deflator Index | Consumer Price Index | Wage earnings Index |
|---|---|---|---|---|---|---|
| 1 | −8·2 | 0·7 | 0·02 | − | − | − |
| 2 | −18·8 | 1·4 | 0·04 | − | − | − |
| 3 | −27·2 | 2·1 | 0·06 | − | − | − |
| 4 | −36·6 | 2·4 | 0·065 | − | − | − |
| 5 | −47·7 | 6·0 | 0·15 | − | −0·001 | − |
| 6 | −51·9 | 6·4 | 0·17 | − | −0·001 | −0·001 |
| 7 | −60·1 | 6·7 | 0·17 | − | −0·001 | −0·001 |
| 8 | −72·0 | 6·0 | 0·16 | −0·001 | −0·001 | − |
| 27 | −124·8 | 2·8 | 0·07 | −0·022 | −0·016 | −0·033 |
| Maximum | −136·8 | 10·1 | 0·25 | −0·030 | −0·016 | −0·033 |
| (Quarter) | (24) | (13) | (13) | (27) | (27) | (27) |

Elasticity with respect to RGM[a]

| | Real GNP | Unemployment | % | GDP Deflator | Consumer Price | Wage earnings |
|---|---|---|---|---|---|---|
| 4 quarters | −0·03 | 0·16 | 0·17 | − | neg. | − |
| 8 quarters | −0·06 | 0·40 | 0·41 | − | neg. | − |
| 27 quarters | −0·10 | 0·19 | 0·18 | −0·08 | −0·08 | −0·16 |
| Maximum | −0·11 | 0·67 | 0·66 | −0·09 | −0·08 | −0·16 |

[a] All elasticities are defined with respect to initial values.
*Source*: Norman [108].

first point to note is that real GNP declines over four quarters by 0·5 per cent and over eight quarters by 1·2 per cent. Since the change in interest rates assumed is in proportional terms both severe and sustained, we may conclude that output over our assumed policy horizon is relatively insensitive to monetary policy. Although the impact of policy is as usual cumulative, this remains true, since the maximum impact on real GNP, attained after four years, is only 2·1 per cent and falls after attaining this value. The impact on real GNP is thus cyclical.

So too is the impact on the percentage of the workforce unemployed. After four quarters this is negligible; and after eight quarters, when the series has already peaked once in the seventh quarter, it remains less than 0·2 per cent.

Not entirely surprisingly, since the wage–price sector of RB74 is essentially an extension of the Phillips curve approach, the simulation suggests that over our policy horizon the assumed monetary restraint has a negligible impact on prices and wages. Over twenty-seven quarters the change in the consumer price index is rather less than 2 per cent and that of the GDP deflator rather more. Over seven years, however, this amounts to reducing the rate of inflation by some 0·25 per cent per annum, and of this change virtually nothing occurs within our policy horizon of two years.

Thus, it seems that over our assumed policy horizon monetary restraint is even more ineffective in reducing inflation than it is in restricting output. Since one of the loudest sounds in the contemporary world is the assertion of the contrary by monetarists and neo-monetarists, this is perhaps a surprising result, particularly since the Henderson–Norman version of the model specifically permits the expected rate of inflation to influence the rate of change of wages and permits expected inflation itself to be influenced by monetary variables. Whether this

**Table 10.4** *The Balance of payments: simulation results RB74 (Norman)*

| Quarter | Private capital inflow ($A m.) | Current account balance ($A m.) | Change in overseas reserves ($A m.) |
|---|---|---|---|
| 1 | 42·6 | 0·8 | 43·3 |
| 2 | 38·2 | 1·9 | 40·0 |
| 3 | 37·5 | 3·1 | 40·2 |
| 4 | 38·1 | 4·5 | 42·7 |
| 5 | 37·1 | 6·4 | 43·4 |
| 6 | 35·6 | 8·1 | 43·7 |
| 7 | 35·5 | 9·7 | 44·8 |
| 8 | 34·8 | 10·2 | 44·7 |
| 27 | 67·1 | 23·3 | 90·4 |
| Elasticity with respect to RGM[a] | | | |
| 4 quarters | 2·3 | n.a. | n.a. |
| 8 quarters | 2·1 | n.a. | n.a. |
| 27 quarters | | | |
| Maximum | 4·0 | n.a. | n.a. |

[a] All elasticities are defined with respect to initial values.
*Note*: All figures have been rounded.
*Source*: Norman [108].

result is acceptable for the late 1960s – the period of the simulation – and, if so, whether it has any relevance to the problems of the late 1970s, are matters to which we return later. At present we simply wish to stress that this *is* the implication of Norman's simulations.

In marked contrast is the apparent ability of monetary policy to influence the external constraint, i.e. the overall balance of payments. There are, obviously enough, two aspects of this. The first is the response of the current account via the fall in imports; the second is the response of the capital account via the impact of higher Australian interest rates on private capital inflow. As Table 10.4 shows, it is the capital account element that dominates the response which brings about a very rapid change in overseas reserves.

According to these estimates the rate of private capital inflow (PKI) increases by some $A40 million per quarter in the first quarter of the simulation and remains at or close to this figure over the eight quarters of the policy horizon. Thus, over the eight quarters some $A344 million are added to reserves, of which some $A300 million are due to the capital account response. In terms of the initial level of reserves this amounts to a 34 per cent increase.

The maximum response of private capital inflow is some $A67 million. This occurs in the twenty-seventh quarter. Hence, in that quarter, i.e. after nearly seven years, reserves are gaining at some $A90 million per quarter. This is at a quarterly rate of some 8 per cent of the initial (1967.I) figure for reserves.

Norman's equations are of course, experimental in the sense that they represent an early attempt to model the response of private capital inflow rather than the outcome of a lengthy programme of specialised research into the problem. We discuss them more fully in a later section. Because they are experimental it seems essential to treat them with great caution. However, unless they represent a very serious overstatement of both the extent and speed of the response by private capital inflow, the inference seems inescapable that monetary action is, relatively to its impact on output and inflation, an effective means of operating on the external constraint via the capital account.

The broad lessons to be derived from Norman's results are fairly clear. Monetary policy is, it seems, relatively very inefficient at influencing inflation, not very effective in influencing real output and relatively extremely effective in influencing the balance of payments under a regime of a pegged rate for the Australian dollar. It is, of course, a matter for conjecture, and controversy, how far these results were correct for the period of the simulation. Their applicability in the late 1970s is *a fortori* even more a matter for conjecture and controversy.

## 10.4  A note on RB76

The second macroeconometric model that we shall consider is RB76, developed in the Reserve Bank by Jonson *et al.* and discussed in a series of research papers.[6]

This model was also the subject of a conference in applied economic research held at Sydney in December 1977. For a full exposition of RB76 and a more systematic review of its properties, both theoretical and empirical, the interested reader should consult the published account of this conference.[7] Our present account is based on earlier papers and two studies that became available prior to their appearance in the conference volume.

In discussing RB74, we characterised it as neo-Keynesian, since it contains a transmission mechanism that is typical of this form of theory. In a somewhat less precise manner RB76 could be characterised as a relatively small neo-monetarist model, since the transmission mechanism that it contains, although it allows for interest rate effects on net fixed capital investment and household expenditures, emphasises the role of monetary disequilibrium, defined as the excess supply of real money ($M_3$) balances. Essentially, this monetary disequilibrium term replaces the wealth effect and the availability effects found in neo-Keynesian models, while the method of including the interest rate in the two expenditure functions, particularly that for fixed capital investment, simplifies the supply-price-of-capital mechanism contained in RB74.

In addition to appearing in the function explaining household expenditure, the monetary disequilibrium term (as defined above) also appears in the equation determining the price of output and the equation explaining average weekly earnings.

The rationale of this emphasis on monetary disequilibrium[8] has been given by Jonson, Moses and Wymer [78] as money's crucial role as a buffer stock and money's informational, and thus expectation-influencing, properties. The former rationale is stressed with regard to its inclusion in the household expenditure function, the latter in relation to its inclusion in the price and wage equations. Just how convincing these arguments are seems highly dubious. For example, in view of the buffer stock analysis, it is surprising to find that the monetary disequilibrium term does not appear in other asset demand functions, such as those explaining the non-bank demand for government securities and net capital inflow. Equally, the expectational–informational justification for the term's inclusion in the wage–price equations is unconvincing. Admittedly, in view of the apparent attachment of the media, the semitechnical press and even many politicians to various forms of monetarism, it would be surprising if, in some sense, monetary variables did not now (i.e. in the late 1970s) enter the expectation-generating process. It seems, however, to assume a remarkable degree of sophistication on the part of transactors to regard the relevant monetary variable as the real excess supply of money rather than (say) some far simpler index, such as the rate of change of the nominal money stock. Moreover, in so far as the emphasis is on the role of monetary disequilibrium in determining inflationary expectations, it is perhaps strange that the wage–price equations do not contain a specific term in the expected rate of price change (for which estimates are available) and an additional equation explaining the new endogenous variable in terms *inter alia* of monetary disequilibrium (as defined). The fact that the expected rate of inflation does not appear, i.e. that the reduced form approach is used, means that the monetary disequilibrium term may be capturing a number of influences, of which its own influence on expectations is only one.

In short, although the monetary disequilibrium term plays an important role in RB74, which thus appears to emphasise the influence of money, it is by no means sure that the monetary disequilibrium term in practice reflects only monetary influences in this narrow sense. It is indeed a reasonable conjecture, but no more, that the term also captures some more familiar wealth effects. Unfortunately, without introducing a fairly considerable additional measure of disaggregation, these conjectures cannot be tested.

It can thus be argued that, although RB76 emphasises the role of money, it does not establish it. The emphasis is typically *a priori*, in that monetary disequilibrium does not seem to have been established as the only element in the transmission mechanism reflected in the estimated contribution of the excess real supply of money.

These points are offered not as criticisms of RB76 but as qualifications to the interpretation of the results that it generates. The model is a major research effort with many interesting and potentially fruitful characteristics. Unfortunately, we cannot review these in any worthwhile way, since our present interest is concerned only with its simulation results.[9] An important paper by V W Fitzgerald and C I Higgins appears in the proceedings of a conference concerned with the properties of the Reserve Bank model RB76. These proceedings are now published as Conference in Applied Economic Research [137]. The Fitzgerald-Higgins study contains simulations of the responses of both RB76 and the NIF model to a defined form of monetary expansion introduced in 1966.III – a date not too far removed from that used in the Norman experiments with RB74.

## 10.5 *RB76 and the NIF model*

The precise form of monetary expansion has been defined by Fitzgerald and Higgins as a: 'Sustained reduction (of one per cent) in official interest rates plus an additional increase in money stock due to bank advances policy.'

Because of a change in the structure of the NIF wage-award equation in 1975.I, the simulations reported end in 1974.IV. There are thus thirty-four quarterly observations in the Fitzgerald–Higgins simulations as opposed to the twenty-seven reported by Norman [108] for RB74. Once again, however, we are primarily interested in the results occurring within our assumed two-year policy horizon.

On initial examination of the responses of RB76 to the defined change in policy, two conclusions emerge immediately: (a) the extremely small impact on real output, which by the eighth quarter has risen by less than 0.5 per cent;[10] and (b) the negligible effect on the price level, which by the eighth quarter has risen by only about 0.24 per cent. Thus, in these two areas RB76 tells much the same story as RB74, at least over our policy horizon.

Two points, however, are worth noting. The response of RB76 is in general cyclical. Thus, the rate of growth of prices, which by the eighth quarter is above its control value, falls to its control value by the twelfth quarter and then remains *below* it. This means that monetary expansion (as defined) has a negligible effect in increasing the rate of inflation over the policy horizon and in the somewhat longer run actually *decreases* it.[11] As a result, the price *level* is below its control value from the fifth year onwards. These seemingly counter intuitive results obviously qualify the apparent resemblance of the model's results to those of RB74.

The figures in Table 10.5, kindly supplied by Dr Jonson, give the external response of RB76 over a two-year policy horizon. Once again the external response is relatively significant. The main element, however, now occurs in the trade balance, with the response of private capital flows relatively small and only a fraction of that indicated by Norman's results. It must, of course, be remembered that in RB76 the rate of exchange is an endogenous variable and that the monetary expansion induces a fall in the exchange rate.

**Table 10.5** *External response of RBA76:*[a] *deviations from control ($A million)*

| Period | Trade balance | Capital flows | Foreign reserves |
|:------:|:-------------:|:-------------:|:----------------:|
| 1 | − 0.5 | | − 0.3 |
| 2 | − 1.2 | −0.6 | − 1.8 |
| 3 | − 1.3 | −1.3 | − 4.7 |
| 4 | − 3.5 | −1.8 | − 4.7 |
| 5 | − 5.3 | −2.2 | − 14.8 |
| 6 | − 10.3 | −2.4 | −21.6 |
| 7 | − 7.9 | −2.5 | −30.0 |
| 8 | − 15.5 | −2.5 | −39.9 |

[a]Simulation of monetary expansion as defined in Reserve Bank of Australia [137].
*Source*: Personal communication from Dr P. Jonson.

Comparison of these figures with the commentary by Jonson *et al.* in Reserve Bank of Australia [137] must be undertaken with care, since, while the data in Table 10.5 are given in terms of absolute changes, the graphical summary in the former is presented in terms of annual growth rates. However, Jonson *et al.*'s comment on this simulation that 'the fall in international reserves – due in this case largely to the response of capital flows to the lower bond rate' – is difficult to reconcile with the data on absolute deviations given here.

It is also clear that, in comparison with Norman's results, the decline in reserves is very much smaller.

The Fitzgerald–Higgins comparison of RBA76 and the NIF model[12] suggests two things:

(1) The output response of the NIF model is considerably greater, reaching about 1.2 per cent by the eighth quarter.

(2) The price response of the NIF model, although only some 0.3 per cent by the eighth quarter, increases steadily throughout the simulation, reaching about 1.75 per cent by the eighth year.

This *form* of price response seems intuitively more plausible than that of RB76. It nevertheless suggests that monetary expansion (as defined) adds only about 0.2 per cent to the annual rate of inflation, most of which occurs after the end of our (assumed) policy horizon.

Examining the relative impact on the balance of payments in the two models is made virtually useless by the fact that the present NIF model contains no equations explaining private capital flows. Thus, in this model the balance of payments responds only through imports and, since some imports are treated as exogenous, only through the category defined as 'endogenous goods'. By contrast RB76 does not disaggregate imports and has a single equation explaining capital flow. Since output responds more strongly in the NIF model, it would be natural to expect a correspondingly stronger response of imports. However, the response of imports of endogenous goods, which is all that the NIF model determines, is only a part of overall imports. This explained element seems to suggest an import response that is very similar to Norman's results with RB74, although marginally slower over the first few quarters. Nevertheless, the absence of equations for capital flows and the limited extent to which imports are explained renders the NIF model, at least in its present form, unsuitable for assessing the impact of monetary expansion (as defined) on Australia's external position.

In sum, the existence of the NIF model does not require us to modify our general view of the impact of monetary expansion on output and inflation, while it is not suitable for the assessment of the external impact.

## 10.6 Conclusions

In all, then, both RB76 and the NIF model tend to confirm the qualitative conclusions that we derived from Norman's simulations with RB74, in the sense that over a two-year period monetary policy seems:

(a) to exert little influence on the price level and hence on the rate of inflation;

(b) to be a relatively inefficient means of influencing output; but

(c) according to RB74, and to a far less extent RB76, to have a significant influence on the balance of payments, possibly more particularly on the rate of capital inflow.[13]

In dynamic form and in quantitative detail the simulation results of the three models differ. RB76 does not generate Norman's large and rapid shifts in capital inflow; and at least at a first inspection, the path of prices in RB76 seems difficult to accept. Nevertheless, at the rather general level of analysis that concerns us the models suggest not only that conclusions (a)–(c) should be provisionally accepted but also that our earlier intuitive judgements concerning the impact of monetary policy on aggregate demand and output may not have been too misleading.

As we have sought to stress, the models generate results for average behaviour and typically estimate the parameters of average behaviour from a data base beginning in 1959 and ending in the early or mid-1970s. It must remain a problem to decide how far these results, even if broadly reliable as general indicators of the economy's response up to (say) 1974, will remain relevant in the late 1970s and early 1980s. Equally, it is a problem to know how the responses of the system may have changed, if they have indeed done so. On these issues there is little to guide us but intuition.

We return to this problem later. In general, however, it must seem dubious whether the behaviour of the models will be a very reliable guide to contemporary (1977–8) and immediate future responses, since the Australian economy has in recent years experienced, not only historically very high rates of inflation and unemployment as well as severe shifts in macroeconomic policy, but also repeated injections of political uncertainty. Indeed, after the experience of 1975–7 it would surely be naive to expect the routine behaviour (presumably) captured by econometric models to remain unchanged.

## Notes: Chapter 10

1 In some models variables typically regarded as policy controlled, and thus exogenous, are endogenised by estimating reaction functions. RB76 follows this procedure with both the medium-term bond rate and the rate of exchange.
2 For an interesting example, cf. Argy and Carmichael [5].
3 Simulations should thus be regarded as yielding orders of magnitude rather than precise estimates.
4 This emphasis on a relatively short period of time may be somewhat inappropriate in the case of RB76, which is designed to emphasise the medium term.
5 Cf. Henderson [54].
6 The most useful reference is Reserve Bank of Australia [137].
7 Reserve Bank of Australia [137].
8 For an excellent review of the monetary dynamics of RB76, consult Davis and Lewis in Reserve Bank of Australia [137].
9 For a comprehensive account of this model and an equally comprehensive critique, cf. Reserve Bank of Australia [137].
10 The impact on unemployment is negligible.
11 In our view the result may derive in the main from a specification of monetary expansion that is inappropriate given the monetary dynamics of RBA76, since a fall in the interest rate in this model reduces the excess supply at real $M_3$ and is thus deflationary. For a discussion of this point, cf. Fitzgerald and Higgins in [137].
12 An acount of this model is given in Treasury and Australian Bureau of Statistics, *An Econometric Model of the Australian Economy* (Treasury–ABS, mimeo, November 1977).
13 At present, as stressed in Chapter 11, the modelling of private capital movements is in an experimental stage. The results for this variable therefore need to be treated with particular caution.

# Chapter 11

# Monetary Policy and Private Capital Inflow

## 11.1　Introduction

On our interpretation of the results to be derived from the existing macroeconometric models, the apparent effectiveness of discretionary monetary action is greatest in influencing the balance of payments constraint and, more particularly, the rate of private capital inflow. This finding, if correct and if it relates to the contemporary as well as the past behaviour of the Australian economy is clearly of considerable significance, in that it must influence the objectives for which monetary policy should be deployed. Because of this potential importance this chapter seeks to bring out in rather more detail the relationships that exist between private capital inflow and monetary variables. Additionally, it reviews some further results of investigations into the determinants of private capital inflow and attempts to compare these with those provided by Norman's work with RB74.

In short, the chapter tries to examine rather further the implications of the apparent existence of a relation between Australian monetary policy and private capital inflow, while concurrently seeking to assess just how far the (apparent) relation has been established by economic investigation.

248

Figure 11.1    Balance of payments: summary ($A million)

Apparent private capital flow (a)
(right-hand scale)

Capital account balance

Current account balance
(right-hand scale)

Changes in official reserves

$A MILLION

YEARS

a  Defined as grand total in Figure 2.6
*Source:* Reserve Bank of Australia, *Statistical Bulletin*

## 11.2  Capital Movements and Monetary Policy

For the whole of the period covered by this study the Australian authorities treated the rate of exchange as a discretionary variable, as opposed to a market-determined or market-influenced price. In the short run the rate was therefore fixed in terms of a major reserve currency — originally sterling, later the US dollar — or a trade-weighted subset of such currencies. Exchange rate changes were discretionary and infrequent. The regime was therefore that of a 'jumping peg' – the typical Bretton Woods arrangement.

Since December 1976 – a date after the formal end of this study – the rate has been managed. Thus far we have only some fourteen or fifteen months' experience on which to form a judgement on how this will perform. It seems, however, that the rate will 'crawl' after market forces rather than respond fairly rapidly and fully to them. It follows that in the present context the jumping peg and the crawling peg are similar in that external disequilibria will be met by reserve changes, not exclusively by exchange rate changes. Thus, under both regimes a change in the rate of private capital inflow must entail a roughly corresponding change in Australia's external reserves and Australia's nominal money stock. More generally, it follows that, in so far as the Reserve Bank of Australia wishes to control the change in the net base or the net LGS (liquid assets and government securities) base, it must seek to offset changes in its overseas reserves arising out of changes in either Australia's balance on current account or capital account.

In order to give some idea of the importance of private capital inflow in this context Figure 11.1 presents quarterly data for the current account balance, capital account balance, the changes in Australia's external reserves and the apparent private capital inflow. This gives some idea of the significance of fluctuations in the last item. Clearly, this is on occasions very considerable indeed. Moreover, in interpreting the data it must be recalled that in some periods the Australian authorities were attempting to restrict private capital movements by such devices as the VDR, partial embargoes and – it is said – deliberate administrative delays in granting exchange control approvals. Therefore, the data understate the extent of variation in planned private-capital movements.

As we have seen, the institutional integration of Australian money and capital markets with overseas centres has developed very extensively since the mid-1960s. This integration is likely to proceed further in the future. It therefore seems reasonable to argue that the *potential* variation in Australia's balance on capital account is unlikely to diminish in future.

Thus, the picture not only makes it clear that fluctuations in private capital inflows have on occasions raised grave doubts about the technical capacity of the Reserve Bank to carry out its intended monetary policy, but also suggests that fluctuations may well become more severe in the future as financial integration proceeds.

The reader should note the obvious qualification that these judgements are conditional upon a jumping or crawling peg regime as we have interpreted it. A fully flexible rate of exchange would in theory eliminate changes in external reserves and thus the difficulty of controlling the net base. In short, the Australian problem is the familiar one of how far it is possible for a small open economy with a highly developed and increasingly internationally-integrated financial system to combine a discretionary monetary policy with a jumping or crawling peg, i.e. with a discretionary exchange rate. We return to this overall policy issue in Chapter 13. For the moment, however, we look very generally at the theory of private capital movements; for not only is there a relationship via the net base between such movements and the Reserve Bank's discretionary changes in its net domestic assets, but there is also a relationship between domestic monetary policy and private capital flows in the sense that the monetary stance of the Reserve Bank will typically influence the private capital flow. This, of course, is the relationship emphasised in Norman's results with RB74. It is also one modelled by Jonson *et al.* in RB76.

## 11.3 *Capital Flows: Theoretical Considerations*

As a matter of definition we may distinguish between private capital flows that are: (a) *exogenous,* in the sense of being independent of any of endogenous variables determined within the macroeconomic model of the Australian economy; and (b) *endogenous,* in the sense of being determined within the model.

In the first case the rate of private capital inflow is by assumption independent of Australian economic conditions. It follows that the rate of inflow will not respond to changes in such conditions including *inter alia* changes in Australian monetary policy. Hence, if all private capital inflows are exogenous, the problem for the Reserve Bank will be the technical one of offsetting or neutralising the impact of any change in the capital inflow on the net base by open market operations, by changes in the required ratio of SRDs or, more rarely, by changes in the reserve requirements of the trading and savings banks. Obviously enough, the Reserve Bank's ability to do this is asymmetrical in the sense that increases in reserves are more readily dealt with than reserve losses, which can only be offset to the extent of the initial reserve holding, supplemented by the authorities' willingness and ability to borrow overseas.

In the second case private capital flows are assumed to be highly and rapidly responsive to Australian conditions, including, of course, Australian monetary conditions. In this sort of situation any rise (fall) in Australian interest rates relative to those in key countries overseas will lead to fund inflows (outflows). In the limit, therefore, we may expect the domestic Australian rate to tend to a fixed relation, not necessarily that of numerical equality, with the dominant international rate, e.g. the rate of Eurodollar obligations of corresponding maturity. If this situation holds, the Australian nominal money stock will tend to be equal to the nominal Australian demand at the given Australian domestic rate, which is now in effect determined in the Eurodollar market.

From this it follows that, where this limiting case holds, the Australian authorities cannot conduct an independent monetary policy defined in terms of *either* the nominal money stock *or* the domestic nominal interest rate. For example, if they attempt to increase the nominal money stock by increasing the Reserve Bank's net domestic assets, the only consequence will be an outflow of private capital that is precisely equal to the increase, thus leaving the net base and the money stock unaltered. In short, in this case the Reserve Bank can vary the *composition*, but not the *total*, of the net base. Alternatively, it can in theory control the rate of private capital inflow simply by increasing or decreasing its net domestic assets.

This inability to control the nominal money stock, or the Australian nominal interest rate, is, of course, conditional on the maintenance of a (slowly) crawling or (rarely) jumping peg. If the rate of exchange is allowed to clear the exchange market, then, as we have noted, an independent monetary policy will become possible. Thus, with a 'managed float', reverting to the nowadays more common nomenclature, a 'clean' float will restore the possibility of an independent monetary policy; conversely, the 'dirtier' the float, the smaller is this possibility.

The two cases discussed above are, of course, polar extremes of unacceptable implausibility. The typical case contains elements of both, and Australia is no exception to this rule. We now consider their implications a little further.

## 11.4  Capital Inflows and Monetary Control

Although the two polar models sketched above generate similar conclusions regarding the practicability of conducting a discretionary monetary policy under an exchange regime of an (infrequently) adjusted peg, they do so for very different reasons and thus, assuming that a clean float is an unacceptable exchange regime in Australia, pose different policy problems.

Under the exogenous capital-flow assumption, discretionary monetary control can only be made technically feasible even in the short run either: (a) by administrative devices aimed at regulating capital inflows or outflows, i.e. exchange control; or (b) by institutional changes that increase the Reserve Bank's capacity to offset or sterilise inflows or outflows.

With the opposite polar assumption exchange controls are, at least theoretical-unnecessary. This is so because, in so far as private capital movements are sensitive to relative interest rates, these can in principle be, at least in part, divorced from market rates for international transactions by such devices as the VDR technique or interest equalisation taxes. Both devices should be effective where capital movements respond to differentials in nominal interest rates.

The implicit assumption underlying the discussion thus far is that the fixed (in the short period) rate of exchange is not expected to alter. If this assumption does *not* hold – and it has clearly not held on several occasions in recent Australian experience – the *ex ante* holding period yields on Australian and overseas assets, which we have so far identified with nominal interest rates, must take account of the expected capital gain or loss arising from exchange rate changes. This introduces a speculative element into the analysis. Moreover, since correctly anticipated changes in exchange rates may provide considerable percentage short-term capital gains, the *ex ante* value of these, adjusted for tax and measured at an annual rate, will dominate the *ex ante* holding period yield. In these circumstances there is probably no practicable technique that, by modifying the relationship between observable nominal rates and effective nominal rates, can effectively reduce speculative capital movements. The only possibilities are: (a) to employ administrative methods, i.e. exchange controls, to limit the scope for such movements; and/or (b) to take action that modifies expectations concerning the exchange rate.

Unfortunately, we know remarkably little about the ways in which short run expectations regarding the rate of exchange are formed.[1] Yet, in view of Australian experience, particularly experience during 1976 and early 1977, this issue is of major short-run importance. It is doubtful,[2] however, how far the formal modelling of capital flows can help with this problem, even if the specified model contains a function purporting to generate exchange rate expectations.

This discussion suggests that, in seeking to establish how far it is possible for the authorities to combine a discretionary monetary policy with a relatively invariant rate of exchange, we need empirical information upon the following issues:

(1) the extent to which private capital flows of a non-speculative nature are (a) autonomous with respect to Australian monetary conditions over the relevant policy period and (b) exogenous to the Australian economy as a whole;
(2) the extent to which endogenous non-speculative private capital flows react to Australian monetary variables and the time form of any such reaction;
(3) the extent of speculative private-capital flows;
(4) the form of any expectation-generating function;
(5) the technical efficiency of both (a) exchange control procedures and (b) rate distortion procedures in influencing capital movements; and
(6) the capacity of the Reserve Bank (a) to offset or (b) to neutralise private capital inflows.

We now attempt a short review of empirical work relating to these issues.

# 11.5 Empirical Results:
## Porter's Model and Norman's Equations

In principle there are three methods by which the relationship between private-

capital inflows and domestic monetary conditions may be investigated:
(a) the specification and estimation of structural equations explaining the major components of private capital movements and the incorporation of the resultant equations into an existing Australian macroeconomic model;
(b) the specification of a model specifically related to the problem of explaining capital inflows by a reduced form equation; and
(c) the estimation of a set of structural equations the form and specification of which is unrestricted by the need to be compatible with existing or even contemplated macroeconomic models.

The available work in Australia appears to employ (a) and (b). Thus, Norman [108] [110] has estimated three structural equations and attached these to the Reserve Bank model (RB74). Against this, Kouri and Porter [94], Porter [131] [132] and Murray [102] have developed reduced form estimates. Additional work is known to be in progress, notably by Hunt [66], and this will develop structural equations aimed at explaining capital inflow.[3]

The Porter model is set out fully in Kouri and Porter [94] and more briefly in Porter [131] [132]. Essentially, it is a small general-equilibrium model containing *two* domestic markets: (a) for base money and (b) for domestic bonds.

Rather general and static domestic demand functions for base money and bonds are assumed, and the domestic wealth restriction ($W_D$) is written

$$W_D \equiv M_D + B_D + F_D \qquad (P1)$$

where $M$ is base money, $B$ is domestic bonds and $F$ is foreign bonds and the suffix $D$ denotes domestic.

There is also postulated a foreign demand function for domestic bonds, which is again static.

The supply of base money ($M^S$) is defined as $M^S \equiv NFA + NDA$ (P2) where $NFA$ is net foreign assets of the Reserve Bank and $NDA$ is net domestic assets of the Reserve Bank.

Net capital inflow is then defined as

$$PKI \equiv \Delta B_F - \Delta F_D \qquad (P3)$$

where $\Delta B_F$ is increase in foreign demand for domestic bonds and $\Delta F_D$ is increase in domestic demand for foreign bonds.

The model is used to generate two reduced-form equations of the form

$$\Delta r_d(t) = d_0 + d_1 \Delta r_f(t) + d_2 \Delta Y_D(t) + d_3 \Delta W_D(t) + d_4\, CAB(t) + d_5 \Delta \text{NDA}(t) \ (P4)$$
$$PKI(t) = a_0 + a_1 \Delta r_f(t) + a_2 \Delta Y_D(t) + a_3 \Delta W_D(t) + a_4 CAB(t) + a_5 \Delta \text{NDA}(t) \ (P5)$$

where the $d_i$ and $a_i$ are functions of the partial derivatives of the asset demand functions with respect to $r_d$ (domestic interest rate) $r_f$ (foreign interest rate) $W_D$ (domestic nominal wealth) and $Y_D$ (domestic nominal national income), $CAB$ is current account balance and $\Delta NDA$ is change in net domestic assets of the Reserve Bank.

The model is then solved by assuming that $\Delta NDA$ (change in Reserve Bank's net domestic assets) is the exogenous policy variable. At the same time the current account balance ($CAB$) is treated as independent of the value of $\Delta NDA$.

No results are presented for equation P4. The several results reported by Porter

**Table 11.1** *Equations explaining net capital inflow (reduced form) (Porter)*

| Equation no. | Constant | $\Delta r_f$ | $\Delta Y_D$ | $\Delta W_D$ | CAB | $\Delta$NDA | Spec[a] | $R^2$ | DW |
|---|---|---|---|---|---|---|---|---|---|
| P5.1 | 73·98 | −20·10 | 0·040 | n.a. | −0·680 | −0·484 | 0·068 | 0·680 | 2·38 |
| | (4·48) | (1·52) | (2·37) | | (8·68) | (6·40) | (7·30) | | |
| | | | | | $\Delta B_D^c$ | $\Delta B_N^c$ | | | |
| P5.2 | 73·63 | −9·08[b] | 0·709 | n.a. | −0·630 | −0·646 | −0·053 | 0·925 | 2·18 |
| | (7·09) | (1·34) | (6·96) | | (13·61) | (18·45) | (7·57) | | |
| P5.3 | 78·16 | −11·84 | 0·057 | n.a. | −0·630 | −0·470 | 216·200 | 0·816 | 1·875 |
| | | (0·79) | | | (6·74) | (5·29) | (6·08) | | |

[a]Spec is defined as follows:
P5.1: foreign exchange reserves in previous quarter
P5.2: dummy for speculative pressure in 1971–2 defined as lagged value of reserves in 1971–2
P5.3: dummy = zero up to 1970.IV and unity thereafter.
[b] Adjusted for variable deposit requirement
[c] $\Delta B_N$ = government deficit plus current account surplus
$\Delta B_D$ = discretionary change in the base.
*Note*: t values are given in parenthesis
*Sources*:
P5.1 from Porter [131], data period 1961.III–1972.IV.
P5.2 from Porter [132], data period 1962.III–1975.IV.
P5.3 from Kouri and Porter [94], data period 1961.III–1972.III.

for equation P5 are given in Table 11.1.

In interpreting these results Porter has argued that the coefficients of $\Delta NDA$ in equations P5.1 and P5.2 and $\Delta B_d$ in equation P5.3 imply that something in the range of 47–63 per cent of an increase in the domestic element in the base is offset by private capital outflows due to: (a) an excess demand or supply for base money, generating direct substitution between base money and foreign bonds; and/or (b) substitution effects due to changes in the unobservable relative holding period rates ($\equiv$ market interest rates) due to a change in the endogenous domestic rate.

Moreover, on the basis of the results of the differing sample periods he has argued that the offsetting coefficient, which on his interpretation is approximately a measure of the Reserve Bank's inability to control the base and thus of domestic monetary impotence, has been rising. This result, if valid, would undoubtedly be of major importance and perhaps constitute a case for either adopting a flexible exchange rate with a relatively very clean float or introducing rather rigorous exchange controls. Fortunately, although the regression results must hold and clearly establish a fairly close relationship between *PKI* (net private capital flow) and the variables on the right hand side of equations P5.1, this does not establish Porter's theory and thus his interpretation of the coefficients on $\Delta NDA$ or $\Delta B_d$.

There are a number of reasons for arguing in this way, the first and most important of which is that equations P5.1 are underidentified reduced forms, in the sense that the partial derivatives of the asset demand functions, which are the behavioural constants of the system, are not determined by the estimates of the $a_i$ regression coefficients. Since it is only about these parameters that we have even the weakest of priors, it is hard to say in what sense the reduced form results support Porter's theory rather than any one of a presumably large number of alternative theories that would imply the same, or very similar, reduced forms.

The second set of reasons concerns doubts over the Kouri–Porter specification. For example:

(1) The exogenous policy variable is $\Delta NDA$ (the net change in the Reserve Bank's domestic assets). This implies that the Reserve Bank operates upon some domestic credit expansion target and chooses its values quite independently of either the state of the current balance or the rate of net private capital inflow. This would be a strange form of Reserve Bank behaviour. Happily, it seems an even stranger description of how the Reserve Bank actually behaves.

(2) Although it is doubtful whether the Reserve Bank was dominated by any form of quantity variable as a proximate target rather than by a target nominal interest rate, it would almost certainly be more sensible to regard it as aiming at a given change (net of $SRD$ calls) in the base. Call this $\Delta B^*$. If we now assume that the Reserve Bank can set $\Delta B = \Delta B^*$ to a close approximation, then

$$\Delta B \equiv \Delta NDA + PKI + CAB \approx \Delta B^*$$

so that

$$\Delta NDA \approx \Delta B^* - PKI - CAB$$

In this case, as Porter [131] has shown, the coefficients on $\Delta NDA$ in equations P5.1 and P5.2 will be biased towards $-1$. Moreover, it seems that unless the variance of $\Delta B^*$ is fairly large, which would indicate rather great variation in choices of policy, the bias will also be large. It follows that the estimated coefficient, in Porter's terminology, may in absolute value be substantially biased. Thus, on an alternative specification of Reserve Bank behaviour that seems at the very least markedly less implausible than that chosen by Porter, the estimated offset coefficient may in fact be a rather poor estimate of the sterilisation coefficient, which on this approach equals $-1$.[4]

(3) The choice of $\Delta NDA$ as a policy variable set independently of $PKI$ or $CAB$ seems strange for another reason. Typically, the Reserve Bank is interpreted as attempting to set 'the' domestic interest rate. Since this is presumably a market rate, it must respond not only to $\Delta NDA$ but also to $PKI$ and $CAB$. It follows that the value of $\Delta NDA$ will be a function of both $r_d^*$ (the target value of the domestic rate) and $(PKI + CAB)$. This argument is symmetric with the earlier one, in that , if accepted, it indicates a similar bias in the estimated offset coefficient.

(4) The acceptance of (3), of course, eliminates the applicability of the reduced form to the Australian case since:

(a) if $\Delta r_d = \Delta r_d^*$ i.e. if the authorities *do* set rates, $\Delta r_d$ can be regarded as the exogenous variable and $\Delta NDA$ eliminated from the equation explaining *PKI*; so that

(b) the equation for *PKI* can simply be rewritten in terms of $\dfrac{\partial PKI}{\partial r_f}$, $\dfrac{\partial PKI}{\partial r_d}$

and the relevant changes in domestic and overseas incomes ($Y_D$, $Y_F$) and nominal wealth ($W_D$, $W_F$).

The general point underlying these comments is, plainly enough, a simple one. There are *two* relationships between domestic monetary policy and capital inflows. The first, operating through the base, suggests that $\Delta NDA$ will be inversely related to *PKI* and *CAB* but probably not in any very stable way, since in some cases the Reserve Bank, in seeking to set $\Delta r_d^*$ or $\Delta B^*$, will aim at lowering rates, or raising $\Delta B^*$ rather faster, for cyclical or other reasons. The second relationship arises because any action to set $\Delta r_d^*$ or $\Delta B^*$ will change $r_d$ in relation to $r_f$ and thus set up an induced capital flow, which in the case of a policy with $\Delta B^*$ as the proximate target may be supplemented by direct substitution between money and foreign assets.

Murray's [102] work is essentially an extension of Porter's, since he has explicit-introduced a simple reaction function explaining the authorities' behaviour and re-estimated a Porter-type reduced form by two-stage least squares (TSLS). Unfortunately, the reaction hypothesis performs poorly – and the TSLS and ordinary least squares estimates of the equation explaining capital flows are very similar. As with Porter, the change in the overseas interest rate is highly insignificant. However, Murray has found a considerably smaller (in absolute terms) offset coefficient. Murray's other contribution is to estimate the proportionate significance of each of the independent variable to the explanation of observed private-capital flows. The method used to do this is to assess, over a selected time period, the contribution of each independent variable other than $\Delta r_f$ that is statistically insignificant. This exercise, for what it is worth, suggests that, apart from the subperiod of 1971.I–1972.IV, the contribution of $\Delta NDA$ was relatively small – 5–9 per cent according to Porter and 3–5 per cent according to Murray.

The period 1971.I–1972.IV saw a cumulative increase in Australia's overseas reserves of ($A5,155 million    $A1,779 million = $A3,376 million). In the same period the cumulative net private-capital flow was approximately $A3,950 million and the cumulative reduction in the adjusted domestic assets of the Reserve Bank $A2,176 million. Thus, simply as a ratio $\dfrac{\Delta NDA}{\Delta OA_{RB}} = -0.65$, suggesting that on

average around two-thirds of the net change in overseas assets was offset. In roughly 1972.II monetary policy became expansionary. For 1972.III and IV, the change in Australia's overseas assets amounted to $A1,230 million. For the same period $\Delta NDA$ amounted to $-\$A417$ million – a marginal ratio of $-0.34$. Thus *after* the change in monetary policy stance the apparent neutralisation rate fell to roughly half its *average* value over the period, while prior to the shift in policy the apparent neutralisation ratio was $-0.82$ – rather more than 80 per cent. This, coupled with the observation that (a) $\Delta NDA$ tends to be rather closely and negatively related to $\Delta OA$, while (b) its relation to $PKI$ is frequently positive, e.g. in 1964–5, suggests that the data reflect, at least in large part, a conscious policy of neutralisation by the Reserve Bank, the quantitative incidence of which in any short period is modified in the light of short-run policy requirements. As we have seen, there are sound, if non-econometric, reasons for accepting this view.[5]

There are also what may, rather generously perhaps, be regarded as econometric results supporting the interpretation.

If the Reserve Bank is assumed to follow a quantity as opposed to a price (interest-rate) policy, we may argue that it will set the base in conformity with it. We shall therefore expect

$$\Delta B^*(t) = \Delta B(t) + e_1(t)$$

where $\Delta B^*(t)$ is target value of the base and $e_1$ is error in setting the Base.

The ultimate targets of the Reserve Bank are not known; nor are the authorities; preferences between them. The usual reaction-function approach, however, would yield an expression of the form

$$\Delta B(t) = \Phi \Sigma a_i [\Upsilon_i^* \ (t) - \Upsilon_i(t)] - \Phi B(t\text{-}1) \tag{II.2}$$

to explain $\Delta B^*(t)$, where $\Upsilon_i(t)$ are the actual values of the authorities' ultimate target variables, $\Upsilon_i^*$ $(t)$ are the unobservable target values of the $\Upsilon_i$, $\Phi$ is a parameter reflecting the political and technical costs of adjusting the base and the $a_i$ are parameters reflecting both the Reserve Bank's preferences and its notional model of the economy.

For a rough test of equation II.2 the following target variables were defined:

$\dfrac{\bar{v}}{\bar{u}}$ $(t)$ $\equiv$ a four-quarter unweighted moving average of the ratio of recorded vacancies to recorded unemployment;

$OR(t)$ $\equiv$ a four-quarter moving average of the total of Australia's reserves;

$CPI(t)$ $\equiv$ a four-quarter moving average of the consumer price index ($CPI$); and

$\bar{\dot{P}}(t)$ $\equiv$ a four-quarter moving average of the actual percentage rate of change in the $CPI$.

The moving average was chosen in the attempt to eliminate seasonal distortions from the $\Upsilon_i$. The $\Upsilon_i^*$ were assumed to be constant. This is, of course, an extremely crude procedure.[6]

In general, on this crude assumption $\dot{p}(t)$ added nothing to the explanation of $\Delta B$. Nevertheless, despite its simplicity the hypothesis provided a reasonable degree of explanation for $\Delta B$. These results are essentially preliminary. All that is claimed for them is that they are suggestive.

The addition of political dummy on $a_1$ for the period when a Labour government was in office proved unhelpful. This suggests that, at least over our sample period, the Reserve Bank may have had a rather stable set of preferences.

Typically, central banks monetise some part of the central government deficit (GD). Therefore, this was included as an explanatory variable in the equation for $\Delta B$, with the results shown in Table 11.2.

**Table 11.2** *Movements in the base (dependent variable $\Delta B(t)$)*

| Coefficient on variable | | 1961.I–1971.IV | | 1961.I–1976.IV | |
|---|---|---|---|---|---|
| Constant | $[\equiv a_0]$ | −431·20 (30) | −439·90 (3·1) | −284·10 (2·1) | −278·50 (1·8) |
| $\overline{v}/\overline{u}$ | $[\equiv a_1]$ | −62·20 (3·1) | −65·20 (3·4) | −20·90 (0·8) | −32·20 (1·0) |
| $\overline{OR}$ | $[\equiv a_2]$ | 0·09 (2·8) | 0·09 (3·3) | 0·13 (4·6) | 0·14 (4·4) |
| $\overline{CPI}$ | $[\equiv a_4]$ | 7·10 (2·6) | 7·40 (2·7) | 6·80 (2·9) | 7·70 (2·9) |
| $GD$ | $[\equiv a_5]$ | 0·03 (0·7) | | 0·12 (4·6) | |
| $B(t-1)$ | $[\equiv a_6]^*$ | 0·19 (2·0) | 0·21 (2·1) | 0·35 (3·7) | 0·38 (3·6) |
| $S_1$ | | −72·50 (3·8) | −77·90 (4·5) | −96·00 (3·4) | 132·30 (4·3) |
| $S_2$ | | −35·70 (0·9) | −61·00 (3·6) | −25·70 (0·6) | −122·20 (4·2) |
| $S_3$ | | −36·40 (2·1) | −38·40 (2·3) | −46·20 (1·8) | −62·70 (2·1) |
| $R_2$ | | 0·679 | 0·675 | 0·673 | 0·557 |
| $DW$ | | 2·173 | 2·15 | 1·75 | 1·81 |
| $SER$ | | 39·2 | 38·9 | 68·0 | 78·4 |
| $N$ | | 44 | 44 | 58 | 58 |

$SER$ = Standard Error of Residuals
\*     The figure given is the value of $\Phi = -a_6$.
*Note:* Figures in parenthesis are t values.
*Source:* Model as in equation II.2.

Doubtless a more sustained investigation and a more realistic definition of the $\Upsilon^*_i$ would, in so far as the Reserve Bank does set the base, yield improved results. Nevertheless, as a first approximation the explanation provided by our simplistic approach seems not unreasonable.

If the Reserve Bank typically attempts to set $\Delta B = \Delta B^*$, then, as we have seen,

$$\Delta NDA(t) = \Delta B^*(t) - \Delta OR(t) \qquad \text{(III.3)}$$

$$= a_i \frac{v}{u}(t) + a_2 CPI(t) + a_3 OR(t) + a_4 GD(t) + a_5 \Delta OR(t) + a_6 B(t-1)$$
$$\text{(III.4)}$$

Hence, if equation III.3 holds, we must expect that equation III.4 will yield: (a) estimates of $\hat{a}_i (i \neq 5)$ that are similar to those reported in the results for $\Delta B(t)$; and (b) $\hat{a}_5 \approx -1$.

The restults for $\Delta NDA(t)$ are set out in Table II.3. Again recalling the simplistic nature of our assumptions, the results of estimating equation III.4 are not un-impressive in that: (a) $\hat{a}_5$ is extremely close to -1 and highly significant; while (b) the remaining $\hat{a}_i$ typically do not differ very seriously from those reported in the explanation of $\Delta B$.

**Table 11.3.** *Movements in net domestic assets (dependent variable $\Delta NDA$ (t))*

| Coefficient on variable | | 1961.I–1971.IV | | 1961.I–1976.III | |
|---|---|---|---|---|---|
| Constant | $[\equiv a_0]$ | $-407{\cdot}90$ (2·9) | $-436{\cdot}20$ (3·0) | $-231{\cdot}70$ (1·7) | $-273{\cdot}50$ (1·7) |
| $^v/_u$ | $[\equiv a_1]$ | $-44{\cdot}90$ (1·9) | $-60{\cdot}60$ (2·9) | $-7{\cdot}70$ (0·3) | $-31{\cdot}10$ (0·9) |
| $OR$ | $[\equiv a_2]$ | $0{\cdot}07$ (2·0) | $0{\cdot}09$ (3·2) | $0{\cdot}12$ (4·1) | $0{\cdot}14$ (4·3) |
| $CPI$ | $[\equiv a_3]$ | $7{\cdot}00$ (2·6) | $7{\cdot}50$ (2·8) | $5{\cdot}50$ (2·2) | $7{\cdot}60$ (2·7) |
| $GD$ | $[\equiv a_4]$ | $0.07$ (1·6) | | $0.14$ (4·5) | |
| $\Delta OR$ | $[\equiv a_5]$ | $-0{\cdot}90$ (11·9) | $-0{\cdot}96$ (16·1) | $-0{\cdot}92$ (17·4) | $-0'99$(16·8) |
| $B(t\text{-}1)$ | $[\equiv a_6]^*$ | $0{\cdot}20$ (2·0) | $0{\cdot}22$ (2·2) | $0{\cdot}29$ (3·0) | $-0{\cdot}37$ (3·3) |
| $S_1$ | | $-87{\cdot}90$ (3·5) | $-79{\cdot}90$ (4·5) | $-94{\cdot}70$ (3·4) | $-132{\cdot}60$ (4·3) |
| $S_2$ | | $-9{\cdot}10$ (0·2) | $-65{\cdot}20$ (3·6) | $-34{\cdot}60$ (0·8) | $-123{\cdot}10$ (4·1) |
| $S_3$ | | $-32{\cdot}10$ (1·9) | $-38{\cdot}00$ (2·3) | $-41{\cdot}20$ (1·7) | $-62{\cdot}40$ (2·1) |
| | | | | | |
| $R^2$ | | 0·930 | 0·929 | 0·925 | 0·894 |
| $DW$ | | 2·20 | 2·15 | 1·92 | 1·83 |
| $SER$ | | 38·7 | 39·2 | 67·0 | 79·2 |
| $N$ | | 44 | 44 | 58 | 58 |

$SER$ = Standard Error of Residuals
\*      The figure given is the value of $\Phi \equiv -a_6$).
*Note:* The figures in parenthesis are standard deviations.
*Source:* Model as an equation III.4.

These results[7] do not, of course, establish that Porter's interpretation of his offset coefficient is inadmissible, for it always is possible to argue that our estimate of $\hat{a}_5$ is close to -1 simply because a change in $NDA$ leads to a more or less precisely offsetting change in reserves that occurs primarily through the capital account. Regression results do not reveal causality. It must therefore be left to the reader to form his own judgement on this point. However, there seems small doubt that Porter's interpretation is erroneous and that his offset coefficient, which implicitly assumes a sterilisation coefficient of zero, is heavily biased.

This interpretation is given further support by the absence of any explicit dynamics in the Kouri-Porter approach. If the Reserve Bank sets the base with the objective of setting either the money stock of 'the' interest rate, it must surely do so in the knowledge that the response of the money stock to $\Delta B$ occurs with a distributed lag, even if the long-run money-supply function is stable. Banks, in short, do not adjust their choice assets fully even within a quarter to a change in the Base. This point is, of course, supported by the researches of Sharpe [151] [152] and Terrell and Valentine [160].

If this is so, Porter's first reduced form (equation P4) is a dynamic mis-specification from the supply side, since in addition to containing $\Delta B(t)$ it should also contain lagged values of $\Delta B$, which it does not.

A similar difficulty arrises on the demand side, where again there is an absence of any explicit dynamics.[8]

Logically, Porter's reduced-form equation for $\Delta r_d$ *(equation P4) is prior to his equation for PKI(t)* (equation P5) in the sense that the latter is obtained by substituting the former into the definition of *PKI(t)*. Hence, if equation P4 has little or no explanatory power, the meaning of equation P5 will become even more dubious.

Porter has presented no results for equation P4, arguing that published interest rates in Australia – typically, government bond yields – do not respond adequately to the market conditions that are central to his model. It is, however, possible to interpret $\Delta r_d$ as the change in the ninety-day commercial bill rate, which *is* responsive to market conditions. If this is done, the results are as shown in Table II.4.

These results are scarcely impressive. They suggest that equation P4 is a mis-specification, which in turn suggests that equation P5 is a mis-specification. Again, this does not *establish* that Porter's interpretation of his results is erroneous. There may be some at present unobserved rate that, if inserted into equation P4, would yield more plausible results; but until this rate can be shown to exist, it is difficult to take Porter's interpretation of his equation P5 results and their extensions in Porter [132] very seriously.[9].

Norman [108] [110] has attempted to develop three structural equations to explain (a) other net direct investment (*ODI*) and (b) portfolio investment and institutional loans (*PI*), which are both themselves disaggregated.

The first of these, which follows an earlier specification by Helliwell and Schott [51], is of the stock adjustment form. Thus,

$$ODI(t) = \lambda_1[k^*_f(t) - k_f(t-1)] \qquad 0 < \lambda_1 \leqslant 1 \qquad (N1)$$

where $k^*_f$ is desired overseas holding of capital in Australia. $k^*_f(t)$ is then specified as a proportion of the Australian capital stock such that

$$k^*_{ft} = \alpha(t)k(t) \qquad (N2)$$

and

$$\alpha(t) = f[rh_d(t), rh_f(t)] \qquad (N3)$$

where $rh_d$ is domestic supply price of capital per cent and $rh_f$ is foreign supply price of capital per cent. Substituting yields

$$ODI(t) = \lambda_1\{a_0k(t) + a_1k(t)[rh_d(t) - rh_f(t)] - k_f(t-1)\} \qquad (N4)$$

This simple hypothesis is then supplemented by two variables to reflect cash flow considerations:

$BFR \equiv$ business financing requirement

$TYCP \equiv$ company income-tax payments.

The full equation then becomes

$$ODI(t) = \lambda_1 a_0 k(t) + \lambda_1 a_1 k(t)[rh_d(t) - rh_f(t)] - \lambda_1 k_f(t-1) + a_2 BFR(t) + a_3 TYCP(t) + \Sigma q_i s_i k(t) \qquad (N5)$$

where the $s_i$ are seasonal dummies. In practice only one such dummy occurs in the estimate.

The explanatory power of Norman's equation (N5) is not impressive; and since $\lambda_1$ is not significantly different from zero – the estimated value is 0.008 with a $t$

**Table 11.4** *Sample period: 1961.III–1975.IV*

| Equation | Constant | $\Delta r_f$ | $\Delta Y_D$ | $\Delta Y_{UK}$ | $\Delta Y_{US}$ | $R^2$ | $R^{-2}$ | DW |
|---|---|---|---|---|---|---|---|---|
| III.P4.I | 0.1713 (0.2114) | 0.5860 (0.1395) | −0.00089 (0.0003) | 0.3465 (0.1410) | −0.0122 (0.0066) | 0.0014 (0.0014) | 0.3722 | 2.068 |
| III.P4.2 | 0.2234 (0.2149) | 0.6389 (0.1352) | −0.00068 (0.00031) | 0.2869 (0.1496) | 0.7966 (0.9817) | $\Delta B - PKI$ −0.00032 (0.0070) | 0.3612 | 1.966 |

*Notes:*
(1) $\Delta B$ = change in base adjusted for changes in SRD ratio;
$\Delta B - PKI \equiv \Delta NDA + CAB$; and
$\Delta r_f$ ≡ ninety-day Eurodollar rate adjusted for VDR requirement.
(2) Figures in parentheses are standard deviations.

*Source:* Models – author's version of Porter's (p.4).

value of 0.42 – the economic meaning of the estimated relationship, if any, is far from clear.

The equation for institutional loans is a flow equation, since according to Norman a stock adjustment hypothesis performed poorly. We have

$$\Delta IL(t) = \lambda_2[IL^*(t) - IL(t\text{-}1)] \tag{N6}$$

where $IL$ is flow of institutional borrowing overseas. The long-run planned value of $IL$ is then written as

$$IL^*(t) = b_0 + b_1[r_{1d}(t) - r_{1f}(t)] + b_2GDP_f(t) + b_3k_e(t) + D_1(t) \tag{N7}$$

where $r_{1d}$ is interest rate on bank-discounted ninety-day commercial bills in Australia, $r_{1f}$ is rate on ninety-day Eurodollar deposits in London, $GDP_f$ is permanent foreign domestic product in current US dollars, $k_e$ is expected rate of appreciation of the Australian dollar (proxied by the Reserve Bank's net forward position in US dollars) and $D_1$ is a dummy variable designed to capture the influence of controls on $IL$ imposed in 1973.

Substitution of equation N7 in equation N6 yields the usual reduced form.

The estimated results have a relatively high explanatory power ($R^2 = 0.87$); and economically they make more sense, since $(1 - \lambda_2)$ is close to zero and insignificant, suggesting that $\lambda_2 = 1$, so that $IL(t) = IL^*(t)$. Apart from the proxy for $K_c$ the remaining coefficients are well determined and of the correct sign. Thus, this particular structural equation probably merits further investigation and refinement.

The equation for portfolio investment is of the same form as equation (N6). Once again, the adjustment coefficient ($\lambda_3$) is indistinguishable from unity. Thus,

$$PI(t) = PI^*(t) \tag{N8}$$

with

$$PI^*(t) = c_0 + c_1[rh_d - rh_f] (t) + c_2GDP_f(t) + c_3MVR(t) \tag{N9}$$

where $MVR$ is ratio of the market value of Australian fixed capital plus inventories to their replacement value.

Unfortunately, of the coefficients, only $C_0$ and $C_3$ are significant: hence equation N9 effect states that the only variable *reliably* influencing $PI$ is $MVR$ and thus, indirectly, Australian asset prices. Unfortunately, the model contains no lags, and hence it is not clear whether it is $PI$ that explains $MVR$ or $MVR$ that explains $PI$. Intuitively, one would expect $PI$ to be related to expectations about Australian equity prices, which dominate changes in *ex ante* holding period yield on equities. Thus, before equation (N9) can be given a more confident economic interpretation, it will be necessary to relate $MVR$ to equity prices, equity prices to expected equity prices, and expected equity prices to the underlying determinants. The last task, in particular, is extremely difficult; but until it is attempted, equation (N9) is best considered simply as a not very reliable fit between two contemporaneous variables, one of which ($GDP_f$) is exogenous and one of which ($MVR$) *may* respond systematically to domestic monetary policy.[10]

As we have seen, Norman has employed his three structural equations together with a modification of RB74 to simulate the consequences of discretionary monetary action. This exercise suggests an approximate interest elasticity of capital flows of slightly less than unity. Moreover, the change in private capital inflow accounts for more than half the rate of change per quarter in foreign reserves, showing that the change in capital inflow contributes rather more than the change in the current balance to the improvement in the external position.

Some fairly strong, and rough-and-ready, assumptions are necessary to estimate the change in the domestic element in the base. By the fourth quarter after the policy change the money stock, according to the simulation, has fallen by some $A241 million. Typically, the base, excluding the trading banks and savings banks holdings of government securities, is around 12 per cent of the money stock. Thus, if the money stock fell by $A241 million the base would have fallen by perhaps $A30 million on the assumption that the average value of the ratio of base to money stock is a reasonable estimate of marginal ratio. Over the same period overseas reserves rose (according to the simulation) by $A211 million. Hence, net domestic assets must have fallen by around $A240 million – or roughly $A60 million per quarter.

If these approximations are reasonable, the observed value of the average ratio of the change in the rate of private capital inflow to the change in the rate of net domestic-asset expansion by the Reserve Bank must be around $-0.55$.

This, it should be noted, is not far from the estimate by Porter, although the implicit mechanism, which treats the domestic interest rate as the proximate target, is the inverse of Porter's, since both $\Delta B$ and $\Delta NDA$ are in effect dependent variables, while $\Delta Y_D$ and $\Delta W_D$ are themselves influenced by the change in $r_d$.

Norman's results therefore do suggest that the Reserve Bank may have decidedly limited ability to pursue discretionary interest-rate policies over any very long period, particularly where these involve a discretionary reduction in the Australian interest rate, since, assuming that the simulations are approximately symmetric, a 1 per cent reduction in the domestic rate would involve: (a) a $A211 million fall in overseas reserves over four quarters; and (b) a $A154 million cumulative fall in private capital inflow.

Moreover, Norman's figures must in some measure *understate* the sensitivity of private capital, in that exchange rate expectations may well be a function of the rate of reserve loss (gain). If this were the case, a speculative element would need to be added to the changes revealed by his simulations.

Any conclusion that we reach must be extremely tentative in view of our theoretical and empirical reservations about the available studies. Two things do seem clear, however

(1) The rate of private capital inflow into Australia does respond to discretionary changes in domestic interest rates.
(2) The response may well be sufficient to make the discretionary movement of Australian rates of very limited use in influencing aggregate demand, particularly where rates are required to fall.

Against this Norman's equations suggest that private capital inflows (even allowing for offsets via the current account) can be fairly readily diminished by a combination of administrative controls and VDR schemes. Thus, a discretionary monetary policy that is restrictive can be followed more easily than one that is expansive, and the VDR device is potentially an effective means of influencing private capital inflows.

Because of our misgivings about the available research in this area it is difficult to put forward estimates of the extent to which either the embargo or the VDR technique as originally employed from September 1972 to November 1974 influenced the rate of capital flow.

Norman [108] has made some calculations by examining the residuals from forecast values generated by his equations. He concluded that, mainly via institutional borrowing, capital inflow was reduced by $A235 million per quarter. This figure may have been itself reduced by a somewhat lower rate of dividend remission, which Norman has estimated at $A54 million per quarter. Hence, the net impact may have been of the order of $A180 million.

Porter [132] also has presented some estimates of the effect of VDR and the embargo, which over a fifteen-month period he has put at around $A500 million – or perhaps $A100 million per quarter. Again, however, these estimates are somewhat dubious, since Porter's main reduced forms typically display insignificant, and/or wrongly signed, coefficients on $\Delta r_f$ (change in foreign interest rate), although $\Delta VDR$ is correctly signed and typically significant; and where the two variables are combined into a single effective rate, the coefficient is correctly signed but again yields only a low $t$-value (1·34). In the disaggregated equations $\Delta r_f$ is significant only in that explaining Australian investment overseas. $\Delta VDR$ is also significant in this equation and close to it in the equation for direct investment and undistributed income. For financial and portfolio movements, which includes Norman's institutional borrowing, it is wrongly signed and quite insignificant. Against this the embargo dummy is correctly signed, significant and large.

Thus, both Porter and Norman have suggested that the combined effects of embargo and VDR in 1972–4 had a sizable impact on the rate of capital inflow – by something of the order of $A100–180 million per quarter – while Porter's equation for total private capital movements suggests a very large response to a change in VDR. Unfortunately, it is hard to know how reliable these results are or even how they should be interpreted.

A cautious interpretation, however, suggests that:
(a) the VDR device is probably potentially rather powerful; but
(b) it is at present hard to disentangle its impact from that of the embargo; while
(c) the present estimates of its impact in quantitative terms are at best highly dubious.

# 11.6 Conclusions

The investigation of the determinants of the rate of private capital inflow is an extremely complex matter. It is therefore hardly surprising that the pioneer work examined here raises almost as many questions as it answers. Very tentatively, however, three conclusions may be drawn:

(1) Private capital inflows have in the past contained a significant element that, if not exogenous in the full sense, appears to be autonomous with respect to domestic Australian monetary policy.

(2) Nevertheless, most investigations suggest a significant endogenous component.

(3) This component exhibits a useful measure of sensitivity to changes in effective relative rates of return and possibly to disequilibria between the real demand for and supply of money.[11, 12]

Plainly, if (3) is correct, the rate of private capital inflow should respond fairly considerably to the use of the VDR technique. The evidence reviewed suggests that it does.

On the side of central-banking technique the Reserve Bank seems generally to have been able to neutralise changes in overseas assets within the calendar quarter in which they occurred.

Unfortunately, the studies reported do not offer any very convincing evidence regarding the extent of speculative capital flows; nor do they throw any strong light on the problem of identifying the determinants of exchange rate expectations.

Overall, then, the evidence, as is so often the case in economics, is far from providing clear answers to the relevant questions. As a result our conclusions, described as 'tentative', contain a considerable measure of judgement.

# Notes: Chapter 11

1 Research into this issue is probably worthy of a high priority.
2 Any function purporting to explain exchange rate expectations seems likely to display considerable instability, since 'the state of the news' may be interpreted very differently at different times.
3 As part of the financial sector of a relatively small model of the Australian economy.
4 In short, the offset coefficient needs to be estimated jointly with the Reserve Bank's reaction function explaining $\Delta B^*$ or conditionally upon some such reaction function that has been independently established. The same point has been made by Murray [102].
5 For example, the very development of the special accounts and SRD requirements.
6 Many criticisms can be made of this simple reaction-function approach.
7 These results are essentially preliminary. All that is claimed for them is that they are suggestive.
8 The demand side implies that all portfolio adjustment is completed with the period of observation – in this case a calendar quarter. This result is not one that typically emerges from applied studies of individual demand functions or models of portfolio choice.
9 Some further experiments, as yet incomplete, with an expanded reduced-form model suggest an offset coefficient of 0.2 or less. It is believed that Hunt's [66] study yields an estimate of

the same order for the impact offset coefficient. This information is derived from a private communication by Hunt.

10 We have assumed a response of this form in our discussion of transmission mechanism, and a similar linkage exists in RB74.

11 Available simulations with RB76 – a model that emphasises the role of the excess demand (supply) of real money balances – do not include this term in the equation explaining capital movements. It is likely, however, that Jonson and his collaborators will develop new versions of the equation that include this term. If they do, the results should provide evidence regarding its importance.

12 Zecher [170] has suggested that an even closer relationship exists between $\Delta NDA$ and outflows of reserves and found a coefficient of approximately $-1$. However, Zecher's model is unconvincing and does not, as he has pointed out, exclude the possibility that $\Delta NDA$ is set to neutralise reserve changes so that the causal relation is the reverse of that accepted by him and by Porter. This, of course, is precisely what our own results suggest.

# PART FOUR

# SOME CONCLUSIONS
# AND SUGGESTIONS

## Chapter 12

# The Australian Experience: A Summing Up

## 12.1 Introduction

Put rather broadly, the central themes of this study have been: (a) to show how the Australian authorities have as a matter of fact deployed monetary policy for the purposes of stabilisation; and (b) to try to form a judgement as to whether monetary policy has in general been wisely used to this end. It is now time for us to at least attempt to summarise our assessment of these issues, in particular of the second.

Before embarking on this task it seems proper to remind the reader of the limitations of our approach.

The first of these is, of course, our artificial compression of macroeconomic policy into the stabilisation framework and our correspondingly narrow definition of the target variables that the authorities have typically sought to influence by discretionary macroeconomic action. Clearly, this simple approach entails a risk that the authorities' objectives in certain periods may be misinterpreted, with the consequence that policies that were in fact *ex ante* entirely consistent may appear to have been inconsistent, i.e. irrational.

The second limitation is perhaps more fundamental in that, although some relevant material has been provided in our outline of Australia's cyclical experience, we have not established that over the quarter-century currently under review it was possible for the Australian authorities to conduct an effective stabilisation policy. That this was possible remains in practice an important implicit assumption, which, although probably so familiar as to escape attention, is nevertheless increasingly becoming a matter of controversy.[1]

Given these two limitations, how are we to approach the task of providing a summing up?

We begin by recalling our assessment of the characteristics, including, of course, the dynamic characteristics, of discretionary monetary action.

## 12.2 The Apparent Characteristics of Monetary Policy in Australia

In earlier chapters we have made use of three types of evidence in an attempt to assess the dynamic response of the Australian economy to monetary action:
(a) those time series which, on the basis of our prior discussion of the transmission mechanism, we have identified as being of major importance – these we have examined most fully for four selected subperiods;
(b) evidence provided by policy simulations of the three available macroeconomic models; and
(c) evidence consisting in particular pieces of quantitative applied economics not related to existing or prospective macroeconomic models.

Much of the evidence is conflicting. Not all of it has as yet been exposed to systematic professional assessment and criticism; and as we have sought to stress, our largely intuitive interpretation of time series contained in Chapters 6–9 may easily contain idiosyncratic elements. In all, however, we interpret the evidence that is at present available as indicating that over a two-year policy horizon monetary action in the past had:
(a) a small, but not negligible, impact on output and employment;
(b) a more nearly negligible impact upon the rate of change of prices; and
(c) although here the evidence is much less cohesive, an apparently fairly considerable impact on the capital account of the balance of payments through the rate of private capital inflow.

It thus seems that, at least over a two-year horizon, the comparative efficiency of monetary action lies in its impact on the external constraint.

Admittedly, if this horizon is lengthened, this judgement will become much more insecure, since in the medium term the simulation results diverge, while some – notably the consequences for the price level in RB76 – seem hard to accept. It would, however, be a very bold man who formulated policy on the basis of macroeconometric models' medium-term predictions. Equally, it would be only a very bold and very secure political leader who felt able to conduct macroeconomic policy on the basis of a policy horizon approaching half a decade. Thus, for both technical and sociopolitical reasons we are probably justified in concentrating on our shorter two-year policy horizon.

If we accept this view, what general judgement can we formulate regarding the way in which the Australian authorities have in fact sought to employ monetary policy?

If we temporarily postpone the issues of the *timing* of intervention, this problem will contain two elements. The first of these relates to the way in which monetary policy was assigned in relation to our three macroeconomic target variables. The second and much more difficult question relates to the *extent* of macroeconomic intervention, i.e. to whether the authorities tended to overestimate their capacity to undertake effective macroeconomic stabilisation in the rather narrow sense in which we have defined it; for if this indeed was the case, monetary policy, however assigned, must have been expected to do too much and to do it too quickly.

We begin by examining the simpler of these two closely inter-related issues, i.e. the question of assignment.

## 12.3 The Assignment of Monetary Policy

In theory the so-called 'assignment' problem is of small significance, since in the absence of uncertainty regarding the response of the economic system to fiscal and monetary action the optimal mix of policies is defined once the authorities' preferences regarding ultimate policy targets are given, as in theory they should be. In the presence of uncertainty, however, the problem facing the authorities is commonly simplified by regarding one form of intervention as particularly relevant to one target of policy, even though in any general-equilibrium system any discretionary action, either fiscal or monetary, will have an impact on all the endogenous variables of the system and thus on all the ultimate target variables.

Accepting this view, policy can be regarded as being rationally assigned if each form of intervention is typically employed in accordance with its relative efficiency – or to use an alternative terminology, its comparative advantage. We are thus asking how far this was typically done from 1950 to 1975.

For most of our period, i.e. until 1971, Australia operated with a pegged rate of exchange. Hence, the principal instruments (in the very broadest sense) that were available to the authorities were fiscal and monetary policies, buttressed from 1952 to 1960 by quantitative import restrictions. Comparative advantage in the case of monetary policy must therefore be defined in relation to fiscal action, for the general acceptance of a Phillips curve approach to the determination of the domestic elements in changes in wages and prices effectively collapsed our three policy targets to two.

Simulations of the kind already mentioned can be used to estimate the characteristic response of the economy to fiscal actions over our defined policy horizon. A number of such simulations have been reported for RB70, RB74, RB76 and the NIF models. These cannot be reviewed here, and the interested reader is referred to other publications.[2] Broadly, these seem to suggest that fiscal action, typically simulated as a defined expansion in the rate of government expenditure or a defined reduction in a tax-generating function, has a comparative advantage over monetary policy in influencing aggregate demand and output over our two-year horizon in relation to its impact on the external constraint. This is not surprising, since monetary and fiscal expansion are likely to have opposite effects on private capital inflows and, via domestic demand, similarly signed effects on the current acount. Once again, however, the medium term effects present a rather different picture both in particular models and between models.

Notice that we are here discussing comparative, not absolute, advantage. This means that we are *not* asking whether fiscal action or monetary action is more efficient in influencing aggregate demand or some other endogenous variable. This question indeed, if asked, permits of no very obvious answer, since there is no unambiguous way of quantifying the degree of monetary intervention (say in terms of lowering interest rates) that corresponds to a given fiscal intervention (say in terms of increasing government expenditures). For the assessment of policy the most sensible method of normalising would presumably be to define monetary and fiscal interventions, which to the authorities seem equally difficult to accomplish.[3] Since the repugnance weighting is *prima facie* unlikely to be invariant either to the direction of policy change or over time, any attempt at such a scaling seems likely to be misleading. This is particularly probable since the administrative dynamics of the two policies differ, while the political strength of governments varies.

What kind of evidence exists on the assignment issue? That is, how can we form a view of the authorities' own estimates of the comparative advantage of fiscal and monetary devices? As usual we are left with two possibilities: (a) to form a judgement based upon an intuitive interpretation of what the authorities did over the twenty-five years under review; and (b) to undertake a more systematic analysis of a range of relevant time series by means of an econometric model of the authorities' behaviour. The latter is known in the literature as the 'reaction function' approach.

Consider first the reaction function approach, on which there is an extensive literature including, for Australia, Jonson [72] and Lewis [96].[4] Essentially, this consists in specifying (a) an assuméd disutility function for the authorities and (b) the model of the economy as perceived by authorities and then assuming that the authorities set their instruments of fiscal, monetary and other possible policies so as to minimise expected disutility, subject to the constraints imposed by the model of the economy as they perceive it. Typically, of course, the disutility function is defined over the gaps between the target values of the authorities' assumed target variables and their observed values – and in some cases the disutility attached by the authorities to changing the value of their instruments. Sometimes, rather unkindly, the latter is referred to as 'bureaucratic inertia'.

The minimisation process referred to above leads to a reduced form equation explaining the setting of any selected instrument by the deviations of the target variables from their target values and by the costs of, or repugnance attaching to, changing instrument settings. Since the reduced form coefficients can be estimated by suitable econometric methods, the reaction function approach has the familiar appeal of at least apparent objectivity and numerical precision allied to an explicit theoretical framework. Moreover, the approach appears to give a useful estimate of the inside lag in policy formation.[5] It is therefore not altogether surprising that it has already generated a very considerable number of applied studies and promises to generate a good many more.

Unfortunately, the approach is riddled with difficulties. For example, the disutility function is usually taken to be quadratic and often to be invariant over the time period investigated. The former assumption seems implausible, while the latter suggests that political changes have typically only a negligible influence on performance – a view that implies that the political process is typically shadow boxing, in the sense that ministers are invariably dominated by a bureaucracy that rarely modifies its own preferences. All this is bad enough; but additionally the policy horizon is usually undefined, the implicit forecasting problem is thus ignored, and the authorities' model of the economy is assumed, like the disutility function, to be invariant over the sample period. The last assumption is particularly worrying, since it seems to imply that the authorities learn nothing from their non-negligible, direct and indirect expenditures on economic research and are curiously unable to learn anything worthwhile from their often traumatic experiences. Since politicians, civil servants and central bank officers are, to say the least, not obviously less intelligent than academic economists, this assumption appears to be a strange selection. Finally, the dynamics of any estimated reaction function are usually arbitrary, and the model is usually technically unidentified in the sense that it is in general not possible to solve for the parameters of the assumed disutility function and the assumed model of the economy from the estimated reduced-form coefficients. Other weaknesses of the reaction function methodology could readily be added; a most useful review is to be found in Lewis [96]. Enough, however, has been said to remind the reader that, despite the contemporary prestige attaching to econometric results, the findings derived from reaction function studies are not necessarily superior to the less-refined inspection of relevant time series buttressed by informed intuition.

The principal reaction function studies for Australia are those of Jonson [72], who has reviewed macroeconomic policy as a whole, and Lewis [96], who has concerned himself with monetary policy alone. Some additional unpublished work of our own is also restricted to monetary policy. Both the Jonson and Lewis results, although the methods employed to obtain them differ, confirm that the setting of a proximate monetary target (Jonson) or an *ex ante* index of monetary policy (Lewis) can be usefully explained by a plausible set of ultimate target variables designed to reflect the level of economic activity, the behaviour of the price level and the external position. Summarisation of these results is difficult, not least because Lewis has presented a considerable range of estimates and also offered results for three distinct data periods, namely, 1956–71, 1956–61 and 1962–71.

Of the three studies mentioned, only Jonson's throws any direct light on the authorities' view of the comparative advantage of monetary policy, defined in this case in terms of the nominal medium-term bond rate as a proximate target. His finding is that for the period 1959–65 'the authorities behaved as if interest policy had a strong comparative advantage over other policies in correcting reserve imbalance'. Again, according to Jonson, this reaction by the authorities seems to have been modified after 1965, and monetary action seems to have been regarded as relatively more effective in influencing the labour market – the proxy for economic activity.

Lewis's results, although not directly concerned with comparative advantage, suggest that after 1962 the external position had rather less influence on the setting of the monetary policy index than before. This seems consistent with Jonson's results.

Jonson's finding is, however, rather surprising, since it is precisely *after* 1965 rather than before that we should expect the increasing international integration of the Australian capital market to give monetary policy action, via the rate of private capital inflow, a greater, rather than a reduced, comparative advantage in influencing the external position.

Based simply upon a review of the time series, it seems that Jonson's results in some degree reflect the emphasis typically placed on monetary policy relatively early in cyclical upswings and the reluctance displayed on a number of occasions by the Australian authorities to make use of fiscal policy until virtually compelled to do so. It is also generally known that prior to the mineral boom in the mid-1960s the external position was thought of as secularly weak. Hence, the authorities were constrained to protect it via the current account, partly by the attempt to use monetary policy to contain activity. Thus, sample periods dominated by the years prior to the mid-1960s may give the appearance of an assignment derived from an authoritative assessment of comparative advantage, when in practice they reflect in the main the authorities' reluctance to accept the need for countercyclical fiscal measures.[6]

In short, the authorities' use of monetary policy does not suggest that the comparative advantage of this device for influencing the external position that seems to have developed from the early 1960s onward has been fully appreciated. The implication of this is that monetary policy has been used more than it should have been in an attempt to influence aggregate demand and domestic price behaviour. This accords with our own review of the time series.

After 1972 the rate of exchange became an effective, as opposed to merely notional, policy instrument in Australia. This regime – briefly, that of the occasionally jumping peg – lasted virtually until the end of 1976, when after the devaluation of November the jumping peg was replaced by a crawling peg, which on some future occasion may nevertheless revert to jumping. The implications of this approach for the future of monetary policy are discussed in Chapter 13. Extension of the sample period for our own exploratory reaction equation for monetary policy alone suggests that, if anything, the inclusion of the data relating to 1972–5 weakens the relationship between monetary policy and the external position; but this result is very tentative and should not be taken as a firm indication.

A not unreasonable conclusion seems to be that since the mid-1960s the apparent assignment of monetary policy has been to some extent inconsistent with what appears to be the comparative advantage of monetary action as indicated by published research.

## 12.4  Dynamic Considerations

Interpreting the dynamics of discretionary monetary action is no less controversial a matter than attempting to infer the authorities' assignment. Once again the same two methodologies are available: briefly, the 'interpretation' of time series on the one hand, and the econometric estimation of reaction functions upon the other. As we have seen, both are easily criticised.

Based upon the inspection of time series, it appears that, given the speed at which, from simulations and other evidence, the economy responds to monetary action, the inside lag of monetary policy has been uncomfortably long. On a number of occasions restraint (on our definition) has been imposed rather too late in the cyclical upswing, while the switch of policy to ease has come well after the cyclical peak (on our dating) and in some cases at, or even after, the cyclical trough. This judgement, however, in addition to the time series methodology contains the implicit assumption that monetary action was in most cases assigned to the level of output in relation to capacity. In so far as the assignment *was* to the external situation or to the labour market, since both tend to lag the output series, our method in effect wrongly dates the authorities' actions and thus overstates the apparent inside lag in relation to the transmission process.

Additionally, by its comparison of time series, our methodology is implicitly discrete in that it compares our datings of major policy shifts with the cycle peaks and troughs. In fact policy changes are more continuous than this method allows. It is therefore of some importance to record that Lewis [96] has not regarded his own investigations in terms of a reaction function as indicating a long inside lag. Jonson's results do, however, suggest a rather slow response; but here again doubts must exist, since in his model the coefficient that determines the dynamics may be subject to bias.

In these circumstances no very definite conclusion is possible. Our intuitive judgement, however, remains that there is evidence of an uncomfortably long inside lag.[7]

The inside lag is in theory decomposable into two elements: (a) the so-called *'recognition lag'* – the time that elapses between the need for a policy change and the recognition of the need; and (b) the *implementation lag* – the time consumed in the formulation, acceptance and implementation of policy. Neither our time series methodology nor the reaction function approach enables us to separate these two elements. Intuitively, however, it seems likely that, if we are correct in our assessment of the inside lag, it is the recognition lag that constitutes the major problem.

In terms of this dichotomy, the process of recognition consists in two problems: (a) identifying the current position of the economy; and (b) forecasting how, in the absence of policy changes, the economy will move over the policy horizon or some somewhat shorter period of (say) four to six calendar quarters. Once formulated, this conditional forecast can then be used to compare the target values of the target variables with their forecast values and thus to estimate the need for a policy change.

Neither of these two problems is at all simple. Statistical time lags calendar time; and although preliminary estimates of the current values of crucial variables are undoubtedly available to the authorities, they are probably often revised and on occasions quite substantially. Thus, identifying the current position of the economy is not easy and must often be subject to a good deal of uncertainty.

It is probable that the forecasting problem is even less tractable. Thus, forecasting export receipts, import prices and the performance of the capital account must present serious difficulties, although we have no directly relevant published evidence regarding the authorities' abilities in this area. Hence, even if the authorities are confident of their underlying model, the conditional forecasts that they devise must have a very considerable measure of uncertainty.

Typically, the existence of uncertainty delays action, since the likely response is to await the arrival of later, and (it is hoped) clarifying, information. Our intuitive judgement is that it is the difficulties associated with the diagnosis and forecasting of an economy as open as the Australian that explain the apparently excessive inside lag. It is also possible that these difficulties are an important element in explaining not only why action has sometimes been delayed but also why, when it has been taken, it has sometimes been excessive and rather too long sustained.

## 12.5 The Choice of Proximate Target

The principal instruments of central-banking control in Australia are, as we have seen, open market operations, variations in the trading banks' required statutory reserve deposits (SRDs), changes in certain interest rate maxima, lending requests to the banking system and, in rare cases, modification in the LGS convention. However, our knowledge of the transformation linking changes in these instruments to the ultimate targets of policy is generally speaking rather imprecise. In these circumstances it is common for the monetary authority to select some intermediate financial variable as its 'proximate target' and to conduct its monetary policy mainly, but typically not exclusively, on the basis of this variable. In reviewing the experience of the last quarter-century we thus need to make some assessment of whether the proximate target of the Reserve Bank of Australia was well or ill chosen. This issue is, of course, extremely controversial, since it is nowadays fashionable to regard the nominal money stock in some sense as the appropriate proximate target not only for monetary policy but often also for macroeconomic policy in general.

Apart from Lewis [96], who, as we have seen, has investigated the setting of monetary policy in terms of an index, most researchers seem to have identified the proximate target of Reserve Bank action since 1961 with the nominal interest rate on medium-term Commonwealth bonds. This, for example, is the variable employed by Jonson [72] in his reaction function study, which also includes tests of alternative proximate targets. It is again reflected in RB71 and RB74. The same identification recurs in a rather more sophisticated form in RB76,[8] and our own estimates tend to confirm that this variable performs better as a proximate target in a simple reaction-function model than either the base, the LGS base, the nominal ($M_3$) money stock or the Reserve Bank's net domestic assets. We may thus accept that, assuming that the formation of monetary policy is sufficiently dominated by a single proximate target to render a simple one variable identification permissible, the interest rate, as defined, was that variable over most of the period from 1961 through 1975.

A one-variable identification is, of course, an oversimplification in the sense most central banks are considerably more eclectic in their policy formation than a single variable implies. Thus, as both the Reserve Bank's *Annual Reports* and Governor Phillips' statements make clear, the Reserve Bank has been concerned with such variables as relative interest rates, the money stock, the flow of housing finance and the flow of trading bank lending. These obvious limitations of the one-variable approach need to be kept in mind.

Given these limitations, there are at least two approaches to the selection of appropriate proximate target of monetary action. The first of these, typically theoretical rather than empirical, is through control theory. This essentially seeks an answer to the question of which proximate target, in this context usually referred to as an 'instrument', the authorities should employ in order to minimise the variance of some ultimate target variable(s) around their target values. The literature on control theory in general and on its relevance for the choice of the optimal monetary proximate target is already considerable, exhibits a far-from-negligible rate of expansion and is technically fairly demanding.[9]

Any attempt to summarise this literature is bound to be superficial. We therefore simply record our judgement that its central message for a relatively small open economy is that we do not know enough about the forms of uncertainty facing the Australian authorities to identify the optimal proximate target, which in any case will not be independent of the authorities' preferences regarding their ultimate targets, even in the simplest case in which the coefficients of the underlying behaviour functions, i.e. the model of the economy, are known constants. Since in practice they are *not* known constants but stochastic parameters, no clear-cut solution from control theory presently emerges. Accordingly, to form a judgement some other approach to the problem must be specified.

To see what is involved we need to recall that conducting a stabilisation policy as defined in this study, although an important function of the Reserve Bank, is not its primary responsibility. The first responsibility of any central bank must be to ensure the stability of the financial system within which it operates, beyond this it also has a major responsibility for promoting and guiding the development of the financial system. These responsibilities, although not infrequently given insufficient emphasis, place considerable constraints on central banks in that their freedom to select their *modus operandi*, which in theoretical treatments appears to be great, is in practice sharply circumscribed. The Reserve Bank is no exception to the generalisation.

It therefore follows that in selecting its proximate target the Reserve Bank must have regard for the implications of its selection for financial markets and financial institutions.

To see what this implies consider the implications of a policy aimed at setting the money stock, defined as $M_3$, within a very small range of error over a period of (say) a quarter. In so far as the money demand function is unstable in the sense of being subject to random shifts,[10] and the interest rate (as defined) is the variable that adjusts to equate money demand with supply, unpredicted shifts in the demand function will generate unpredicted shifts in the interest rate. In the alternative case, in which the Reserve Bank sets the interest rate as its proximate target, unpredicted variations in the money demand function are offset by induced but unpredicted changes in the money stock resulting from induced open-market operations by the Reserve Bank. In short, when the demand function for money is unstable in the sense defined, there is an implicit relation between the unpredicted variation of the interest rate and the unpredicted variation in the money stock. The greater the accuracy with which the former is set, the greater will be the variation in the latter, and vice versa.[11] Since the money supply is itself an endogenous variable and the money supply function also is subject to variation, this may well add to the problem.

The literature bearing on this problem in Australia at present primarily relates to the demand function and the supply function for money. There has as yet been no published work regarding the cost, in terms of money stock variation, of setting the rate of interest or the alternative procedure.

On the money demand function Valentine's [166] results suggest that, in terms of the familiar partial-adjustment stock-demand model, any $M_3$ demand function may involve a serious mis-specification resulting from inappropriate aggregation. This is on one interpretation confirmed by the results of Norman and Purvis [109], which are difficult to interpret in terms of economic behaviour and which, even when treated as simply a macroeconomic forecasting equation, involve sizeable percentage errors. A more massive study by Sharpe and Volker [153], which presents a wide array of results, leads to the conclusion that 'it required 22 parameter estimates in a total sample of 92 observations to produce a stable result and, in the recent period from 1971.IV to 1975.I a total of six additional dummy variables was added'.

Additionally, the Sharpe–Volker paper suggests rather slow adjustment of demand in the partial adjustment case, which implies a rather small short-run interest elasticity in terms of the bond rate. Thus, the demand side implications suggest that the unpredicted short-period shifts in demand may well be significant and that the resulting short-period changes in the bond rate to equilibrate these would be large if the money stock were the proximate target.

On the supply side there are studies by Sharpe [151] [152] and Lewis and Wallace [97], with some related findings on the lags in bank portfolio adjustments due to Terrell and Valentine [160]. Again, any attempt at a summary could only be superficial. We therefore simply record our assessment, based mainly on Sharpe's later results, as follows:

(1) The error in the quarterly setting of $M_3$ as given by the regressions is probably of the order of 3 per cent.
(2) The lags in the money supply function are relatively long.
(3) The lag forms suggest that attempts at changing the money stock at all quickly would require large and oscillatory changes in the base.

It should, however, be noted that Lewis [96] has found shorter lags.[12]

Admittedly, errors in the money supply function might be so correlated with errors in the money demand function as to reduce the variation in the interest rate resulting from a policy of seeking to set the money stock as a proximate target. However, no evidence suggests that this was the case over the period under review.

Our conclusion, which is essentially judgemental, is that from 1965 to 1975 the Reserve Bank was almost certainly correct in emphasising the interest rate rather than the money stock or some base concept as its main proximate target. This course was probably essential in view of the Reserve Bank's concern to promote the development of both the bond market and the money market. This judgement, which relates to the past period and not necessarily to the future, is not weakened by the econometric findings that are at present available.

This judgement can, of course, readily be challenged on the grounds that concern with orderly markets leads to the interest rate being adjusted too little for an effective stabilisation policy and, more particularly, to inappropriate movements in the *ex ante* real rate.[13] As we have seen in Chapter 4, this is arguable, although not decisive.

## 12.6 Techniques

Our discussion of the Reserve Bank's apparent choice of proximate target makes sense only upon two assumptions:

(1) The Australian and world capital and money markets are imperfectly integrated.

(2)   The Reserve Bank is able to exercise an adequate degree of control over whatever base concept best explains the behaviour of the relevant money stock.

We have already given our reasons for accepting (1). How far are we justified in asserting that (2) held over the period of our study?

Essentially, in this connection, the issue is how far was it typically possible for the Reserve Bank to neutralise the impact upon the base of changes in overseas reserves originating on either the current or capital account of the balance of payments. This question is, of course, limited to the short period, since cumulative reserve losses cannot be accepted indefinitely. Neutralisation thus requires the Reserve Bank to have the capacity to change the net domestic asset component of the base by an amount that is equal to, but of opposite sign to, the changes in overseas reserves. Whether it will choose to do so or not depends on its target value for the base. In some cases neutralisation may be negligible in the sense that the observed value of the change in net domestic assets divided by the observed change in overseas reserves may be close to zero. At other times this ratio may be less than $-1$ or even positive. This is simply because the variable that the Reserve Bank controls is the base, so that, if $\Delta B^*$ is the change in the base required by the Reserve Bank, then, since

$$\Delta B = \Delta OR + \Delta NDA$$

it follows that

$$\Delta NDA^* = \Delta B^* - \Delta OR$$

where $\Delta NDA^*$ is the required change in net domestic assets.

As a small open economy Australia has experienced very sharp changes in overseas reserves; a classic example of this was, of course, the period 1950–2. More recently, changes were also very marked from 1971.I to 1972.V. The potential technical problem was therefore very severe particularly in the earlier years in which the Australian bond market had a very small capacity to absorb open market operations.

It is, of course, a familiar story that the special accounts – SRD techniques were developed out of experience in the Second World War, largely to give the Reserve Bank (Commonwealth Bank) an extramarket neutralisation technique in this sense. The power of this technique was made clear by Governor Coombs in his evidence to the Radcliffe Committee and has been discussed *inter alia* by Rowan [140]. It may be concluded that in general the Reserve Bank has been able to neutralise (in this sense) changes in overseas reserves in the way that it wished.

There is, of course, nothing new in this assertion. The same conclusion has reached by Lewis and Wallace [97] and Lewis [96]. It is confirmed by our finding that, if a reaction function for the base is estimated in terms of some rather simple-minded proxies for plausible ultimate targets, an estimated equation for $\Delta NDA$ in terms of the same proxies plus the change in overseas reserves yields similar coefficients for the proxies with a coefficient close to $-1$ on the reserve change.[14] Typically, it seems, the Reserve Bank has set the base rather than net domestic assets[15] and has neutralised reserve changes to do so. This would not have been possible if the Reserve Bank's technical means had not been adequate.[16]

The justification for examining the base in this way is simply that, whether Reserve Bank wishes to set the nominal interest rate or money stock (as defined), inversion of the money supply function must imply an appropriate required change in the base.

Accepting the efficiency of the Reserve Bank's technique for formal neutralition purposes, there remains the question of whether the effectiveness of the SRD system might not be improved by eliminating the income effects on the trading banks associated with its present form or alternatively, if these cannot be eliminated, whether the device might be more fruitfully replaced by a *statutory* minimum LGS requirement variable at the Reserve Bank's wish. We return to this issue in Chapter 13.

## 12.7 *Monetary Policy and Macroeconomic Policy*

Our final problem in this assessment is to evaluate the *extent* to which monetary policy was used in our study period for essentially anticyclical purposes. More concisely, we ask whether in some sense monetary policy was asked to do 'too much' in this area.

For this question to have any meaning we need to interpret the term 'too much'. We do this by reverting to our earlier argument that the primary responsibility of any central bank must be to preserve the stability of the financial system within which it conducts its operations. The Reserve Bank is, we repeat, no exception to this rule. It therefore follows that the *extent* of overall macroeconomic intervention for stabilisation purposes and the *emphasis* placed upon monetary policy in this policy mix must not be such as to compel the Reserve Bank to run the risk of failing in its primary responsibility. If there is evidence that in some situations this important constraint on monetary action was neglected, then in those situations we define monetary policy as being asked to do 'too much'.

We have already noted that the Australian economy is not easy either to diagnose or to forecast. Moreover, we have argued that this is particularly likely to be the case when the major sources of cyclical movement in output and prices originate overseas. In such cases action is likely to be taken too late and thus to be taken in a context in which quick results are required.[17] Since, as we have seen, the transmission process relating monetary action to ultimate targets is relatively slow, quick results, at least in terms of these targets, will entail marked and rapid shifts in policy stances. Thus, in expansionary periods financial markets may experience excessive ease and thus encourage correspondingly excessive reliance on short term finance, often for speculative purposes. Similarly, in the subsequent severe restraint it may prove impossible for many borrowers to refund their short-term indebtedness, with a consequential risk of a collapse in financial confidence and a sudden demand for liquidity that puts a severe strain on even highly responsible financial intermediaries. It is important that the monetary authority should not be asked to change policy stance so fast and so extensively as to invite financial instability in this way.

If we examine Australian macroeconomic policy since 1961 – approximately the year in which the Reserve Bank became able to conduct a 'monetary' as opposed to a 'banking' policy – the years covered by this study fall into two periods. In the first, which runs approximately from the beginning of 1962 to 1970–1, overall macroeconomic policy was remarkably successful; in the second, which runs to the end of our study, such policy must, at least with the benefit of hindsight, be regarded as remarkably unsuccessful.

It is clearly something of a puzzle why the economic advisers who (apparently) performed so well in 1962–71 should (again apparently) have performed so poorly in later years. Unfortunately, the puzzle is outside the scope of this study. Two points may be argued, however:
(1) In the period of success (1962–71) there is little evidence of either:
    (a) excessive macroeconomic intervention; or
    (b) excessive reliance on monetary policy.
(2) In the later period there is certainly evidence to suggest that:
    (a) in 1972–5 there was excessively sharp variation in the stance of monetary policy; which
    (b) led to a severe risk of financial instability towards the end of 1973–4 and in early 1974–5; with
    (c) particularly severe strains on the permanent building societies, the flow of mortgage finance and private investment in dwellings.
It is difficult to form any general judgement on macroeconomic policy as a whole over this later period, for two reasons:
(1) Our analytical framework is essentially concerned with macroeconomic policy as a means of anticyclical stabilisation.
(2) Other social and distributional objectives exerted an important influence during this period.
It is, however, not unreasonable to argue that this period, together with 1950–2, suggests very strongly that inflationary impulses originating from overseas cannot be effectively resisted within the framework of a rarely adjusted adjustable peg.

It is also arguable that the later period was one of peculiar difficulty, in that the collapse of the Bretton Woods system, the increase in the world rate of inflation and the growth in international monetary uncertainty coincided with marked shifts in the emphasis and techniques of domestic policy. In such circumstances it would be reasonable to expect routine responses to have been replaced by decision behaviour on the part of many transactors; and in so far as such a change did occur, there must be a derived expectation for the scale of error typically attaching to crucial behaviour functions and familiar diagnostic and forecasting techniques to increase. If these conjectures are correct, both control theory and common sense imply that for any given disutility function and shortfalls in performance, the scale of intervention, i.e. the degree of fine tuning aimed at by the authorities, should have been reduced.

Evidence on the emergence of decision behaviour and the growth in uncertainty is not easily provided. Intuitively, however, it seems that both occurred on a significant scale[18] and that the authorities, in so far as they failed to appreciate this change in economic circumstances, were excessively confident of the responses to the economic policy and thus intervened to an excessive degree. Fairly obviously, this judgement is an extremely speculative, even though it has been reached with the full benefit of hindsight. It is therefore an issue on which the reader is urged to deploy a full measure of constructive scepticism.

# 12.8 Conclusions

None of the conclusions set out in this chapter is particularly novel, even though some of those put forward may well prove to be a matter of controversy.

Our principal findings, given our assessment of the dynamics of the transmission process of the 1960s and early 1970s and the comparative advantage of monetary policy, are: (a) that monetary action in the area of stabilisation does not seem to have been correctly assigned after 1961; so that (b) excessive reliance was placed upon it in the attempt to fine tune economic activity.

In general, however, this does not seem to have compelled the Reserve Bank to undertake policies that entailed a risk to financial stability, although this generalisation clearly fails in the period 1972–5.

As we try to show in Chapter 13, these conclusions, even if correct, may be of rather small help in formulating policy in the future.

# Notes: Chapter 12

1 Cf. Modigliani [100], Mayer [99] and Rowan [144] where this issue is discussed.
2 RB76 is comprehensively reviewed and compared with the NIF model in Reserve Bank of Australia [137]. For RB71 and RB74, consult Henderson [54] [55] [56], Henderson and Norman [57] and Norton and Henderson [115]. For the NIF model, consult the various joint papers from the Treasury and Australian Bureau of Statistics, in particular *An Econometric Model of the Australian Economy* (Treasury–ABS, mimeo, November 1977).
3 This implies that the costs of alternative forms of intervention, as perceived by the authorities, are related to the genuine social costs of alternative actions.
4 An extensive summary of other such studies is given in Lewis [96].
5 In the limited sense of how long a time elapses on average between the emergence of some gap and the authorities' reaction to it, Lewis [96] has found a relatively short lag.
6 And prior to 1965, preoccupation with a weak current-account position.

7 Assuming a domestic assignment.
8 The model includes a reaction function explaining the setting of the medium-term bond rate.
9 Some relevant studies are Poole [128], Karecken *et al.* [87] and Turnovsky [161] [162] [163].
10 This is not instability as usually defined in econometric studies.
11 There is in fact a trade-off, the econometric characteristics of which for Australia have not yet been established.
12 Our own preliminary attempts to estimate a deposit supply function for the major trading banks suggest a considerable adjustment lag and a rather poorly defined process. These results are, however, very tentative.
13 This was a major element in the criticisms of the Federal Reserve Board's emphasis, prior to the introduction of the 'proviso clause', on setting money market conditions. On this point, consult OECD [118].
14 Although our results are once again essentially preliminary, they are set out in Tables 11.2 and 11.3.
15 Setting net domestic assets would be a strange policy.
16 It must be recalled that the VDR instrument and the embargo have both been used to reduce capital inflows and thus the magnitude of the problem facing the Reserve Bank. On the general issue, see Swan [156].
17 This has probably been the case in the United Kingdom on a number of occasions.
18 The relatively poorer performance of consumption and investment functions gives some support to this contention. Cf. Freebairn [42] and Higgins, Johnston and Coghlan [59].

# Chapter 13

# Concluding Observations

## 13.1 Introduction

Our purpose in studying the past is the wish to improve performance in the future. Now that we have completed our review of monetary policy over the quarter-century from 1950 to 1975 it seems only natural to ask whether this review and the conclusions derived from it have any clear-cut implications for the future conduct of monetary policy.

The aim of this chapter is to attempt an answer to this question. Not very surprisingly, since some of our conclusions are tentative, some elements in our answer are correspondingly cautious and even hesitant; but this simply reflects the complexity of the issues and our present ignorance.

## 13.2 Macroeconomic Policy and the Future

Much of the evidence that we have on the response of the Australian economy to changes in the stance of monetary policy is derived either from macroeconometric models of the economy as a whole or from methodologically similar studies of its subsectors. The behavioural regularities captured by these models have been estimated from data from the 1960s through to the early 1970s. For most of these years the Australian economy performed more than acceptably; in particular it experienced low rates of unemployment and tolerable rates of price change. Moreover, for much of the period the exchange rate was pegged. Thus, the routine behaviour presumably captured by the models probably reflects that which was appropriate to a relatively satisfactory economic environment in which there occurred few violent changes in macroeconomic policy, while most changes

287

that did occur were familiar in form and technique and readily comprehensible in terms of the prevailing economic orthodoxy.

Since about 1973 conditions have been very different. Both unemployment rates and rates of price change have reached values that are historically abnormal; and at the moment of writing (mid-1978) both, but more particularly the unemployment rate, remain at historically high levels. Over the same period there have been several discretionary adjustments of the exchange rate followed by a formal change in exchange rate policy, deliberate attempts by the authorities to modify the share of wages and a far-from-negligible injection of political uncertainty. In short, conditions at present seem sufficiently unlike those of the past to make it extremely unlikely that the routine behaviour of the earlier period constitutes reliable evidence regarding the likely contemporary responses of the economy to changes in macroeconomic policy in general or monetary policy in particular.

If this view is correct, it must severely restrict the immediate relevance of our earlier analysis. This is the more likely, since the macroeconometric models that we have briefly examined contain only rather rudimentary aggregate supply hypotheses and are, implicitly if not explicitly, concerned mainly with the determinants of demand. In the existing situation, at least if we are correct in regarding it as characterised by an unusually high degree of political and economic uncertainty, the management of aggregate demand may be, and probably is, much less important than identifying and adopting a policy stance that improves the potential response of real output and employment to demand changes by restoring the profitability of production at the margin and reducing the uncertainty generally bearing on the business community.[1]

The macroeconomic policies that are most likely to be successful in restoring confidence and thus in the return to more routine forms of behaviour are inevitably controversial. We have no wish to enter this controversy at any length. However, in so far as business uncertainty derives from the frequency of shifts in policy stance or techniques, a major requirement may well be greater stability in both. This suggests a rather longer policy horizon, if politically feasible, together with the adoption of policies that have some concensus support and are thus less likely to be reversed. Within a fairly wide range it may in fact matter less what policy stance is actually chosen than that the chosen stance has these medium-term implications and a measure of concensus support and thus offers a reasonable prospect of being maintained. If these arguments are correct, it seems to follow that the selection of contemporary policy may be much more a matter of what particular policies would best meet these conditions, given the contemporary political situation, than one of searching for some control-theoretic optimum on the basis of what econometric research has to tell us about past macroeconomic responses.

In short, our view is that the examination of behaviour from (say) 1960 to 1973 is unlikely to provide a useful guide to the immediate formation of either macroeconomic policy or monetary policy. This does not entail that these studies have no relevance to the future. If the contemporary and, it is hoped, transitory problems can be successfully met, relatively well-identified and reliable routine responses to policy stimuli may not only re-emerge but also bear a useful relation to those revealed by recent modelling. In discussing the relevance of our review and its findings to the future, it is in this sense rather than in terms of some conjectural calendar dating that the future should be defined.

## 13.3 The Assignment Problem in the Future

The dynamic characteristics of the economy's response to monetary policy have already been summarised and do not require restatement. It is, however, worth recalling that our acceptance of a significant response of private capital movements to changes in Australian monetary conditions must be treated with caution, since the evidence is conflicting. If we accept that this effect is now present to a significant degree, then, since we must expect the international integration of capital markets to continue in the future, we must expect its significance to rise. Thus, this conjecture, taken together with our earlier conclusions, suggests that the comparative advantage of monetary policy in influencing the balance of payments is likely to increase.

The view is, however, conditional upon the policy followed with regard to the exchange rate. Our assumption here is that, for as long as Australia maintains a managed float, the float will typically be relatively dirty. This amounts to saying that Australia's exchange-rate policy is assumed to be a discretionary flexible peg rather than a freely flexible rate. In the short run, small but frequent adjustments in the rate will doubtless be in the direction indicated by market forces. The discretionary element will therefore lie mainly in the occasional jump. Since we are assuming that such jumps, or discrete adjustments, will not be excluded from policy consideration, we can formulate the assignment problem by asking in what way, in the light of our findings, Australia should assign its three instruments – namely, monetary policy, fiscal policy and the exchange rate – in relation to our assumed macroeconomic targets of economic activity, the rate of change of prices and the balance of payments. We begin our examination of this problem with an account of the exchange rate instrument.

Traditionally, the rate of exchange is considered to be a variable influencing the current account of the balance of payments partly through substitution effects and partly through real balance effects (on the demand side) and relative cost effects (on the supply side). A devaluation, it is argued, makes imports relatively dearer than domestic products; hence, expenditure is reallocated in favour of import-competing domestic products.

Both import competing and exporting become relatively more profitable in relation to the production of non-traded goods. Hence, resources, including, of course, capital, shift from the domestic non-traded goods sector into import competing and export producing. Unfortunately, this shift in domestic resources comes about because of a reduction in the domestic costs of production in relation to overseas costs, which is predominantly a reduction in labour costs. It therefore seems that a crucial element in the analysis is that the real wage must fall and remain permanently at a lower level in relation to the rest of the world. If the real wage falls, but not permanently, the relative cost effects will be transitory. Moreover, if the real wage is restored to its predevaluation relativity at all speedily, the shifting of resources away from the production of non-traded goods will not occur. In this situation the devaluation will have its direct impact on the domestic price level rather than the current account of the balance of payments, although, so far as this is the case, there will be a corresponding real-balance impact upon aggregate demand and thus indirectly upon expenditure and imports.[2]

The characteristics of the rate of exchange as a policy instrument operating over a policy horizon of (say) one or two years therefore depend crucially on two dynamic processes: (a) how rapidly after a devaluation money wage adjustments restore the real wage; and (b) how rapidly productive resources shift out of non-traded production into import competing and exporting. Recent experience seems to suggest that in Australia (a) is a more rapid process than (b) – in short, that devaluations are, over the policy horizon defined above, typically more effective in raising the Australian price level than they are in improving the current account or shifting the factor distribution of income.[3] Indeed, the authorities' anxiety to influence wage determination in a way which reduces the real wage, implies a recognition that this is so. It is, of course, always possible by such means to retard the dynamic process outlined in (a). Experience with wages policies, however, seems to suggest that such retardation is often short lived and that it may well impose longer run costs in terms of a deterioration in industrial relations.

These issues are unfortunately matters of continuing economic controversy. Equally, it is improbable that the argument can be applied *mutatis mutandis* to an exchange appreciation which may well have a longer-lived impact on the relative real wage and to this extent promote resource shifts.

Nevertheless, in the light of our present knowledge of the dynamics of the relevant processes it seems to be reasonable to regard discretionary changes in the exchange rate primarily as a means of influencing the rate of change of the domestic price level rather than the current balance.[4] If this is indeed its present comparative advantage, the appropriate policy assignment of discretionary changes in the rate will be to the rate of inflation – or more precisely, the impact of external inflation on the Australian wage–price process. Since Australia's recent inflation was in large measure the dynamic consequence of overseas inflation as well as exogenous domestic shifts in wage determination,[5] this assignment seems, if generally accepted, to offer some prospect of insulating Australia from future external price fluctuations.

In the discussion that follows we assume that the discretionary element in the setting of the exchange rate is typically assigned in this way, i.e. to moderating external influences on Australian prices. It follows that the remaining issue is how monetary and fiscal policy should typically be assigned.

We have already argued that monetary policy has a comparative advantage over fiscal policy as a device for controlling the balance-of-payments position. We have also suggested that, as the international integration of capital markets proceeds, this comparative advantage is likely to increase. It follows from this that, to the extent to which fiscal and monetary policies can be regarded as independent devices, the appropriate assignment of monetary policy must be the the external account.

Accepting this, it follows that the independent element in fiscal policy is assigned to the level of economic activity, since we are defining 'the future' for which these assignments are suggested in a way that assumes that an aggregate demand policy will typically be necessary. This view is in some degree controversial, since there is a group of economists who believe that the private sector is stable in the sense that the range of fluctuation in aggregate demand cannot be sensibly diminished by government intervention.[6]

The proposed assignment is open to the criticism that it is clearly at variance with the contemporary monetarist orthodoxy, which, after interpreting monetary policy in terms of some (not always clearly) defined money-stock concept, typically assigns this to the rate of change of prices. What appears to be crucial here are: (a) the response of the expected rate of price change to the rate of change of the defined money stock; and (b) the response of the observed rate of wage–price changes to changes in the expected rate of inflation. As remarked earlier, it would, given the prevailing monetarist flavour of many politicians' pronouncements and much economic journalism, be a matter for considerable astonishment if some such mechanism were not operative in Australia.[7] However, the continuous assertion of monetarist propositions does not of itself establish either the existence of this mechanism or its quantitative importance. At the moment of writing (mid-1978) published research on the Australian wage–price process does not confirm either the quantitative importance or the reliability of the money stock–expectations–inflation mechanism, although the results reported by Jonson and Mahoney [77] and Taylor [158] [159] certainly suggest that such a mechanism exists. This judgement may easily be upset by further research findings; and were this to occur, it would then be necessary to reconsider the assignment suggested above. Alternatively, the repeated and confident assertion of the existence and significance of the mechanism may persuade transactors to modify the process by which they form their expectations in a way that is consistent with the mechanism itself. Both are real possibilities. Our judgement, however, is that the research findings that are at present available do not support a strong monetarist position or a monetarist assignment.

# 13.4 The Proximate Target of Monetary Policy

On the assumption that the assignment suggested above is acceptable, we may now ask what is the appropriate proximate target for the monetary authority. As a preliminary to investigating this issue we shall devote a second look at the concept of external balance.

We can begin by defining

$$\Delta OR \equiv CAB + PKI + Z$$

$\Delta OR$ is change in external reserves (adjusted for an revaluation effects), $CAB$ is the balance on current account, $PKI$ is apparent private capital inflow, and $Z$ is remaining items on capital account (net).

Clearly, in a growing economy there will be some desired trend rate of growth in reserves. External balance may then be thought of as consisting in the condition

$$\Delta OR(t) \approx \Delta OR^*(t)$$

where $\Delta OR^*(t)$ is the required rate of growth.

It is obvious that, since $\Delta OR$ has a large capital-account component as well as a current account component, this can be met, even approximately, only if $CAB$ and $PKI$ move inversely to each other during the cycle. Fortunately, there may be some tendency for this to occur; for in cycles that are primarily of domestic origin and are not due to monetary disturbances, Australian interest rates should rise relative to overseas rates and induce a qualitatively equilibrating capital movement. Whether this will be of an appropriate magnitude is, of course, a separate issue. However, in so far as cycles are external in origin, capital movements may well reinforce the reserve changes brought about by cyclical changes on current account. This is particularly likely in so far as Australian cycles lag overseas cycles and/or the Reserve Bank of Australia is unable to offset reserve gains arising from current transactions. We may conclude that maintaining $\Delta OR(t)$ close to $\Delta OR^*(t)$ will require policy action aimed at adjusting the current and capital accounts to each other. Typically, it is the latter that will need to be adjusted to the former, since the current account position will be roughly determined by the level of capacity utilisation and the phase of the overseas cycle. In short, in assigning monetary policy to external balance we are implicitly assigning it to the capital account, more particularly, to the rate of apparent private capital inflow.

We can define apparent private capital inflow as

$$PKI \equiv \begin{matrix} \text{Direct} \\ \text{investment} \\ \text{in} \\ \text{Australia} \\ \text{by} \\ \text{overseas} \\ \text{companies} \end{matrix} - \begin{matrix} \text{Direct} \\ \text{investment} \\ \text{overseas} \\ \text{by} \\ \text{Australian} \\ \text{companies} \end{matrix} + \begin{matrix} \text{Institutional} \\ \text{loans} \end{matrix} + \begin{matrix} \text{Portfolio} \\ \text{investment} \end{matrix} + \begin{matrix} \text{Balancing} \\ \text{item} \\ \text{on} \\ \text{capital} \\ \text{account} \end{matrix}$$

According to economic theory, each of these elements is a function of the relative *ex ante* rates of return on investment overseas and in Australia and on the expectations regarding the exchange range of the Australian dollar, i.e. upon the relative *ex ante* rates, including expected capital gains or losses due to exchange rate changes. This speculative element in capital movements can be extremely large, hard to control and even harder to resist. Thus, if Australia is to have a useful measure of control over its exchange rate, the cumulative development of expectations of exchange rate changes will need to be avoided.

At present we know remarkably little about the factors determining expectations of exchange rate changes.[8] This is not surprising, since the supply of information, both economic and political, that could be relevant is virtually limitless and since there is no plausible single way of forming a reasonable, let alone a 'rational', expectation-generating function. Despite our ignorance, however, we may argue, at least tentatively, that expectations of exchange rate changes are likely to be encouraged by cumulative reserve losses or gains. Hence, external balance requires: (a) not only maintaining $\Delta OR$ relatively close to $\Delta OR^*$ in the medium to long term; but also (b) ensuring that over any relatively short period of (say) one year cumulative reserve gains or losses are below some critical value, which at present we cannot quantify. In putting things this way we are – let us be clear – not arguing that (b) is a sufficient condition for avoiding the emergence of speculative expectations; we are merely arguing that in practice it is likely to prove a necessary one.[9]

Now that we have given a rather clearer interpretation of the external balance requirement, let us consider what this implies for the Reserve Bank's choice of proximate targets.

The alternative proximate targets typically considered are either the change in some nominal money-supply concept or some nominal interest rate. We have already given reasons for thinking that, if *one* of these were to be selected, it would in the light of existing knowledge be wiser to select the interest rate rather than the money stock. This conclusion, which derives from our own assessment of the reliability and dynamic forms of the Australian money demand and supply functions, implies that the money stock is passively adjusted to the short period demand for it. This approach would, however, be somewhat naive in an intellectual climate dominated by some forms of monetarism, since in such a climate the behaviour of the money stock may exert an influence on expectations.[10] In these circumstances the path of wisdom would probably be to continue to aim at setting the interest rate with the intention of influencing capital flows, but to do this subject to the induced rate of change of the money stock being acceptable to the authorities. This, as readers will doubtless recognise, is similar to the strategy adopted by the Federal Reserve Board during the period in which it typically defined its operating target as 'money market conditions' but made its instruction to ease, tighten or maintain these, subject to the proviso that some specified monetary aggregate did not deviate significantly from its projection.[11]

This discussion, of course, assumes that the Reserve Bank is not compelled to follow a publicly proclaimed and narrowly defined target rate of growth for some nominal money stock (say $M_3$). Clearly, such a requirement would be a severe constraint on its ability to follow a policy defined in terms of interest rates.[12] Moreover, it seems likely that discrepancies between the target rate and the observed rate of growth in the relevant money stock would dominate short term expectations regarding interest rates[13] to a degree that could further constrain interest rate policy.

Thus far we have spoken of 'the' interest rate without any specific identification. This is customary but unacceptable, since, precisely because we have assigned monetary policy to the capital account of the balance of payments, the rate(s) that the monetary authority must ultimately seek to influence is the rate that exerts the quantitatively most significant and reliable influence on private capital movements. Which Australian rate this is is a question of fact and one on which the research findings that are at present available do not provide a clear-cut guide. We must expect it to be a private sector rate rather than a Commonwealth bond rate; and once the rate had been identified, the Reserve Bank would then need to identify the transformation process relating the rate to its instruments. Alternatively, if we can assume a reliable rate-structure equation relating the relevant private-sector rate to the medium-term bond rate ($r_{GM}$), we shall be able to regard the latter as the appropriate operating target. This is the procedure that we in fact adopt, but in accepting this identification it should be noted that we are following convention rather than the findings of research in that we do not have extensive empirical evidence on the Australian rate structure.[14]

# 13.5 Private Capital Inflow and the Effective Rate of Return

The assignment tentatively proposed for the future thus consists in regarding monetary policy as essentially concerned with the management of the balance of payments, i.e. with the attempt to adjust private capital inflow to the current account position.[15] This approach is consistent with our assumption regarding the exchange rate regime, the general thrust of research findings regarding private capital inflow and our conjecture that the international integration of capital and money markets is a continuing and even accelerating process. It is necessary, however, to point out that the ability of the Reserve Bank to influence private capital flows in this way, even in the absence of speculative expectations, may well be rather limited.

This is because, as we have repeatedly sought to stress, the fundamental responsibility of the Reserve Bank is to maintain the stability of the financial system through which it operates. This responsibility must impose limits upon its ability to bring about (a) sharp changes in market-determined interest rates, and (b) similarly large changes in the base.

Since we have already argued that in 1973–5 the Reserve Bank probably reached or exceeded these limits, our proposed assignment must be seen in the context of a smaller range of variation in future in the proximate target(s) of the monetary authority. This immediately raises the problem of whether, consistently with the retention of the money and capital market mechanism, a way can be found to increase the impact on private capital movements of a given change in Australian market rates.

If we assume that the typical transactor expects no change in the ruling exchange rate, the overseas investor purchasing assets in Australia must expect a holding period yield ($\hat{r}_{j(Aust)}$), which consists in a current rate of return plus an expected rate of capital gain or loss. To purchase the Australian asset he has to forgo an overseas rate ($\hat{r}_{row}$). It follows that by reducing the effective return on Australian assets *below* $\hat{r}_{j(Aust)}$ the rate of capital inflow can be varied at the margin. If we neglect the system of dual exchange rates, this can be done either by introducing a special form of taxation – an example is available in US experience – or by employing the variable deposit requirement (VDR) technique. Since the latter has been employed on several occasions in Australia,[16] we shall consider it alone.

The VDR technique, like the Interest Equalisation Tax, requires an administrative mechanism. Its acceptability must therefore depend on the costs of this mechanism and on its effectiveness in the sense of its ability to make the VDR requirement, if imposed, effective over an appropriate range of transactions. There is no available evidence on these issues, although it has been suggested that certain forms of capital movement undertaken by multinational concerns operating in Australia may be extremely difficult to supervise and thus substantially reduce the effectiveness of the device. Against this the reader is referred to the far from negligible impacts tentatively estimated by Norman [108] and Porter [132].

Despite the administrative requirement, the VDR is a market process in the sense that the transactor contemplating the movement of funds is able to reach his decision on the basis of the effective rates of return on domestic and overseas assets. For example, a capital inflow can be discouraged by imposing a VDR proportion ($u$) such that, to overseas residents considering moving funds to

Australia, the effective $\hat{r}_{j(Aust)}$ is reduced to $\hat{r}_{j(Aust)}(1-u)$, while for Australian residents the opportunity cost of borrowing abroad becomes $\hat{r}_{row}(1+u)$. Similarly, $u$ can be used to discourage capital outflows by requiring capital exporters to meet a VDR requirement on their transactions. It cannot, unless $u$ can be negative, be used to encourage capital inflows from foreign residents, unless the initial value of $u$ is not equal to zero. In this case some stimulus can be provided by reducing $u$. Thus, varying $u$ has some limitations. It nevertheless seems a potentially powerful device of some flexibility. Moreover, since no government revenue is directly involved, its use is not likely to be distorted for revenue purposes. Finally, it leaves the decision to move funds or not to the transactor to determine in the light of the relation between $\hat{r}_{j(Aust)}(1-u)$ and $\hat{r}_{row}$. It thus should not inhibit the integration of Australian financial markets with those overseas, as, for example, a formal apparatus of exchange controls and embargoes would do. This is an important consideration for a country that is likely to require a fairly considerable secular rate of capital inflow for development purposes.

Thus, interpreting our proposed future assignment of monetary policy we are seeking to increase the effectiveness of monetary action by using variations in the VDR requirement to supplement the impact of variations in $\hat{r}_{j(Aust)}$. In this way discretionary operations that influence $\hat{r}_{j(Aust)}$ may be rendered more effective while variations in $\hat{r}_{j(Aust)}$ can be constrained within a range that is compatible with the Reserve Bank's responsibility for financial stability.

## 13.6 Some Matters of Technique

Our proposed assignment already implies that the VDR technique should be used more flexibly to supplement movements in domestic rates, and this suggests that the ability to determine the value of the VDR ratio ($u$) should be allocated explicitly to the Reserve Bank. How frequently and how widely it would be both desirable and practicable to vary $u$ are empirical matters on which only broad conjectures are possible. Recalling, however, our earlier definition of 'the future' for which our assignment is proposed, it seems not unreasonable to hope that variation in capital flows will be rather less severe than in recent years. Our suggestion, however, entails that the administrative mechanism that is necessary to implement the VDR technique is retained in being.

Our identification of the proximate target of policy as 'the' interest rate, although subject to a proviso clause, requires us to consider whether the Reserve Bank's ability to influence the rates of return on marketable obligations, particularly on those of the private sector, might not be improved by some minor changes in existing techniques. Two changes that might contribute at least marginally to the outcome are briefly outlined below.

At present the Reserve Bank does not publish the rate that it charges on loans to authorised dealers in the official money market, and the rate is at least notionally confidential. Despite this, information on this rate is not hard to obtain, although the accuracy of the information is not always beyond doubt. Changes in the rate would be a useful indicator of changes in the Reserve Bank's stance, knowledge of which might well speed the response of the market in ways that were helpful to the authorities. It thus seems doubtful whether the present confidentiality of the rate serves any useful purpose. On the contrary, since it seems likely to give rise to both rumour and uncertainty concerning the Reserve Bank's intentions, publication should be considered. Now that the official money market is well established,[17] it is difficult to see objections to a more open approach.

A second change in technique that might be beneficial would begin by giving explicit recognition to the adverse income effects imposed on the trading banks by the SRD device. Theoretically, these income effects must encourage the trading banks to respond to increased SRD requirements by increasing their relative holdings of more risky and higher-yielding bank assets. Empirical evidence on the significance of this effect is lacking. In general, however, it is undesirable for a control device of this type to generate side effects, particularly if these are likely to reduce its efficiency in its main role. There thus seems a good case for either: (a) paying a market rate of return on holdings of SRD, thus eliminating or reducing the income effect already discussed; or (b) removing the minimum LGS ratio requirement from the realm of convention by giving it the force of law and giving the Reserve Bank power to vary it.

If either (a) or (b) were adopted, it would be necessary to devise a formula by which the trading and savings banks recompensed the Reserve Bank for services rendered to them. Again, if in return for restrictions upon entry it was argued that banking profits should be controlled, it would be necessary to introduce an explicit fiscal procedure to ensure this. Possibly, these difficulties make the administrative costs of introducing even the change called (a) exceed the gains in efficiency to be derived from it. It is, however, generally desirable for a method of central-banking control to have a single impact on banking behaviour, and either (a) or the more difficult (b) would ensure the result.

The seasonal and random fluctuations in the LGS holdings of individual trading banks are severe. Moreover, seasonal patterns, although marked, are not invariable. In these circumstances trading banks are frequently in considerable uncertainty regarding the origin of a given change in their LGS holdings and thus the appropriate reaction to it.[18] This unavoidably reduces both the speed and the reliability of the banking system's response to changes in LGS holdings engineered by the Reserve Bank. In theory at least it would reduce the risks of erroneous identification of LGS changes by a trading bank if seasonal loans were available to the banks from the Reserve Bank at market rates. Where such loans were not run off at the end of the period of seasonal stringency, *ex post* the borrowing would be non-seasonal. It would then be open to the Reserve Bank to charge a penalty rate(s) on such outstandings if it wished. Admittedly, such a system might not initially prove attractive to the trading banks, which are apparently adverse to borrowing from the Reserve Bank for whatever purpose. This objection might well become less important as the facility became more familiar; and if, as we have argued, it had the effect of reducing erroneous portfolio adjustments, it should contribute to the advent of speedier and more reliable responses by the trading banks to Reserve Bank policy. This should render the Bank's quantitative control more precise.

Since we have proposed an operating strategy that aims at setting the interest rate subject to an acceptable rate of expansion for some defined monetary aggregate, the Reserve Bank may wish to introduce other changes in technique that should have the result of increasing the reliability of the money demand function. Given this objective there is, at least qualitatively, a case for the progressive abandonment of interest rate maxima on trading bank and savings bank obligations and loans. This is because the maxima, when effective, imply not only a discontinuity in the rate structure but also an element of rationing. Both, but more particularly the latter, inhibit the portfolio allocation process that theoretically underlies the demand function for any broad monetary aggregate and to this extent makes the emergence of a reliable relation less likely.

None of these suggested changes in Reserve Bank operating techniques is particularly novel. Equally, apart from the proposal relating to VDR none is specifically dependent upon our proposed assignment, although it is true, as we shall see, that an alternative assignment would provide a case for some additional and rather more fundamental changes.

# 13.7 The Future of Macroeconomic Policy

Our discussion of the use of monetary policy has implicitly assumed an approach to macroeconomic policy in the sense that, although vague and imprecise, there is underlying it some notion of the extent and frequency of discretionary policy changes. We now try to make these vague notions more precise.

The empirical evidence that we now have on a number of crucial issues is not only unsatisfactory in itself but may have limited applicability to the future, even as we have defined it. The major issues under this head are:
(a)  the determinants of private capital inflows;
(b)  the factors influencing exchange rate expectations; and
(c)  the impact of monetary variables (and their correct definition) on inflationary expectations and on the domestic wage–price process, whether by inflationary expectations or not.

Beyond making the obvious recommendation that each of these problems, and the nature of the aggregate supply function, merits considerable further research, we suggest that, precisely because of our lack of confidence in our present degree of understanding, we should expect, and in fact recommend, that in the future both the extent and frequency of shifts in macroeconomic policy should be less than in the past. It is indeed against the background of a much reduced degree of attempted fine tuning that we have put forward our rather muted proposal regarding the assignment of monetary policy.

We must now face the sociopolitical objection that the prevailing climate of opinion in economic affairs is strongly interventionist and may well remain so. If this proves to be the case, a general reluctance to engage in fine tuning, together with a tendency to plan policy on the basis of a more medium-term horizon than in the past, may be difficult to maintain.

It seems likely that a lesser readiness to change policy would be more acceptable to the general public if the technical difficulties of diagnosing the current position of the economy and making conditional forecasts of its development over the policy horizon were realised. Accordingly, in the interests of promoting such understanding it is suggested that the Australian authorities, including the Reserve Bank, give consideration to making public, after some suitable lag, details of:

(a) preliminary and other data utilised by them in the process of diagnosis;
(b) their forecasts of exogenous variables over the policy horizon;
(c) their derived forecasts of crucial endogenous variables; and
(d) the actual out-turn of both.

If, indeed, both processes are as difficult in Australia as we have suggested earlier, *ex post* reviews of this type should have an educational effect that would confer upon the authorities benefits that far outweighed the costs of any embarrassment due to perceived failures in forecasting or diagnosis.[19] Gradually, this process should ensure that the authorities would no longer be expected to manage the economy within limits that in practice were typically beyond attainment.

## 13.8 *A Final Warning*

The proposals in this chapter derive from the conclusions of Chapter 12, and these in their turn are dependent upon the analysis of Chapters 1–11. For reasons already stated, both our conclusions and our proposals are tentative. The point that we wish to stress here is that it would be possible, in some instances even by quoting the same research, to reach very different conclusions regarding how the Australian economy works and to derive from them very different recommendations regarding assignments.

For example, if it were our judgement that the domestic capital market was virtually completely integrated with overseas markets, then, as is well known, an independent monetary policy would be incompatible with a pegged rate of exchange. If at the same time exchange rate expectations were found to depend significantly on some notion of purchasing power parity, while the expected rate of inflation responded quickly and predictably to changes in some nominal money stock and itself influenced the wage–price process, we should then have a very different 'model'.

Such a model might indicate assigning the rate of exchange to the balance of payments (which would imply a clean float) and monetary policy (with the money stock as proximate target) to the prices objective. If, at the same time, it were argued that the private sector was sufficiently stable to make an aggregate demand policy otiose, fiscal policy would in the longer run be a matter of determining the relative size of public and private sectors and in the short run be merely an element in money stock control. Institutionally, a model of this type implies *inter alia* a development of a foreign exchange market in which official intervention is minimal.[20]

What matters to Australia is that the assignment of policy – or more generally, the strategy determining its conduct – should be research based rather than fashion based. Economics is a subject that is particularly susceptible to shifts in intellectual fashion – shifts that all too commonly have little systematic evidence to support them. It is also susceptible to old habits of thought and the tendency to retain familiar intellectual structures despite their emergent irrelevance.

It is believed that our conclusions and proposals derive from a suitably cautious and impartial assessment of the evidence that was available up to the end of 1977. Nevertheless, it must be stressed that economic research is a continuous process, and as a result new studies now in prospect or in progress may very well modify our present findings on the essentially quantitative issues that are of crucial importance in determining the future role of monetary policy. It must be left to the future reader to determine how far this has occurred.

# Notes: Chapter 13

1 This is *not* to be taken as an assertion that macroeconomic demand management is unnecessary; cf. Rowan [144].

2 And perhaps an indirect effect, via capacity utilisation, on the rate of change of wages.

3 The qualification 'typically' may be important, since it is likely that the dynamic process (a) will be slower in a recession.

4 For a fuller discussion, consult Kasper [88] [89] and Swan in Kasper [90].

5 Just *how* large a measure is controversial. On this point, see Argy and Carmichael [5] and Nevile [105] and the debate between them.

6 Cf. Modigliani [100].

7 In forecasting the rate of inflation it would be sensible, if not rational in the technical sense, to take account of many variables other than past rates of inflation. One such variable would surely be the rate of change of some nominal money stock; but whether this variable, when defined, would add much to the explanatory power of past rates of inflation plus a simple error-learning process is quite another matter. Some preliminary results of our own suggest that up to 1976.III it did not.

8 The proxies used in some applied studies seem either to be quite *ad hoc* or to *reflect* the existence of speculation rather than *explain* speculative expectations.

9 The speculative expectations of 1976.III seem to have been primarily political in origin.

10 Admittedly, if the relevant money stock target is $M_2$, $M_3$ or some broader aggregate, the money stock can be modified by developing new financial assets that are not (by definition) money but offer a combination of liquidity, capital certainty and a rate of return that is superior to

that of (say) fixed deposits, savings bank deposits and building society obligations. The economic significance of such window-dressing operations is, if we reject a purely mechanical naive monetarism, uncertain. The issue of Australian savings bonds was essentially an exercise along these lines. We do not consider such devices or the issue of indexed bonds as means of money stock control.

11 For a discussion of this policy, cf. Axilrod [12] [13] and OECD [118].

12 Such a target, apart from the sort of operation discussed in note 10, very sharply reduces the independence of fiscal policy and commonly condemns any central bank to pressing continuously for reductions in the government deficit, whether the deficit is autonomous or simply induced by a recession.

13 And when, the exchange rate is relatively flexible, possibly exchange rate expectations also.

14 Cf. our brief note on this issue in Chapter 3.

15 This is a simplified statement. There are good reasons for arguing that the Commonwealth government should borrow overseas for similar purposes.

16 The variations in the VDR requirement and the embargo are given below as reported by the Reserve Bank.

Controls over overseas borrowing were first imposed in September 1972 when an embargo was placed on borrowing for two years or less. In December 1972 the VDR device was placed upon borrowing for over two years. The VDR was initially set at 25 per cent, and the deposit so defined earned no interest.

Since its initiation, the main changes have been:

October 1973: VDR raised to $33^1/_3$ per cent.

June 1974: VDR reduced to 25 per cent.

August 1974: VDR reduced to 25 per cent.

November 1974: VDR suspended, and embargo reduced to six months.

January 1977: VDR reintroduced at 25 per cent, some borrowing for capital expenditure made exempt, and embargo increased to two years.

June 1977: VDR suspended, and embargo reduced to six months.

Source: Reserve Bank of Australia, Exchange Control (Sydney: RBA, October 1977).

17 And closely integrated with the unofficial market.

18 The Reserve Bank, as is well known, is in virtually continuous contact with the trading banks and will to the limit of its ability aid the banks in their task of diagnosis, in particular in assessing whether the change is or is not transitory.

19 The difficulty here is that in any period some private forecaster may do better than the authorities, even though over a reasonable number of forecasts all forecasters are likely to do worse.

20 Cf. Snape [154] in Kasper [90].

# Bibliography

## General sources

Australian Bureau of Statistics, various publications.
*Australian Economic Review* (1968+).
*Australian Financial Review* (various issues).
Reserve Bank of Australia, *Annual Reports* (1949–50 to 1975–6).
Reserve Bank of Australia, Occasional Papers.
Reserve Bank of Australia, *Statistical Bulletin* (1949–50 to 1976).

## References

[1] Adams, C. and Porter, M. G., 'The stability of the demand for money', in Reserve Bank of Australia [136].

[2] Aigner, D. J. and Bryan, W. J., 'A model of short-run banking behaviour', *Quarterly Journal of Economics* (1971).

[3] Allan, R. H., 'The economics of intervention in the short-term money market', unpublished PhD thesis (Australian National University, June 1977).

[4] Andersen, L. and Jordan, J. L., 'Monetary and fiscal actions: a test of their relative importance', *Federal Reserve Bank of St Louis Review* (November 1968).

[5] Argy, V. and Carmichael, J. L., 'Models of imported inflation for a small country, with special reference to Australia', in Kasper [90].

[6] Arndt, H. W., 'The banks and the capital market', ES & A Bank Research Lecture, 1958 (University of Queensland, 1960).

[7] Arndt, H. W., 'Overdrafts and monetary policy', *Review Banca Nazionale del Lavoro*, vol. 17 (1964).

[8] Arndt, H. W. and Stammer, D., *The Australian Trading Banks* (Melbourne: Cheshire, 1974).

[9] Artis, M. J. and Lewis, M. K., 'The demand for money in the United Kingdom, 1963–73', *Manchester School*, vol. 44 (1976).

[10] Artis, M. J. and Wallace, R. H., Chapters 18-19 in Runcie [146].

[11] Auld, D. A. L., 'A measure of Australian fiscal policy performance, 1948–9 to 1963–4', *Economic Record* (1967).

[12] Axilrod, S. H., 'Monetary aggregates and money market conditions in open market policy', in Federal Reserve Bank [40].

[13] Axilrod, S. H., 'The FOMC directive as structured in the late 1960s: theory and appraisal', in Federal Reserve Bank [40].

[14] Barry, P. F. and Guille, C. W., 'The Australian business cycle and international cyclical linkages, 1959–74', *Economic Record* (June 1976).

# BIBLIOGRAPHY

[15]   Barton, L., Derody, B. and Sheehan, P. J., 'Some estimates of the full-employment budget position for the Australian economy', *Australian Economic Review*, no. 1 (1976).

[16]   Beck, M. T., Bush, M. G. and Hayes, R. W., *The Indicator Approach to the Identification of Business Cycles*, Occasional Paper, No. 2 (Sydney: Reserve Bank of Australia, June 1973).

[17]   Bischoff, C. W., 'Business investment in the 1970s: a comparison of models', *Brookings Papers on Economic Activity* (1971).

[18]   Brainard, W., 'Uncertainty and the effectiveness of policy', *American Economic Association Papers and Proceedings/American Economic Review* (May 1967).

[19]   Brainard, W. and Cooper, R. N., 'Empirical monetary macroeconomics', *American Economic Review* (May 1975).

[20]   Branson, W. H. and Hill, R. D., *Capital Movements in the OECD Area* (Paris: Organisation for Economic Co-operation and Development, December 1971).

[21]   Brunner, K. and Meltzer, A. H., 'The meaning of monetary indicators', in G. Horwich (ed.), *Monetary Process and Policy* (Irwin, 1967).

[22]   Bush, M. G. and Cohen, A. M., *The Indicator Approach to the Identification of Business Cycles*, Occasional Paper, No. 2 (Sydney: Reserve Bank of Australia, 1968).

[23]   Carlson, K. M., 'Estimates of the high employment budget, 1947–67', *Federal Reserve Bank of St Louis Review* (June 1967).

[24]   Christ, C., 'Econometric models of the financial sector', *Journal of Money, Credit and Banking* Vol. III (1971).

[25]   Coombs, H. C., 'The development of monetary policy in Australia', ES & A Bank Research Lecture, 1954 (University of Queensland, 1955); reproduced in Runcie [146].

[26]   Coombs, H. C., 'Conditions of monetary policy in Australia', R. C. Mills Memorial Lecture (University of Sydney, April 1958); reproduced in Runcie [146].

[27]   Coombs, H. C., 'A matter of prices', paper presented to the 34th ANZAAS Congress (Perth, 1959); printed in *Economic Record* (December 1959).

[28]   Coombs, H. C., *Memoranda of Evidence: Committee on the Working of the Monetary System* (Radcliffe Committee) (London: HMSO, 1960).

[29]   Coombs, H. C., 'Other people's money', Sir John Morris Memorial Lecture (Canberra: ANU, 5 April 1962).

[30]   Coombs, H. C., 'Maintaining stability in rapidly developing economies', paper presented to the 18th International Banking Summer School (Melbourne, 1965).

[31]   Coombs, H. C., 'Central banking: a look back and forward', *Economic Record* (December 1969).

[32]   Corrigan, E. G., 'The measurement and importance of fiscal policy changes', *Federal Reserve Bank of New York Review* (June 1970).

[33]   Danes, M. K., 'The measurement and explanation of inflationary expectations in Australia', *Australian Economic Papers* (June 1975).

[34]   Davis, R. W. and Wallace, R. H., 'Lessons of the 1960 bank credit squeeze', *Australian Economic Papers* (June 1963).

[35]   Defris, L. V., 'Leading Australian cyclical indicators, 1960–75', *Australian Economic Review*, no. 4 (1975).

303

[36] Dewald, W. G., *LGS Assets and Monetary Policy*, NSW Economic Monograph, No. 285 (Sydney: March 1967).

[37] Dewald, W. G., 'The short-term money market in Australia', ES & A Bank Research Lecture (University of Queensland, 1967).

[38] Drake, P. J., 'The cost of capital controls', in Kasper [90].

[39] Enzler, J., Johnson, L. and Paulus, J., 'Some problems of money demand', *Brookings Papers on Economic Activity*, no. 1 (1976).

[40] Federal Reserve Board, *Open Market Policies and Operating Procedures: Staff Studies* (Washington: FRB, July 1971).

[41] Fellner, W. and Larkins, D., 'Interpretation of a regularity in the behaviour of M2', *Brookings Papers on Economic Activity*, no. 3 (1976).

[42] Freebairn, J. W., *Determinants of Consumption Expenditure* in Reserve Bank of Australia [136].

[43] Friedman, M., 'The role of monetary policy', *American Economic Review* (March 1968).

[44] Goldfeld, S. M., 'The demand for money revisited', *Brookings Papers on Economic Activity*, no. 3 (1973).

[45] Gramlich, E., 'The usefulness of monetary and fiscal policy as discretionary stabilization tools', *Journal of Money, Credit and Banking* (May 1971).

[46] Gruen, F. H. G., 'What went wrong? Some personal reflections on economic policies under Labour', *Australian Quarterly* (December 1976).

[47] Guille, C. W., 'Instruments and objectives of economic policy: some lessons of recent world experience', in Kasper [90].

[48] Hacche, G., 'The demand for money in the United Kingdom: experience since 1971', *Bank of England Quarterly Bulletin* (September 1974).

[49] Hall, A. R., 'The Australian economy, 1960-5', *The Bankers' Magazine* (October 1965).

[50] Haywood, W., 'The deviation cycle', *Australian Economic Review*, no. 4 (1973).

[51] Helliwell, J. and Schott, K., *Some Causes and Consequences of Direct Investment Inflows to Australia*, Research Discussion Paper, No. 20 (Sydney: Reserve Bank of Australia, 1971).

[52] Hendershott, P. H., 'The inside lag in monetary policy', *Journal of Political Economy* (October 1966).

[53] Hendershott, P. H., *The Neutralized Money Stock* (Irwin, 1968).

[54] Henderson, J. F., *Some Preliminary Results from the Model RBA.1 The Channels of Monetary Policy* (Sydney: Reserve Bank of Australia, mimeo, February 1974).

[55] Henderson, J. F., *Lags in the Effects of Policy: Empirical Evidence from the Econometric Model RBA.1* (Sydney: Reserve Bank of Australia, mimeo, February 1974).

[56] Henderson, J. F., 'The development and use of macroeconomic models in the Reserve Bank of Australia', paper presented to the Pacific Basin Central Bank Conference on Econometric Modelling (Federal Reserve Bank of San Francisco, May 1975).

[57] Henderson, J. F. and Norman, P. M., *The Equations of RBA1/74 Model of the Australian Economy*, Research Discussion Paper (Sydney: Reserve Bank of Australia, November 1975).

[58] Henderson, R. F., 'Monetary policy in Australia, 1960-1', *Economic Record* (September 1961); reprinted in Runcie [146].

[59]   Higgins, C., Johnston, N. H. and Coghlan, P. L., 'Business investment: the recent experience', in Reserve Bank of Australia [136].

[60]   Hill, M. R., *The Commonwealth Bond Market*, Economic Society of Australia and New Zealand Monograph No. 306 (ESANZ, August 1969).

[61]   Hill, M. R., 'Housing finance institutions', in Hirst and Wallace [65].

[62]   Hirst, R. R., 'Post-war monetary policy in Australia', *Economic Record* (May 1953); reprinted in Runcie [146].

[63]   Hirst, R. R., 'The short-term money market', in Hirst and Wallace [65].

[64]   Hirst, R. R., 'Finance for economic development', in Hirst and Wallace [65].

[65]   Hirst, R. R. and Wallace, R. H., *The Australian Capital Market* (Melbourne: Cheshire, 1974).

[66]   Hunt, B., 'Capital account flows and the Australian balance of payments', preliminary results privately communicated by the author.

[67]   Johnston, N. H. and Perrin, J. R., *The Portfolio Behaviour of the Official Short-term Money Market* (Canberra: Australian Bureau of Statistics, 1976).

[68]   Johnston, N. H. and Spasojevic, J., *The Asset Portfolio Behaviour of Permanent Building Societies* (Canberra: Australian Bureau of Statistics, 1976).

[69]   Johnston, N. H. and Spasojevic, J., *The Portfolio Behaviour of the Australian Savings Banks* (Canberra: Australian Bureau of Statistics, 1976).

[70]   Johnston, N. H. and Zarb, J. F., *A Framework for the Monetary Sector of the NIF Model* (Canberra: Australian Bureau of Statistics, 1975).

[71]   Jonson, P. D., 'Our current inflationary experience', *Australian Economic Review*, no. 2 (1973).

[72]   Jonson, P. D., 'Stabilization policy in Australia: an objective analysis', *Manchester School* (September 1974).

[73]   Jonson, P. D., 'Some aspects of the recent inflation', in Reserve Bank of Australia [136].

[74]   Jonson, P. D. and Butlin, M. W., *Price and Quantity Responses to Monetary Impulses in a Model of a Small Open Economy*, Research Seminar Paper (Sydney: Reserve Bank of Australia, March 1977).

[75]   Jonson, P. D. and Danes, M. K., *Money and Inflation: Some Analytic Issues* (Sydney: Reserve Bank of Australia, September 1976).

[76]   Jonson, P. D., Mahar, K. L. and Thompson, G. J., 'Earnings and award wages in Australia', *Australian Economic Papers* (June 1974).

[77]   Jonson, P. D. and Mahoney, D. M., 'Price expectations in Australia', *Economic Record* (March 1973).

[78]   Jonson, P. D., Moses, E. R. and Wymer, C. R., *A Minimal Model of the Australian Economy*, Research Discussion Paper (Sydney: Reserve Bank of Australia, 1976).

[79]   Jonson, P. D. and Taylor, J. C., *Modelling Monetary Disequilibrium*, Research Discussion Paper, No. 7705 (Sydney: Reserve Bank of Australia, 1976).

[80]   Jonson, P. D. and Taylor, J. C., *Inflation and Economic Stability in a Small Open Economy: A Systems Approach* (Sydney: Reserve Bank of Australia (April 1977).

[81]   Jorgenson, D. W., 'Anticipation and investment behaviour', in Duesenberry, Fromm, Klein & Koh, *The Brookings Quarterly Model of the United States* (Chicago: Rand McNally Co., 1963).

[82]   Jorgenson, D. W., 'Capital theory and investment behaviour', *American Economic Review* (May 1963)

[83] Jorgenson, D. W., 'Econometric studies of investment behaviour', *Journal of Economic Literature* (December 1971).

[84] Jorgenson, D. W. and Siebert, C. D., 'A Comparison of alternative theories of corporate investment behaviour', *American Economic Review* (September 1968).

[85] Jorgenson, D. W. and Stephenson, J., 'The time structure of investment behaviour in US manufacturing', *Review of Economics and Statistics* (February 1967).

[86] Juttner, D. J. and Tuckwell, R. H., 'Partial adjustment, multiple expectations and the demand for money in Australia', *Kredit und Kapital* (January 1974).

[87] Karecken, J., Muench, T., Supel, T. and Wallace, N., 'Determining the optimum monetary instrument variable', in Federal Reserve Bank [40].

[88] Kasper, W., 'The exchange rate: a "new" instrument of economic policy', *Australian Economic Review*, no. 4 (1974).

[89] Kasper, W., 'The emergence of an active exchange-rate policy: some quantitative lessons', in Kasper [90].

[90] Kasper, W. (ed.), *International Money: Experiments and Experience* (Canberra: Department of Economics RSSS, Australian National University, 1976).

[91] Kasper, W., *Issues in Economic Policy* (Melbourne: Macmillan, 1976).

[92] Kennedy, R. V., 'Quarterly estimates of national income and expenditure, 1950-1 to 1957-8', *Economic Record* (June 1969).

[93] Keran, M. W. and Babb, C., 'Explanation of federal reserve actions', *Federal Reserve Bank of St Louis Review* (October 1969).

[94] Kouri, P. J. K. and Porter, M. G., 'International capital flows and portfolio equilibrium', *Journal of Political Economy* (May-June 1974).

[95] Laidler, D. E. W., 'Information, money and the macroeconomics of inflation', *Swedish Journal of Economics* (January 1974).

[96] Lewis, M. K., 'The lags and effectiveness of monetary policy in Australia', unpublished PhD thesis (University of Adelaide, 1977).

[97] Lewis, M. K. and Wallace, R. H., 'Monetary policy in a dependent economy: the Australian case', unpublished paper made available by the authors (1973); for an abridged version of this important paper see *The Bankers' Magazine* (September-October 1973).

[98] Mallyon, J. S., 'Statistical indicators of the Australian trade cycle', *Australian Economic Papers* (June 1966).

[99] Mayer, T., 'The structure of monetarism', *Kredit und Kapital* (October 1974 and January 1975).

[100] Modigliani, F., 'The monetarist controversy: or should we forsake stabilization policies?', *American Economic Review* (March 1977).

[101] Mundell, R. A., 'The appropriate use of monetary and fiscal policy for internal and external stability', *IMF Staff Papers* (March 1962).

[102] Murray, G. L., *Monetary Policy and Capital Inflow* (mimeo).

[103] Nevile, J. W., *Fiscal Policy in Australia: Theory and Practice* (Melbourne: Cheshire, 1974).

[104] Nevile, J. W., 'Inflation, company profits and investment', *Australian Economic Review*, no. 4 (1975).

[105] Nevile, J. W., 'Australian inflation: made at home or imported?', in Kasper [90].

[106] Nevile, J. W., 'Measuring the income effects of fiscal policy', paper presented to the Conference of Economists (Hobart, 1976).

[107] Nevile, J. W. and Stammer, D. W., *Inflation and Unemployment* (Harmondsworth, Middlesex: Penguin, 1972).

[108] Norman, P. M., 'The policy implications of a model of Australia's balance of payments', paper presented to the ANZAAS Congress (Canberra, January 1975).

[109] Norman, P. M. and Purvis, D. D., 'The behaviour of monetary aggregates in Australia: some new evidence', paper presented to the 5th Conference of Economists (Brisbane, August 1975).

[110] Norman, P. M., 'A Study of some international influences on the Australian economy, 1967–73', unpublished MSc dissertation (University of Southampton, 1976).

[111] Norton, W. E. (ed.), *Three Studies of Private Fixed Investment*, Occasional Paper No. 3E (Sydney: Reserve Bank of Australia, 1971).

[112] Norton, W. E., *Some Principles of Economic Policy*, Occasional Paper, No. 6 (Sydney: Reserve Bank of Australia, March 1973).

[113] Norton, W. E., Cohen, A. M. and Sweeney, K. M., *A Model of the Monetary Sector*, Occasional Paper, No. 30 (Sydney: Reserve Bank of Australia, 1970).

[114] Norton, W. E. and Henderson, J. F., 'A model of the Australian economy: a further progress report', paper presented to the Australasian Conference of Econometricians (Monash University, August 1971).

[115] Norton, W. E. and Henderson, J. F., *A Model of the Australian Economy: A Progress Report*, Occasional Paper, No. 3G (Sydney: Reserve Bank of Australia, 1972).

[116] Oram, J. T., 'The bond market and the bank's market operations', a lecture to the Insurance Institute of Victoria (July 1976).

[117] Organisation for Economic Co-operation and Development, *Monetary Policy in Japan* (Paris: OECD, 1973).

[118] Organisation for Economic Co-operation and Development, *Monetary Policy in the United States* (Paris: OECD 1973).

[119] Organisation for Economic Co-operation and Development, *The Measurement of Domestic Cyclical Fluctuations* (Paris: OECD, July 1973).

[120] Perkins, J. O. N., *Anti-cyclical Policy in Australia* (Melbourne: Melbourne University Press, 1975).

[121] Perkins, J. O. N., *Macroeconomic Policy in Australia* (Melbourne: Melbourne University Press, 1975).

[122] Perkins, J. O. N., *Macroeconomic Policy in Australia, 1971–4*, University of Melbourne Research Paper, No. 28 (Melbourne University Press, January 1975).

[123] Phillips, A. W., 'Stabilisation policy and the time form of lagged responses', *Economic Journal* (June 1957).

[124] Phillips, J. G., 'Recent developments in monetary policy in Australia', ES & A Bank Research Lecture, 1964 (University of Queensland, 1964); reproduced in Runcie [146].

[125] Phillips, J. G., 'Developments in monetary theory and policies', R. C. Mills Memorial Lecture, (University of Sydney, April 1971).

[126] Pierce, J., 'Some rules for the conduct of monetary policy', in Federal Reserve Bank of Boston, *Controlling Monetary Aggregates* (Boston: FRBB, 1969).

[127] Pissarides, C. A., 'A model of British macro-economic policy, 1955–69', *Manchester School* (September 1972).

[ 128] Poole, W., 'Optimal choice of monetary policy instruments in a simple stochastic macro model', *Quarterly Journal of Economics* (May 1970).

[129] Poole, W., 'Rules-of-thumb for guiding monetary policy', in Federal Reserve Bank [40].

[130] Poole, W., 'Interpreting the Fed's monetary targets', *Brookings Papers on Economic Activity*, no. 1 (1976).

[131] Porter, M. G., 'The interdependence of monetary policy and capital flows in Australia', *Economic Record* (March 1974).

[132] Porter, M. G., *Capital Movements: A Further Note*, Seminar Paper, No. 53 (Melbourne: University of Monash, 1976).

[133] Purvis, D. D., 'The role of the monetary base in Australia', *Australian Journal of Management* (April 1976).

[134] Raasche, R. H., 'A Review of empirical studies of the money supply mechanism', *Federal Reserve Bank of St Louis Review* (July 1972).

[135] Radcliffe Committee, *Report on the Working of Monetary System* (London, HMSO, 1959).

[136] Reserve Bank of Australia, *Conference in Applied Economic Research* (Sydney: RBA, September 1976).

[137] Reserve Bank of Australia, *Conference in Applied Economic Research* (Sydney: RBA, December 1977).

[138] Reuber, G. L., 'The objectives of Canadian monetary policy: empirical "trade offs" and the reaction function of the authorities', *Journal of Political Economy* (April 1964).

[139] Rose, P. J., *Australian Securities Markets* (Melbourne: Cheshire, 1969).

[140] Rowan, D. C., 'The monetary problems of a dependent economy: the Australian experience, 1948–52', *Review of Banca Nazionale del Lavoro* (October–December 1954); reprinted in Runcie [146].

[141] Rowan, D. C., 'Central banking in export economies', address to the NSW Branch of the Economic Society of Australia and New Zealand (May 1955).

[142] Rowan, D. C., 'The future of monetary policy in Australia', *The Bankers' Magazine* (February 1956); reprinted in Runcie [146].

[143] Rowan, D. C., 'Radcliffe monetary theory', *Economic Record* (December 1961).

[144] Rowan, D. C., 'Monetarism and monetary policy', ANZ Bank Research Lecture (University of Queensland, July 1977).

[145] Rowan, D. C. and Edwardes, W., 'Inflationary expectations and the term structure of interest rates: the UK experience', in Bagiotti and Franco, *Pioneering Economics* (Edizioni Cedam, Padua, 1977).

[146] Runcie, N. (ed)., *Australian Monetary and Fiscal Policy* (London: University of London, 1971).

[147] Sharpe, I. G., *The Channels of Monetary Influence: An Evaluation of the Monetary Sector of RBA1* (Sydney: University of Sydney, mimeo, 1972).

[148] Sharpe, I. G., 'A mortgage model: some theoretical and empirical results applied to Australian savings banks', *Australian Economic Papers* (December 1973).

[149] Sharpe, I. G., 'A quarterly econometric model of portfolio choice: part I', *Economic Record* (December 1973).

[150] Sharpe, I. G., 'A quarterly econometric model of portfolio choice: part II', *Economic Record* (March 1974).

[151]   Sharpe, I. G., *Secondary Reserve Requirements: The Monetary Base and the Money Supply in Australia*, Economics Working Paper, No. 7 (Sydney: University. of Sydney, 1974).

[152]   Sharpe, I. G., 'Australian money supply analysis: direct controls and the relationship between the monetary base, secondary reserves and the money supply', unpublished research study (September 1976).

[153]   Sharpe, I. G., and Volker, P. A., 'The impact of institutional changes on the Australian short-run money demand function', paper presented to the 6th Conference of Economists (Hobart, 1977).

[154]   Snape, R. H., 'Australian exchange-rate policy, 1957–77', in Kasper [90].

[155]   Stammer, D. W., 'The exchange rate and demand management policies', in Kasper [90].

[156]   Swan, T. W., 'Overseas investment in Australia: Treasury economic paper, no. 1', *Economic Record* (June 1972).

[157]   Swan, T. W., in Kasper [90].

[158]   Taylor, J. C., 'Price expectations, causes, measurements and effects', paper presented to the 47th ANZAAS Congress (Hobart, May 1976).

[159]   Taylor, J. C., *Calculations for Expected Inflation: Wales/ACMA Series 1966.IV–1976.IV*, Research Paper (Sydney: Reserve Bank of Australia, mimeo, 1977).

[160]   Terrell, D. and Valentine,T., 'Australian trading banks' demand for excess LGS assets: a cross-section time series analysis', paper presented to the 6th Conference of Economists (Hobart, 1977).

[161]   Turnovsky, S. J., 'Optimal choice of a monetary instrument in a linear economic model with stochastic coefficients', *Journal of Money, Credit and Banking* (February 1975).

(162)   Turnovsky, S. J., 'Monetary policy, fiscal policy and the government budget constraint', *Australian Economic Papers* (December 1975).

[163]   Turnovsky, S. J., 'Stabilization policies and the choice of monetary instrument in a small open economy', in A. Bergstrom (ed.), *Stability and Inflation* (Wiley, 1978).

[164]   Valentine, T. J., 'The loan supply function of Australian trading banks: an empirical analysis', *Australian Economic Papers* (June 1973).

[165]   Valentine, T. J., 'The demand for very liquid assets in Australia', *Australian Economic Papers* (December 1973).

[166]   Valentine, T. J., 'The demand for money and price expectations in Australia', *Journal of Finance* 32(3) (June 1973).

[167]   Vernon Committee, *Report of the Committee of Economic Enquiry* (Government Printer, May 1965).

[168]   Waterman, A. M. C., 'The timing of economic fluctuations in Australia, January 1948 to December 1964', *Australian Economic Papers* (June 1967).

[169]   Waterman, A. M. C., *Economic Fluctuations in Australia, 1948–64* (Canberra: Australian National University Press, 1972).

[170]   Zecher, R., 'Monetary equilibrium and international reserve flows in Australia', *Journal of Finance* (December 1974).

# Index

aggregate demand: Australian 'cycle' 25-31; Behaviour of, in 1958-60 149-150; behaviour of, in 1968-1971 169; and investment in stocks 26-27, 29; measurement of in cycle 25; and simulations (RB.74) 238-240
anti-cyclical stabilization policy: *prima facie* case for 24
assignment of policy instruments 273-277
assignment problem and policy instruments in future 292
Australian 'cycle' and capacity utilisation 20-23
Australian 'cycles' dating of, 20-25
Australian current account: Australian 'cycle' 35-37; import restrictions 11, 37; inventory investment 37; monetary policy stance 82; secular weakness of 82
Australian financial development: *and* layering of claims 50; relative importance of main financial institutions 50, 52
availability effects: bank advances 77; mortgage market 107; reduced importance of 106; transmission mechanism 106-107

balance of payments and simulations (N.I.F. Model) 246; and simulations (RB.74) 241-242; and simulations (RB.76) 245; and private capital flows in 1971-1973 193-194, 196-197; capital account and capital flows 37-38; current account *see* Australian current account; capital account and Reserve Bank Model (RB.74) 114
banking base (net) defined 78; exogenous elements in 79
base concepts defined 78

building societies, borrowing rate (deposits) 1968-1971 168; deposit inflow in 1968-1971 168; dominance of, by permanent building societies 59; econometric studies of 59, 61; and financial crises 211-212; financial stability of, 59; financial stability of, and monetary policy 59; fund inflows to 61-62; in 1973-5 62; and seasonal factors 61; and econometric modelling 61; lending policy of, 61; and dynamics of operations 59; and mortgage approvals 59; monetary policy 59

central bank, responsibility for financial stability 283
Commonwealth Bank of Australia, *see* Reserve Bank of Australia
cost of borrowing effect, transmission mechanism 107; interest rates 107

development finance companies, growth of 50; money market corporations 50; overseas capital markets 50, 66

economic models, and policy horizon 236; Reserve Bank Model (RB.70) 110-113; Reserve Bank Model (RB.74) 236-242; Reserve Bank Model (RB.76) 242-244; and simulations 234-236; Treasury-Bureau of Statistics (N.I.F.) Model 244-246
exchange rate, assignment of 290-291; as discretionary instrument 290-291; and future 289-291

310